Praise for
The New American Story

"Bradley does the hard work of delineating exactly what needs to be done to reform health care, education, pensions and the political process . . . before showing exactly where the money would come from. . . . Others can take a leaf from . . . Bill Bradley and get serious about how to fix the country."
—*Newsweek*

"Bill Bradley is one of our most valuable public citizens. What he has given us in this wise and thoughtful book is a chilling portrait of a nation that has lost its way politically, economically, and socially —and a road map to help us find our way back."
—DAVID HALBERSTAM

"The book lays out a new story, designed to reawaken idealism and optimism. It is a plan to redistribute responsibilities among citizens, corporations and government so no one is a perpetrator and no one is a victim."
—*Daily Record* (Morris County, New Jersey)

"Bill Bradley's book is a powerful call to arms—a wise, passionate, insightful polemic that everyone who is serious about politics and our country will read and debate in the months and years ahead."
—DORIS KEARNS GOODWIN

"A thoughtful look at American politics for citizens of whatever political persuasion."
—*Booklist*

"[A] thoughtful policy agenda . . . insightful . . . Bradley puts forward a tough, plainspoken indictment of the Republicans and a vigorous and substantive Democratic reform program that deserves to be read and debated."
—*Publishers Weekly*

THE
NEW AMERICAN STORY

THE
NEW
AMERICAN
STORY

Bill Bradley

Random House Trade Paperbacks New York

For my daughter, Theresa Anne,

and my friend Herb Allen

2008 Random House Trade Paperback Edition

Published in the United States by Random House Trade Paperbacks, an imprint of
The Random House Publishing Group, a division of Random House, Inc., New York.

RANDOM HOUSE TRADE PAPERBACKS and colophon are trademarks of Random House, Inc.

Originally published in hardcover in the United States by Random House, an imprint of
The Random House Publishing Group, a division of Random House, Inc., in 2007.

LIBRARY OF CONGRESS CATALOGING-IN-PUBLICATION DATA

Bradley, Bill.
The new American story / Bill Bradley.
p. cm.
Includes index.
ISBN 978-0-8129-7579-6
1. United States—Politics and government—2001–
2. Politics, Practical—United States. 3. Political culture—United States.
4. Political parties—United States.
5. United States—Foreign public opinion. I. Title.
JK275.B69 2007
973.931—dc22 2006037621

Printed in the United States of America

www.atrandom.com

2 4 6 8 9 7 5 3 1

Book design by Laurie Jewell

CONTENTS

FOREWORD

When I traveled the country in the last year talking about *The New American Story*, I discovered a poignant paradox. Whereas people I talked to desperately wanted to hear the truth from their political leaders about today's very real problems—regarding health care, education, pensions, oil dependence, the environment, the economy, national security—they had no expectation that effective action would ever be taken. Sadly, such widespread public skepticism is self-fulfilling, inviting politicians to avoid the exercise of political will and, in turn, inculcating a kind of political cynicism. These two negatives feed each other, producing a downward spiral. The result is that as a nation we are less than we can be, even at a time when we know what to do and can afford to do it. I wrote *The New American Story* in an attempt to show how to counter both that public hopelessness and that political cynicism.

One of our problems as citizens is that we can ask the questions, but we don't feel confident about arguing with or picking apart the answers that candidates or elected officials give us. For example, when we hear from a candidate that it's essentially not possible to provide health care for everybody, or to reform our public schools, or to reduce our dependence on oil dramatically, we should challenge his or her "can't do" story.

The New American Story gives the citizen the information to counter such "can't do" answers—and to deepen the questions so as to get to the real heart of the issues. As in "If countries poorer than we are can provide health insurance for everyone, why can't we?" Or "If establishing a standard of 45 miles per gallon for all new cars will eliminate our need for oil imports from OPEC, why didn't we do it long ago?" Or "If setting national standards for our public schools is common sense in a competitive world economy, why would anyone oppose it?" *The New American Story* encourages us to maintain hope in the face of politicians who say we can't do the most basic things to secure our country's future.

Citizens who want to break the spiral of public skepticism and political cynicism need to ask tough questions of their presidential candidates—questions about intent, specific plans, past record, understanding of leadership. These questions are not personally invasive, "gotcha" questions; they flow, rather, from an awareness of what is necessary to bring about a successful presidency.

So before you cast your vote for president, you might ask yourself the following questions about each candidate:

1. **Can the candidate put a good team together to govern?** Has he ever done team-building before, in government or the private sector? Can she delegate to appointees and hold them accountable? Presidents rise or fall on the strength of their administrations. Above all, they need relevant competence and flexibility from their White House advisers and cabinet members. It helps if a president has had some experience with his team and has a clear sense of their loyalty to him and his objectives. Some leaders can surround themselves with people who are the best—people who are even smarter than they are—and manage them with skill. Others select the wrong people and never think about how to mold them into a coherent organization.

2. **Does the candidate have a personal feel for the country?** Does she understand our history and what has led other presidents to failure or success? The broader the candidate's life experience, the better chance she has to represent all the people fully. Learning about parts of the country for the first time in

the campaign necessarily will produce superficial knowledge. It is important to understand, for instance, how critical water is west of the 100th meridian, or the enormous differences between farming in Iowa and farming in California, or how the needs of suburbia differ from those of small towns or large urban areas. In order to internalize the country, you have to have absorbed its contradictions.

3. **Does the candidate know the world?** There is no substitute for engaging in dialogue with foreign leaders, understanding how the world looks from a non-American perspective, and knowing the consequences of previous administrations' policies. If a candidate has little foreign policy experience— as was true of candidates Ronald Reagan, Bill Clinton, and George W. Bush—the key is making the right choices for secretaries of state, defense, and the treasury, and national security adviser. Absent a candidate's announcing key cabinet posts during the campaign, it is difficult to know whom someone will nominate for these important positions; still, close scrutiny of those giving advice in the campaign will give you an indication of the caliber of possible appointees. A candidate who learns on the job with inadequate advisers is a dangerous choice to lead the country.

4. **Is the candidate surrounded by advisers who are secure enough psychologically, competent enough professionally, and curious enough personally to reach out to the broadest range of non-campaign talent?** Such advisers, once in power, are more likely to continue reaching out. All they have to do is pick up the phone and ask questions. No one will refuse their calls. Too often, campaigns and even administrations are cordoned off by palace guards, who actually hurt their president's chances for success. If a candidate's team respects the people and seeks ideas from them, it will stand the best chance of realizing the potential of the national moment it is striving to preside over.

5. **Does the candidate have a sense of humor—one that can be used in partisan political combat, legislative negotiations, and internal administration debate?** FDR skewered many a political opponent with his wit, thereby making his point with-

out becoming angry or disagreeable. Above all, is the candidate secure enough not to take himself too seriously? Lincoln comes to mind here. A sense of humor flows from a feeling of command, and when the president has one, everyone relaxes, which is when real creativity flows.

6. **Can the candidate prioritize—tell you what she'd do first, second, third?** Every president hopes to accomplish many things: cutting taxes, establishing universal health care, improving schools, reforming immigration laws, reducing oil consumption, putting Social Security on a firm footing, building respect for America around the world. If a president tries doing all of that simultaneously, failure is inevitable. The key is setting the order in which they are to be accomplished. The candidate's schedule of priorities should be logical, coherent, and politically sensible—even as she recognizes that unforeseen circumstances may well dictate new choices.

7. **Has the candidate ever demonstrated political courage?** Knowing how to do what we need to do is not rocket science; having the courage to do it is the difficult part. You need to know whether a candidate has ever demonstrated political courage, and you need some idea of the extent and power of the forces operating against the candidate at that time. Courage entails having a clear-sighted view of the risks of making the right decision but making it anyway: Think of LBJ on civil rights. Having walked that lonely road of leadership several times before becoming president is the best guarantee that a candidate will seize the moment as president.

8. **Will the candidate's election—in itself—transform the citizenry's sense of what is possible in the country?** When Jack Kennedy won in 1960, there was a palpable feeling that a new generation was taking over. It was a tonic to the national psyche. Would the election of the first woman have that effect? Would the election of the first Hispanic? Would the first election of an African American—one who also comes from a new generation? The potential of true transformational leadership flows from the qualities of the leader and the aspects of the national moment.

9. **Does the candidate understand a few big issues or a host of smaller ones, and which mind-set fits the national moment?** Ronald Reagan knew two big things: that the role of government in our lives should be smaller and that pressure on the communist system would someday break the USSR because communism was a failed philosophy. FDR, on the other hand, in combating the Great Depression, tried on new policies like new suits of clothes, never worrying about appearing inconsistent. A leader of the Reagan kind will put together a more focused administration with a clear strategy, better able to function in a world where old structures need to change in big ways. A leader of FDR's kind will constantly alter tactics to find the right combinations to solve problems. Such a president functions best in a chaotic, crisis environment—one in which there are few clear answers. These two are signal examples, but the core question is whether a candidate's mind-set and leadership style fit the national moment.

If citizens and the media took time to ask themselves these nine questions about the presidential candidates, voters would be better able to tell whether a candidate had the inclination or ability to deal with the genuine challenges facing the country. Getting the answers would also help make the New American Story a reality. Americans want to confront our major problems. They want a government that puts country ahead of party and tells people the truth about the complex issues we must deal with. With answers to foundational questions about its candidates, the American electorate will properly make the decision that it alone is entitled to make—a decision on behalf of the whole, not in the individual's interest, or in the group's interest, but what is in the best interests of us all.

INTRODUCTION

Politics is stuck. It's not that there's an absence of political will and good intent. It's that too many people who want change don't believe change can happen. So all the policies that would make our lives better just pile up, with no movement forward, no action, no change.

I wrote this book in the hope that it would help break up this logjam, so that the many people of great talent and high values who serve in office today would be encouraged to do what must be done for the country's long-term future—and that it would encourage private citizens to try to make a difference, not only in their own communities, but also in the larger world of which we're all a part.

So many people in America want to improve their own and others' lives but don't know how. Or if they do know what needs to be done, they don't think it's possible. I want to challenge both these assumptions. There are things we *can* do, and this book demonstrates, from a budget standpoint, how easily they can be done. It's not rocket science.

Yes, I know it's difficult to reach political consensus on issues as challenging as health care, education reform, ending our addiction to oil, and producing balanced economic growth. But the American people and their leaders have done far more difficult things in the past. Winning World War II and achieving racial justice required a much larger transformation of our society than most of the policy initiatives I'm recommending in this book. If we do the right things, the battles of today will lead to the accepted consensus of tomorrow. The problems we face today are solvable.

But solving them requires not just policy proposals but also politics. Politics is the way you get things done in a democracy. That's why this book is about both policies and politics and is addressed to policymakers and ordinary citizens alike. I've tried to be as specific as I can about how we can achieve the changes that most Americans say they want, so the book is detailed in some places. (I want people to read this book in total, but if in the "New Agenda" section you get bogged down in the details, then just skip over some of them.)

My hope is that the agenda I've laid out in Part II will be adopted and become the law of the land. If it were, our country would be more just, our people would have more opportunity, and our place in the world would once again be based on our example and not simply on our economic and military superiority.

I was a senator for eighteen years, so I realize how some of my bolder policy suggestions would play in a normal political context. But I don't think the context is normal these days—nor should we put all of our hope in one party. Republicans are in the White House and, until recently, controlled the House and Senate—and now Democrats control the House and Senate and, in the next presidential election, may win the White House. But what will be different? What is the agenda? What can be agreed upon by both parties?

This last question is important because absent filibuster-proof majorities, only the policies for which there is a rough bipartisan consensus will last. In the Senate, for example, if you have a 51-to-49 majority, you can ram something through on a party-line vote, but when the other party comes into power your policy reform is undone. Ultimately, politics is not about one party beating the other but about listening to the American people enough to know what policy changes will command bipartisan support over the long run.

It is this *listening* that has led me to write this book. I have listened to the American people all my life, from my days on the road as a basketball player through my years in the Senate to my campaign for the presidency, and even now, among other ways, in preparing my weekly Sirius Satellite Radio show *American Voices*. Those long years of listening have led to the proposals in this book.

I call this book *The New American Story* because I believe we've been told a story about America that simply isn't true. But we've been told it so often that it seems true. It's a story of no possibility—of too few resources and no political will; of fear and lack of compassion; of individual consumerist values at home and "America only" policies abroad. But Americans are better than the current story says we are, and Americans have begun to question this story. Now we need a new story about who we are and what we might do together as a country.

For those who say Americans are too diverse to rally around a new American story, I say, "That's not so!" People in America may speak with different accents, but they all care about a few basic things—family, work, health, and the education of their children. Whether in the small town in Missouri where I grew up or the large metropolitan areas of New Jersey I represented for so many years, people shared these same concerns.

For years, I've listened to the stories that people told about their lives. From stories, you learn something deeper than what you learn from laws or speeches or newspapers or blue-ribbon-panel reports, because when you listen to people's stories, you can see it if they get tears in their eyes or they smile. You see the effects of policies because you see how these policies work in the human context. If the job of a politician is to serve humanity, then politicians have to pay attention to human beings, with all of their aspirations and shortcomings.

Every time I talk to people who have no health insurance, or to families without the means to find a good education for their children, or to pensioners who have lost their pensions, or to the many others whose lives would be so much better if we made a few basic changes in policy, I think that somewhere along the way we must have lost our capacity to imagine something better for our country. But things can change: The 2006 midterm elections are striking evidence of that.

I grew up near the Mississippi River. Often I would go down and sit by the Mississippi and think of all of the rivulets that flowed into the little streams that then flowed into the bigger streams that flowed into the Missouri and the Ohio, and then of how those bigger rivers would flow into the mighty Mississippi. And I would imagine those who came to the Mississippi for the first time—the trappers and the traders and the founders of little communities and the immigrants who came to work in the small-town factories along its banks. I would watch the current—how it never stopped. The river never stopped. It just kept going. And that's America's destiny—to keep going, pursuing the dream of our Founders.

The river also teaches us about death and rebirth—floods rise and fall, factories come and go, communities flourish and dry up, things die and get reborn in a new form. In a fundamental sense, we're on the brink of a rebirth in this country. We've had a down cycle—but American idealism isn't dead. It can be reawakened. Every American citizen is like one of those small rivulets that, flowing together, can make something mighty.

There's an emotional dimension to this for me because I'm outside the political pressure cooker now with no ax to grind and no political ambition to accomplish. What's here comes from my soul and from a new sense of freedom. This book simply reflects my faith—based on what I've learned during all the years I've been listening, on the road and in politics—that the American people are basically good and that if they are given the right information in the right way, they will make the right decisions.

I'm interested in the heart of America as well as in its laws. The answers to our problems rest in our hearts as well as in our heads, and until we understand that, we'll make marginal improvements, but we won't make the quantum leaps that our Founders made and hoped we would continue.

I know the stories Americans tell about themselves and their country, and I know that the story we've been told, about what's real and what's possible, does not reflect the best of America. This book offers a new American story.

Part I.

THE NEW AMERICAN STORY

Once upon a time, there was a country known for its openness and ingenuity. Its power rested on its continental size, its thriving economy, its generous-hearted people, its fair and democratic government. Its distance from the dangerous places in the world reassured its citizens. People everywhere recognized that this country was different from all others. It became a beacon to the world and sought to follow policies that benefitted everyone in the world, not just itself. The citizens of this fortunate nation were welcomed everywhere they went. The country's appeal was universal. When some bully started a war that endangered the country's security or that of its allies, it went to war, and all its citizens knew why their government had taken them to war. The government told the truth to them. It asked them to sacrifice for the nation, and they did. Other countries expressed their gratitude to this country's various heads of state, and, over time, the citizens came to assume that this preeminent and admired position was their God-given right. . . .

Chapter 1.

THE STORY WE'RE TOLD

All Americans want a good life for themselves and their families. They want to be proud of their country and to believe that it can live up to its ideals. A friend asked me recently if I thought dealing with our national problems was possible in the money-soaked political and media world we live in. I said "Yes," emphatically—anything is possible in America. But no one is going to make us do the right thing. It's our choice.

Either we can ignore our country's problems until they're so big that they're almost impossible to solve or we can make the substantive decisions now that will secure America's future. At this watershed moment, political courage and political action have to take precedence over ideology. Politics, like many other human activities, can become inflexible. Once that happens, what needs to be done to save the whole cannot break through. We are at such a moment.

How can ordinary citizens bring about a change in the political culture that will give us a fresh start and realize our best hopes as a nation? Will one of our two major parties seize the high ground with an agenda that takes the country to a new level of greatness?

In this book, I will talk about where we are, what we must do now, and why it's good politics to do it. I will talk about what role politics plays in our society generally, and I will show how the Republican Party's dedication to building party structure usually has allowed it to outstrip the Democrats, who dream instead of finding a charismatic leader. I will describe how the warring factions within the Republican Party now endanger a structure carefully built over thirty-five years, threatening even the party itself—and how the only way the Democratic Party can overcome the inertia of its recent history is to connect emotionally with voters, which requires a clarity rooted in values, based on convictions, and expressed in explicit programs that can help people where they live their lives.

. . .

A key to our country's future is the word "common"—that which we share as Americans. It's not just the so-called blue states that have compassion, and it's not just the so-called red states that want to fight terrorism. One of the biggest lies perpetrated on the public in recent decades is the red/blue division of our country—the idea that we are hopelessly split by warring ideologies, unforgiving in our criticism of each other, unwilling even to listen to the other side of the argument. The media amplify this lie and, in doing so, have helped to drive a spike through the heart of civility and compromise. The political elites may indeed be at one another's throats, but the American people are not.

We are obliged to recognize our common human aspirations as well as our abundant human frailties. Friends may have different political opinions, but they often walk for a while in each other's shoes. We give our neighbors the benefit of the doubt every day. When you're watching your son's Little League baseball game, you don't say to yourself, "I wonder if the parent sitting next to me is a 'red' or a 'blue.'" Even family members hold different views on hot topics—on abortion, immigration, the war in Iraq, what to do about income inequality—but they still love, honor, and communicate with one another. Within families, differing political views are often treated as lovable idiosyncrasies rather than battle cries. An aunt of mine is a staunch conservative. We don't spend a lot of time talking politics (except when I'm kidding her), but I don't love her less because her political philosophy differs from mine.

There is a new story—a New American Story—which says that America is a family, too, and that it has, collectively, the same generosity of spirit. All we have to do is bring it out, not stifle it with fear or poison it with animosity. That doesn't mean that our politics will be less important or that Republicans and Democrats will come to agree on most issues. Far from it. Politics has never been more important, and differences openly expressed are the only way a democracy can make a choice. It just means that demonizing the other side doesn't facilitate the process that leads to informed consent of the governed.

The story we're told today by our current leadership is largely a can't-do story. In this book, I want to shine a light on this negative story and show how misleading it is. To do that, I had to put myself in the shoes of its proponents. I had to feel the way they feel about what they're telling us, and I have done my best to represent it accurately. I tell an alternate story—one that offers hope and sets out to inspire all Americans to work toward securing, as promised in the Preamble to our Constitution, "the blessings of liberty to ourselves and our posterity."

During the forty-two years I travelled around America—first as a basketball player, then as a United States senator, then as a presidential candidate—I formed a strong sense of what it meant to be an American. I visited every state in the union and travelled to thirty-one foreign countries—some regularly. I came to my own conclusions about what the United States meant to the world. As a candidate for the 2000 Democratic presidential nomination, I talked about the goodness of the American people—the heroic acts that seldom got reported, the courage shown against all odds, the generosity to strangers, the capacity to dream. I still believe in those American traits I observed firsthand over many years—traits that are part of our heritage.

But while Americans have inspiring stories to tell about their individual lives, these days you rarely hear an inspiring narrative about America itself. When I ran for president, I had a positive story in mind about what kind of country America had been, was, and could be. Losing the race did not diminish my desire to tell that story, to demonstrate that we can lead our nation and the world in new ways.

But first we need to examine the story we are told today—over and over, both in the media and by the present administration and its supporters—about America. What does it say is possible for us to achieve, both individually and as a nation? What does this story say about who we are, what we believe is important, what we are willing to sacrifice for? What are we proudest of? What do we have to offer other nations?

As I hear it, the story we're being told about America now goes something like this:

Today we are the most powerful nation in the world. Our economy dwarfs all others. Our military faces no serious challengers. We won the cold war. We need other countries less than before. We straddle the world like a colossus. Although it's true that many countries don't like us, that's the price of success, of leadership, of being number one.

Our democracy represents the world's most advanced form of governance. The free market, with its efficient allocation of resources, brings the greatest good to the greatest number of people. The most important values are individual economic freedom and faith in God. Government help to those in need can be replaced by the charitable, faith-based impulse of millions of Americans. Charity will suffice, because Americans are the world's most generous and devout people.

It's no coincidence that we have more millionaires than any other country. It's no surprise that we win more gold medals than any other Olympics participant. It's neither coincidental nor surprising that millions of people worldwide want to immigrate to America: After all, our songs are sung everywhere, our movies are watched around the globe, and everybody wears our blue jeans. We have what the world wants.

The most important thing to remember about our post-9/11 role in the world is that we are at war. The president's first job, as commander in chief, is to protect us from physical threats. Nothing is more essential than our national security. Without it, we will perish. People who oppose the war in Iraq are dangerously wrong. Would they prefer to fight the terrorists in Iraq or here in the United States?

There is evil in the world, and evil nations are doing evil things. We have to put the full weight of the United States on the side of righteousness and democracy, not only to ensure our own safety but to establish the freedom of people everywhere. The normal rules of war and of our judicial system cannot always be observed in this conflict. Terrorists have no appreciation of the sanctity of human life. Unless we take extreme measures, our enemies will inflict much pain, suffering, and death. America's very existence is at stake in this struggle. On the issue of constitutionality, we have to recognize that the president's fundamental responsibility is to protect the American people. Without guaranteed security, there would be no Constitution.

This is the story we're being told about our role in the world — but does operating under it really assure our long-term security? To continue:

America is not perfect, but none of our problems is unmanageable. Their seriousness is often exaggerated, generally for political reasons. Yes, our budget deficit is large, but as a percentage of our gross domestic product it is smaller than the deficits of the early 1980s. Yes, our trade deficit is at an all-time high, but in a world with $9.8 trillion in savings, foreigners may well be willing to continue lending us the money to finance our consumption of their exports. The U.S. economy is so big that foreign ownership of our assets still represents only a fraction of our total assets. That household indebtedness as a percentage of GDP is higher than it has ever been tells us only that the American consumer is the backbone of the economy. Just look at the crowds in the malls.

What's important for economic growth is to lower the tax burden on everyone, particularly on those who have the capital needed for investment. Without lower taxes, these people will have no incentive to invest — and their capital is the engine of our economy. Tax cuts produce economic growth, and accelerating growth leads to higher incomes and more tax revenue. Most people would rather keep the money they earn than send it to government to waste on programs that never seem to achieve their goals.

In fact, we really no longer need much government. Government

*only makes things worse. Most people can't even name a single govern-
ment program, other than Social Security or Medicare. Presidents
Clinton and Bush II agree on one thing—that the era of big government is over. Federal bureaucrats are the problem. They call themselves
civil servants, but they're really underachievers with secure jobs who
exert power by intrusive regulation that goes far beyond the intent of
the law. If government would just get out of the way, many of our problems would solve themselves. Government bureaucrats don't trust the
people to make decisions that are in their own long-term interest. They
insist they know what the people need better than the people themselves do.*

These are the claims of the story we're being told. But in the interdependent world we live in, can we really do without government? Without it, who would establish the rules for commerce?
And are we really prepared to assume direct personal responsibility for the lives of those who have fallen by the wayside? Aren't
there some things, besides national security, that only government
can do?

*Because most of us are skeptical of what government can accomplish
and don't want to finance its programs with higher taxes, any politi-
cian who argues that taxes ought to go up will lose. Look at Walter
Mondale. He lost to Ronald Reagan in 1984 because he told the
American people that as president he would raise taxes. George W.
Bush saw his father lose the presidency to Bill Clinton in 1992 because
Bush Senior had broken his pledge of "no new taxes." Many of the
House Democrats who lost their seats in the 1994 midterm elections
will tell you it was because they voted for the Clinton budget package,
which included higher taxes on the wealthy. Politicians underestimate
the American people when they say that without adequate taxes roads
will continue to deteriorate, schools will remain mediocre, pensions
will become even less secure, and those without health insurance will
stay uninsured. With the help of private enterprise, we will find a way
to strengthen vital services, and by cutting taxes we will starve those
parts of government that waste taxpayers' money. The Bush tax cuts*

have kept the economy healthy. Those who complain that nearly 55 percent of that money went to the wealthy ignore the fact that wealth is the driving force of capitalism.

That's the story on the economy. It goes hand in hand with the story we're told on the social safety net:

As for social programs, just look at Lyndon Johnson's War on Poverty. That's a war we have been losing from the moment of its inception. Since 1965, when LBJ moved poverty to the national agenda, we have spent trillions trying to end it. Every year we spend $180 billion to aid the poor with food, housing, health care, and other needs. And the result? There's as much poverty as ever. Poverty is not an economic problem, it is a cultural problem. Imagine the opportunities available to a fifteen-year-old girl who has a child out of wedlock, drops out of school by the time she's turned seventeen, and goes on welfare. They're bleak. If you want to solve poverty, promote marriage. Throwing money at the problem will never solve it.

Also, the prevalence of racism is grossly exaggerated—witness Colin Powell and Condoleezza Rice. The practice of affirmative action destroys the self-esteem of women as well as minorities. Our universities should admit students solely on the basis of grades and test scores, not some misguided policy of encouraging diversity. People ought to be rewarded (hired, promoted, admitted) because they're the best, not because of their gender or the color of their skin.

And what about energy and the environment?

As for the energy "crisis," those who assert that we're about to run out of oil ignore American ingenuity. Here and abroad, there are many places where oil exploration has just begun, and with friendly governments in those countries, we will have access to more oil resources. That's what we expect to happen in Iraq. In existing oil fields, new technology will allow us to get more out of old wells. If government provides enough economic incentives and relief from excessive environmental regulation, an abundant supply of oil is assured. Alternative energy sources are fine, but they cannot, in the foreseeable future, significantly reduce our need for oil.

Global warming is another myth. Scientific opinion is divided; no one really knows what affects the earth's climate in the long term. But we do know that forcing our economy to meet arbitrary standards on carbon dioxide emissions will cost American jobs now. We need to resist those who would endanger the U.S. economy to further their own radical (and erroneous) environmental agenda.

So that's the story we're told about the health of the planet. What's the story about the well-being of individual Americans?

To salvage pensions, people should be encouraged to invest in the stock market. Working people should be permitted to invest a part of their Social Security taxes on their own—another way in which government can help to empower the individual. The old social-insurance model embodied by the Social Security system is broken and can't be fixed. In the past, the young were willing to pay into the Social Security trust fund to take care of the old because they knew they would in turn be taken care of by the young when they retired. Nowadays, with more and more baby boomers retiring, the workforce soon won't be large enough to guarantee retirees the benefits they've been promised. Privatized Social Security is the only chance younger workers now have to receive a decent retirement income, and defined-contribution private pension plans are better than defined-benefit plans. Neither government nor the paternalistic company should be in charge of investing for the individual. People can be trusted to take care of their own money.

The numbers on health care can be deceptive. Uninsured Americans, like those below the poverty line, are different people at different times in the year. Moreover, many of them are young people who don't want to pay for health insurance even if it were offered at a bargain-basement price. When people really need help, they can go to local emergency rooms, where they will be taken care of. People tend to overutilize the health care system nowadays, because someone else is paying for it. What we need are tax-exempt health savings accounts.

The market will sort out who gets what coverage. The era of going to the doctor for every ache and pain and sending the bill to the rest of us will be over. A national health insurance plan would force people to give up the health insurance they have now and with which most of them are happy. Our retirees are covered by Medicare, which faces open-ended and unsustainable costs. It, too, would benefit from lower utilization. With seniors paying more out of their pockets for health care, government would have to pay less. Health savings accounts will help them do that.

Finally, here's the story on education:

Public education, as now constituted, is a monopoly that wastes money and produces meager results. What is needed is competition among providers. The use of vouchers for private and parochial schools — or, alternatively, the establishment of private corporations to run public elementary and high schools — would subject public education to market forces, thus guaranteeing improvement. Control should stay at the school board level. People closer to the culture of the students are best able to select teachers and establish curricula that will provide a quality education in each of the more than 14,300 school districts in America. One more thing: Social engineering to guarantee racial integration has never worked and should be abandoned. It's time to take civil rights out of the schools and put performance back in.

• • •

How do we feel overall about this story? Let's look at it more closely.

One reason it all seems so plausible is that we've heard it so many times. But while it may seem plausible, is it true? And is it consistent with the best of American history and reflective of what most Americans really want today? What are the consequences of accepting it, and what kind of country will it make us twenty years from now?

If we get beneath the surface of this story we're being told, we see that it's a paradoxical amalgam of soaring confidence and avowed limitations packaged in religious and moral certitude. It doesn't embody the "rugged individualism" that built this country, or the high aspirations John Winthrop had for the Puritans' New World as "a city upon a hill," or the spirit of tolerance that permeated the founding of Rhode Island by Roger Williams and Pennsylvania by William Penn, or the selfless feeling of community that Alexis de Tocqueville caught in his descriptions of early-nineteenth-century America. It is none of these things. It is, rather, a story about war, inequality, pollution, corruption, and hyperindividualism that plays out every day in the news. Instead of being blunt, experimental, forward-looking, egalitarian, and optimistic, as we were throughout our history, we are being presented as manipulative, predictable, obsessed with wealth, and preoccupied with all the bad things that could happen to us. Is this a true story about you and me?

Is there a better, truer story?

Of course there is.

The New American Story

The New American Story begins by facing our reality squarely. No lying. No fudging the numbers. No excuses for inaction. No wallowing in bad news. No spinning of good news. Just the facts. As Senator Daniel Patrick Moynihan once said, "You're entitled to your own opinion but not to your own facts." The number-one principle of the New American Story is that country comes before party. When there is a choice between them, a patriot chooses country.

Americans are not narrow and selfish, preoccupied only with today because we're fearful of the future. We are generous and expansive, capable of realizing our dreams because we can envision how each one of us can have a better tomorrow. We believe, and we have shown, that the human spirit can achieve great things. We are aware that the freedom to realize our individual potential must be balanced by the obligations we have to one another.

While the market is indeed the most efficient allocator of resources and the engine of economic growth, it's not the answer to every economic problem. The New American Story says that public investment in the health and education of individual Americans is good for all Americans and that those early in life and near the end of life need our collective support. It says that without sufficient national savings, we can't have the investment necessary to build a brighter future. Reducing the federal deficit is the quickest way to increase national savings, and the key to most fiscal issues is our income-tax system, which is currently a crazy quilt of contradictory, overly complex provisions. That system is at the root of our inability to increase national savings and investment and halt the growth of inequality. Whereas Republicans won't increase taxes, and Democrats won't cut spending enough, we should do both.

Globalization and technological advance offer the promise of greater prosperity for millions of people around the world. For this prosperity to be realized, countries must ensure that the benefits of open trade go to all their citizens and not just to the political elites, and the international system must establish rules that make these two transformative forces work for the poorest as well as the richest countries. The fates of all countries are bound together as never before.

The New American Story says you don't have to go to war to show you're a patriot, but you can't shy away from military force in times of imminent danger to the country. Global terrorism is a genuine threat to our lives. Opportunity can't deliver its richest dividends in a world of fear and violence.

There is a dangerous irony in the fact that whereas cultural issues, such as gay rights and legalized abortion, are important to *some* Americans, good jobs, pensions, health care, and education are important to *all* Americans—yet the political wrangling is disproportionately over the former. The New American Story confronts the special interests of each party, whether these interests are the public teachers' unions that resist changes in education or the corporate lobbyists who gut environmental laws. It asks all of us to go to a higher ground of patriotism, where we can see a time horizon further than the next election. Public policy should address the big issues that affect the maximum number of Americans.

To bring about the New American Story, we need all Americans to be involved. Less than half of the electorate regularly exercises the basic right to vote. We need to reform the electoral process: when we vote, the rules under which we vote, how we raise money for political campaigns, how the media cover our political life. It is important to remember that sovereignty rests with the people, not the elected. Just as rain nourishes our crops, so does the attention of the people nourish our democracy. Without citizen involvement, democracy will die. With it, great things are possible — for all of us.

Chapter 2.

THE HERITAGE

The new story we tell about America is really an old story we seem
to have forgotten—one that Thomas Jefferson and the other Founders told. It says we are a country unlike any other, dedicated to the
proposition that all people are created equal and with certain in-
alienable rights, including life, liberty, and the pursuit of happiness.
The Declaration of Independence does not say "life, liberty, and
property." It says "the pursuit of happiness," which means that, from
its very beginning, America has been in pursuit of an ideal. When
America was founded, there was a sense that it was fundamentally
something new in the history of the world. We were from the beginning a society based on individual liberty, which government was established to protect as the greater part of its purpose.

As the country grew and became more complex, we extended the
idea of liberty further—to more citizens and into new forms. Usually these changes happened because a leader arose who knew that
change was required. In the 1830s, when the commercial class did
what it wanted with the country and the little guy was trampled, Andrew Jackson arrived and, even with all his contradictions, broke the
hold of eastern financial capital over the lives of everyday working
people. In the 1860s, when slavery besmirched America's moral self-
image and civil conflict threatened the very existence of the country, Abraham Lincoln extended liberty to the slaves while keeping

the union together. In the early twentieth century, when the powers of commerce again dominated most of American life, Teddy Roosevelt's confidence, energy, and vision shifted power back to the people through his battle against Standard Oil and "representatives of predatory wealth." Woodrow Wilson continued the forward momentum of progressivism by giving women the right to vote, and thirty years later Franklin Delano Roosevelt gave millions hope in the Depression and led the country with skill through its biggest war.

Each of these men—three Democrats and two Republicans—succeeded because they told a story about America different from the one that ruled the day. The story they told evoked the grand sweep of our history: It was about how the promise of the Founders played out in their own times; it was about improvement in the daily lives of average people; it was about freedom in all its wondrous manifestations. These leaders challenged the conventional wisdom, finding in the unflagging spirit of the electorate the energy to build a better country.

The spirit of America has always been optimistic, pragmatic, and generous. We have no king, no hereditary aristocracy, no official religion—only citizens. Granted, some of these citizens wield immense power and others have none, yet upward mobility is a peculiarly American faith, and in every generation that faith is renewed. The advances of science and technology continually create a new world with new opportunities to achieve financial success. America is also the land of second chances: If you fail here, you can start anew. If you go bust, you can make another try, and no one counts your previous misfortune against you. America's economy and culture are resilient. There is no such thing as an "impossible idea" in this country; consequently, there are always a whole lot of ideas around, and many of them turn out to be very good indeed. America moves forward carried by the genius of a few and the adaptability and openness of many.

Whether we realize our ideals in this lifetime is immaterial, as long as we never give up trying. Susan B. Anthony and many of the other leaders of the fight to expand the benefits of citizenship to women did not live to receive the vote, but their daughters and nieces did. We Americans can never sit back and contemplate our achievements, because there is always more to do. We came together to form a more perfect union, but none of us individually or collectively will ever be perfect. The most we can hope for is to be complete—to know that as individuals we have done our best, both for ourselves and for our fellow citizens. We live with our limitations and our dreams simultaneously and still find in each day the joy of being alive in such a country.

There are many things right about America—the ingenuity of our people, the diversity of our culture, the genius of our democracy, the richness of our land, with its huge resources. The Founders gave us political institutions flexible enough to allow us to adjust to new times. If we remain true to their values and attuned to what wants to be born, we can use those institutions to adapt to new challenges. Remember, when the United States Constitution was adopted, only white males with property could vote. Whether it was abolishing slavery, limiting the power of corporations, cleaning up the environment, waging war, securing peace, managing the economy, or using the resources of active government, we have shown an impressive creativity in building a better, stronger, and more just country. Sometimes the forces of a reactionary status quo triumphed—even for decades—but when the bulk of the people was not being served, sooner or later they woke up, found a voice, asserted themselves, and moved the country forward. All it took was committed individuals, a just cause, active followers, a lot of hard work, and a little luck. In addition, at critical moments in our nation's history, real leaders emerged—George Washington, Thomas Jefferson, Andrew Jackson, Abraham Lincoln, Teddy Roosevelt, Woodrow Wilson, Franklin Roosevelt, Harry Truman, Dwight Eisenhower, Lyndon Johnson, Ronald Reagan.

The advances of the last forty years only confirm our optimism: Our air and water are cleaner. Individual rights have become a part of our legal fabric. Breakthroughs in health care and nutrition have extended life expectancy. In the whole of the twentieth century, as Colin Powell pointed out at the World Economic Forum in Davos, Switzerland, the only land America ever sought in the wake of military victory was enough for a cemetery to bury our dead. We have made mistakes, as any country as powerful and fractious as we are would. But none have been fatal or even close to it. Today's mistakes seem more egregious and occur more frequently, but America still has a large bank account of untapped greatness.

American exceptionalism has come to be synonymous with American arrogance in recent years, but the real uniqueness of Americans is our lack of pretension, our respect for the spiritual, our willingness to help a neighbor, and (some might say) our earthiness, with all that implies about our essential humanity. The New American Story we tell now doesn't flinch from saying that all is not well if it isn't—or that we can do better, if we can. At its core is a confidence as hard as New Hampshire granite and as wide as the Kansas horizon—a conviction that we still have something to give to the world: not weapons or money or pollution, but our shining example.

Jefferson always said that the best way for Americans to lead was by the power of example. I believe he was right. For those who diminish our example as part of the new story, I can only say, "Excuse me. Read our history. See when you get a lump in your throat or tears come to your eyes." It's not when the millionth millionaire is created or when we've invaded yet another overmatched country; rather, it's when we have acted responsibly, expanded our tolerance to new levels, arranged for more of our citizens to have a better life, made a collective sacrifice for strangers in need, or lost lives battling foreign tyranny when it threatened our existence and that of our allies. Our example makes the new story come alive. If each of us looked in the mirror, what would we, in our best moments, want to see? What would we want that example to be?

America at its best is a caring community. We see it every day in acts of one individual toward another. But there is something larger. A friend of mine told me about a mother and her nine-year-old son who went to Washington, DC. They came out of a subway, and there sat a homeless man begging for money. The little boy saw the man, reached into his pocket, and pulled out the money he had been saving over the last year to spend during the trip. He looked up at his mother, and she said that what he did was up to him. He gave the man half of what he'd saved. They walked around the corner, and there sat three more homeless men begging. The boy looked sadly at his mother and said, "I don't have enough money." She said, "Take this as a lesson. There are some things in life that you can't do alone." This is what government is for—to help us do together what we can't do by ourselves.

Government provides the way for us to help those in need, in amounts that can make a difference. That doesn't mean you stop helping people one at a time, but it does mean that government is not something to be denigrated. Amid all the micromanagement, self-indulgence, turf battles, and timidity in the federal bureaucracy, there are dedicated people working long hours to make the world a better place. Hold them accountable, yes, but don't stigmatize them. Only through government can we assure health care and pensions for everyone. Only government has the legitimacy and consensus-building ability to deal with national problems too big for the individual or private charities to solve and requiring too much selflessness to be left to the private sector. We have done big things before as a national community. We put Americans on the moon, won difficult wars, built the intercontinental railroad, invented the Internet, passed civil rights laws, helped millions get a toehold on a better life—and we can do it again.

A good society recognizes the elderly for what they have given and the sick for what they can still give, and values all people just because they're human beings. A good society as rich as ours recognizes that as long as sick children can't see a doctor or workers laid off after thirty years lose their pensions, we are diminished as a nation. It is possible for our educational system to have exceptional teachers with the best technology, giving individually tailored instruction in diverse ways which make education so exciting that kids won't want to leave at the end of the school day and assuring that graduates are produced who are knowledgeable, motivated, and creative. It is possible to protect the natural world, which every year as the seasons change reminds us of death and rebirth and the return of all things. What is at stake on a personal level is the continued availability of those experiences of nature for our children. What is at stake on a higher level is life itself on our planet.

Some people might say that we can't keep the New American

Story's promises on pensions, health care, and education without endangering our ability to compete in the world economy. To the contrary, fulfilling these promises will improve our competitiveness. Each proposal is an investment in our most precious asset—our people—and by fulfilling our commitments to one another, we will make all of us stronger. We won't be like Europe, with its overly generous, and in the long run unsustainable, welfare state, which micromanages the workplace to a degree that discourages job creation. We won't be like China, with its buccaneer capitalism, paltry safety net, and deteriorating environment. We will be our own best selves, smart enough to keep our economy dynamic and wise enough to prepare all of our citizens to contribute their very best.

There comes a time in our country when self-interest must yield to collective interest, when denial must yield to common sense, when individuals working together can realize their power and act. We are at such a time. The New American Story offers us a vision of what it would be like to fulfill the promise of the Founders. It encourages all of us to realize our potential as citizens and human beings. It applauds excellence and rewards innovation. It recognizes that war represents a failure of imagination—but that sometimes peace is not immediately attainable. It guarantees a strong military, even as it seeks to avoid deploying our forces. It urges us to lead the world by our example as a pluralistic democracy with a vibrant economy that takes more and more people to higher economic ground. The new story reminds us of what we can be as a nation when we realize our potential. It strengthens the bonds of our solidarity as Americans by telling us that we share a common life and a common destiny—a part of which allows each individual to soar as high as his or her abilities will allow and another part of which demands fulfillment of obligations to our neighbor.

The New American Story asks all Americans to join the team of active, conscientious citizens who want to build a better America. It doesn't matter if you're Republican or Democrat or independent. All you have to do is look at the world around you—with our prestige falling, the climate heating up, 46 million Americans without health insurance, millions of children stuck in schools that don't teach, countless hardworking Americans whose pensions have been cut in half or cancelled and who are forced to work two jobs to equal what they were once paid for one. All you have to do is take in all of this and then decide that none of it is tolerable. All you have to do is seek real solutions, not rhetorical talking points, election-year slogans, or public relations spin. The New American Story says that all these problems are opportunities to show the world and ourselves that freedom and fairness are not mutually exclusive and that the short term doesn't have to be the enemy of the long term.

There might be no single answer to all of America's challenges, but whatever is proposed must be bold enough to alter real conditions in a reasonable period of time. The fate of our country requires us to make sure that all Americans have the chance to do great things. America has always been shaped by the hard work of individuals and by our collective aspirations. Now is the time to come together and aspire again. We must invite all Americans to seize this moment, to get into the action, to fight for a bigger vision and, in the process of the struggle, be transformed. Ultimately, the New American Story is about more than how we organize our parties for battle; it's about our self-respect and our ability to lead in the world. It speaks to our hearts as well as our heads. Our common humanity asks us to do more than win elections; it requires us afterward to use the power the people have given the elected to make life better for all Americans and all the people of the world. It is an awesome responsibility—and at the same time it's a glorious opportunity.

So let's look at six issue areas important to America's future. I'll repeat the story we're told about these subjects, and then I'll offer an alternative from the New American Story.

Part II.

THE NEW AGENDA

Chapter 3.

AMERICA'S ROLE IN THE WORLD

The thrust of the story we are told today about America's role in the world is that, because we are the world's dominant power, the views of other countries are no longer as important to us as they once were, and that our national objectives must take precedence over international rules and agreements (including some we created and shaped after World War II). We are told that we have an obligation to promote our values worldwide, by force if necessary, that we are at war with the evil forces of international terrorism, and that the war in Iraq is part of that struggle.

What good is it, the story asks, to have the world's strongest military if you never use it? The world respects us because we're not afraid to stand up for our values. While it's true that many countries don't like us, that's the price we pay for leadership. We have what the world wants. That's why millions want to immigrate to our shores. Our democracy represents the world's most advanced form of governance. We are putting the full weight of our nation on the side of righteousness and democracy, not only to assure our safety but also to bring freedom to people everywhere.

The flaws in this story are numerous. In a recent essay titled "Why Bush's Grand Strategy Fails," G. John Ikenberry, a professor at

Princeton's Woodrow Wilson School of Public and International Affairs, sums them up with admirable succinctness:

> The contradiction in the Bush foreign policy is that it offers the world a system in which America rules the world but does not abide by rules. This is, in effect, empire. As such it is both unsustainable at home and unacceptable abroad. A unipolar order without a set of rules and bargains with other countries leads to a system of coercive unipolar American dominance. As the Iraq episode shows all too clearly, under these circumstances other countries will tend to "under supply" cooperation. They will do so either because they decide to free ride on the American provision of security, or because they reject the American use of force that is unconnected to mutually agreed upon rules and institutions—or both. So the United States will find itself—as it does now—acting more or less alone and incurring the opposition and resistance of other states. This is the point when the conservative unipolar vision becomes unsustainable inside the United States. The American people will not want to pay the price for protecting the world while other countries free ride and resist.

Globalization

The biggest flaw in the story we are told now is that it unfolds in ways that seem ignorant of the forces shaping the world. The world is more interdependent than ever, and the challenges it faces today require multilateral answers. Only countries acting together can effectively share intelligence on terrorists, regulate the flow of refugees, facilitate the growth of legitimate trade, reduce global warming, counter global organized crime, stop the spread of pandemic disease, limit arms trade, manage the interdependence of the world economy, stem the influx of counterfeit goods and illegal immigrants, and ameliorate the desperate poverty of over a billion of the world's people. Every time we announce a new military doctrine—such as preemptive war, however intellectually defensible in the new world of terrorism and advanced technology—without consulting our traditional allies, an alliance that was once rock solid becomes more frayed and strained. America can continue to act unilaterally, but the more we do so, the less we'll be able to accomplish, and eventually even we will be unable to do as we like in an increasingly chaotic, uncooperative, polarized, and angry world.

Globalization is nothing new. It existed even when Marco Polo went to China. What is different about globalization today is the degree to which, because of the confluence of economic, political, and technological factors, nation-states are losing control of their own economies. Interest rates in Tulsa or Miami or Philadelphia are set by international capital flows as much as by the chairman of the Federal Reserve. In fact, the monetary authorities must respond to those capital flows by either lowering or raising interest rates. Multinational corporations shop the world for the lowest labor costs and choose low-tax nations in which to situate their facilities. Global competition limits the ability of a national legislature to set high tax rates on resident corporations. If a government raises taxes, the corporation can simply move to another jurisdiction. Individual workers born in one country labor in another. Indeed, there are more people today living outside the country in which they were born than at any other time in history, and these migrations have profound impacts on the host countries.

Not only is the economic system global but so is the environment. If we clean up our car exhausts but China doesn't, global warming will not markedly improve. If we clean up our smokestacks while Brazil continues to burn its rain forest, global warming will increase at the same time habitat is destroyed and with it the species from which we derive many of our medicines.

Organized crime is also global. Moisés Naím, editor of *Foreign Policy* magazine and author of the startling book *Illicit: How Smugglers, Traffickers, and Copycats Are Hijacking the Global Economy*, tells of Africans from Cameroon or Nigeria who sell counterfeit Prada bags on the streets of New York that have been produced in China from designs stolen in Milan. Some experts estimate that at least 20 percent of world trade is illegal. Governments have been unable to stop the theft of intellectual property because the criminal networks are international whereas the authority of states in this area is national.

Today what moves across international boundaries is not just goods and people but also styles, ideas, information, and disease. Kids in Kazakhstan wear Michael Jordan T-shirts. Americans eat Afghan food. Brazilians dance to Bruce Springsteen. Europeans listen to Cesaria Evora. My friend Palaniappan Chidambaram, India's finance minister and a former Congress Party MP, told me once about campaigning in his district, in Tamil Nadu. After shaking hands with his constituents, as politicians do worldwide, he went into a tea shop to have a cup of tea. He was served by the thirteen-year-old son of the proprietor. Chidambaram asked the boy what he wanted to be when he grew up. "I want to go into computers," the boy said.

"Why?" asked Chidambaram.

"So I can be like Billy Gates, the richest man in the world," the boy replied. The story of Microsoft, on the shores of Puget Sound, in the state of Washington, in the United States of America, had travelled 8,000 miles around the globe and ignited the imagination of a little boy in a tea shop in southern India.

Technology, especially information technology, supercharges both the positive and negative effects of globalization. Today, financial panics could begin if thousands of computers that were keyed into an automatic program spit out the instructions to sell; in a nanosecond, the bottom would drop out of the financial markets. Criminals or hostile powers could wreak havoc in our country simply by attacking the software programs of our financial institutions or energy grids.

The spread of disease is the dark side of the free flow of goods, capital, and labor. Someone with SARS can get on a plane in China and end up in New York thirteen hours later. AIDS moves from country to country with the inevitability of natural sexual contacts. Avian flu breaks out in some remote village in Indonesia and American businessmen cancel their trips to a conference in Jakarta because they're worried about contracting the disease. The emergence of Ebola virus or some other new mutated disease creates fear in the minds of health planners at the World Health Organization, the U.S. Centers for Disease Control and Prevention, and beyond.

Each of these examples of interdependence has real impact on the health and well-being of the American people. Each poses a new challenge for policy makers to integrate into an overall view of how to protect America's future. In spite of all these strong indications of the force of globalization, in 2002, according to David Sanger of *The New York Times*, the word "globalization" didn't even appear in the Bush administration's national security strategy report. The administration has done little in the way of sharing the fruits of globalization with more than its corporate supporters. It has called for democracy in Iraq but resists democratizing international economic institutions—a case in point being the International Monetary Fund. In the last several decades, the austerity of the IMF's conditions for assistance indicates a lack of concern for the welfare and even the lives of average people.

Don't misunderstand me. I believe that if our government and others were to make sure that economic growth was shared fairly, globalization and technological change would be capable of raising living standards for the greatest number of people in the history of the world. These two forces could also lay the foundation for the widest dispersion of democracy the world has ever known.

But let's think a little about another possibility. Think of young Saudis radicalized by the Soviet occupation of Afghanistan, the first Gulf War, and the placement of American forces in the country that contains Islam's two holiest sites, Mecca and Medina. They get their news about America from CNN; they learn about counterterrorism from U.S. government Web sites; they transfer money through an international banking system; they train in cells in Germany and flight schools in Florida; they board international aircraft and fly to the United States, where some stay in Boston and others rent cars and inexplicably drive to Portland, Maine, where they board planes headed back to Boston, rejoin their colleagues, continue on to Los Angeles, and divert the planes into the World Trade Center. That is globalization and technological change as well.

Terrorism

Another problem with the story we are told about our role in the world is that we have declared a war on terrorism but have been given no clear definition of terrorism. Any repressive regime, from Egypt to Kazakhstan, is thus free to label its domestic critics as terrorists and ruthlessly suppress them, all the while justifying internal persecution by declaring itself America's "ally" in the "war on terror." Vagueness is often useful in diplomacy; it is disastrous in defining national doctrine. We call the opponents of unfriendly regimes (such as Iran) "freedom fighters." The domestic opponents of our authoritarian allies (such as Saudi Arabia) are "terrorists." Our rhetoric is all about democracy, but our actions suggest that we are quite comfortable with authoritarian regimes. This flagrant inconsistency damages our credibility around the world and provides support to those who charge us with hypocrisy.

All terrorism is not the same. Our failure to make distinctions muddles our policy. The global terrorist network, like the international criminal network, consists of very bright people. Indeed, two-thirds of the hijackers and planners for 9/11 had attended college. Many in the global network's leadership were radicalized in the context of a European society that opened up to them but regularly humiliated and marginalized them and regarded them as "other." Exposure to the West fed their resentment and outrage. Al Qaeda is not like the IRA, the Basque separatists, or even the Palestinians: All these are nationalist organizations that exist in relation to a nation-state. Al Qaeda is more nihilistic and messianic—dedicated to destroying our values and the opportunities that flow from them.

The terrorism of today is a distributed threat—remember all those information networks? It is nothing like Hitler with his armies poised on the border ready to invade Poland, or Saddam with his army on the border with Kuwait; rather, it consists of thousands of franchises spread across the world, each one possessing the means to ignite a terrorist event. Many of the necessary materials are already in place, and so are the perpetrators, who wait for a signal, which can be something as innocuous as a small flower that one day appears in the lower right-hand corner of a Web site on ancient Islamic texts.

The current strategy for dealing with the global terrorist network is simply to destroy it. I agree. But in this task armies of occupation and "shock and awe" air campaigns are not as important as intelligence, police work, commando operations, and targeted military strikes. In the nineteenth century, we stopped piracy on the high seas by giving the pirates no safe haven. If we want to do the same to the terrorists, allies are indispensable. If we truly believe that terrorism is the greatest threat the United States faces, then every foreign policy decision must take into account its effects on our allies.

But prosecuting the war on terrorism requires something more than destroying Al Qaeda and its imitators. The international terrorist swims in a sea of non-terrorist Muslims who are often poor and uneducated. They give the terrorist cover and sometimes, carried along by the popular mood, volunteer to martyr themselves for the cause. But they are different from Al Qaeda. When it comes to this group of potential terrorists and terrorist sympathizers, winning the war on terror requires us to respect Islam and understand its pluralism, to help restore the hope of Muslims everywhere for a better life here on Earth, and to make progress toward resolving the Israeli-Palestinian issue. To achieve these ends, we should urge Israel to give up more land for peace with secure borders. We should also confront the authoritarian regimes from which we get half our imported oil, demanding that they provide education and jobs for their citizens and stop buying domestic peace by allowing radical Islam to be preached in their mosques and Jihad to become a way of life for segments of their population.

The Bush administration has repeatedly declared that, in a post-9/11 world, everything has changed. It is certainly true that the way other nations look at us has changed—and not for the better. We have damaged our reputation for doing the right thing. In the name of fighting terrorism, we have proceeded to violate the rights of foreign nationals and our own citizens as no administration has since FDR's, when Japanese Americans were sent to internment camps during World War II. The Patriot Act of 2001, according to a civil rights consortium cited by Haynes Johnson in *The Age of Anxiety: McCarthyism to Terrorism*, gave the federal government new powers "to read your medical records, screen your credit card bills, search your home or business without telling you, patrol your Internet use, wiretap your phone, spy on you and your house of worship, examine your travel records, inspect your bookstore purchases, snoop on your library records, [and] monitor your political activities," all in the name of fighting terrorism. And you don't have to be a suspected terrorist to be subject to these new intrusions on your privacy. Since 9/11, in an echo of the midnight raids and summary deportation of foreign nationals by Woodrow Wilson's attorney general, A. Mitchell Palmer, during the Red Scare of 1919, we have detained in this country more than 5,000 foreign nationals, often for longer than six months, with extremely restricted opportunities for them to see, phone, or receive mail from their families or a lawyer. None of them has been convicted of terrorist acts.

Abroad, we have flouted the Geneva Conventions on the treatment of enemy combatants, Abu Ghraib being the signal—but not the sole—example. The practice of sending our prisoners to countries whose intelligence agencies will torture them has become a cynical way of denying that we torture prisoners. The result: The world—and not just the Muslim world—has now formed a new and unflattering picture of America. We have given a lot of ammunition to our worst enemies by our actions. Even our closest allies are ashamed of us for the gross abuses of international standards. Britain's minister in charge of policy in the Middle East, Kim Howells, has called for the closing of the Guantánamo detention center on the grounds that it contradicts everything America has always stood for. Our European allies are in various degrees of open rebellion against our policies. If this is leadership, where are the followers?

Iraq

The story we are told says that our invasion of Iraq was part of the war on terrorism, and a Harris Poll in July 2006 found that 64 percent of Americans still believe that there was a strong link between

Saddam Hussein and Al Qaeda. Yet each rationale offered before the war by the Bush administration and its supporters has proved false. Apart from the nonexistent weapons of mass destruction, there is the fact that the war's radicalizing effect on the Islamic world has heightened the possibility of fundamentalist control of Pakistan, which does have nuclear weapons. We were also said to be going into Iraq to prevent it from becoming a haven for terrorists—but now Al Qaeda and other terrorist groups from all over the Islamic world use the TV scenes of carnage there as a recruiting tool and the insurgency itself as a training ground for new fighters, who flock to Iraq because it is easier to kill Americans there than anywhere else. Establishing a friendly government in Iraq was supposed to give us military bases from which we could stage interventions from the Persian Gulf to Central Asia—but no independent Iraqi government will ever be able to allow that in the face of the inevitable objections of its own people. Creating a democracy in Iraq, it was argued, would have ripple effects throughout the region that would eventually benefit Israel—but the Iraqi people are overwhelmingly pro-Palestinian. It was supposed to be a restriction of our sovereign power to consult with Iraq's neighbors before the war so that they would be clear about our intentions—but now the opposition and hostility of those governments endanger our prospects for success. Indeed, the biggest beneficiary of the Iraq War has been Iran. It got rid of a feared enemy who killed 300,000 Iranians and injured another half million during the Iran-Iraq War of 1980–1988, and it markedly increased its influence among the Shia of southern Iraq. Finally, toppling Saddam Hussein was supposed to give us a friendly government in control of the second-largest proven oil reserves in the world, so that when supply was tight we could get it to pump more oil, thereby moderating prices. In fact the war and the insurgency have caused oil production to drop below prewar levels, creating the largest cumulative oil disruption since World War II—bigger even than the drop during the Iranian revolution of 1979 or the nationalization of Iran's oil fields in the 1950s. What will the widening civil war in Iraq produce for America, other than lost soldiers, lost wealth, and lost respect in the world?

It seems we've fallen into Al Qaeda's trap. Fouad Hussein, a Jordanian journalist, described in a 2005 book Al Qaeda's twenty-year plan to dominate a part of the world stretching from Spain to Indonesia. An early phase of the plan envisions the United States abandoning, as an Al Qaeda manual says, "its war against Islam by proxy" and going to war with a Muslim country in the region directly. The following phase involves a confrontation between the United States and Iran. In each phase, Hussein argues, Al Qaeda believes it will benefit. By doing exactly what they expected us to do, we've allowed the enemy to predict our actions and plan their responses before we've even taken them.

Our involvement in Iraq appears to have been based on several false assumptions.* We thought it would turn out like the first Gulf War, in which "shock and awe" led to immediate surrender. Instead, it is more like the war in Chechnya, where the application of massive force for a decade has yet to snuff out an insurgency. We thought the desire for democracy would produce the same results as it did in Eastern Europe, where country after country quickly embraced democracy and dampened sectarian differences. Instead, it is more like the war in Afghanistan, where the Taliban and other elements of the society stay outside the democratic process and use violence against the government. Finally, with the Balkans of the 1990s as our guide, we thought that a peaceful majority could overcome the violence of a few local insurgents and foreign jihadists. Instead, Iraq insurgents and foreign terrorists learned the lesson of Hezbollah in Lebanon in the early 1980s and Pakistani terrorists in Kashmir in the last decade. From those examples, they concluded that violence causing maximum deaths and economic damage can rout a superpower (as it did the United States in Lebanon) and prevent peace talks from succeeding (as with India and Pakistan). There is no evidence that our war planners ever considered the world as it might look to our adversaries. The Iraq War is the most serious foreign policy blunder I have seen in my lifetime.

Beyond the immense cost in American and Iraqi lives, we need to be aware of the hidden costs of our preoccupation with Iraq. The

---

*See *Risk Intelligence: Learning to Manage What We Don't Know* by David Apgar (Harvard Business School Press, 2006).

time, money, manpower, and brainpower that go into the war short-change our needs elsewhere: in Northeast Asia, where China is flexing its muscles as a world power and where tensions between China and Japan could get out of control; in Russia, where the state is becoming increasingly authoritarian and less and less cooperative with us; in Europe, where our unilateralism of the last six years with regard to the Kyoto Protocol, the Comprehensive Nuclear Test Ban Treaty, the International Criminal Court, the treatment of enemy combatants, and various trade disputes has weakened historical bonds; in Latin America, where Venezuelan president Hugo Chávez thumbs his nose at the United States and inspires imitators throughout the region; and finally in Iran, North Korea, and other countries where the cause of nuclear nonproliferation is being lost.

Let's look more closely at three of these neglected opportunities:

Over the last several years, there has been an ominous deterioration in relations between China and Japan. Nationalist passion has inflamed historical as well as current hostilities between the two countries. In its National Defense Program Guidelines released in late 2004, Japan identified China, along with North Korea, as a threat. Early in 2004, to support the U.S. effort, the Japanese sent troops to Iraq, thereby liberally interpreting their constitutional proviso that renounces war and implies that the Japanese military will be used only for self-defense. Later that year, a Chinese nuclear attack submarine entered Japanese waters. In 2005, the Chinese cancelled a visit by Japan's foreign minister, and earlier that year China's vice premier, on a trip to Japan, cancelled a meeting with then Japanese prime minister Junichiro Koizumi because of the Japanese leader's repeated trips to a shrine honoring Imperial Japan's war dead, including veterans of the brutal occupation of China from 1937 to 1945.

When Japan joined the United States in declaring peace in Taiwan as a shared strategic objective, Beijing accused Japan of violating the one-China policy it had previously agreed to. When Japan, which is the second largest contributor to the United Nations's budget, tried to get a permanent seat on the UN Security Council, Chinese citizens, probably at the government's urging, began a petition drive to oppose it. And in April 2005, Chinese citizens took to the streets. Rocks were thrown at the Japanese Embassy in Beijing, and Japanese flags were burned. Later that year, Prime Minister Koizumi appointed foreign policy hawks to prominent positions in his government. Each country claims rights to natural-gas deposits in the East China Sea, and in November 2005, a Chinese satellite-tracking ship cruised through the area. By 2006, conflict had simmered down somewhat, and the new Japanese prime minister, Shinzo Abe, has said he wants to improve relations with China, but tension still bubbles beneath the surface. Abe's declared objective of rewriting the constitution so Japan can have a military with offensive capability has set off alarm bells in China.

The historical animosity on both sides cannot be underestimated. Two years ago, I attended a dinner party for Mianheng Jiang, the vice president of the Chinese Academy of Sciences. After some reasonably sophisticated general conversation about politics, economy, art, and science, the host asked each of the nine guests around the table to make an observation or ask a question. When my turn came, I conveyed my concern about the Sino-Japanese relationship. The vice president's eyes narrowed; he slammed his hand down on the table so that the silverware jumped as he barked, "Exactly! You're exactly right! I teach my children never to forget what the Japanese did in China in the 1930s and 1940s. Never!"

The United States, preoccupied with Iraq, has done little to defuse this situation. We could have acted as an honest broker, urging each country to observe a cooling-off period after the persistent outbreaks of animosity between them. We could have asked the Japanese to be more forthcoming about their actions during their occupation of China. We could have urged each country, as we did France and Germany at the end of World War II, to revise the way it treats the other in its history books. We could have worked toward the creation of a regional energy consortium or begun a North Asian security dialogue. We did none of these things. To the contrary, our alarmist statements about growing Chinese military capabilities feed nationalist sentiment in Japan. With no apparent design, we have allowed ourselves to be pulled into a deeper and deeper alliance with Japan, with the unacknowledged effect being containment of China. Instead of positioning ourselves in the middle of the dispute and trying to cool it down, we are standing alongside one of the disputants, which has effectively heated it up.

Latin America, especially Venezuela, is another example of opportunity lost. In Venezuela, we tried to influence politics in a ham-fisted way, silently condoning a briefly successful coup and after its failure blatantly siding with the ultraconservative elements of society. Our ineptness has contributed to the rise of Hugo Chávez, an anti-American populist who in 2006 shocked the United Nations with a speech that eight times referred to President Bush as a devil. With little attention devoted to the region because of Iraq, we have played virtually no role in the events of the last two years in Bolivia, Brazil, Ecuador, and Argentina, where fed up with the corruption, exclusion, and incompetence of previous regimes, the citizenry has elected governments that are suspicious of the United States and question the wisdom of free trade.

During this time, we made no apparent diplomatic initiatives. It was as if the only things we wanted to talk about with Latin America were drugs and immigrants, both of which we wanted to keep out of the United States. We had no expressed plan for the region that would convey to the peoples of Latin America that we understood their aspirations for a better life, and that we were with them. We failed to assert powerfully why market reforms are still the best path, as long as the benefits are shared with the people, as opposed to accruing to a small elite. All we managed to provide was an occasional photo opportunity for one or another Latin American head of state in the Oval Office. A photo opportunity is no replacement for an engaged policy.

Some of our actions have backfired. For example, we slapped Chávez's Venezuela with sales restrictions on spare parts for its old F-16 American-made fighter jets, thereby forcing him to turn to Russia to buy their newer SU-30 fighter jets. It was reported in the Russian business newspaper *Vedomosti* that Chávez also will buy Russian surface-to-air missile systems that could shoot down American planes and cruise missiles. By selling the jets, Russia is telling the United States, "If you play in our backyard in Central Asia, we can play in your backyard, too." Meanwhile, Chávez has succeeded in wooing the region with money. He sends oil to Fidel

Castro at cut-rate prices and literacy volunteers to Bolivia. United States aid to Latin America amounts to $1.9 billion, almost half of it military aid. With oil at over $60 per barrel at the time of this writing, Chávez has spent $25 billion selling cheap oil, buying foreign bonds, and assisting efforts to improve the health and education of his neighbors. His money and his hostile, confrontational attitude toward the United States could lead to a growing anti-American movement in Latin America.

The proliferation of nuclear weapons represents the third opportunity lost because of the Iraq War. Since taking office, the Bush administration has rejected the very concept of nonproliferation. It has taken the view that it is not the weapons themselves but the countries which possess them that create the danger. For Bush, overthrowing a government—regime change—became a nonproliferation policy, but unilateral U.S. invasion of every country we suspect of developing weapons of mass destruction cannot be a sustainable policy on either economic or political grounds. By opting for this direction, the administration has turned its back on the entire international regime (safeguard agreements, export controls, International Atomic Energy Agency inspections, supplier club regulations, and, most important, the Nuclear Non-Proliferation Treaty itself) that over thirty years reduced the number of nuclear weapons in the world and the number of countries with weapons programs. It may be too late to prevent Iran and North Korea from becoming nuclear nations, but if there is a chance, it will require multilateral action within a robust international nonproliferation regime.

Our withdrawal from the Anti-Ballistic Missile Treaty, rejection of the Comprehensive Nuclear Test Ban Treaty, and stated desire to develop new nuclear bombs (the most destructive of the so-called bunker busters) created the impression that not only did the administration abandon nonproliferation as a policy but it wanted to sabotage chances for nonproliferation. Consumed by Iraq, the Bush administration apparently wanted no consensus to emerge out of the 2005 Nuclear Non-Proliferation Treaty Review Conference and actively undermined any chances of achieving it, thereby guaranteeing its failure. Since the United States is the world's largest nuclear power, without us there can be no real progress on the proliferation issue. It was left to the Carnegie Endowment for International Peace, a nonprofit foundation, to put forward a nonproliferation plan and then do the painstaking work of trying to build an international consensus on the direction of nonproliferation policy. But a farsighted nonprofit can't begin to compare with the U.S. government in clout or reach.

Neglect wasn't the only failure of this administration. In agreeing to a deal that implicitly ratified India's nuclear policy, the Bush administration set back the goal of nonproliferation worldwide. We put ourselves in the indefensible position of saying that it's OK for India to have nuclear bombs but not Iran. Whether the Indian agreement was a part of an anti-China containment policy or a hedge against a fundamentalist regime in nuclear Pakistan, the deal was a blow to nonproliferation. If Shia Iran now gets a nuclear weapon, then the Saudis and Egyptians will need a Sunni bomb, and Turkey will seek one, too. Add to that Israel's bombs, and suddenly the region will be a hair trigger away from a doomsday scenario—not unlike Europe on the brink of World War I. It took the Great Depression to catalyze international economic cooperation. One hopes that we won't have to wait until a devastating nuclear disaster before we remember the value in cooperation.

Politics: Soft Power—Hard Power

In an administration which believes that the only legitimacy for U.S. policy stems from the consent of the governed here at home and not from international opinion, domestic interest groups and politics have come to dominate our foreign policy to a troubling degree. For forty years it has been the policy of this country that the final status of the West Bank should come out of negotiations between Israel and the Palestinians without predetermining the boundaries. The Bush administration abandoned this policy and explicitly promised Prime Minister Ariel Sharon that the borders of Israel and Palestine established in any eventual peace settlement would not be the same as those in 1967. The apparent reason for this policy shift was the need to pander to the Christian right—an important part of the Republican Party's base—which believes that

God gave the land to the Jews and that the Jews' return to the Christian holy land is the necessary precursor to the conflict that will lead to the second coming of Christ (which would mean, to these same religionists, the eternal damnation of those Jews who choose not to accept Jesus as their Lord and Savior). For loyal allies such as Tony Blair, who forcefully supported the Iraq War but has sought a more evenhanded policy on the Israeli-Palestinian conflict, our defection was a stab in the back.

The story we're told is a one-dimensional approach to the world. It says that, for most of what threatens us, there is a military solution. It is easy for the United States to intimidate a small country but not so easy to convince its citizens of our genuine interest in their well-being. We forget that America's unique appeal was never based on our military or economic power but on what Joseph Nye, former dean of Harvard's Kennedy School of Government, and others have called our "soft power": our credibility coupled with our attractiveness as a productive and free society.

In 1992, I sponsored a law creating the largest student exchange program in history between the United States and the countries of the former Soviet Union. By 2003, when I attended the tenth anniversary of that program in Kiev, more than 14,000 high school juniors from Russia, Ukraine, Kazakhstan, Georgia, Turkmenistan, and the other republics had lived a year with an American family. The most striking thing about the 400 kids who came to Kiev as representatives of the 14,000 was what they recalled about their stay in America. They were impressed by our material abundance, our democracy, and our popular culture, but it was the nonprofit sector that inspired them. It was eye-opening to them that citizens would raise money and create organizations to help strangers with no expectation of getting something back for themselves. After returning home, many of these young people had raised money and started their own organizations. A young man from Uzbekistan was drilling water wells to provide safe drinking water for the rural poor. A group of young men and women from Ukraine went from school to school lecturing about the dangers of AIDS. I remember one girl in particular. She was disabled. When she returned to St. Petersburg, she told us, she founded an organization to help the disabled in that city "live a normal life," because in her year in the United States she had been inspired to believe that she herself could.

The ultimate soft-power challenge is to show countries with little experience in civil society or the rule of law or free speech how to build democratic institutions—an independent judiciary, an elected legislature, a vibrant press—that will allow them to move from their totalitarian past to a democratic future without violence. With each exercise of hard power that is unrelated to self-defense or is pursued unilaterally, we lose respect in the world. The time is past when other countries hungered for our approval. Instead, the rest of the world looks at us with growing wariness. They wonder what we will do with all our power. Will we use it to promote only our own well-being, or will we work to build a world in which they, too, can realize their dreams?

Even in a post–cold war world, being the world's chief military superpower has obvious advantages. No country is under any illusion that it could win a shooting war with the United States. It was, after all, the threat of U.S. military action that forced Iraq to open itself to intrusive inspections for weapons of mass destruction. But in our hubris, we sometimes forget that conflicts escalate in a political context and always have unpredictable consequences. Who would have thought, before the first Gulf War, that the stationing of U.S. troops in Saudi Arabia, the home of Islam's holiest cities, would have caused an obscure malcontent named Osama bin Laden to redirect his hostility from the House of Saud to America? Who would have voted to invade Iraq in 2003 if it had been clear that we'd be caught in the middle of a civil war whose roots go back more than 1,000 years?

The more we go it alone, using military force as a first resort, the less likely it is that our allies will support our other goals. When we flex our military muscle, especially if there is no direct threat to us, we are seen as a country bent on world dominance, determined to export our political values and promote our economic self-interest, no matter the cost or the wishes of those we're exporting to. But for our military power to be a force for good requires an internationally accepted legitimacy for its use. The UN could have provided that in Iraq, but we preempted its work by our invasion. By ignoring international norms and institutions, the Bush administration has taken a first step toward dismantling the international institutional architecture that gives the world an escape route from disaster through miscalculation. Deciding when and how U.S. military power will be deployed is one of the fundamental challenges to the international system. The United States should be leading the effort to achieve legitimacy for our actions. Sadly, we are doing the opposite.

The more we fritter away our moral authority, the smaller the room for diplomatic maneuver and the weaker our impact on the world. As Reinhold Niebuhr wrote in *Moral Man and Immoral Society*, "A country will have authority and influence because of moral factors, not its military strength; because it can be humble and not blatant and arrogant. . . . And a nation without morality will soon lose its influence around the world." A June 2006 *Financial Times/ Harris* Poll found that, on average, a third of the people in five European countries—France, the United Kingdom, Italy, Germany, and Spain—see the United States as the number-one threat to world peace. Our standing was even worse in 2003, when a Eurobarometer Survey revealed that 55 percent of the British respondents saw the United States as such a threat.

It is not surprising, then, that China and Russia have energized the five-year-old Shanghai Cooperation Organization, which includes several central Asian countries, with Iran knocking at the door. While today the group focuses on energy and preventing expansion of U.S. influence, it could easily become a military alliance that could challenge NATO tomorrow. But Chancellor Angela Merkel of Germany told a New York audience recently that her country's relationship with Russia, which is based on oil and gas imports and economic cooperation, is unchallengeable. She sees Russia as a partner, not a threat. If you add these developments to the arc of anti-American regimes powered by oil in Latin America, you see that the legacy of the last six years could well be the long-term isolation of the United States in the world.

The World After 9/11

In today's world, no president (or prime minister or chancellor) can give citizens a 100 percent guarantee that a terrorist bomb won't explode in St. Louis or Tokyo or Paris or Sydney tonight. We have to learn to live with a greater sense of insecurity. It has become more or less habitual for airline passengers to scan one another suspiciously. For those of us who cross the Golden Gate Bridge or drive through the Lincoln Tunnel or go to the top of the Sears Tower, the thought of possible terrorist action is never far out of mind. Such a new reality can make people edgy. But before we are carried away by anxiety, it's important to remember that we have been here before.

Like many of you, I am a child of the cold war. In Crystal City, Missouri, in the 1950s, the threat of nuclear war was vivid. I kept a diagram of my own private bomb shelter, which, in a child's naïve way, I knew my father would build for the family if things got really bad. In that drawing, I had designated where I would put my cot, my favorite snacks, my favorite books, my basketball. (Even after a nuclear holocaust, you understand, there would be basketball.) But I had to live with the fear.

Finding a sense of peace in a time of growing insecurity is not an easy task. We cannot deny the reality of the threat—but neither should we exaggerate it. The prospect of terrorism need not distract us from our hopes and ambitions for ourselves and our families; indeed, we have to hold both possibilities in mind simultaneously and not be carried away by either.

Only cooperation, strength, generosity, and vision can move the world in the right direction. The key to all of that is leadership, and no leader is more powerful than the president of the United States. He can have an impact on the world by what he does and what he says, by how well he listens and to whom, by the caliber of the people around him, by how attuned he is to people's aspirations worldwide, by how he defines America and its role in the world.

After President John F. Kennedy's assassination, I remember the stories of journalists and foreign aid workers who found his picture on the walls of rural huts in Latin America and in the slums of Karachi, Cairo, and Cape Town. He had struck a sympathetic chord in people worldwide, and his untimely death marked the end of our post–World War II innocence.

Lyndon Johnson was the inheritor of the goodwill stemming from November 22, 1963, but he was also the right man at the right time. He knew how to get things done, and he was possessed of a large spirit. For a brief time between Kennedy's assassination and the galloping tragedy of Vietnam, it was possible to believe in a better world. After the national trauma came the success of LBJ's powerful domestic agenda—Medicare, Medicaid, federal aid to education, the civil rights acts. He made difficult decisions consistent with the best of America's ideals. His vision matched the moment. He transformed the country for the better.

That was more than forty years ago, and much has changed in America. But I thought of those days many times after September 11, 2001—another national tragedy, even more suddenly, shockingly violent than Kennedy's assassination. President Bush's speechwriter referred to 9/11 as a "teachable moment," which is a time when people listen to their leaders in ways they do only when they're ready to be led. I agree. Fear makes people seek the protective reassurance of a leader, who intuits when it is right to comfort, to challenge, to ask for sacrifice. There is an outpouring of caring, support, national unity. It is at such moments that a president can put his imprint on history. He can fit his dreams for the country to the opportunity the tragedy presents, as Johnson did in 1964, in the wake of JFK's assassination.

When the World Trade Center towers fell, I was in England, having been bumped off a flight to New York just before takeoff. When shopkeepers and clerks in London saw I was American, they offered their condolences and prayers for the United States. Some talked about how Americans had come to Britain's rescue in World War II. Others talked about our "special relationship" as English-speaking peoples. Many told me how much America meant to them. The next day, *Le Monde*, France's greatest newspaper, had a headline that read, WE ARE ALL AMERICANS.

In the ensuing weeks, New York was a different place. New Yorkers always pull together in a crisis—a blackout, a transit strike, a blizzard—but September 11 created a deeper response: People seemed more open, more vulnerable, more in need of human connection. They grieved together, prayed together, sought understanding together. They looked to the president. It was a teachable moment.

George Bush, in the days, weeks, and months that followed the attacks, conveyed strength and resolve. Every time he spoke, I'm sure I felt like a lot of Americans—I wanted him to do well. His clarity and decisiveness led us to Afghanistan, where the perpetrators were holed up. The world supported him, and the U.S. military made short work of the Taliban government and many Al Qaeda loyalists. It was a time of national and international unity, and the president passed the test of leadership as commander in chief in a crisis.

But an American president is also leader of the world. He commands respect not just because of how strong we are but also because of how good we try to be—remember the pictures of JFK in those villages. To be a transformative leader is to give the world a vision of what it can become. It has to be a vision clear enough, expansive enough, inclusive enough so that a kid in Jakarta, a lawyer in Rio, a factory worker in Korea can see that their future can be better, too, if the vision is realized. At their best, American presidents have done that. President Truman, for example, showed what could come out of the rubble of World War II: not just increased American military might but the Marshall Plan to get Europe back on its feet and international economic institutions such as the World Bank, the International Monetary Fund, the General Agreement on Tariffs and Trade—all of which promised a more prosperous life for all the people of the world.

After his initial show of strength and single-mindedness in attacking Al Qaeda bases and liberating Afghanistan from the Taliban, George Bush essentially wasted the world leadership potential of his teachable moment. Maybe he didn't see it. Maybe he didn't have anything more to say. Maybe he didn't want to take the political risk. Maybe his advisers were too focused on narrow national concerns to see the broader potential. Whatever the reason, here was a lost opportunity of colossal proportions.

When the world said, "We are all Americans," how did our president respond, beyond provoking war and vengeance and messianism? He might have issued a call to escape the oil addiction that has been a root cause of two American wars in the last fifteen years and continues to imperil the national interest of the richest nations as well as the developing ones. He might have issued a call to reform the United Nations by making it less bureaucratic and more action-oriented and accountable. He might have issued a call for a new set of institutions, even a new group of big nations (the United States, China, Japan, Europe, Brazil, India), that would begin to talk about what they shared and how they could work together on common problems. He might have issued a call to end poverty in the world, with a time line to engage other countries in the effort and inject a sense of urgency into its implementation. He might have issued a proposal to protect habitat, slow down global warming, prevent the despoliation of our seas, with assigned national responsibilities. He might have issued a domestic call to service, capturing the mood of the days after 9/11 and challenging each of us to be better and more generous—instead of the simple injunction to consume more goods and services to keep the U.S. economy going. He might have acknowledged the power of the spiritual in our world and emphasized the common values of the world's various religions and ethical traditions, out of which might well have come an agreed-upon agenda for action. He might have done any of these. Each would have lifted our spirits and allowed America to lead in a way that inspired people around the globe. The teachable moment is a time to dream a big dream and call others to action. LBJ knew that in domestic affairs forty-some years ago, and it's a genuine tragedy that George W. Bush didn't see it in foreign affairs in 2001.

THE NEW STORY

So, what is the new story that we can tell about our role in the world? Do we continue to live every day just for ourselves? Do we continue to miss the opportunity to learn what other countries can teach us?

Most Americans are citizens primarily of their local communities. That's where they raise their children, interact with their friends and neighbors, worship their God. This kind of citizenship is what impressed Alexis de Tocqueville when he saw neighbors helping neighbors raise a barn. Americans are also familiar with what it means to be a citizen of our nation. It is a kind of civil religion. Once, in Washington, DC, I hosted a thank-you dinner for twenty of my supporters. After dinner I rented a bus, and we toured our national monuments. It was a cosmopolitan, successful group who had seen the world, but not one of them had visited our national shrines at night. Years later, people told me that if it hadn't been for that evening, they never would have felt as they did when they walked up the steps of the Lincoln Memorial and read the excerpt of Lincoln's magisterial second inaugural address:

> With malice toward none, with charity for all, with firmness in the right, as God gives us to see the right, let us strive on to finish the work we are in, to bind up the nation's wounds, to care for him who shall have borne the battle, and for his widow and his orphan, to do all which may achieve and cherish a just and lasting peace among ourselves, and with all nations.

I also remember one night in the Senate when I was entertaining some Russian visitors. In the middle of the evening, after a discussion about the founding of American democracy, I suggested we visit the Jefferson Memorial. In the deserted open-air rotunda, we looked up and read Jefferson's words on the challenge of change to a democracy:

> I am not an advocate for frequent changes in laws and constitutions, but laws and institutions must go hand in hand with the progress of the human mind. As that becomes more developed, more enlightened, as new discoveries are made, new truths discovered and manners and opinions change, with the change of circumstances, institutions must advance also to keep pace with the times. We might as well require a man to wear still the coat which fitted him when a boy as civilized society to remain ever under the regimen of their barbarous ancestors.

As we walked back down the steps, I ran into Supreme Court Justice Byron White, who had brought his own out-of-town guests to the monument that night. The fact of a U.S. senator and a Supreme Court justice meeting on the steps of the Jefferson Memorial, both proud of our national heritage and anxious to share it, gave me a good feeling about our country. In the presence of the great words spoken by our great leaders, we are reminded that America remains an unfinished and unrealized idea.

Now for the first time in our history we need to be a third kind of citizen, a citizen of the world. We cannot escape our interconnectedness with the rest of humankind. For some of us Americans, the world extends only to the boundaries of our nation. We regard other countries as inferior powers, inferior people. We know little about them. The cultures are alien, the languages beyond our comprehension. We still think we can exist as an island in a sea of humanity, a part of which every day gets smarter and stronger and another part of which falls deeper into poverty and misery. Although markets pull us toward a world with no boundaries, the world is still an abstraction for many of us. In contrast, our jobs, our families, our churches, our friends are concrete, full of meaning, situated in a familiar place.

But the new story says that the three—community, nation, and world—must be connected. You no longer can be a responsible member of a smaller community without being a world citizen, too. In the words of the political philosopher Michael J. Sandel in his book *Democracy's Discontent: America in Search of a Public Philosophy*, "The civic virtue distinctive to our time is the capacity to negotiate our way among the sometimes overlapping, sometimes conflicting obligations that claim us, and to live with the tension to which multiple loyalties give rise."

The more we can be world citizens, the better we can secure our future. Being a citizen of the world does not mean weakening our attachment to our personal communities but rather strengthening our attachment to the rest of humanity. It does not mean throwing our hands up in the face of immense problems; it is possible to imagine a world where evil exists but doesn't preoccupy us. We take measures to protect ourselves, but we don't wallow in fear. We recognize the fleeting nature of all things on Earth and recall in our own lives how the most memorable moments have been the human interactions, not the search for success or security or entertainment. We are bounded by time and feeling. Our sense of self-interest and our obligations to others exist in the same heart. When we take those insights and apply them to the world, our responsibility to strangers, to future generations, and to our best selves becomes clear. To live for ourselves today, we must live for others as never before.

In the new story, it is not acceptable for our country to relate to the world primarily with force. We also want to share the joy, spread the creativity, celebrate what we have in common. What we as Americans can give to the world is the ability to see the big possibilities, to see what we can achieve together if we maintain our goodwill and keep our focus. There will still be a multiplicity of religions and cultures; the only requirement is mutual empathy and respect. We can uphold the importance of family and neighborhood, but we can also make a world in which there are sufficient jobs, quality education, good health, and peace for everyone—a world where nuclear weapons are not just controlled but eliminated. None of these goals will ever be completely attained, just as the ideals of our Declaration of Independence will never be completely realized. But the striving is what counts and what transforms the way we act toward our allies or our enemies. The pursuit of American ideals automatically leads us to pursue the good of the whole world.

The New American Story says that holding all three levels of citizenship is a necessity. It gives us a clear agenda and helps us prioritize. It challenges us in new ways. The New American Story says that we avoid war whenever possible, and wherever it breaks out we try, with our allies, to stop it. It affirms that children, wherever they live in the world, should no longer grow up to fight the disputes of their grandparents. It says that as the dominant power we have to acknowledge that the rules apply to us as well as others and to go out of our way to listen to other nations who might otherwise fear or resent us. It insists that the fruits of scientific advance are for the many and not just for the few. It asserts our obligation to future generations and our commitment to safeguard our planet against the unintended consequences of our own actions.

Three principles guide the new story: global cooperation, global responsibility, and our special American role. The following megapolicies will help us to realize this new story.

Global Cooperation

1. We need a new set of international agreements to deal with the most pressing international issues, such as preventing proliferation of nuclear weapons, combatting terrorism, and stopping genocide. What are envisioned here are not supranational organizations or world governance but a series of agreements among participating nations that share values and reach consensus about how military power will be deployed, and under what circumstances. These issues could be explored by nations in small meetings that prepare the agenda and options for a larger conference. The model would be the Bretton Woods Conference, which established the economic institutions that have given the world its largest sustained period of economic growth in modern history.

2. The purpose of one of the most important agreements would be avoiding disaster caused by climate change. The Kyoto Protocol should be ratified by all countries and then immediately superseded with a much stronger regime that places hard caps on the emission of carbon dioxide and sulfur oxides, relies on markets for its implementation, and establishes mechanics to assure compliance. This time the United States should ratify it immediately, implement it unilaterally, and lead the effort for worldwide adoption.

3. Our global economy must share its benefits more widely. Only in that way will economic growth, even for rich countries, be sustainable. We need to persuade the developed world to increase investment in global health, education, and protection of the environment through existing international institutions. Established by world leaders attending the UN Millennium Summit in September 2000, the Millennium

Development Goal, that every child in the world should receive at least a primary education by 2015, could be achieved with an outlay of $10 billion to $15 billion a year. World health could improve substantially given inexpensive public-health investments to guarantee clean water. The Nobel Prize–winning economist Joseph Stiglitz has pointed out that revenue to achieve these ends could come from auctioning off things such as fishing and mining rights in international waters or carbon permits for use of fossil fuels. An adequately funded environmental lending institution could help reduce global warming by paying for some of the incremental costs incurred by the poorer countries. We also need to address systemic global economic problems such as those in agriculture; commodity subsidies in rich countries must be reduced to give poor nations a chance, through their agricultural exports to the developed world, to lift their citizens out of poverty.

4. Something often missing in statecraft is an acknowledgment of people's deepest feelings. A religious revival is sweeping the world. To ignore it is to miss a golden opportunity to get beyond fanaticism, national disputes, and great-power rivalries. There must be a concerted attempt to develop an action agenda for the world community rising out of the common values of its major religions.

Global Responsibility

1. As the world's largest consumer of oil, we must go further than other countries in lessening our dependence on oil and simultaneously enlist other countries to begin an aggressive worldwide effort to break the stranglehold that oil addiction has on all of us.

2. We must develop incentives — both carrots and sticks — to encourage all countries, developed and developing, to invest the fruits of their market economies in the health and education of their people instead of bestowing them on rich, politically connected subsidy seekers.

3. We must mobilize a relentless campaign against corruption in both public and private life.

Our Special American Role

1. America must lead by the power of its example, with the realization that imitation by others will be more successful than intimidation of others.
2. We must recognize that most of the twenty-first century's major challenges require international cooperation and then build the means to achieve it.
3. We must use talk before action, diplomacy before war.
4. We must maintain our military through investment in high-tech weapons, intelligence resources, and training of military personnel.
5. We must continue the war on terrorism together with our allies but end the war in Iraq. Given the history of Iraq and the nature of the conflict, leaving has fewer long-term downsides than staying.

If Americans can work together to realize these goals, our new story will bring about a new day for the planet we inhabit and— once again—the respect of the nations we share it with.

It's our choice.

Chapter 4.

THE ECONOMY

With regard to the economy, the story we're told is simple: Cut taxes, especially for the wealthy, who have the capital for investment. "After the Internet bubble burst in 2000, when the economy turned down, it was tax cuts that brought us back," goes the argument. "They always do." Individuals who save for health care, education, or retirement merit even further tax reduction.

The story says that if we reduce or eliminate government regulation, businesses will be able to spend their time increasing productivity and creating jobs, instead of languishing in a web of bureaucratic micro-management. It says spend freely on war, Medicare drug entitlements, corporate incentives, and earmarked projects in the districts of key congressional allies, and cut spending on poverty programs, which have been shown not to work. If you're poor, pull yourself up by your own bootstraps, as people like Justice Clarence Thomas did. Any help should come from family members or your church. Poverty is not an economic problem. Many of the poor are victims of their own bad choices. If you want to solve poverty, reward traditional two-parent families. In a dynamic capitalist society, the hardworking people will rise to the top and should be rewarded. Economic sectors might go up or down, but if you're patient and informed about the stock market, you can always make money in the long term. That's what Americans do—it's one of the reasons we're the greatest country in the world.

The main problem with this story is that it ignores economic fundamentals and minimizes the fact that we are the world's biggest debtor nation. We can't continue to run increasingly large budget deficits and trade imbalances, or have the lowest personal savings rate of all industrial countries except Australia, without the sky falling someday. The only question is, When—and how bad—will it be?

A country's economic health requires investment in its future. Our enormous federal budget deficits and a rising national debt amount to a giant tax on the future—our children's future. The national debt will have to be brought under control eventually, through either tax increases or reduced spending or inflation. Current and future U.S. government obligations amount to half a million dollars for each household in America; the 2007 deficit is projected to be some $286 billion. In March 2006, Congress raised the amount the federal government is allowed to borrow by nearly $800 billion, which, given recent federal budget deficits, will last us for perhaps another three years.

The potential liabilities for the federal government are enormous, and I'm not referring to just Social Security, civil-service pensions, Medicare, and Medicaid. For example, if a few more airlines went bankrupt, they could wipe out the government fund at the Pension Benefit Guaranty Corporation, which insures the private pensions of 44 million Americans. The government-chartered Fannie Mae and Freddie Mac, which buy mortgages, are also in trouble. In February 2004, then Federal Reserve chairman Alan Greenspan told the Senate Banking Committee that the two posed a "systemic risk." One gets the queasy feeling that the public is not being told all the facts about these two shareholder-owned public institutions, because if it was, financial panic might ensue, given that together they have $1.5 trillion in outstanding debt obligations and hold $2.6 trillion in guaranteed mortgage-backed securities.

Individuals pile up debt, too. In his recent book *The Untied States of America: Polarization, Fracturing, and Our Future,* Juan Enriquez, chairman and CEO of Biotechonomy, a life-sciences research and venture capital firm, reports that, between 1992 and

2004, household indebtedness doubled, to more than $10 trillion. In October 2004, the average personal savings rate was 0.2 percent, which means that if you had an annual income of $65,000 (nearly 50 percent more than the median income for 2004), you would put away only $130 in savings per year. The average household owed over $84,000 in October 2004, including some $8,000 in credit-card debt.

Add up the indebtedness of the public and private sectors, and the numbers become ominous. The financial analysts Bill Bonner and Addison Wiggin, in *Empire of Debt: The Rise of an Epic Financial Crisis*, state that the total value of all assets in the United States is some $50 trillion. The present value of the federal government's promised expenditures in Social Security, civil-service pensions, and health care is more than $37 trillion. If you add to this the indebtedness of state and local governments, corporations, and individuals, the United States is practically bankrupt. For almost a generation, America has cheated our future and lived only in the here and now.

Economic growth depends on the level of investment in both physical capital—machines, infrastructure, technology—and human capital, which consists of the combined skills and health of our workforce. Investment today produces growth tomorrow. Spending today is gone by tomorrow. Only foreign loans keep us afloat. When winter came, Aesop's grasshopper was left out in the cold, while the ant, having invested in the future, was warm inside his abode.

And investment depends on savings. The Harvard economist Benjamin M. Friedman points out in *The Moral Consequences of Economic Growth* that for many decades corporations and individuals saved 16 to 18 percent of the national income. After allowing for replacement of plant and equipment, their combined savings rate was nearly 10.0 percent, on average, throughout the 1960s and 1970s. In the second half of the 1980s, it dropped to 7.9 percent, and in the mid-1990s to 4.8 percent. As combined savings dropped, investment in physical capital declined, too. There is a limited pool of savings from domestic sources available for investment. The borrowers of that capital are individuals, businesses, and governments. When governments run deficits, they are borrowing to pay for the part of government for which they don't have enough in tax revenues. When there aren't enough personal savings and governments borrow massive sums, there is less capital available for the private sector. Demand will bid up prices, interest rates will rise, fewer investments will be made, and the economy will stagnate.

Because America doesn't have sufficient savings, we import about $2.3 billion every working day to finance these debts, which means that, before the federal government spends any taxpayer money on education or health care or the military, it must pay interest to foreign creditors. The result of this infusion of foreign savings is that interest rates don't go up here, so Americans continue to borrow and then overconsume. Foreigners now own half of America's publicly held debt of $4.2 trillion, with Japan holding $639 billion and China $323 billion. If you add corporate and quasi-public debt, China has nearly $1 trillion in dollar-denominated financial assets. In Japan, the Finance Ministry and its director of foreign exchange, Masatsugu Asakawa, controls over $500 billion in U.S. Treasury debt. If he or any of our creditor nations' central banks ever decided to diversify aggressively into euros or yen or gold, the dollar would drop and interest rates would rise in order to make U.S. government debt more attractive to other investors. Rising interest rates would make it more expensive to buy, carry, or refinance a home. With more money going to finance housing, less will be available for consumer spending, which could drop sharply.

Consumption now represents 71 percent of the U.S. gross domestic product, and savings 1 percent. The Chinese, by contrast, have a consumption rate of only 38 percent of GDP, a personal savings rate of 35 percent, and a fixed-investment rate of 48 percent, compared with America's fixed-investment rate of 17 percent. We fill our homes with flat-panel TV screens, MP3 players, and computerized refrigerators; they fill their bank accounts with U.S. Treasury bonds. In essence, the Chinese manufacture our products and do our savings. They save more of their salaries. We borrow, to consume more of their goods. It is a virtuous circle—for them. They get jobs. We get debt.

The U.S. trade deficit implies that at some point we will have to take in more by selling U.S. goods abroad than we spend on importing foreign goods. To date, given the low private savings rate, the giant government deficits, and the looming entitlements due to baby-boomer retirees, that day seems a long way off. In such a climate, there is little chance that sufficient investment can be sustained.

How did we get to our present position as the world's largest debtor nation?

By the late 1980s, at the end of Ronald Reagan's second term, the budget deficit had climbed to $155 billion, pushing real interest rates (the interest rate above inflation) to a forty-five-year high of 4.4 percent. His successor, George H. W. Bush, aware that the numbers didn't include another expensive item—the bailout of the Federal Savings and Loan Insurance Corporation, which was off-budget— saw the danger to the country's well-being and, to his credit, acted. He slowed the growth of government spending, raised the ceiling on income subject to the Medicare tax, and increased tax rates on the wealthy. When Bill Clinton came to office, in 1993, he followed a similar fiscally responsible budget policy. He reduced the growth of spending, increased the gasoline tax, took the income ceiling off the Medicare tax, and raised the income-tax rate for people making more than $250,000 per year.

Clinton's 1993 budget was unusual in that not one Republican voted for it. They claimed that the tax package would stop investment and short-circuit the incipient recovery from the 1990–91 economic downturn that had claimed Bush I's presidency. Instead, the economy entered a period of sustained growth, with business investment leading the way. By 1997, the deficit had shrunk from $290 billion, which is where it was when Clinton took office, to $22 billion. By 2000, there was a $236 billion surplus. With no need to finance a budget deficit, the surplus made more capital available to the private sector, and net national investment rose to a level it hadn't reached since the 1970s. The result was robust economic growth, and because of the expansion of the earned income credit, which aids low-income working families, the growth was more fairly shared. For the first time in twenty-five years, weekly wages rose.

Poverty decreased. In many ways, this budget was Bill Clinton's finest hour.

In 2001, George W. Bush assumed the presidency and immediately proceeded to squander the surplus. After 9/11, people wanted money spent on the war on terror—but they wanted money spent on education and health care, too. Bush obliged, but he also insisted on three big tax cuts. By 2004, the deficit was $412 billion, the largest share of our national income since 1993. The Congressional Budget Office reported that during Bush's first term, from January 2001 to January 2005, the budget went from a ten-year projected surplus of $5.6 trillion to a projected deficit of $2.6 trillion. The tax cuts accounted for half the swing. (The March 2006 ten-year projection, from 2007 through 2016, was for a $3.4 trillion deficit.)

Inequality

The story we're being told on the economy ignores the rising inequality of wealth and the erosion of the middle class. A lot of Americans never made a financial killing during the high-flying dot-com days or the recent real-estate boom. Fifty-one percent own no stocks at all—none. Given international competition, technological developments, and the relentless corporate drive to cut costs in the short run, it becomes more difficult for the benefits of economic growth to reach all Americans. As of 2003, 15 million people in America lived in poverty even though the head of the household was a full-time worker.* There are millions more white-collar workers who have no job security and fear losing their jobs tomorrow. For them, the only question is, If it is your turn to go, will the company give you an hour, a day, or a week to clean out your desk?

The period from the start of the 1970s to the early 1990s saw the living standards of most Americans stagnate. Median income and average weekly wages remained flat or declined. When you factor in the rising costs of health care, fuel, and college education, as well as state and local taxes, the standard of living for many Americans ac-

---

*This number was up 50 percent since 1975.

tually declined.* The bottom 40 percent of working America earns below $24,960 per year. At a time when middle-class income was stuck, the Bush tax cuts, combined with CEO stock-option profits, raised the income of the well-off. The result: Inequality increased dramatically. The perverse aspect of these developments is that productivity has risen, but the workers who created it haven't shared in it.†

In 1971, the minimum wage's purchasing power in today's dollars was $7.21. Now it's less than $5.00, and at the time of this writing the federal minimum wage has not been raised in ten years. A full-time minimum-wage worker takes home $10,700 per year, a figure below the poverty line for a father or mother with one child. In 2006, 11 percent of U.S. households did not have enough food and 26 million Americans received food stamps. Only 36 percent of un-employed workers now collect unemployment benefits at all, and for women the proportion is even less. Even young professionals feel the pressure: In the decade after 1993, average income for Americans between the ages of eighteen and twenty-five rose 29 percent, while housing costs for the same group rose 39 percent. The current average retirement savings account has $95,000 in it. If you don't count the small number of accounts with very high holdings that disproportionately distort the average, it drops to $27,000. Americans with more than $250,000 in their retirement accounts are only 11 percent of the labor force.

A large part of the middle class believes that the future will not be as good as the past. In a 2005 poll conducted for *Parade* magazine, Mark Clements Research reports that 56 percent of middle-income ($30,000 to $99,000 annually) Americans think "things will be worse for their own children." And they appear to be right: The rela-tive standard of living of Americans is declining. In 2004, for the first time since the early 1900s, the United States was not among the

---

*From 2000 to 2004, property taxes alone went up 28 percent, while income rose only 16 percent.

†From 1995 to 2006, the average annual growth in productivity exceeded the growth of real com-pensation by 300 percent. Even in the economic recovery of 2004–5, middle-class wage income did not match the historical trends of other recoveries.

top five per-capita-income countries. The citizens of Luxembourg, Denmark, Ireland, Switzerland, and Norway all made more that year than we did.

Increasingly, not only do people not understand the economic forces that shape their lives (globalization and technological change) but the effect of those forces is to destroy bonds of community and isolate individuals, making them even more powerless. Whether it's Wal-Mart's impact on Main Street, the challenge of DVDs for movie theaters, or the call-center operators in Kansas losing out to a company in India, what once seemed permanent no longer is, and one's worst nightmare often becomes reality. The journalist Simon Head, in his brilliant book *The New Ruthless Economy: Work and Power in the Digital Age,* shows how the industrial proce-dures of the assembly line have been adapted to the service sec-tor, making individual workers' skills less valuable. The computer systems and software that were supposed to liberate employees have imprisoned them in a world of rigid scripts, speeded-up functions, and invasive monitoring. Just think of how many times you have called a bank, an airline, or a cable television company and heard a recording say that the call was being monitored for quality pur-poses. How many times have you asked the person at the other end of the line a question that obviously wasn't in the script and he or she didn't have a clue how to answer it? Instead of flexible procedures and flattened organizations, the software has rewarded hierarchy and diminished the importance of workers' individual contributions.

I know a ticket-counter employee for a major airline who built a large and loyal customer base with her personality and conscien-tiousness. When a new supervisor, reading from a reengineering manual, told her that she could no longer come out from behind the counter to greet her customers or interact with them in any way other than by a scripted dialogue, she quit. The fewer the skills a ser-vice worker needs, the less necessary any individual worker is to the company's performance. The result is less leverage for workers in labor negotiations and greater job insecurity. And this is no longer happening just to a segment of the middle class. It is happening to a clear majority of the electorate, including middle management and administration, employees of small businesses, and lower-paid professionals, such as physicians working for HMOs.

What's most worrisome is that people seem fatalistic about their predicament. Recently I asked another airline ticket-counter agent about her pension. She said that, after twenty-eight years at the company, she expected only pennies on the dollar and that her husband, who had been a mechanic for another airline, would lose the bulk of his pension, too. I asked her how she felt about this. She shrugged her shoulders and said, "Well, what can you do?"

How did we move from John Kennedy's claim for economic growth, in defense of his proposed 1963 tax cuts, that "a rising tide lifts all boats" to today's economy, in which the gap between rich and poor has never been greater? The promise of America was that if you worked hard and played by the rules, you could have a good life. No more. Repeatedly, corporations have broken promises to their workers, and some have even voided legal contracts. Unions have chosen to protect seniority rather than widen membership. The media have largely scanted these issues, preferring to entertain rather than to explore the complexities and inequities of our national economy. The government has given disproportionate attention to the welfare of the wealthy. True, if you want to encourage investment, it is the wealthy who inevitably benefit, because they own much of the personal savings. But there is no excuse for failing to conduct rigorous oversight of and increase resources to education, beginning with prekindergarten, which in the long run will result in greater national productivity and, given that income goes up with each additional year of school, greater equality.*

As for poverty, the old story properly emphasizes encouraging the poor to graduate from high school, delay childbearing, and marry. Who could argue with those objectives? But the old story both ignores the difficulty of getting a foot on the first rung of the ladder

---

*To ensure that globalization and technological change produce the maximum level of fairly shared economic growth, the government must create what I called in a 1993 speech "an economic security platform," providing health care for all; pension security; and a flexible education system with dramatic improvement in K–12 school performance, more high school graduates going on to college (especially in math and science), and innovative programs to offer retraining and education to people displaced by globalization or technological change.

and denies the advantage of class. A rich kid gets his asthma treated early, by the best doctors, and goes to a private school, where he has access to individual tutors. He finds his math talent recognized and enriched in grade school, takes expensive SAT-prep courses, and has his alumnus uncle pull strings to get him into a prestigious college. A poor kid can have just as much ambition and drive and natural ability but a lot more obstacles. And it's not only the absence of a well-connected uncle. Sometimes it's a home with no books and parents who don't emphasize the value of education; sometimes it's a neighborhood featuring drugs, violence, and third-rate schools, where you can't find a place to study; sometimes it's peer pressure to hang out with friends instead of stay in with the homework. Sometimes it's all of these things.

Government is not a "paternalistic" force in such lives; rather, it is the equalizer that gives a child's talents a chance to develop. It allows the poor to get prenatal medical care and their children to receive early immunizations, to prepare for school in Head Start classes, to learn from a mentor or coach in a Job Corps program, to have access to computers in grade school, to have a math tutor in high school, to receive the grant money needed for a college education. Those trapped in the old story don't realize how difficult it is to break out of poverty these days without a helping hand from government.

As for racism, it's important to remember that, for America to realize its potential, we must be good as well as prosperous. Most of us have been taught that how we treat others will determine in large part how others treat us. Racial unity is a commonsense notion. If you believe you are your brother's keeper, then you have to walk the talk. If you believe we should lead the world by the power of our example as a successful pluralistic society, then you know we still have work to do. But if morality or world leadership fail to convince you of this commonsense notion, try self-interest. By 2015, fewer than 55 percent of the people who enter the U.S. workforce will be native-born whites. If labor economics means anything, the economic future of the children of white Americans will increasingly depend on the talents of nonwhite Americans. That's not ideology, it's demographics.

America is becoming more pluralistic, not less. Did you know that there are more Muslims in the United States than Presbyterians? Americans of Hispanic descent are the largest minority, and in some states, given their high fertility rates, they will soon reach 50 percent. In the Silicon Valley of California during the 1990s, nearly 30 percent of all start-ups were formed by entrepreneurs of Asian ancestry. Recently I saw a newspaper story that captured our national moment on diversity. It was about a Korean American restaurateur in Houston who hired Mexican American workers to prepare Chinese-style food for a predominantly black clientele.

The continued existence of racism limits what some of our citizens can be, and in so doing keeps us from achieving our full potential as a country. I remember conducting a public hearing at Morgan State University in Baltimore on the future of the African American male. One of the witnesses sticks in my mind and reminds me of the legacy of racism in America. The witness was a handsome fourteen-year-old black male in a white shirt and tie. I asked him what he wanted to be. "Oh," he said, "my first choice would be to become an NBA player, but I don't know if I'll be tall enough. My second choice is that I've always wanted to join the FBI or the CIA." He paused and then said, "I know if I have the ability, I'll make the NBA, but even if I have the ability, I don't know if I can get into the FBI or the CIA." We need every American, regardless of race, to know that, if he or she has the ability, he or she can get the job. Diversity has become one of our richest assets, and either all of us will advance together or each of us will be diminished.

Financial Risk

Yet another problem with the story we are told on the economy is that it ignores the steep rise in household indebtedness and the general proliferation of risk. The federal tax cuts that the vast majority of middle-class Americans got in the last several years were peanuts. Millions of Americans have had to keep their heads above water by borrowing more. Household indebtedness as a percentage of GDP is at its highest level ever in our history.* The home equity loan has replaced the company raise as the way families pay for the consumption that remains the backbone of the economy. That's all well and good, until interest rates rise, and then a lot of mortgages will be in default and a lot of pain will be distributed.

The real-estate bubble succeeded the Internet bubble as the way Americans thought they would get rich, and debt fuelled the speculation. The analysts Bonner and Wiggin quote from a real-estate loan ad on the Internet: "Borrow up to $250,000. Less than perfect credit is okay. . . . No income verification. . . . No home equity requirement. . . . 24 hours approval." One-fourth of homes bought in 2004 were for investment, not for occupancy by the owner. Interest-only loans became the rage. One in five new homeowners by mid-2005 had a mortgage whose debt service took half the buyer's disposable income. At the height of the real-estate boom, it was commonplace for people to buy houses or condos and flip them in a year. Bonner and Wiggin note that in Paradise Cove, California, even mobile homes appreciated 100 percent per year in the first five years of the decade, with some going for over $1 million. Warren Buffett, ever the astute capitalist, has cashed in on the latest bubble. "I recently sold a house in Laguna [California] for $3.5 million," he told his shareholders in April 2005. "It was on about 2,000 square feet of land, maybe a twentieth of an acre, and the house might cost about $500,000 if you wanted to replace it. So the land sold for something like $60 million an acre."

The problem with a bubble is that most people act as though it will last forever. They seem to feel that the price of Internet stocks or condos in Boca Raton or the value of their home will only go up. When told that the fundamentals are out of whack and some correction is necessary, they say it will be a soft landing—no crash in prices, just a slackening off in sales. But the real-estate market today gives every sign of a hard landing. Prices have begun to drop in many places. The result is excess inventory, followed by the sellers offering incentives for prospective buyers that will reduce the cost of

---

*Since 1990, average household income has gone up 11 percent, while average spending per household has gone up 30 percent.

the transaction without lowering the offering price. When those marble countertops or rebates no longer attract buyers, the offering prices will drop. In a world of lower prices, investor-owned condos will be put on the market in order to get sales before the prices drop even lower. When California's last real-estate bubble burst, in 1990, prices declined or stayed flat for most of the next six years. When the bubble burst in Japan in the late 1980s, real-estate prices plunged and have yet to recover.

Hedge Funds

A second source of economic risk—and a powerful symbol of our economic times—is the hedge fund, an all but unregulated pool of capital. While hedge funds are subject to insider-trading rules and the antifraud sections of the securities laws, they can, unlike mutual funds, invest as much as they want in any one stock and then leverage—that is, borrow to increase their investment using the original investment as collateral. Anyone can set up shop as a hedge-fund manager; if somebody can convince people to give them money, he or she is in business. No government registration or background check is required. Hedge-fund fees and the percentage of profits that hedge-fund managers take are often quite high.*

Hedge-fund totals have gone from $58 billion in assets under management in 1991 to $1.2 trillion at the end of 2005. There are now nearly 9,000 hedge funds. While there are honest (and brilliant) hedge-fund managers out there who charge reasonable fees, take a reasonable share of the profits, and make money for their clients, there are, given the explosion of dollars under management, probably too many others who take their clients' money and invest

---

*In 2005, the lowest earner of the top ten hedge-fund managers made $300 million. The highest earner that year made $1.5 billion. If you invest $100,000 with a hedge fund, your money is often locked up for five years. If the hedge-fund manager takes a 3 percent annual fee and 25 percent of the profits, the fund has to make a 20 percent gain over five years before you as much as break even. When taxes are factored in, the return has to be even higher. And that's before you consider that, during the life of the fund, the salary, office, travel, and lifestyle of the manager can be paid out of your money over and above the fees and profits. If you invest in a fund of funds (a hedge fund of other hedge funds), you will pay more fees and give up more of the profit before you see any profit yourself. That hedge-fund manager who made $1.5 billion in 2005 charged a 5 percent management fee and took 44 percent of the gains for himself.

it recklessly. You never hear about the hedge funds that fail. (In 2005, there were 848.) All you hear about are the stars.

When you invest in a mutual fund, you worry about underperformance. When you invest in a hedge fund, you should worry about loss of capital. In order to make a name for themselves, hedge-fund managers often initially take inordinate risks, using leverage for an even bigger payoff. After they acquire a three-year track record of double-digit growth, they are awash in money from investors clamoring to get into their next fund. If their first fund was $100 million, for example, with the manager getting a 3 percent annual fee, the new fund might be $1 billion, with the manager still getting a 3 percent fee. Now the manager will shift from risk to caution, for fear of losing the capital upon which that new $30 million annual fee depends. So initially the system encourages excessive risk, whereas, ultimately, capital is not allocated to its best use.

Warren Buffett says that leverage is the way smart people go bankrupt. Just ask the two future Nobel Prize winners who were on the board of Long-Term Capital Management in 1998. That year, the multibillion-dollar hedge fund nearly collapsed in a matter of weeks. Buffett refers to leverage as a spike in the middle of your car's steering wheel. The sharp end points toward you. The greater the leverage, the longer the spike. If you hit a bump or slam on the brakes, you're dead. There are too many hedge funds that are drastically overleveraged. Today even funds of funds use leverage. One is reminded of the story of the Three Little Pigs. Too much capital today is living in a house made of straw.

On one level, hedge funds have little national economic importance, because only the rich can play the hedge-fund game—unlike an investor in mutual funds, you have to have a $1 million net worth to be eligible. Wealthy investors usually don't care what compensation a manager takes, as long as they get hefty returns. If the fund tanks, it represents only one component of their diversified investment portfolios. They know the risks. They take their chances. Still, hedge-fund behavior can hurt anyone who owns a stock. These lightly regulated entities tend to spook easily and move in herds. And the ones that are highly leveraged need to move the fastest. With $71 billion in domestic pension funds invested with hedge funds, a small event can get out of control quickly, like a raging virus, and destroy the retirement dreams of millions.

The most sobering aspect of the phenomenon is that hardly anyone knows who these 9,000 hedge-fund managers are. Before the hedge-fund boom, Alan Greenspan could call the key players in the economy to calm the financial markets. Today, with over $1 trillion in almost unregulated money sloshing around the financial system, under the control of thousands of unknown hedge-fund managers, a speculative run on the dollar is not impossible. If one investor, George Soros, could force a devaluation of the British pound in the early 1990s, imagine what hundreds of hedge-fund managers could do to the dollar today. In the devaluations that led to the 1997 world-wide market tumble, one currency speculator told a reporter for *Time* magazine that he and his colleagues were like "wolves on the ridgeline looking down on a herd of elk . . . by culling the weak and infirm, we help maintain the health of the herd." No patriotism here, only narrow economic self-interest. That kind of attitude is troublesome if the culled part of the metaphorical herd is a company; if it is the U.S. dollar, it is a national disaster.

The dubious premise behind the government's indifference toward the hedge-fund and real-estate booms is that we have found the tools to control the modern economy so that the system will never break no matter how many risks it absorbs. Proponents of this view point to the 1987 stock market crash, when the Federal Reserve flooded the markets with liquidity and stabilized the panic. They talk about 2001, when the biggest fiscal and monetary stimulus in history brought the economy back from its burst-Internet-bubble lows. Yet the closer a government allows the economy to get to the edge, the easier it is for the unexpected event, amplified by investor irrationality and software that automatically sells at a certain price, to trigger a crisis.

So if the story we are told about the economy ignores the burgeoning personal and national debts, the increasing inequality, and the explosion of risk, what might a new story be?

THE NEW STORY

The new story is about economic growth fairly shared and responsibly achieved.

Economic growth can indeed generate a rising standard of living for most Americans. A rising standard of living fosters tolerance: If middle-class Americans are doing well, government efforts to help the poor don't bother them. If economic growth enables upward mobility, all Americans become optimists. Economic growth gives us the resources to educate our children, guarantee a secure retirement for our elderly, provide health care for everyone. With growth, we can afford most public goals; without it, those goals compete with one another for limited resources, and the country becomes a meaner place. In long economic downturns, racists and xenophobes have a field day.

The right levels of employment, inflation, and productivity are necessary for the new story, but they are not sufficient. Quality of life must also be good. Growth as we measure it through our accounting of assets and liabilities doesn't always take into account what is important to the society as a whole. The Canadian philosopher John Ralston Saul, in his 1995 book, *The Unconscious Civilization*, observes that

> growth, as we currently understand it, classifies education as a cost, thus a liability. A golf ball, on the other hand, is an asset and the sale of it is a measurable factor of growth. A face lift is an element of economic activity while a heart bypass is a liability which the economy must finance. Holidays are among the pearls of the service industry, while child care is a cost. . . . If growth can be conceived in a wider, more inclusive form, then it will abruptly become possible to reward those things which society finds useful.

Or as Benjamin Friedman puts it in *The Moral Consequences of Economic Growth*:

> Because economic growth positively affects the character of the society as a whole—and, crucially, because neither openness nor toler-

ance nor democracy is a good that private markets trade and price—there is a consequent role for policy measures to seek growth beyond what the market would provide on its own. . . . The challenge is to seek growth-promoting policies that are consistent with a fairer, more open society, and, where possible, that further these ends as well.

Such "growth-promoting policies" fall into three categories: the legal system, the social system, and national defense. The last is obvious. If a country is destroyed by war, economic growth will be extinguished. A strong defense guarantees the physical safety needed for normal economic activity. The social system means health and education: Without good schools, there will be fewer new ideas; without health, productivity drops. With adequate investment, both will create the stability necessary for growth. A functioning legal system has direct relevance to the economy in many ways. If crime is not punished, it endangers personal security and encourages more illegal activity, whose ultimate effect on the economy is to reduce its efficiency. Economic activity produces inevitable disputes that can be resolved through the legal system. Having a reliable way to deal with those disputes increases economic activity. Private property rights are the bedrock of legal protections for investment. Constitutionally guaranteed freedom of movement along with gender, racial, and ethnic equality guarantee that all the nation's talents will be utilized to generate the maximum growth.

The new story asserts that globalization and technological change will create economic possibilities that cannot be imagined now. One reason the Soviet Union fell was that its economy, with prices controlled by bureaucrats and corruption rife, couldn't produce the growth to support the large increases in military expenditures necessary to match U.S. technological advances. In this sense, President Reagan's Star Wars project and military buildup helped to bankrupt the Soviet state. Some on the left say that our own economy is propped up by what President Eisenhower termed the military-industrial complex. The truth is the opposite. The military economy sits atop the basic-research economy, the technological-development economy, and the adequate-capital-investment economy of our country. The new story says that making Americans more knowledgeable about math and science and keeping foreign math and science graduate students in the United States after graduation is the key to future economic success. This emphasis on education is international. In *Flight Capital: The Alarming Exodus of America's Best and Brightest* (2005), the former Citicorp employee and Wharton business school professor David A. Heenan writes:

> Half of the Americans who shared Nobel Prizes in physics and chemistry in the past seven years were born elsewhere. Nearly 40 percent of MIT graduates are from abroad. More than half of all PhD's working here are foreign born, as are 45 percent of the physicists, computer scientists, and mathematicians. One third of all current physics teachers and one fourth of all women doctors immigrated to this country.

With more and more foreign-born professionals returning to their countries, there ought to be a sense of urgency about our educational system and the need for more math and science competence and ambition. Any American high school student in the top third of his or her academic class should be able to attend college with tuition and fees paid by all of us. Additional incentives should be offered to students majoring in math, science, engineering, and critical foreign languages, with even more assistance available for graduate study in those fields. Between now and the time we produce more American-born PhDs, we must attract and keep foreign talent. Instead of making it easier for talented foreigners to work in the United States, post-9/11 immigration policies have made this more difficult, another unintended consequence of the war on terror.

On the one hand, the new story says that technological innovation fuels growth and creates jobs. Recall that thirty years ago the Internet, MRIs, iPods, cell phones, DVDs, CDs, and countless other new devices, medicines, and materials didn't exist. If we dramatically improve our schools, attract more Americans to math and science, and continue to invest in research in the private, public, and university sectors, thirty years from now there will be new jobproducing industries that few could predict today.

On the other hand, we could be like Brazil. In *The Untied States of America*, Juan Enriquez writes:

Decades ago [Brazil] decided to become the best in the world. Scouts scoured each and every village to find the most talented kids. It did not matter if they were rich or poor, were black, brown, or white, lived in a village or a big city, had powerful parents or were orphans. If they were good, they were supported, mentored, tracked, and trained. And eventually, the country won. Time and again . . . [u]ntil there was no doubt they were the best. Brazil beat the world five times. The tragedy is that Brazil chose to do this in soccer. In 2003, 92% of Brazil's schools had no access to the Internet and 52% did not even have a phone line. If you live in North East Brazil, your life span is likely seventeen years shorter than that of a southern Brazilian.

Countries rise and fall.* In the thirteenth, fourteenth, and fifteenth centuries, China was number one in the world. No country could compete. The Chinese composed an encyclopedia of 4,000 volumes. And then they pulled back, reducing contact with the outside world. Europe kept developing, while China languished for centuries. Even with the growth of the last decade, China and India together account for only 5.8 percent of global trade.

Citing the Latin American historian John Coatsworth, Enriquez reports that

Mexico, Peru, Brazil, and Colombia had universities, courts, printing presses, centralized tax systems, and hospitals up and running decades before the *Mayflower* was built. Mexico's National Autonomous University was up and running in 1553. Harvard? 1636. In 1700, the British, Spanish, and Portuguese colonies of the Americas were about equally productive. Cuba was producing 67% more wealth per person than the U.S. Through 1800, Cuba's GDP per capita exceeded that of the U.S.

---

*Enriquez points out that "around AD 1000, the best mathematicians, astronomers, hydrologists, botanists, engineers, architects, doctors, and pharmacists congregated in the great universities in Damascus, Shiraz, Esfahan, and Córdoba. But when Arabs quit learning, researching, incomes began to erode, for centuries. And they continued to fall . . . [they were] 11% of rich countries' . . . incomes in 1980 . . . 5% in 1990. 4% in 2000. Despite oil." He also notes that China around the first millennium produced "as much steel as Europe would produce five to six hundred years later."

And then a drop in investment and human creativity took its toll. Enriquez cites the economic historian Angus Maddison, who wrote, "During the post-independence chaos, most Latin American countries simply missed the industrial revolution. By 1820, the U.S.'s GDP per person was about twice that of Mexico: by 1900 it was just under four times as much." In each of these cases—the Arab world, China, and Latin America—it was as if the society had said, "No more science. Let's stop," and they did.

Technology will always give us the "new new thing," and if we keep reasonable tax rates, investment capital will continue to fuel new ideas, new businesses, new jobs, and more economic growth. Fortune 500 corporations do not create jobs; many of them have fewer jobs than they did a decade ago. They generally grow only through mergers and acquisitions or foreign expansion, which usually result in cutting jobs. Even high-tech companies, such as Microsoft, Google, or eBay, reach a point where the number of jobs no longer expands. Most jobs are created by small business. Start-ups are born every week and produce hundreds of thousands of jobs. Entrepreneurs are the secret ingredient in our economy. When I was in public life, I wanted to change the world. Now, as a merchant banker, I'm still trying to do that. You do it by finding entrepreneurs who want to change the world and financing them.

In 1998, I gave a speech on venture capital at the University of Zurich. I asked the assembled members of Swiss academia how many of them owned their own companies. No hands were raised. I asked them whether, if they went bankrupt, they could get money for a new venture. They looked at me incredulously, as if to say that in Switzerland such a person would have a big red "B" stamped on his forehead, and the financial world would shun him. I then informed them that, in California's Silicon Valley, many professors owned their own companies and that bankruptcy was considered the equivalent of a graduate degree.

The market—with its transparent pricing mechanism, vibrant capital markets, and flexible workforce—is the best allocator of resources. We should keep it free and open. But it doesn't work for everyone. It is not the sole answer for our health care, education, and pension crises, and it is not omnipresent, omniscient, or omnipotent. Warren Buffett likes to say that each of us should imagine it's twenty-four hours before we're born and a genie comes to us and says that we can pick the rules of the society we'll be born into. We can design the political system, the economic system, the culture, the social system, and it will remain that way our whole lives and for the entire lives of our children. You ask the genie, "What's the catch?" The genie replies, "Just before you're born, you have to go over to that box, which contains 6 billion tickets, representing all the people of the world on the day of your birth, and draw one. It will tell you whether you're going to be American or Brazilian, Chinese or German, tall or short, male or female, black or white, rich or poor." So, what kind of society would you design for a world in which you don't know which ticket you'll draw? Would you put all of your trust in the market if you knew your ticket told you that you'd be born in the barrios of Los Angeles or the poorer neighborhoods of South Chicago, or as a woman in the Taliban's Afghanistan, or a Christian in Somalia?

• • •

The new story says that the economy can turn around quickly. Given the right policies, we can reach the point where a rising tide of economic growth does indeed lift all boats.

How to Reduce the Deficit

The most important step the federal government can take to generate growth is to reduce the federal budget deficit. Individual Americans are unlikely to become 35 percent savers, like the Chinese, overnight. Our culture and history argue against it. The only way to get a quick and dramatic increase in national savings is to reduce the percentage of savings that government sucks up to finance its deficit. Only reducing the federal deficit can have a substantial impact on increasing national savings in the immediate future. The alternative is to continue to borrow abroad and, with each passing year, see our net worth as a nation go down. However, if we make simple changes, the deficit will drop, economic growth will be stimulated, and additional resources will be available for pressing human needs.

By reducing the deficit, we generate more capital at lower interest rates, which will increase investment, which in turn increases economic growth—which in turn brings in more revenues to reduce the deficit. Another virtuous circle, but this time it's ours, not China's. The largest drivers of that deficit on the spending side are defense, health care, and programs for the elderly. By 2016, without legislative change, these three, along with interest payments, will take up 88 percent of the budget.

Although reducing defense spending in a time of war is difficult, it is important to remember that the United States spends nearly as much on defense as all the rest of the countries in the world combined. Including the cost of the Iraq War, our defense spending is approaching record highs—higher than the Reagan buildup of the 1980s or the increases of the cold war period. We could cut defense 10 percent and still spend twice as much on defense as Russia, China, Japan, India, Germany, and England combined. What this implies is that the Iraq War has provided the cover necessary to increase defense expenditures across the board. Spending on weapons alone has soared 43 percent in the last five years, to $147 billion— most of it unrelated to Iraq. Surely there are unnecessary weapons systems; in some cases, the reason for jettisoning a weapons system is redundancy. Multiple services don't all need a weapons system that has the same purpose. The mission can be accomplished for the foreseeable future with existing systems and greater cooperation among services. Other systems need to be cancelled because they were conceived for a cold war world very different from today's, with different military challenges. The Pentagon has yet to make the procurement choices that are both less expensive and better fitted to the new challenges of terrorism and insurgency. At a minimum, we can forgo the F-22 Air Force fighter aircraft, the V-22 Osprey aircraft, and the DDG-1000 Navy destroyers.

In addition to the hardware scrutiny, we should take a close look at the amount of money we spend in administrative support of our combat troops. According to Business Executives for National Security, a group that reviews the Pentagon from the perspective of experience in the private sector, as much as 70 percent of the defense budget now goes to support housing, travel, payroll processing, and inventory management. Many of those and similar functions could be privatized. The result could be significant savings.

The connection between the Iraq War and the slower pace of military reform is real. Before President Bush ordered that his time and energy be devoted to Iraq, former defense secretary Donald Rumsfeld had declared war on pork-barrel military spending and sought a modernization of our forces based on cost efficiency. He was the perfect person to achieve these objectives. Then, instead of reforming the military, he got trapped into trying to reform the world—a task I believe he never would have chosen.

Direct support for the elderly—Social Security, Medicare, Medicaid nursing-home care, and federal government pensions—currently accounts for 43 percent of the federal budget, headed to 48 percent by 2015. From 1994 to 2004, average per capita benefits for the elderly have gone up 4.5 percent annually for Social Security and 6.7 percent for Medicare, while the rest of the budget went up 3.9 percent annually. The columnist and radio host Matthew Miller, in his courageous book *The 2% Solution: Fixing America's Problems in Ways Liberals and Conservatives Can Love*, writes that "the federal government spends about eight times more on seniors as on children under eighteen." Indeed, the United States now spends a smaller percentage of its national income on non-elderly domestic spending than it did in 1940. We have to get control of the disproportionate increase in programs for the elderly.

The two largest programs—Social Security and Medicare—have been enormous successes. In 1965, 44 percent of the nation's elderly had no health insurance; now all of them have coverage. In 1959, more than 33 percent of the elderly lived below what was considered a minimally acceptable living standard; today the children and grandchildren of the elderly are more likely to live in poverty than the elderly themselves. Still, some 30 percent of the elderly get 90 percent of their income from Social Security and would be unable to buy health insurance absent Medicare. The elderly must contribute to the solution of our budget deficit without the most vulnerable among them being endangered.

Any effective solution will call on the patriotism of older Americans. Most of them are parents of workers paying high Social Security taxes and health premiums, and grandparents and great-grandparents of children whose future depends on a good education. If we can show that everyone has to help to bring about the new story, the elderly will see their contribution in a new light.

In order to remain solvent for the next seventy-five years, the Social Security system needs four simple measures: increase the minimum eligibility age of sixty-seven, due to go fully into effect in 2027, by one month every two years until in 2099 it is seventy; make 2.0 percent of the 6.2 percent Social Security tax assessed to individuals apply to all income, not just up to the current cap of $94,200; bring all newly hired state and local government employees into the Social Security system over a five-year phase-in period; and finally, change the way the annual cost-of-living increase is calculated. It should be based on the so-called chained consumer price index, which takes into account purchasing substitutions (such as buying more chicken when beef prices go up or spending less on food in order to pay higher gasoline prices).

There are no easy answers to the Medicare problem. The options are increased premiums for Medicare recipients, higher taxes on working Americans, reduction of benefits for Medicare recipients, or reform of the whole health system. The optimum path would be to make Medicare changes a part of overall national health care reform, in which health care providers compete on the basis of outcomes to give the best care at the lowest price. In the absence of that option, a more modest way to reduce spending on Medicare is by increasing the choice of health care plans for Medicare recipients. Instead of one-size-fits-all, allow individuals to choose among plans that have larger copayments and deductibles, or that limit the choice of doctors and hospitals, and make more generous plans available to those willing to supplement their basic Medicare benefit with private funds. The costs of these plans would be different. In addition, make hospitals report their outcomes per dollar spent, so that health plans can identify which institutions provide the best care at the lowest cost. Under such a system, doctors and hospitals would compete for Medicare patients—much as they compete for non-Medicare patients—instead of avoiding them, as they do now. Absent universal health care, these changes won't solve Medicare's long-term problem, but they will buy us another twenty-five years. If these changes don't reduce costs and improve quality after a few years, then the only alternative is a more regulatory approach, with tougher controls on prescription drug costs and hospital reimbursement rates. In the long run, it will probably take a combination of reform, tough regulation, and increased choices to do the job.

There also needs to be a reduction in the number and value of the so-called earmarked appropriations that go to pet projects of members of Congress. Logrolling has always been a part of the legislative process, overseen by the chairmen of the House and Senate Appropriations Committees. It has gotten out of hand. A series of special projects in his or her district became almost a right for a Republican member of Congress in the last decade. Earmarks are a conscious part of most reelection strategies. The value of these projects was $67 billion in 2005. During Republican control of Congress from 1996 through 2006, they increased (according to the conservative commentator George Will) by 873 percent. Occasionally some provisions serve the public interest, but many more could better be done by the private sector, or by state or local governments, or ought not to be done at all. Worse still are the earmarks that reward friends and campaign contributors. While the amounts of money spent on earmarks pale in comparison to the costs of defense, Social Security, and health care, they are often a waste of taxpayer money and a stain on the reputation of Congress.

The deficit is so large that spending cuts alone won't eliminate it. In addition to cutting spending, we will have to raise taxes, but politicians fear nothing more than the T-word, seeing it as political death. Generally that political cliché is the truth, but in the conservative states of Virginia, Idaho, and Colorado, Democratic and Republican governors raised taxes to do specific things—education in Virginia and Idaho, road building and maintenance in Colorado. It appears that you can raise taxes *and* get reelected if you are clear about how the money will be spent, if your priorities have broad support, and if the electorate is confident that the money will be spent wisely.

If a political leader simply connected the dots so that the American people had a picture of our real situation, I believe that people would do the right thing. Look at the Social Security compromise in 1983, which cut benefits, raised taxes, and increased the minimum elegibility age to sixty-seven by 2027. Once people knew that the integrity of the system was at stake, they accepted the remedy. The key is to make our predicament clear. To ensure the growth that brings rising standards of living, we must increase savings—not by a little but by a lot. The quickest way to do that is by reducing the federal budget deficit. Given the war in Iraq and the demands of Social Security and Medicare—and given the country's needs in education, pension security, and health care—there is only one way to reduce the deficit and increase investment at the same time, and that is by raising taxes as well as cutting spending. For those who argue that raising taxes will cripple the economy, I point out that real per-person economic growth increased at the same rate during the 1990s, when taxes were raised, as it did in the 1980s, when they were cut. It is important to remember that there could have been no Clinton boom had George Bush I not raised taxes and reduced spending in 1990.

I believe that a tax increase spent on health care, education, pension security, and deficit reduction would receive broad public support. Indeed, a poll taken by the Pew Research Center for the People and the Press before President Bush's first tax cut in 2001 showed that more people wanted the surplus to go for spending on domestic programs, paying down the national debt, or bolstering Social Security and Medicare than wanted their taxes cut.

Tax Reform

The need to raise taxes also creates the opportunity to reform the income-tax system, which is unfair (equal incomes don't pay equal tax), inefficient (the market knows better where to put capital than do members of the Finance or Ways and Means Committees), and overly complex (few people fill out their own returns, and tax fraud has reached between $40 billion and $70 billion per year). By cutting tax rates and eliminating most of the nearly $1 trillion in individual and corporate tax loopholes, we do two things simultaneously. We allow people to keep more of each additional dollar they earn, and we deal a blow to the special interests. As Justice Oliver Wendell Holmes Jr. said, "Taxes are the price we pay for civilization."

The government subsidizes many activities by allowing you to pay less tax if you do them. Buying a home is an example. There, the government allows you to reduce your taxable income by the amount of your mortgage interest and property taxes, which means you pay tax on less income. These tax savings are the government subsidy to home ownership. In any tax reform it would be possible to protect such middle-class "tax expenditures"—that is, deductions, exclusions, and credits; besides mortgage interest, these include charitable contributions, state and local taxes, health insurance, and pension buildup—even as we lowered tax rates. In a system with just three rates, these items could be deductible only against the bottom two; everyone would thus get the subsidy, but for the wealthy it would be worth less. For example, if the rates were 10, 20, and 30 percent, a dollar's worth of deductions would save, at the most, twenty cents in taxes for someone in the 20 percent bracket and ten cents in taxes for someone in the 10 percent bracket. Those in the 30 percent bracket would still get the deduction, but it would be worth only twenty cents. They could not deduct it against the top rate of 30 percent.

In the 1986 tax reform, we cut rates to 15 and 28 percent and eliminated about $30 billion per year in loopholes, and the wealthy, even though the top rate was reduced from 50 percent to 28 percent, ended up paying a bigger percentage of the total income taxes collected.

There are rates that everyone, including most of the wealthy, can agree are fair. I believe that the best tax rate is the lowest tax rate for the greatest number of Americans. Increasing the earned income tax credit assures lower-income working Americans that they, too, can keep more of each dollar they earn. If we simply split the difference between the amount of personal income taxation we had at the end of the Reagan term, which was 8.0 percent of GDP, and the amount at the end of Bill Clinton's presidency, which was 10.3 percent of GDP, and constructed a new income-tax system around raising that amount of revenue, we could, along with spending cuts, realize the new story with ease. By eliminating most of the tax deductions, exclusions, and credits (now worth $911 billion), we could reduce rates, make the system fairer, and raise revenue. By simply reducing these "expenditures," or tax subsidies, in the tax code, we could spend more through appropriations for education, health, and pension security.

If we went back to a level of income-tax revenue halfway between that at the end of the Reagan years and that at the end of the Clinton years, we could also reduce the growing inequality of the last decade. As the Princeton economist Paul Krugman has pointed out, the amazing fact is that 40 percent of the benefit from George W. Bush's tax cuts flows to taxpayers with incomes over $341,000. Fifty-three percent goes to the top 10 percent of taxpayers. Indeed, the amount of the tax cuts going to the top 1 percent of American taxpayers exceeds what the federal government spends on elementary and secondary education and homeland security combined. In addition, by increasing the minimum wage and the earned income tax credit, we could further reduce inequality and give people incentives to work. And more IRS agents and better computer systems would increase tax collection from the wealthy. Commissioner Charles Rossotti says that for an investment of $296 million the service could collect $9 billion more annually.

Another tax innovation would be aimed at people who have *only* wage, interest, or dividend income and take no itemized deductions. There is no reason for them to fill out tax returns; the IRS has all the information about them that it needs, and it can prepare individual tax returns from those W-2 and 1099 forms and send the returns to the taxpayers. If taxpayers wanted to fill out their own forms at that point, they could; more likely, they would simply sign and return the prepared forms. Not having to pay a tax preparer would amount to a kind of tax cut. California put such an initiative on the ballot in 2004, but groups such as H&R Block with a vested interest in the current system managed to kill it.

If politicians were bolder, they could take on an even more ambitious and complex tax reform—moving taxation away from work to pollution and natural resources. In general, we ought to tax less whatever we need, such as wages, and tax more whatever is dangerous to us, such as pollution, resource depletion, trans fats, and tobacco. In this vein, we could implement a $1 per gallon gasoline tax (or an equivalent carbon tax, which is a tax on any energy source that emits carbon dioxide) or equivalent taxes on other major air pollutants: volatile organics, nitrogen oxide, lead, sulfurous dioxide, and particulates. These taxes could be phased in over five years, with the revenue going to reduce employment taxes (Social Security, Medicare, or unemployment insurance) for employees and employers alike. The gasoline or carbon tax would encourage the nation to reduce its dependence on insecure sources of foreign oil, and with payroll taxes now amounting to 15 percent of labor costs, the lower employment taxes would be an incentive for businesses to hire workers.

Such a shift in taxation—away from jobs and toward pollution, energy, and natural resources—would draw many of the 24 million part-time employed into the full-time workforce, and millions more who are not in the labor force would be more likely to find jobs. After a few years of adjustment in the case of a gasoline or carbon tax, cars would be more fuel-efficient, so consumers would pay what they used to pay for the same amount of driving, and the broad middle class would continue to pay lower employment taxes. The result would be increasing demand for goods and services; shrinking dependency payments, such as unemployment compensation or welfare; lowered social costs, such as crime or avoidable illness; and a more equitable tax system—one that encourages rising employment.

Reducing employment taxes also makes sense on grounds of competitiveness and equity. Employment taxes now hit our most successful companies hardest. A company such as Microsoft or

McKinsey needs talented people desperately, and there is a limited pool of individuals with the requisite skills. As part of the company's compensation package, it has to pay enough salary to offset the employment taxes paid by the employee. If it doesn't make up the taxes in higher wages, the employee can go somewhere else, where the employer will cover the amount owed in employment taxes. Meanwhile, at a lumberyard where there is an excess of labor, the lumber company doesn't have to pay higher wages and the bulk of the employment taxes hit the workers. Perversely, it is the lowest-paid workers and the companies most essential to economic growth that are hit hardest by employment taxes.

Better yet, if politicians wanted a comprehensive and fair way to reduce the deficit and invest in health care, education, and pension security, they could combine income tax reform and gasoline- or pollution-tax increases with a reduction in employment taxes, a 10 percent cut in defense spending, a 30 percent cut in what the federal government spends on corporate subsidies such as those for mining, timber, and use of the digital spectrum, a limit on the corporate deduction for the most expensive medical plans, and a cut in farm subsidies—which today go to only 25 percent of American farmers, with $7 billion of the total $14 billion going to the richest 3 percent, including large agribusiness.

In addition, the budget process should be governed by the pay-as-you-go rules that existed in the 1990s. Under those rules, any tax cut or spending increase had to be offset by a spending cut elsewhere in the budget.

Finally, the entire federal budget should be on the Internet, with keyword accessibility. For example, if you searched for "breast cancer" or "housing," you would be directed to all the places in the federal budget where money is spent for those purposes. That way, citizens could have the information with which to understand the trade-offs in taxes and spending and hold their legislators accountable.

The key to passage of these measures would be to have them all in one package, so that choices—between more money for health care, education, and pension security on the one hand, and spending cuts and higher taxes on the other—could be made clearer. If we included spending cuts or increases in one bill and tax reform in another, the connection between what we were giving up in tax increases and what we were getting in spending increases would be lost. The debate should be about the whole, not the parts. Issues such as sharing the burden fairly between the young and the old, and trade-offs between weapons systems and health care, or corporate welfare and human welfare, would be clearly set out.

Here are my specific policy recommendations:

1. Continue to invest in science and technology—basic research and development—in the public and private sectors alike.
2. Provide free tuition up to $12,000 (the average tuition cost for a four-year public college) for any high school student in the top third of his or her graduating class, and more generous incentives for math, science, engineering, and foreign-language students in both undergraduate and graduate studies.

3. Reduce the federal budget deficit.
   - Reform the income tax code to provide lower rates, fewer loopholes, and more revenue.
   - Impose a $1 per gallon gasoline tax or the equivalent in energy or pollution taxes and then offset either one by a reduction in employment taxes such as those for Social Security, Medicare, or unemployment insurance.
   - Raise the age threshold for receiving Social Security and the income threshold for paying into it, bring new state and local employees into the system, and change the way the annual cost-of-living adjustment is calculated.
   - Make Medicare changes as a part of overall health care reform by offering choices to the elderly and creating competition on outcomes and prices among the providers, recognizing that, absent reform, the only alternatives would be some combination of increased premiums on Medicare recipients, higher taxes on working Americans, and reduction of benefits for recipients.

- Reduce defense spending by 10 percent.
- Reduce farm subsidies for the wealthiest 3 percent of farmers.
- Control budget earmarks, or cut them outright.
- Cut corporate subsidies by 30 percent.

4. Help working families.
   - Increase the earned income tax credit.
   - Increase the minimum wage.

5. Regulate hedge funds.
   - Require all hedge funds that manage pension fund money to come under federal ERISA regulation.
   - Force hedge-fund managers to register with the Securities and Exchange Commission so that authorities would at least know who they are in the event of a financial crisis.

6. Make changes in tax administration and budget rules.
   - Have the IRS fill out tax returns for those with only wage and/or 1099 income and no itemized deductions, thereby saving taxpayers the cost of tax preparation.
   - Cut tax fraud in half by beefing up the IRS to go after the big abusers.
   - Return to the pay-as-you-go budget rules that existed in the 1990s.
   - Put the entire federal budget on the Internet, with keyword accessibility.

Let me offer a word of caution: If we fail to take steps to increase our national savings, reduce systemic financial risk, and generate broad-based economic growth, there is a collision waiting to happen between us and the Chinese. As noted, we send them dollars by buying their exports, and they buy U.S. government debt with that money. Right now, they own more than $300 billion of very-low-interest U.S. government debt and nearly another $700 billion in corporate and quasi-government debt. At some point, they will seek a higher return, at first by diversifying, not out of dollar assets but among dollar assets: They will buy fewer bonds and more stocks. They won't be satisfied with only portfolio investment. They will want to buy companies—as they tried to do in 2005 with the oil company Unocal. Congress will huff and puff and threaten. This time, the Chinese, tired of all the saber rattling over Taiwan and trade deficits, will say, "Fine. You don't want our money. We'll sell more of your bonds, even at a poor rate of return, and put that money in euro- or yen-denominated assets, or even buy gold, platinum, and diamonds." To argue that they would never do this because selling off our Treasury bonds would reduce the return on their investment is to ignore their fierce nationalism. What are a few dollars, compared with national pride? Dubai and other Middle Eastern countries, who are fed up with U.S. bullying over port deals, accusations of shielding terrorists, and intractability on the Israeli-Palestinian problem, will intensify the precariousness of our position by selling some of their U.S. bonds, too. When these countries begin selling U.S. government debt, the dollar will drop and the Federal Reserve will have to raise interest rates to attract non-Chinese, non–Middle Eastern capital. When interest rates go up, many people will liquidate their real estate at low prices. With less money, they will cut consumer spending, and nothing will replace it. The recession will deepen. Bankruptcies and foreclosures will rise, and we'll have a major economic crisis on our hands.

For those who say this could never happen, I say, In the absence of increasing national savings and continued technological advance, just you wait. One day we could wake up to find that our worst economic nightmare has become a reality, with its attendant reduction in living standards for all Americans.

But there is another alternative. We *can* liberate our economy from the stranglehold of increasing debt while continuing to invest in our people's health, education, and economic security. With research producing technological breakthroughs, our productivity would continue to accelerate, and with a new transparent budget and income-tax system, people would be better able to see how their tax dollars were raised and spent. Regulation could rein in the most egregious financial risk taking without numbing entrepreneurship.

Most people remember the last Reagan years as a time of lower taxes and the last Clinton years as a time of great prosperity; by initiating tax reform in order to return to a level of taxation halfway between the two, we can both invest in our future and assure the savings necessary for that investment. Such a course seems like a no-brainer to me.

The choice is ours.

Chapter 5.

OIL AND THE ENVIRONMENT

The story on oil says that the doomsayers are wrong—we're not really running out of oil. There is plenty of it in places all around the world and even here at home, and more sophisticated technology will allow us to extend the life of existing wells. All we have to do is make sure there are enough incentives for oil companies and enough U.S. government clout to assure them security and access internationally. No sacrifice is required of the American consumer; no tax increases or additional federal regulations are necessary. Alternative energy sources are fine, but in the foreseeable future they cannot reduce our need for oil.

Such a view is colossally shortsighted. Estimates of how much oil remains are debatable; the real issue is oil dependence and its distortion of our economy and our foreign policy. President Bush was right when he observed, in his 2006 State of the Union speech, that "America is addicted to oil." The United States is the world's largest and most profligate consumer of oil, using 25 percent of the world's supply, while China, with four times as many people, consumes only 7 percent.*

---

*Although China is growing fast; the U.S. Energy Information Administration forecasts that by 2030 China will consume 15 million barrels of oil per day, more than the current level of U.S. imports.

The largest tax that Americans have paid over the last five years has been assessed not by our government but by OPEC, the Organization of Petroleum Exporting Countries. In 2001, OPEC's average price per barrel of crude oil was $23.12. In 2005, it was $50.71, the equivalent of a tax increase of more than $55 billion. If you bought just 16 gallons of gas per week (a tankful), in 2005 you were paying over $500 more per year for gasoline than you were in 2001. Our dependence on oil is the wild card in our economy. When you factor in the taxes to pay for two wars in the Persian Gulf in fifteen years, a part of whose purpose related to oil, this addiction has cost taxpayers far more than simply the amount we paid in increased gasoline and heating oil prices.

While the first oil war, in 1991, was financed in large part by countries in the Gulf region, the oil war that began in 2003 had cost us, by the end of 2006, some $400 billion, with no letup on the horizon. Yet our government has done almost nothing to deal with the central problem of our dependence on oil and especially our dependence on insecure sources of foreign oil.

The Bush administration has not presented the whole picture to the American people. It has failed to point out that we're not talking about just oil. There are connections among energy security (the amount of oil we import), climate protection (the amount of carbon dioxide entering our atmosphere), and protection against the proliferation of nuclear weapons technology (the number of nuclear power plants and uranium enrichment facilities in the world that are monitored and have safeguards against diversion of their spent fuel to weapons development). If we're going to break our oil addiction, we need to act on all three fronts. If we don't keep the price of oil high, the conservation that the market would otherwise dictate will be lost. If we replace oil with equally polluting tar sands or shale oil, we will continue to promote climate change. And we need to create a comprehensive global nonproliferation regime, so that nuclear energy can reduce our oil dependence by making electricity more plentiful and cheaper (and therefore, among other things, making electric cars more competitive). Unless we reduce oil use and carbon dioxide emissions while avoiding nuclear disaster, we don't have the right policy.

Far from seeing these connections, administration officials continue to tolerate and even foster an oilcentric world. They offer no sense of urgency about consuming less oil. They urge opening the Arctic National Wildlife Refuge to drilling, though its potential daily production wouldn't make up even 5 percent of our daily consumption. Beyond that, the administration touts its support for ethanol, which has been subsidized since the late 1970s; advocates alternative fuels such as liquefied coal, which produces twice as much heat-trapping gases as gasoline; makes a largely symbolic goal-setting nod toward raising auto fuel efficiency standards, which it ignored for six years; and seeks out photo opportunities at the National Renewable Energy Laboratory, which is grossly underfunded. This is not the kind of leadership that allowed us to win World War II.

You would think, from what little the Bush administration has asked the American people to do, that it fails to see the connection between our oil addiction and the loss of American lives in Iraq. A war to sustain our oil dependence is apparently preferable to the administration than the exercise of leadership that would reduce that level of dependence. It can muster the political will to go to war, but it can't muster the courage to tell the American people the truth about what is required of each of us to break our oil addiction. By failing to do so, it is enabling that addiction.

In the 1980s and 1990s, the United States built up a Strategic Petroleum Reserve, which by 2005 contained 700 million barrels of oil. With that buffer stock, we protected access to supply for our national security and created a threat that we could release some oil if prices spiked because of political blackmail. The reserve was rarely used, because the law of supply and demand usually took care of unpredictable shortages. For example, when prices went up in the late 1970s and early 1980s, consumption dropped, and the existing supply was sufficient. Such shortages were temporary, so as more oil gradually came back online, prices dropped and consumption resumed its upward trajectory. Today the market and the Strategic Petroleum Reserve can't cope with our energy realities without great pain. Prices have always risen in times of increased demand or sudden reduction in supply. But if demand increases faster than new supply is available over a sustained period, prices could stay high for a long time. The question is, How fast can new supply come online and how much can demand for oil be reduced without cratering the economy or threatening our domestic welfare or national security?

In the 1950s, a geologist named M. King Hubbert predicted that oil production in the United States (excluding Alaska) would peak between 1965 and 1970. It did, in 1970. Recently, Kenneth S. Deffeyes, a geology professor emeritus at Princeton University, applied Hubbert's methodology to worldwide oil resources and concluded that world oil production would peak in late 2005 or early 2006. If his predictions are accurate, a severe price squeeze will be the result.

Some oil company analysts disagree. They point out that in 1980, when the world consumed 63 million barrels per day, some said we were running out of oil. Today we consume 86 million barrels of oil per day, and we haven't run out yet. It's estimated that by 2030 we will consume 118 million barrels per day. The oil companies say those numbers give you some idea of how wrong the pessimistic estimates are. With new supply coming online, the predicted price disaster never seems to last beyond a few weeks or months. Oil companies also point out that advances in technology allow ever more efficient recovery of oil in ever more difficult to reach geological structures. They are confident that technology will produce significant new recovery techniques no one can now predict. Technology has always come to our rescue, so why shouldn't it continue to do so? Moreover, say the oil companies, there are reserves of black gold in remote regions of the world. All they need for recovery of this oil is a U.S. government that concerns itself with the security of company personnel in those regions and gives the companies a free hand in every other way.

The issue, however, shouldn't be the adequacy of global oil reserves but the timing of their extraction. For an oil company to sit on vast reserves, unable to get at them because of a shortage of capital or adequate technology, doesn't help the world much. One oil company, Royal Dutch/Shell, got into trouble when it failed to make this distinction in its listed reserves, and it is not the only company that has reported total reserves instead of recoverable reserves. In addition to limitations of technology and capital, there is a shortage of petroleum engineers, and the market reflects it. Today a just-graduated petroleum engineer from Texas A&M might get $70,000 plus a $15,000 signing bonus and a $10,000 moving allowance—the highest compensation for any graduate with only a bachelor's degree.

Whatever the outcome of the debate about when the world's oil supply will run out, the increased demand from mature economies, such as the United States, Europe, and Japan, combined with burgeoning demand from developing economies, such as India and China, will soon exceed available supply unless current trends change. In China, for example, there will be ninety times as many cars on the road in 2010 as there were in 1990, and by 2030 there will probably be more cars in China than in the United States. Worldwide, gasoline prices will rise dramatically—unless the shortage is controlled by various government allocation schemes, with their attendant inequities and lines at the pump.

In a continuing atmosphere of shortage and persistent skyrocketing prices, what is unthinkable now might be viewed as necessary. The columnist Martin Wolf of the *Financial Times* has speculated that the United States might conclude that oil allocation by the price mechanism destroys our economy and endangers our national security, and that our only alternative is to seize foreign oil fields and tankers. But even the U.S. military might find it difficult to guarantee physical control of oil production on the ground and transportation on the seas for us and us alone. Such a course would pit the United States against the rest of the world, an untenable circumstance.

Our addiction to oil takes its toll on our economy because when the price of oil rises, the prices of almost everything else rise, too. Airlines and utilities pass on the increased costs to their customers. Even some taxi drivers assess fuel surcharges on top of each fare. In a world market, the problem is not just our imports but our total consumption. The OPEC tax is calculated by multiplying the world price (higher in times of disruption) by the number of barrels we consume. Even if we have no imports, we're still hit hard when prices rise sharply. Our addiction also distorts our foreign policy. Outside the context of the current war in Iraq and the struggle with movements such as Al Qaeda, America has no essential conflict with the countries of the Middle East in the traditional nation-state sense—no territorial dispute, no historical animosity. In fact, as long as Israel remains impregnable, why should America care what happens in the sands of Saudi Arabia? The answer is oil.

We are about 100 years into the fossil-fuel economy. It has become a part of our national fabric, as it has in almost every country around the globe. John P. Holdren, director of the Science, Technology, and Public Policy Program at the Kennedy School of Government, points out, in an essay titled "The Energy Innovation Imperative," that "the replacement cost of today's global energy-supply system—all of the power plants, transmission lines, drilling rigs, pipelines, refineries, coal mines, and so on—is in the range of $12 trillion." He further notes that oil production, refining, distribution, and retailing is over $4 trillion of that amount. The replacement cost for the oil-supply system is nearly twice as big as the current U.S. budget, eight times greater than the current U.S. defense budget, and almost a third the value of all the homes in the United States.*

The world has made a massive continuing bet on oil and gas. To change direction will not be easy. Besides the sheer amount of capital that has been sunk into infrastructure, the thirty- to forty-year life span of those investments means that the transition from oil will be a long-term process. It takes time to develop more fuel-efficient airplanes or to phase out the gas-guzzling SUVs and bring on the electric hybrids—and you can bet that those who benefit from the oil economy will use their considerable political clout to postpone the transition as long as they can. Yet if America were to see its economic and national security future clearly, getting beyond our oil dependency would be a national priority.

*By comparison, worldwide pharmaceutical and biotech investment is $55 billion and worldwide agricultural investment is $300 to $400 billion.

Geopolitical Instability

Oil dependence contributes to geopolitical instability. Nearly 40 percent of the world's exports of oil go through the Strait of Hormuz, between Iran and Oman. United States, British, Dutch, and French oil companies explore for oil on every continent but Antarctica. Japan seeks oil in the Caspian Sea, the Persian Gulf, and the Russian Far East. China, a growing importer, scours the world, gobbling up as much oil as possible: a $100 billion oil deal with Iran; a tar-sands deal with Canada; part of an oil field in Nigeria, including off-shore rights; even investment in Sudan's infant oil industry. With each passing day, the danger rises of a Chinese conflict with Japan over natural gas in the disputed waters of the East China Sea. It's instructive to remember that the Japanese attack on Pearl Harbor, which precipitated our entry into World War II, was in part a response to FDR's cutting off shipments of oil supplies to Japan.

Russia, a net exporter of oil, is riding the crest of the gigantic increases in oil prices and sees no need for economic reform as its vast oil and gas resources bring billions into government coffers. State oil revenues represent nearly 40 percent of all the money raised by the Russian government. Russia has become a one-resource economy, like Saudi Arabia or Iran or Venezuela. If oil prices stay high, corruption will increase. The social and political structure will harden, and the state, feeling flush from new oil wealth and the sense of security it brings, will redouble its efforts to silence domestic dissent. Although the Russian economy as a whole is still only the size of Mexico's, the combination of oil revenues and a budding rapprochement with China makes for an unpredictable future.

Venezuela's Hugo Chávez looks more and more like a Fidel Castro, but a Castro with plenty of oil. As long as oil prices remain high, his power will only increase. He actively pursues a strategy of grouping other Latin American states into an anti-U.S. posture and seeks alliances with China, India, or whomever else he can influence with access to Venezuelan oil.

The countries of the Persian Gulf, especially Saudi Arabia, have used petrodollars to finance extreme religious education all over the

Muslim world. Yet they haven't educated their own people enough to create a broad-based economy. Math and science have taken a backseat to Jihad in too many schools. As is the case in Russia, oil revenues have anesthetized the Saudis to the need for economic diversification. Selling oil requires only as long as it takes to draw it out of the desert and ship it. Building a broad-based economy on the foundation of an educated citizenry requires decades. When they ignore the educational needs of their country, trample their citizens' rights, and put off democratic reform, is it any wonder that no genuine middle class has developed in Saudi Arabia and that many Saudi youth have turned to radical Islam?

Finally, there is India, the pluralistic democracy on the borders of Central Asia. India needs oil from Russia, Iran, and anywhere else it can get it, and it will adopt policies that ensure the supply. Agreements with the United States on developing nuclear power or sharing military technology won't keep India from dealing with any country that can supply it with oil and gas.

There's a limit to the amount of money the American people will be willing to spend for military adventures in the Persian Gulf—or, for that matter, for filling up their cars at gas stations. We could lead the world into a different energy future—one based on more efficiency and new sources of energy. But to do so requires us to lead by example—to conserve energy and promote alternative energy sources.

I came to the Senate in 1979, in the midst of an oil-supply disruption in the Persian Gulf. President Jimmy Carter decontrolled oil prices in April 1979. The price of oil skyrocketed to $39.50 per barrel, which in today's dollars would be close to $100. There were lines at the gasoline pump. Many people directed their anger at the oil companies for raising their prices and called for a return to price controls. Congress resisted that call but offered incentives for conservation, created a Synthetic Fuels Corporation to reduce our dependence on foreign oil, and assessed a windfall-profits tax on oil companies. In the deliberations over these last two pieces of legislation, the assumptions were that oil prices would rise to $100 per barrel by the year 2000 and that all kinds of alternative fuels—shale oil, tar sands, fuel cells, solar, wind, biomass—would therefore be competitive. The only problem was that by the mid-1980s oil had dropped to less than $10 per barrel and people wanted to return to their gas guzzlers. The auto companies accommodated them, and the SUV was born. The 15 percent reduction in oil consumption achieved between 1979 and 1985 began to erode quickly. With the drop in price, there were not enough government subsidies for non-oil sources of energy to make up the difference between the price of cheap oil and the price of more expensive alternative sources of energy. But without a federal mandate, auto companies don't produce enough fuel-efficient cars, and other companies generally don't bother making less wasteful versions of furnaces, hot-water heaters, air conditioners, and the like.

Times have changed. If Professor Deffeyes is right that world oil production has peaked—at a time when demand from China and India has accelerated—the path ahead is toward dangerously higher prices. Even if he is wrong and oil production continues to rise, burgeoning demand may still exceed discovery of new supplies. A worldwide depression could cut the demand for oil, but short of that, the supply and demand curves for oil may have crossed permanently. OPEC used to manipulate production to get a price high enough to earn obscene profits but low enough to make sure alternative sources of energy would not be competitive. Now, given its current capacities, OPEC can no longer produce more oil in order to stabilize prices at lower levels. Indeed, there are fewer than 2 million barrels per day of spare production capacity in the whole world. Yet no matter whether peak worldwide oil production has already occurred or will occur in five years or twenty years, the peril of continued oil addiction to our economy, our security, and our environment demands that today we reduce that dependence.

Those who argue that our oil addiction can be reduced by production of oil from tar sands, heavy oil, coal, or oil shale ignore the fact that those sources are even more polluting than oil. They are also extremely energy-intensive to produce and, in the case of tar sands and synthetic fuels, very water-intensive. Recall that our energy policy ought not to be just about energy security—it should also be about our environmental security and nuclear safety. What good does it do to produce oil from coal or tar sands if the amount of carbon dioxide belched into the air only hastens the heating up of the world's climate? A shift to natural gas would be cleaner than a shift to coal or tar sands. Since 2000, almost all added electrical power capacity in the United States has used natural gas, and vast investments are being made in liquefied natural gas facilities. Both developments seem to ignore the fact that many of the same countries that now control oil also control natural gas; recently, the United States has become an importer of gas. Another current favorite alternative to oil is ethanol, but according to Lee Raymond, former CEO of Exxon, for ethanol to meet even 10 percent of the nation's demand for gasoline would require planting corn in an area bigger than Indiana and Ohio combined. The possibility of producing ethanol from nonedible crops and plant waste offers more hope, but its production costs are currently estimated at twice those of corn-produced ethanol. And Michael McElroy, a professor of environmental studies at Harvard, writes that 75 percent of the reduced fossil-energy consumption that results from use of ethanol is offset by the cost of producing the ethanol and transporting it.

Finally, some suggest nuclear power as a part of our energy solution. According to Anne Lauvergeon, CEO of the AREVA group, one of the world's largest nuclear power companies, technology has created nuclear plants that are so safe an airplane could make a direct hit and no radioactive materials would be released into the atmosphere. The greatest obstacle to wider use of nuclear power is the need for safe long-term storage of spent fuel, which will remain radioactive for thousands of years. Deep geological storage in places such as in Nevada's Yucca Mountain offers a way to sequester it, but surface or near-surface retrievable storage may be a better answer.

America has a choice: Do something now to eliminate our addiction to oil or witness global conflict that will make the two recent wars in the Persian Gulf look like teapot tempests.

The story we are told on global warming says it is a myth, unproved. Scientific opinion is said to be divided. Meeting the arbitrary stan-

dards for carbon dioxide emissions promoted by radical environmentalists, it is said, will cost America jobs.

The story on the environment and development says that the government should reduce the burden of environmental regulation and that there are no limits to the urbanization of America west of the 100th meridian. Just continue to drill water wells, build subdivisions, dam rivers, mine for minerals, drill for oil and gas, cut the timber, and graze the range.

This story flies in the face of copious scientific evidence. What is amazing to me is how smart people can so easily deny reality. Can they really be that greedy or that dismissive of science or that shortsighted? Naomi Oreskes, a professor of history and science studies at the University of California at San Diego, pointed out in an article in *Science* magazine in 2004 that out of 928 randomly selected peer-reviewed articles on climate change appearing in scientific journals over a ten-year period, not one doubted that humans were the cause of global warming. Yet the brothers Jules and Maxwell Boykoff, writing in November 2004 for the organization FAIR (Fairness and Accuracy in Reporting), analyzed articles in newspapers such as *The New York Times, The Wall Street Journal, The Washington Post,* and the *Los Angeles Times* from 1988 to 2002 and found that "53 percent of the articles gave roughly equal attention" to the explanation that climate change was caused exclusively by natural fluctuations, not human conduct. Clearly the public relations teams have been working overtime. Most of those people who ignore the peril to the environment have insured their homes, their cars, and their lives, but they seem to want no global insurance against environmental disaster and no regional insurance against continued drought or sustained flooding. As countries argue over emissions timetables, they fail to facilitate the adoption of technology that would lessen hydrocarbon use.

Shortly after Hurricane Katrina wreaked its devastation, I watched as former president Clinton was interviewed on TV by Larry King. Clinton talked about global warming and how it threatens us all. He said that polls indicated the desire for a clean environment, but if you polled people on what they were willing to do to clean it up, or if you proposed a trade-off with jobs, the numbers dropped. As a voting issue, global warming just didn't yet seem sufficiently urgent. That night I read between the lines of what Clinton was saying, and it gave me a rush of optimism.

During his eight years as president, Bill Clinton had never emphasized global warming. He gave up on trying to push the Kyoto Protocol through the Senate. He threw in the towel on a carbon tax. He just wasn't interested. He delegated the subject of climate change to Vice President Al Gore, who did (and still does) have a sincere and deep personal interest in such matters. So how do you explain the concern Clinton expressed on the Larry King show? When Bill Clinton starts talking about an issue, it is not always because he has a record of championing it, or even an interest in it. Sometimes it's because he thinks it's good politics. And there's nothing wrong with that. Maybe more politicians will see the political payoff and act. Our survival depends on it.

The story we are told on the environment says that recently we have created realistic solutions to environmental problems — solutions that are both effective and not harmful to our economy. But the truth is that the Bush administration has the worst environmental record of any administration since passage of the first significant environmental laws, in the 1960s under Lyndon Johnson. It has failed to renew the Superfund corporate tax that helped pay for the cleanup of toxic water dumps. It has weakened rules under the Clean Water Act that held large pork producers responsible for dumping untreated fecal matter into our streams. It has attempted to gut the rule that forces old power plants, largely in the Midwest, to adopt modern pollution controls when their facilities are modernized. It has succeeded in gutting the protection against mountain-removal mining in Appalachia. It has reduced civil citations against polluters by 57 percent and criminal prosecution of polluters by 17 percent. It runs a federal government that gives away $65 billion a year in traditional subsidies to big oil and a minimum of $16 billion a year to western natural-resource industries, such as mining and timber. It mouths a belief in the free market, but its corporate supporters benefit from substantial federal subsidies — our tax dollars —

and pass along the cost of the resultant pollution to the taxpayers. We pay twice.

The Bush administration has turned over the government posts that are supposed to look out for our national patrimony to the people who want to steal it. *The New York Times* reported in March 2006 that at the Interior Department since 2000 "at least six high political positions have been occupied by people associated with businesses or trade associations tied to public lands or resources." For example, a department solicitor general, William G. Myers, was a lobbyist and lawyer representing ranching and mining companies as well as the National Cattlemen's Beef Association. Thomas Sansonetti, an assistant attorney general for environmental and natural resources, represented Big Coal. And James Connaughton, the chairman of the Council on Environmental Quality, lobbied for major electricity users and companies opposing Superfund cleanup rules. According to a September 2003 article in *Mother Jones*, Connaughton "helped develop the White House's position on climate change (ignore), Superfund (shrink), and air-quality rules (relax)."

To cite an egregious example in which I have something of a personal stake: In 1992, Representative George Miller (D.–Calif.) and I succeeded in getting a law passed that changed the way water from California's Central Valley Project, the largest of the nation's water projects, was allocated and created an environmental fund to protect wildlife in the Central Valley. The fiercest opponent of that law was Jason Peltier, the manager of a trade association that represented the large water interests. Peltier vowed that he and his clients would resist implementation with all the legal and political weapons at their disposal. He then proceeded to oversee the filing of lawsuits that prevented implementation of provisions such as restoration of the Trinity and San Joaquin rivers and various reforms in water contracts. (The Trinity restoration is still in limbo; after fourteen years of litigation and conflict, the restoration of the San Joaquin was finally announced in 2006.) As principal deputy assistant secretary for water and science, Peltier now helps award the Interior Department's water contracts. It appears that one of his major aims is to give the Westlands Water District, which happens to be a former client, a twenty-five-year lease—and an option for an additional twenty-five years—on 1.15 million acre-feet of water (each acre-foot is 326,000 gallons) at a low price, which the water district can then use for its own agricultural production or resell at a profit to municipalities and corporations or other Central Valley farmers. In a state where water is the lifeblood and four-fifths of it goes to agriculture, even though agriculture represents only 2 percent of California's GDP, Peltier wants the federal government to make a fifty-year noncompetitive commitment to one rural water district.

What shocks me is that people aren't angrier about the destruction of their environment—the one thing, beyond life itself, that is given to all of us. Don't they notice that more and more species of butterflies and birds have declining populations? Aren't they aware that the glaciers of the Arctic north are melting? Don't they see our public lands being despoiled by timber companies, oil companies, and mining companies? Don't they know that the coal companies have evaded environmental laws to turn the streams of Appalachia into a toxic brew? Don't they realize that when marshlands go, so does flood protection, as well as the food cycle for the creatures of the sea and the air? Don't they recognize that rampant industrial fishing and rising pollution are turning vast areas of the oceans into dead zones? Don't they witness the growing intensity and frequency of hurricanes, tornadoes, floods, and droughts? Can't they understand the impossibility of promoting a sustainable environment when developing countries believe it's their right to industrialize just as we did? Don't they see the Amazon rain forests burning, with tropical habitat being reduced to a charred wasteland? Don't they know about the increasing extinction of species, as many as 50,000 per year, from the blue pike to the Colombian grebe? Don't they know that a part of Los Angeles smog comes from particulate matter blown over from China by the prevailing winds? Can't they draw a connection between the summer of 2003 (the hottest European summer in 500 years), with the thousands of lives it took, and the process of global warming? Can't they draw a connection between the smog that shrouds their cities and their own use of products whose manufacture pollutes the environment?

Just as with the supply and demand curves in the oil market, there will come a tipping point, when the earth will be rendered all but uninhabitable—at least by human beings. Then it will be too late. Our profligacy will have brought us to the point of no return. Once we are there, it won't matter how rich we are or where our children go to school or whether we believe in God. The facts that are now being questioned will at last be indisputable, and life on this planet as we have known it will change for the worse. Armed camps will hoard the remaining resources, and millions of people will die. We will no longer have the luxury of saying "tomorrow"—in fact, we do not really have that luxury today.

To their shame, the United States and Australia stand alone among the developed economies in denying the urgency of greenhouse warming. The kings of the status quo in the natural-resource industries have bought the Bush government, and it follows their orders. These interests are concerned not so much about the fate of humankind as about their companies' prospects and their own personal bank accounts. The irony is that they, too, will suffer because of the world they have wrought. Their beachfront homes will be submerged by rising sea levels and the force of more frequent and intense hurricanes, their desert golf courses won't survive the sinking water tables, their ski resorts will run out of snow. When the reality of the world we have created bursts on our awareness, there will be no more lobbyists able to guarantee a few more years of business as usual.

The Shortage of Water

Mark Twain once said about the American West that "whiskey is for drinking; water is for fighting." No matter whether Jason Peltier stays in his post at the Interior Department or not, there is a limited supply of water. An August 2006 article by Claudia Deutsch in *The New York Times* reports that the Environmental Protection Agency has stated that if current water consumption patterns don't change, thirty-six of fifty states will have water shortages by 2013. According to Tim Barnett, a marine physicist at the Scripps Institution of Oceanography, there is a 60 to 80 percent chance that by 2025 Los Angeles will see reduction of available water. Other cities in the West, such as Phoenix, already cope with occasional water shortages. If people keep migrating to this fragile land, there will come a day when either rationing water will be necessary or the prices will rise so high that thousands will go thirsty.

For example, a series of Colorado River Basin compacts has divided the Colorado River water among seven states and Mexico. The compacts initially assumed there would be 18 million acre-feet of water available for distribution each year. Several decades later, the figure was lowered to 15 million acre-feet. That best-case scenario allowed the 1928 Boulder Canyon Project Act to give each of the Lower Basin states what it wanted: California, 4,400,000 acre-feet; Arizona, 2,800,000 acre-feet; Nevada, 300,000 acre-feet; with the rest going to the states of the Upper Basin (Colorado, New Mexico, Utah, and Wyoming). A 1944 treaty then allotted Mexico an additional 1,500,000 acre-feet over and above what was given to the Lower and Upper Basin states, bringing the total allocated water to 16.5 million acre-feet. Because of an extended drought, these politically attractive assumptions have now proved optimistic; the average distribution has been closer to 15 million acre-feet, and in many years has been much less. Because of the reduced volume, Lake Mead and Lake Powell are each more than ninety feet below capacity. Put simply, there is less and less water.

As the long drought has reduced available water, more and more people have poured into the region, attracted by the weather and the lifestyle. Terry Bracy, formerly a key aide to Representative Morris K. Udall (D.–Ariz.), recalls a meeting of senators and congressmen prior to the passage of the 1968 Colorado River Basin Project Act, which clarified certain provisions of the earlier compacts. When the development potential of the area between Yuma, Arizona, and Laughlin, Nevada, came up, one participant remarked that you could forget about development there, because "it's hotter than hell and no one will live there but lizards and rattlesnakes." Four hundred thousand people now live along the 170-mile Yuma–Lake Havasu City–Laughlin stretch of the Colorado River. In the winter months, 100,000 RVs from all over the country arrive in Quartzsite, Arizona, alone. The result of this septic-tank-supported development is dangerous levels of nitrates flowing into the watershed and groundwater contamination approaching the danger zone.

All over the West, to raise money for water-quality projects, states sell off land to developers, who build more shopping centers and more houses, which creates more demand for water and more pollution problems. This path is not sustainable. Water pricing must better reflect cost; conservation must improve; and use of water for agriculture (80 to 90 percent of water use in the West) must become more efficient, so that more water can be allocated to commercial, industrial, and residential users. There is no alternative.

Worldwide, the problem of water, both its quantity and its quality, is the hidden threat to all of us. Worldwide withdrawal of water has quadrupled between 1940 and 2000. As people get wealthier, they use more water—for irrigation, bathing, cleaning, and cooking, as well as drinking—and as populations increase, there are more people using more and more water. Pamela LeRoy and Robert Engelman of Population Action International assert in a paper titled "Sustaining Water: Population and the Future of Renewable Water Supplies" that there is "no more fresh water on the planet today than there was 2000 years ago," when the earth's population was less than 4 percent of its current total of 6.5 billion people. The United Nations Population Fund has warned that by 2025, 5.0 billion of the then 7.9 billion people in the world will not have enough drinkable water. As Professor Mark Taylor of Williams College points out, "The problem is most acute in Asia which has approximately 60 percent of the world's population, but only 36 percent of its renewable fresh water." Countries of the Middle East sit on a sea of oil but have very little renewable water. One reason Israel holds on to the Golan Heights is that it houses the headwaters of the Jordan River. Some entrepreneurs argue that oil tankers should return to the Persian Gulf full of excess water from parts of North America and Europe. Use of the Mekong River creates friction between Vietnam and Cambodia, and in Europe pollution of the Dnieper in one country affects all downstream countries. Without some international agreements on water, Twain's saying could prove correct on a global scale.

THE NEW STORY

There's a new story about oil and the environment. It begins with a president who tells the American people the truth—that our oil addiction makes us a weaker country and that with enough will we can break the habit. It begins with a government that asks the American people to be a part of the solution. There is no free lunch here. The new story says that a shift to more benign forms of energy is possible, that conservation still offers us a vast potential savings of oil, that we don't have to accept a dirty industrialization phase for developing countries, that it's not too late to deal with global warming, that dwindling water resources can be conserved.

The new story points out that global warming is fundamentally an air-pollution problem, and we have solved air-pollution problems before, at less cost than anyone thought possible. Technological advance has always given us pleasant surprises, once we decide as a nation that we want to reduce a particular pollutant and set tough regulations to achieve that reduction. In the 1960s, urban smog was a major health threat. "Either we stop poisoning our air," President Johnson warned when he signed the Air Quality Act of 1967, "or we become a nation in gas masks groping our way through the dying cities." Then the catalytic converter was invented, and smog dropped by nearly 50 percent. The same was true for chlorofluoro-carbons in the 1980s. Since we banned them, some studies show that the hole in the ozone layer over Antarctica has begun to close. Acid rain has decreased, too, because the credit-trading system of the 1990 Clean Air Act Amendments gave companies profit incentives for pollution reduction. Up to the tipping point, the environment is incredibly resilient. There is no reason why we could not at least prevent global warming from worsening. Author and lecturer Gregg Easterbrook, writing in the September 2006 *Atlantic*, lamented that Democrats minimize how solvable the problem of global warming is, while Republicans exaggerate the cost of solving it and ignore the efficacy of regulation.

What it takes is for us to lead the way by example and then share our scientific breakthroughs with the world. When we set limits on pollution, economic incentives shift to finding the technological fix.

Just think how much better it would be for the country if companies were to invest more in research on pollution control than in Washington lobbyists to resist bringing about a cleaner world. And if we fund the fix to help ourselves, we could sell it to the world, in an act combining leadership and good business.

The new story says we can still act, even at this late hour, to mobilize our nation and the world to protect our global patrimony. The new story reminds us that when we encounter nature, we come face-to-face with something that lasts longer than we do and is bigger than we are—something that connects us to the past, to other living things, and to that which most makes us human. The story says that the land is our teacher; it teaches us the value of things that can't be bought or sold, traded or exchanged. What's the dollar value of the Arizona desert? What price would you put on the endless marshes of the Everglades? In an earlier time, we might have said: Zero. Nothing. They're worthless. Today we look at the lonely beauty of the desert or the cypress swamp and say: It's priceless.

But the American people owe something to the land. For nearly 400 years, we have torn through it, slashing, cutting, burning, digging, drilling, fencing, paving. We cannot re-create what has been destroyed. As the visionary environmentalist Aldo Leopold put it, "Wilderness is a resource which can shrink but not grow." Who will ever again look upon the long-grass prairies? Who will ever see mile after mile of virgin hardwood? How many of our children will see the grizzly, the wolf, or millions of buffalo, or the passenger pigeons that used to cover the skies, or the ivory-billed woodpecker that Audubon painted so lovingly and so long ago?

The new story is based on sustainable development, particularly in the American West, where 35 percent of Colorado, 50 percent of Wyoming, and 92 percent of Nevada are public lands owned by the federal government. Even though more than 106 million acres in America have been declared official wilderness, the frontier is long gone. In 1950, 105,000 people lived in Phoenix; today it is a metropolis of nearly 1.5 million people with a metropolitan area population of 3.7 million. The same explosive growth has taken place in Tucson, Albuquerque, San Diego, Las Vegas, and Reno. There are more city dwellers in the West today as a percentage of the total regional population than in any other part of the country. This arid land must be managed to protect what waters it still has, or that way of life will be destroyed by the developers who are converging on it from all directions.

The sustainability movement holds that one generation must be the trustee for the next. It attempts to promote both conservation and job creation by increasing the productivity of the land. It begins by determining the natural and cultural legacy to be sustained and then studies ways in which a stream, say, can be used in mining or power production and still be a blue-ribbon trout stream, or how a forest can provide lumber and still offer habitat. At the core of the sustainability movement is the commonsense observation that the rights of a property owner must be balanced against the needs of society.*

As Charles F. Wilkinson writes in *Crossing the Next Meridian*, a remarkable book about the land stretching from Colorado to California and from Montana to New Mexico, "Were not [John Wesley] Powell and [Wallace] Stegner right, after all, about their central point—that the aridity and terrain dictate a finiteness beyond the 100th meridian? Is not the finite in view?"

The only thing that will guarantee the West a brighter future is the goodwill of all stakeholders and the long-term time horizon of the sustainability movement. Many western governors and mayors of both parties now understand the stakes and are moving in creative ways to reduce the strain on their resources, and many private citizens are seeking voluntarily to restore habitat and ecosystems. Imagine what could happen if Washington was a partner in their efforts and not an opponent.

The old economic and political way of doing business cannot improve current circumstances. The get-in-and-get-out mentality of the miner must give way to a different time scale. Geologists talk of "deep time." When you descend into the Grand Canyon, you are walking past hundreds of millions of years, recorded in the layers of earth as if some ancient force wanted us to know its story and to remind us that, against such a backdrop, the evening news, the mus-

---

*See my book *Time Present, Time Past* (Knopf, 1996).

ings of pundits, even our own individual lives are but a nanosecond. All of human history is represented on the canyon wall in just one narrow slice of rock. In this context, oil is another reminder of what has gone before, been trapped in the geology, and waits there for us to use up. It's not inexhaustible.

What we often forget is that there is a relationship between oil and water. Our continued dependence on the combustion of fossil fuels changes the climate in ways that will alter precipitation patterns and could hasten water shortages in some places and rising sea levels in others. Each system of exploitation and dependence, though huge and complex, is also fragile, whether it's depleting an aquifer in the American West that has built up over thousands of years or destroying the Arctic tundra, which, once damaged by oil development, could be lost forever.

$\bullet \quad \bullet \quad \bullet$

The following specific policy changes can reduce the power of oil dependence over our lives and protect the natural world:

1. Since transportation accounts for 67 percent of the oil we consume and surface vehicles alone account for 56 percent, by increasing mileage standards for vehicles to 40 miles per gallon we can significantly reduce our oil consumption. We now have a fleet average of 25.2 miles per gallon. After the Carter administration began to apply CAFE (Corporate Average Fuel Economy) standards in 1979, the fleet average rose from 20.1 miles per gallon to 26.6 miles per gallon within three years—but then the SUV entered the picture, and Congress placed it in the less fuel efficient light-truck category. If our automobile fleet average—including SUVs—equalled that in Europe (43 miles per gallon), we would reduce our oil consumption by more than 25 percent. That act alone— which could be accomplished by a single piece of legislation— would result in our having no need to import oil from OPEC. Let me repeat: "no need to import oil from OPEC."

2. A gasoline tax of $1 a gallon, or the equivalent carbon tax, whose revenues were redistributed to people of low and mod-

erate income (as advised in Chapter 4) directly, through lower employment taxes, would send a clear signal to Detroit that demand for fuel-efficient cars would remain high. With a rebatable tax phased in, people could plan what changes they would make in their lives to survive in a world of permanently high oil prices. Within four years, the auto industry could substantially raise the fleet average, and middle-class America would end up spending the same amount of money on gas as they had before the tax and would also receive a tax cut, represented by the lower employment taxes (Social Security, Medicare, or unemployment insurance).

3. Establish a fee-rebate system in which the buyers of the least fuel-efficient cars within each size class pay fees that go as rebates to those who buy the most fuel-efficient cars within that class.* Such a system would be a major incentive to buy the most fuel-efficient cars. R. James Woolsey, the former director of the CIA and a big advocate of reducing our dependence on foreign oil, said in testimony before the Senate Energy and Natural Resources Committee that a hybrid vehicle such as a Prius can get 50 miles per gallon, and if it was made of lightweight carbon composites used in the manufacture of aircraft, it could get 100 miles per gallon. He goes on to say that if it was a plug-in flexible-fuel vehicle, it could get an incredible 1,000 miles per gallon. It's an industry ready to be born.

4. Level the playing field among competing energy sources. Without subsidies, oil would cost between 15 and 20 percent more than it does now. Indeed, Dan Kammen of the University of California at Berkeley says that if we add the costs of environmental damage and the oil wars, the true cost of oil

---

*Amory B. Lovins, the CEO of Rocky Mountain Institute, a nonprofit organization fostering the efficient and sustainable use of natural resources, suggests in *Winning the Oil Endgame* that the federal government establish an annual fuel-economy benchmark (e.g., 23 miles per gallon for the mid-size SUV class, or a consumption of 0.043 gallons per mile) above which the fee would be charged and below which the rebate would be given. For example, if you are charged a $1,000 fee per 0.01 gallons per mile over a benchmark of 23 miles per gallon for a midsize SUV, then a Nissan Pathfinder that gets 18 miles per gallon — that is, consumes 0.056 gallons per mile — is 0.013 over the benchmark, and therefore its owner pays a $1,300 fee. The proceeds of the fee would then go to purchasers of more fuel-efficient vehicles.

is nearly 50 percent more than the market price. If we subsidized solar and wind power or biomass or fuel cells to the same extent that we do oil, they would become more competitive and could replace at least a small part of our oil consumption. We should either reduce subsidies for oil or increase them for other sources of energy. My choice would be to cut existing subsidies rather than create new ones.

5. Continue to provide incentives for conservation. A provision in the Synthetic Fuels Corporation Act of 1980 accepted for the first time the idea that in economic terms a barrel of oil saved is the same as a barrel of oil produced. Conservation gained a new rationale, and when oil prices rose, the market responded: Many companies and individuals instituted radical conservation measures.* But given the potential for energy efficiency in residential and commercial building design and structure, the potential for fuel conservation is just beginning. The savings will take longer to realize, because buildings last longer than cars and are not nearly as oil-dependent, but they do account, according to the U.S. Department of Energy, for 40 percent of total energy consumption. If you reduce demand for electricity, then that much more will be available for electric cars. If people could plug in their electric cars every night because of increased electricity capacity, our consumption of oil, and therefore its price, would drop, and we'd be taking one big step toward making oil-exporting states less in charge of global peace.

6. Make a commitment to safer, cheaper nuclear power and to the long-term disposal of nuclear wastes. For this to be a global solution, nuclear nonproliferation efforts would have to be stepped up. Leaders would have to see that safe nuclear energy represents a key element in the fight to end our oil addiction and that a comprehensive nonproliferation agreement, including enforcement, is critical to realizing the potential of nuclear energy.

---

*As a result, according to the Energy Information Administration, a barrel of oil today already does two times as much work as in 1975.

7. Establish a tougher mandatory standard to cap emissions of greenhouse gases than exists in the Kyoto Protocol, set up a trading system for its implementation, and then implement it on a national basis. By acting first and negotiating second, we'd lead the rest of the world in the commitment to reduce global warming.

8. Build policies of sustainability into all contracts for government subsidies to the oil, timber, mining, grazing, and water interests. We should insist on conservation and on reclaiming the land harmed by overuse.

9. Appoint government officials who will enforce existing environmental laws and see that our public lands continue to be protected for all of us.

10. Finally, show other countries that we are serious about decreasing our own consumption and ready to transfer technology to developing countries so they can avert the dirty phase of industrialization.

Once again, the choice is ours.

Chapter 6.

PENSIONS

The story we are told on pensions says that individuals, not a company or the federal government, should be in charge of their own financial destiny. When companies began to supplant defined-benefit pension plans with defined-contribution plans, allowing employees to make their own investment decisions, it was a step in the right direction. The story says that Social Security is broken. The younger people are, the less they'll get from it. In the 1980s, retirees got four times what they put into the Social Security trust fund. People who retired in 2000 can expect to get only 1.2 to 1.4 times the contributed amount. Many boomers who retire after 2010 will actually lose money.

For anyone under forty, Social Security is a hollow promise. Given the current benefit and tax levels and the increasing number of Social Security recipients, there won't be enough money to pay Social Security pensions at some point. The system isn't stable for the long term. Private investment accounts are the only way to secure young people's retirement. We all know that in the long term the stock market goes up. Just look at all the executives and investors who have made millions in the market. That can happen to the average guy, too. Giving the money to the individual to invest as he or she sees fit is important not only for ensuring a more robust Social Security system but for empowering the individual. It is the core of the "ownership society."

What is wrong with this story?

In America, retirement has become a lifelong goal, the cultural equivalent of paradise in many people's minds. You work hard for years so that you can retire near your grandchildren or move to Florida or Arizona and enjoy yourself. Work gave you the means to take care of your family, and retirement gives you the free time to do what you always wanted to do but couldn't because of the daily demands of work. When you don't like what you do every day, or when the stress becomes too great, or when you like what you do but you're just tired, you dream of retirement.

But to have a comfortable retirement you need income, and retirement income can come from only three sources: your own savings, Social Security, or your company pension. Today none of them is secure.

The unfortunate fact is that most Americans now save very little over a lifetime. Fully 51 percent of Americans own no stocks of any kind. They will depend totally on pensions, and 35 percent of all Americans have no pension other than Social Security. For most of the other 65 percent, private pensions are the key to comfortable retirement.

But when it comes to funding private pensions, not enough money has been put away—either by the companies or by the employees themselves. Once people calculate what they need for a secure retirement and compare that with what they have in a pension account, they often find that they come up short, and then it is often too late to realize their financial goals through prudent investing. That's when the stock market gambles start.

There are two kinds of private pensions in America: the defined-benefit pension and the defined-contribution pension. Both are based on the premise that the stock market always goes up in the long run. Both are in trouble.

Defined-Benefit Plans

In a defined-benefit plan, a company agrees to pay an employee a pension that is usually based on the person's ending salary and the number of years of employment with the company. It is a kind of annuity, usually paid monthly for life. The company regularly sets aside money in a fund and has it professionally managed, so that it will grow sufficiently to pay the retirees the promised (and legally binding) amount. In the 1980s, 83 percent of all workers who had a private pension had a defined-benefit plan. In 2003, that proportion was 38 percent.

The defined-benefit plan came about in the early 1940s. It promised pensions that would support a middle-class—not just subsistence—lifestyle. The immediate postwar period was the high point of organized labor; over a third of all workers belonged to a union, and unions demanded generous pensions. Attempts to raise wages had been blocked by federal wage and price controls. When management said the company couldn't afford to offer pensions, labor leaders such as Walter Reuther of the United Auto Workers assured the company that the pensions wouldn't put it at a competitive disadvantage because the union would demand the same pensions of all auto companies. It was called the pattern plan. Management went along with generous pensions because, unlike wages, the costs were borne in part by the federal government, in the form of an immediate deduction from company taxes for whatever the company put away for worker pensions, and no tax was assessed on the increase over the years in the pension fund's value.

In such a world, pensions for autoworkers, steelworkers, and other industrial union workers became very generous. Then came the foreign competitors, who had no such pension obligations. They paid lower wages, and their products were just as good as those of American manufacture. When labor lost its monopoly, the pensions became a gigantic and unsustainable cost to the American companies struggling to survive in a global market. As a result, many employees who thought their golden years would be secure—and who had agreed to lower wages over the years because they had been promised generous pensions—found the companies' promises empty. There wasn't enough money in the funds to pay their pensions.

That's when millions of American workers realized that jobs aren't forever and that the absence of economic security can be a daily reality; indeed, the pace of change was disorienting. If you worked for an airline or steel company, an auto company or one of its parts suppliers, a manufacturer of telecommunications equipment or consumer electronics, you lived through a time when the bottom fell out from under your world.

Most men who worked in the steel plants of Gary and South Chicago thought they had lifetime financial security. So did autoworkers, and so did men and women who worked for Western Electric. They had good unions that got them good wages, health care, and a pension. Today the jobs are gone, the health care is often lost, and the pensions are in danger, too. It didn't happen suddenly, like a bomb exploding; it was a gradual erosion—so gradual that most people couldn't see it happening until it was too late for them to do anything about it.

Suppose you're a man who worked a lifetime with your hands. It takes a toll on you. You get older sooner standing next to a blast furnace or on the assembly line. There is no time to exercise, and your diet is probably full of all the wrong things. Still, you go on. You go to work each day because you're proud of what you do. You like the camaraderie. You sleep well at night, knowing that you've taken care of your family. You send your kids to college, even though you never finished high school. You take care of your wife and occasionally help some in-laws with a loan that never seems to get repaid. You go to church each Sunday, and you put a little in the collection plate, because your job enables you to give thanks to God in this tangible way.

You've been retired now for ten years. You're near seventy-five and beginning to get frail. You get Social Security and Medicare, and you have a good company pension. Then one day you wake up to read in the paper that your parent company has gone bankrupt. It couldn't compete with the Japanese, or the Brazilians, or the Russians, or the Chinese. Two thousand people have been laid off, which you think is a damn shame. Eight paragraphs further into the story, it says that the company can't pay its pensions, and the government will have to take them over. The next paragraph says that the Pension Benefit Guaranty Corporation will probably pay only 30 percent of the agreed pension. It doesn't have enough resources to pay 100 percent of what you were promised. You look in the mirror and realize that your life has just collapsed. You're too old to go back to work, even if the jobs had not disappeared. Your savings are meager. So is what you're getting from Social Security. You look at your wife, and you both cry.

That scenario is occurring all over America these days. In 2005, I was on a domestic flight when one of the flight attendants asked if she could speak with me. She thought I was still a U.S. senator, and she wanted me to be aware of the predicament she and her colleagues faced. It turned out that she had worked for the airline for thirty-two years, had given up some of her wages in the last union negotiation, and now her health care insurance required an exorbitant premium and a high copay. The previous fall, the airline had sent her a letter thanking her for her years of service and then dropped the bombshell: If she did not retire by January 1, she would lose her pension. Because she needed the wages and hadn't yet become eligible for Medicare, she had had to continue working past the deadline. Thirty-two years had just gone down the drain.

After the passage in 1974 of ERISA, the Employee Retirement Income Security Act, which established legal responsibilities for companies to make good on their pension obligations, it was inconceivable that employers would renege on their pension promises. To do so would make them pariahs even in the competitive world of big business. A company made a commitment to its workforce. Companies such as IBM made an explicit connection between employee loyalty and retirement security.

When the late 1990s produced a speculative frenzy in stock prices, companies kept raising their assumptions about estimated returns on their pension fund investments and putting away less and less for their employees. The market was doing it for them. Then the bubble burst, and companies were faced with the consequences. Today many of them have set aside too little money to pay negotiated and promised benefits. The older their workforce, the more serious the problem. These companies have a Hobbesian choice. Either they can set aside more money for pensions and report lower earnings, undoubtedly sending their stock prices lower, or they can continue the fiction of great stock market returns, hoping that investors won't read the fine print in their quarterly earnings reports and short their stock. Some companies, such as General Motors, find their very existence at stake.

When the performance of financial markets is inadequate over a long period of time, neither setting aside more money nor hoping the investing public won't notice is as likely an alternative as simply turning the whole pension liability over to the federal government's Pension Benefit Guaranty Corporation. The PBGC estimates that total underfunding in single- and multi-employer pension funds may be as high as $600 billion. As more and more companies turn over their pension liabilities, the resources of the PBGC have become insufficient, and it has insisted that the employees settle for only a fraction of their expected pensions. If many companies default to the PBGC simultaneously, it will be bankrupt, and their employees, along with the 44 million Americans whose pensions the PBGC currently insures (many of whom have worked for forty years in expectation of a legally contracted pension), will have no guarantee that their pension or any part of it will be there for them. Pension resources cannot be built up overnight, and when they turn bad, they cannot be salvaged overnight.

Only the government can back up the private system. To marshal the political support to fix a pension system preemptively becomes a serious political challenge. Even the pension bill that Congress enacted in the summer of 2006 left large areas of pension policy unaddressed. Our slow-motion pension meltdown reminds me of the savings and loan meltdown in the 1980s, when the government ignored the problem until it had become a full-blown disaster.

When it comes to the public pensions of state and local governments, the problems are even bigger. Whereas international competition made transparent the overly generous defined-benefit pension promises of the private sector, the public sector has no such early-warning system. Today the public unions have negotiated pensions so generous that when taxpayers wake up to their ultimate cost, there is going to be an uproar. An airline employee who got twenty cents on the dollar from the PBGC for his bankrupted pension will not be happy when he learns he's paying taxes for a public employee's pension so generous it can never be fully paid without raising his taxes even more.

Defined-Contribution Plans

For all these reasons, the story we're told today says, defined-contribution plans, the most prevalent of which is the 401(k), are better than defined-benefit plans. They remove money from "paternalistic" company control and give it to the employee, leaving the choice of investments up to the "self-reliant individual."

As retirement vehicles, defined-contribution plans have numerous problems. First, as Alicia Munnell and Annika Sundén of the Center for Retirement Research at Boston College emphasize in a March 2006 research brief, they are far from being mandatory savings plans. There are too many outs. Employees don't have to participate. Rulings by the IRS in 1998 and 2000 were supposed to help here. They permit employers to offer pension plans that automatically deduct a part of each employee's salary and invest it in a pension fund; any employees who don't want to participate have to opt out, whereas previously employees had to ask to have savings deducted from their salaries. By 2005, only 16.9 percent of all 401(k) plans had put in automatic deductions, and the year before, fully 21 percent of those eligible workers under the plans elected to have no 401(k) deductions. Only 11 percent contributed the maximum, which is usually 6 percent of salary with a 3 percent employer match. Among people earning between $40,000 and $60,000 annually, the average contribution was less than 1 percent of salary.

The second problem with defined-contribution plans is that most people don't diversify their investments. In 2004, 31.6 percent of all defined-contribution participants held no stocks. Many invested almost solely in money-market funds, which are safe but provide low yields and therefore cannot compound to reach the person's desired retirement nest egg. Twenty-one percent of defined-contribution-plan participants put 80 percent of their funds in equities, with many concentrating too much in their own company stock. They will suffer a double loss if the company falls on hard times. They might lose their jobs and in addition see the value of their pension plan drop precipitously. If you don't believe that can happen, just ask the former employees of Enron and WorldCom.

And a third problem is the practice of cashing out when you change your job. In 2004, 45 percent of those who changed jobs cashed out their 401(k) plans instead of rolling them over into an IRA (individual retirement account). Thus the value of compounding is lost.

Once the company has contributed to the employee's defined-contribution plan, it no longer has legal responsibility for the pension. With a defined-contribution plan, all the risk rests squarely on the shoulders of the employees. It's up to them to decide how to invest the money, which is quite different from defined-benefit plans, in which the workers make no financial decisions before retirement—they simply retire and begin collecting their promised pensions. But most people don't have the time or savvy to manage their own money. Companies may offer their employees advice on money managers. Occasionally, a union will send its membership a pamphlet outlining the various choices and asking members how they want their money managed. Do they want it invested in foreign or domestic stocks; in bonds or stocks; in high-growth, high-risk stocks; or in value stocks that often pay dividends? If they choose the right options, they will have a good retirement; if they make poor choices, they will have a miserable retirement. There is no certainty. Given that defined-contribution plans have mushroomed over the last twenty-five years—in 1980 only 40 percent of all workers had defined-contribution plans and now it's 90 percent—the collective risk for people with no investment experience is considerable.

One might also argue that these plans are simply tax shelters for the well-off. The typical plan is not an annuity paying a guaranteed amount based on the individual's last salary; instead it is a draw-down system, in which the individual takes lump-sum distributions spread over a period of years. The rest of the money stays in the account, compounding annually, tax-free. The pension experts John Langbein and Bruce Wolk point out in their textbook *Pension and Employee Benefit Law* that if one spouse dies, the surviving spouse can transfer the funds in the 401(k) into an IRA, where they can grow, tax-free, until drawn out during the surviving spouse's retirement. If he or she then converts the IRA into a joint account with the kids, the draw-down can be spread over their lives, too, so that it goes on for decades—long after the original earner is dead. In this respect, defined-contribution plans do hardly anything for the bottom half of the population, who have little need of such tax shelters. In a February 2006 lecture at the University of Texas in Austin, Langbein observed that these

> minimum distribution rules allow a million-dollar defined-contribution account to be paid out across a forty-four-year period, from the participants' first withdrawal at age seventy until the last dollar is paid out to the children. During [that] period, assuming an eight-percent growth rate on investments, the $1 million generates a total of more than $11 million in distributions.

Quite a wealth-transfer device! "This is the dirty little secret of the defined-contribution-plan revolution," Langbein said. "Defined-contribution pension plans have ever less to do with pensions and are ever more becoming general-purpose tax shelters for the affluent."

With defined-contribution plans, many people don't get serious about saving until later in life, by which time it is often too late to amass adequate savings for a decent retirement.* The Federal Reserve's 2004 Survey of Consumer Finances states that if you're a worker between the ages of forty-five and fifty-four, you will need to have put away at least $169,000 toward your retirement but that the

---

*Munnell and Sundén show that someone who retires at a salary of $58,000 and has made the 6 percent maximum contribution to his or her pension account, with a company match of 3 percent over four or five decades, will have $380,000 at retirement, a comfortable sum. But not many employees are that prudent.

average person in this age category has accumulated only $49,000. Likewise, if you're between fifty-five and sixty-four, you ought to have $314,000 set aside, but in fact the average person in that age-group has set aside only $60,000. If the latter group bought an annuity with that money, it would pay them only $400 a month for the rest of their lives—not exactly an amount that will get them to Florida.

The final problem is that defined-contribution plans are not covered by the Pension Benefit Guaranty Corporation. Millions of people direct the investment of their defined-contribution plans as if the company and/or the federal government stood behind it. They don't. The saddest fact is that most people are totally unaware of the problems attendant on our private pension system. Most assume that their pensions are fine. No one has explicitly told them that the rules have changed, that they're on their own.

Going from defined-benefit to defined-contribution plans means that we give up the certainty of a lifelong pension for the chance to speculate in the financial markets. Corporations win, because they shed responsibility for their employees' pensions. Government wins, because it no longer has to insure pensions under the PBGC. Individuals, by contrast, can lose big. They no longer have certainty, and they might run out of money before they die. Moreover, neither defined-benefit nor defined-contribution plans offer any protection against inflation, and neither makes any attempt to educate the recipient.

The Stock Market

All private pensions are premised on the story line that has pervaded our culture about people who have gotten rich in the market. Chief executive officers and hedge-fund managers grace the covers of national magazines because they have made hundreds of millions from stock appreciation. Before the 2000 tech-stock crash, college professors drew comfort from the size of their defined-contribution pension funds. Lunchroom conversations among midlevel employees were peppered with stock tips, and even doormen and cabdrivers shared the mania. Now that the market is up again, so is the mania. Hundreds of books and investment letters purport to have the secret of gigantic returns. Infomercials tempt us with surefire ways to make a million in technology, energy, consumer goods, or whatever stock is the flavor of the month. The 1930s, along with the more recent financial downturns, are ancient history. It is this certainty that the stock market is a sure thing over the long run that lends people a false sense of security about their retirement.

I remember the 1987 stock market crash. I heard the news just as I had finished touring cranberry bogs in New Jersey's Pinelands. I sat in the car and listened to the commentator predicting that it was 1929 all over again. As it turned out, the Federal Reserve pumped massive amounts of liquidity into the system and the worst was avoided. Several weeks later, a constituent who had been paying attention to recent events wrote me a letter. "Dear Senator Bradley," it said. "I have a way to guarantee low unemployment, low interest rates, high productivity, low inflation, and high economic growth." Interested, I read on. "Encourage people to invest in the stock market," my correspondent advised, "and if it goes down, have the government bail them out."

As George Bush continues to suggest that people manage a part of their own Social Security money, it's worth examining the claim that a permanently rising stock market will come to the rescue of the Social Security system.

Social Security is a government promise—one that we all make on behalf of one another—not an investment strategy. It is all about security, not risk. It says that however your life has gone—whether you've been a construction worker who has only been able to make ends meet or a stockbroker who lost his nest egg through bad stock picks or a homemaker who becomes a widow—all of us together will ensure that you have a subsistence income in your retirement. Social Security has kept many of the elderly out of poverty and remains the sole source of income for millions. About 26 million Social Security recipients get at least half their income from it. If the elderly had to manage their own Social Security dollars and the market crashed, one thing would be certain: They would expect to be made whole, just as my constituent argued. They would petition Congress, and Congress would respond, making up a part of their losses either by raising taxes (the worst thing to do in an economic downturn) or by cutting Social Security benefits so that less government money would go further. The first alternative would be seen by employees as a betrayal of hardworking Americans, and the second would be seen by the elderly as a betrayal of the government's promise to them of a minimal retirement.

What proponents of Social Security privatization ignore is its uneven impact on seniors depending on when they retire. These proponents point out that the long-term real rate of return on corporate stocks is between 7.0 and 7.5 percent annually. They argue that if "an average income couple"—a couple starting with income of as much as $20,000 apiece and ending with a $40,000 income for the husband and a $30,000 income for the wife—could have diverted their Social Security payroll taxes into an equity account over a forty-two-year period, they would have accumulated $829,800 at retirement, which would be double what Social Security would pay out and would allow them to buy an annuity that would pay them $102,000 a year.

Sounds good, if we assume 7 percent growth and all Social Security payments going into equities. But how do we manage the transition? Who pays all those people who've been promised a retirement income, if workers suddenly stop transferring their Social Security payroll taxes to the Social Security trust fund and instead invest those amounts for themselves? In 2001, when we had a projected ten-year surplus of $5.6 trillion, we could have earmarked that surplus for the Social Security trust fund to cover the projected payments to people over a certain age and then allowed the rest of the people to open private accounts. There was never a better time to deal with the transition to private accounts, and Paul O'Neill, Bush II's first secretary of the treasury and a dedicated and creative public policy thinker, suggested a similar idea to the president. In counselling against a 2002 tax cut, he pointed out that if government used the surplus to give every child $23,000 on the date of his or her birth, at a cost of $92 billion per year, and each account got a

6 percent compounded annual return, by retirement those people would have a million dollars each. He argued that that was how the surplus should be used, and not for tax cuts. The president scoffed. Aware of the political payoff in tax cuts and the hot-button political sensitivity of Social Security, Bush looked at his political adviser Karl Rove and said, "We *are* in politics, aren't we, Karl?"

Beyond the issue of a feasible transition to private accounts, the volatility in the market poses a problem. While it's true that the market goes up over the long term, it is also true that for long periods the market can be flat or in decline. A look at Standard & Poor's 500 Index tells you that it wasn't until 1953 that the market got back to its 1928 level. The 1968 peak was not seen again until 1972, and it wasn't until 1980 that the index got back to the 1972 level. Investors counting on 7-percent-a-year income growth from 1967 on got much less; those were the years of low stock market advance. If you then retired in 1979, your retirement was much more pinched than that of someone who retired in 1997 and got the benefit of the long bull market.

If people aren't putting away enough in personal savings, and private pensions have exaggerated stock performance over the long term, and Social Security is in trouble, what is the new story about pensions in America?

THE NEW STORY

The new story asks questions about what it means to be an American. Do we throw all the responsibility for even a minimal retirement back on the individual, no matter his or her education level? What happens when a lot of individuals lose their money? What do we owe the elderly stranger simply because he or she is a human being? Our decisions about pensions will involve not only how much money people need in retirement but what kind of society we want ours to be.

A good society recognizes its elders for what they have given. It protects them from harm in old age, just as they protected their children. Ideally, all elderly people would have loving, financially stable family members to care for them in old age. Unfortunately, that's not how things always are. The way you judge a society is by how it treats the young and the old. Social Security makes me feel better about myself as an American. The fact that we've found a way to avoid elderly poverty should make us all feel proud. It is an expression of our ultimate sense of community. People should not have to gamble with that achievement for the prospect of doubling their money in the stock market. When retirement comes, seniors deserve certainty. In the new story, they wouldn't have to worry about the stock market's performance.

The new story says that the first thing we owe the elderly (who eventually are all of us) is caring, which is Social Security. The second thing is candor.

There is no free lunch. You can't have comfortable private pensions without setting aside more money in pension accounts over a lifetime, whether that money comes from the individual or the employer. The history of defined-benefit and defined-contribution plans underlines that fact. In the former case, companies undersaved; in the latter, individuals are collectively failing to put enough money away. Americans need to consume less and save more.

The truth must be told about the stock market. It is a lottery— wonderful but never a sure thing. Investing on their own, millions of individuals will make wrong guesses. Some people will be saving when the market is flat. Swarms of advisers will produce widely disparate results for the people doing the saving. Some will create a herd mentality that could lead people off a cliff. Others will promise returns they know are impossible to deliver. Human nature won't change, especially where money is involved.

What policy choices do we need to make in order to realize this new story in pensions?

In 1982, my fourth year in the Senate, we learned that the Social Security trust fund was about to go broke. A presidential commission was convened. I conducted sixteen Social Security forums across New Jersey with seniors. I had a professor from Rutgers, our state university, describe the problem, and then I put a series of solutions on the blackboard. Conventional wisdom predicted that no one in the room would support cutting benefits. But I discovered that these New Jersey seniors thought as Americans, not just as seniors. They were as concerned about burdening their kids with higher taxes as they were about having their benefits reduced. Because they trusted the information I gave them, and because they wanted to be fair, they agreed in those sessions to reduce benefits, raise taxes, and increase the retirement age. The commission suggested a similar path, and when Congress enacted its recommendations, the life of the trust fund was extended for decades. The same thing could happen today.

As I suggested in Chapter 4, four simple steps can be taken to keep Social Security solvent for the next seventy-five years: Raise the minimum eligibility age of sixty-seven years (set to be reached in 2027) by one month every two years until 2099, when it would be seventy years; make 2.0 percent of the 6.5 percent Social Security tax apply to all income, instead of taxing it just up to the current $94,200 level; bring new state and local government employees into the system over a five-year period; and change the way the cost-of-living increase is calculated, basing it on the chained consumer price index, which accounts for people shifting purchases to cheaper goods when prices go up. Another part of the solution would be to increase economic growth. With more Americans, on average, making higher and higher salaries, more money would come into the trust fund and the system's insolvency date would be extended even further.

The most politically tricky of these changes will be raising the minimum eligibility age to seventy, but real leadership on Social Security means bringing it up-to-date with the work world of today. In 1935, when the system was instituted, many Americans worked in manufacturing jobs, most of which were unhealthy and undoubtedly shortened the natural life span. Now many more Americans work in the service sector (which is arguably safer) than in the manufacturing sector. The average life expectancy in America in 1935 was 61 years (59.9 for men and 63.9 for women). Now the combined average is 78. No social-insurance system can pay current beneficiaries for twenty-plus years of retirement without raising taxes or cutting benefits. By raising the minimum age of eligibility to seventy, we recognize that life phases are not just work and retirement but include the period from sixty to seventy-five, when many people want to continue working (if perhaps with a reduced load) and not simply for economic reasons. Work enhances vitality and gives life meaning. Fewer and fewer people in their sixties and seventies feel "old." Upping the eligibility age recognizes that new state of affairs and will help to save Social Security. For those Americans in their sixties who have worked at jobs that damaged their health so much they can't work beyond sixty-seven, there should be a narrowly liberalized eligibility for disability until they reach seventy.

With regard to private pensions, it's important to remember that pension obligations are legal obligations, and government should insist that they are respected even if it means bankruptcy and transfer of control of a company's assets to the pension creditors. We need an infusion of cash to bolster the Pension Benefit Guaranty Corporation, which now has a $60 billion deficit and $450 billion in unfunded single-employer liabilities. Then we should force corporations to close any shortfalls in their pension funds and make larger contributions to the PBGC. In arriving at its pension obligation, the company should take into account the age of its workforce. The larger the employee group close to retirement, the more the company should contribute to the fund. Companies should stop lumpsum payouts if their pension assets fall below 70 percent of their obligations. Transition to the new system by delaying the date that problem companies (such as airlines) must comply should not become the first step on the path toward permanent exceptions. As noted, the pension bill that Congress passed in 2006 did not go far enough in protecting employer-based pensions, and Congress hasn't even begun to think about public-pension alternatives should companies find the reform proposals so onerous that they stop offering pensions. While the law beefed up the savers' credit for low-income Americans by $10 billion, it didn't cover the 50 million Americans who pay no taxes because their income is too low. At the same time, the bill gave $36 billion to upper-income Americans by raising the amount of money they can put away in their IRAs and 401(k) accounts tax-free.

But we need something beyond employer defined-benefit or

defined-contribution plans. Some have suggested a hybrid approach, in which the company guarantees a base amount in a defined-contribution plan, which is managed by professionals selected by the company and insured by the PBGC. While this approach is more flexible, it would be better to match pension liabilities, which are long-term, against assets that are long-term and secure, which means greater investment in fixed-income assets, such as long-term, inflation-proof government bonds. That's the only way to achieve a measure of retirement certainty. Taking bigger and bigger equity risks to pay off overly generous promises or overly optimistic expectations is a recipe for disaster.

We need a retirement system in which all Americans have the same incentives to save. The tax deduction for IRA or 401(k) plans is worth more for the wealthy. A dollar deducted for someone in the 35 percent bracket is worth thirty-five cents in saved taxes; for someone in the 15 percent bracket, its value is just fifteen cents. Such incentives don't increase savings, they shift them around. The wealthy save anyway and, acting rationally, transfer their assets to the tax-favored savings vehicle. To rectify this upper-income bias, we should eliminate the tax exclusion for IRAs and 401(k) plans while keeping the tax-free accumulation of earnings in those accounts. In place of the deduction, William G. Gale, Jonathan Gruber, and Peter R. Orszag, writing in a white paper prepared for the Hamilton Project of the Brookings Institution, propose a government match of "30 percent for all qualifying contributions up to either 10 percent of adjusted gross income or $20,000 annually for 401(k) accounts and $5,000 for IRAs." The cost of this system would be offset by the elimination of the tax exclusion. In other words, for every dollar you save in a 401(k) or IRA, the government will give you thirty cents. The government match would be placed directly into accounts administered by the federal government's Thrift Savings Plan, thereby eliminating the need for more bureaucracy. Or you might make the match into a refundable tax credit that would offset any tax owed by the amount of the credit dollar for dollar, or if there is no tax liability, money would simply be sent to you in the form of a check from the government. You could draw on a limited amount of those federal accounts for health and education purposes, just as you can on current 401(k) plans or IRAs. Such a system might increase overall savings by turning middle-income people who now aren't tempted by a tax deduction worth only fifteen cents into new savers.

A further step to assure retirement security would be to follow up on Paul O'Neill's suggestion to President Bush in 2002: The U.S. government should provide every child born in America a $5,000 American Birthright grant. It would be put in an account that compounds tax-free and is administered by the Thrift Savings Plan of the federal government. As with state pension funds, the money would be invested in financial instruments such as indexed equity and bond funds. If the funds generated 5 percent annual growth for seventy years, the account would provide a nest egg of about $152,000 over and above Social Security. If the fund earned 6 percent, the amount would be $295,000. In that sense, it would be a second tier of federal retirement security.

The U.S. economy has been good at inventing credit products, such as home equity loans, consumer loans, and credit cards, but less innovative in providing long-term financial products for retirement security. The result is that we are stuck with either defined-benefit or defined-contribution approaches. There should be alternatives. Companies should establish retirement systems whose stability doesn't depend on making the right guesses about the stock market. Rather, all an individual should have to decide is the size of his or her desired retirement income and his or her minimum retirement income. No longer will the key to retirement be trying to figure out whether investing in distressed Argentinian real estate or biotech will beat the market. Fixed-income investments should cover the minimum-need income relatively risk-free, and a basket of riskier assets could be added to realize the desired level.

Individuals should be able to refer to their own Internet accounts to see how much they need to save each year, given different levels of returns, to produce each of those incomes. That way they can make the savings versus consumption trade-off more easily. If they are not saving enough, they may choose either to work longer or to reduce their desired retirement income. This exercise would remind people that there is no such thing as a free lunch. Before retirement, the savings would be converted into an inflation-protected annuity, which is a guaranteed real amount of money each year for life. To augment savings and pension dollars, people could also take advantage of the value of their houses with reverse mortgages or sell their life insurance policies as additional sources for annuity dollars. We need the best of the defined-benefit plans, which is annuitization, and the best of the defined-contribution plans, which is the portability of pensions from job to job.

Here are some specific policy changes:

1. Bring new state and local employees into the system, apply a part of the Social Security tax to all income, use the chained consumer price index as the basis for calculating the cost-of-living increase, raise the minimum eligibility age for Social Security, and narrowly liberalize disability eligibility for workers from sixty-seven to seventy who have had health-damaging jobs.
2. Provide the Pension Benefit Guaranty Corporation with an infusion of capital.
3. Require corporations to close shortfalls in their pension plans.
4. Stop lump-sum payments to pensioners of all the assets in their defined-contribution account if a company's pension fund assets fall below 70 percent of its obligations.
5. Replace the federal tax exclusion for contributions to 401(k) plans and IRAs with a direct federal matching program worth the same for all Americans, based on how much they save up to a certain level.
6. Establish a $5,000 American Birthright account that compounds tax-free for every child born in America.
7. Develop new private pension approaches that are neither defined-benefit nor defined-contribution but that allow people to determine easily the amount they need to save annually to reach their desired retirement income. Invest most of the contributions in fixed-income assets that

will be exchanged at retirement for inflation-proof annuities.

We can continue down the current path on pensions and some-day find our golden years threatened, or we can face some hard truths and make effective changes now to secure our future.

The choice is ours.

Chapter 7.

HEALTH CARE

The story we are told about health care begins with the view that consumers should be in charge of their own health. It says that, under the current system, the uninsured can get adequate treatment in emergency rooms. It says that most young Americans don't want to pay for medical insurance, even at a bargain price, and only a minuscule number of Americans want socialized medicine. If we simply give individuals the option of opening private health savings accounts—that is, tax-favored accounts for health care expenses—and cut costs for companies by having them provide less expensive high-deductible insurance policies for their employees, we would reduce the overutilization of the health care system while encouraging people to save. Individuals would pay for much more of their own medical insurance and be responsible for their own health. If we treated them as informed consumers, they would respond as they already do in countless other areas.

The assumption underlying private health savings accounts is that Americans consume too much health care. The story goes that if we raise the price of health care to consumers by making them pay more out of their own pockets for medical care, they will use less of it—just as they do when the cost of any product rises. But, of course, health care is not like any other consumer item. You can go without new shoes, a new car, a new refrigerator. But when you break your arm, you can't wait until prices go down to have it put in a cast. Or, as D. Ferrel Atkins of Charleston, Illinois, recently put it in a letter to *The New York Times*, if someone "were having symptoms of a heart attack, do we really believe that he would call emergency rooms for competitive prices before calling the ambulance? Nonsense!"

Adding high-deductible insurance policies and health savings accounts to our current health care system is a dubious solution to an impending crisis. Millions of Americans—those who are uninsured, unemployed, or homeless—are not in the system at all. This story offers no help to them.

Moreover, the story ignores the reality that many families can't even make ends meet now. The story asks a two-earner family of four making the median income (in this case, $46,326) to save for health expenses formerly paid by employers, just as it asks the same parents to save for their retirement and for their children's education. It won't happen. The people who can't afford to put a substantial amount away in health savings accounts simply won't see a doctor. As the cost mounts, these middle-class workers—and their children—will receive less health care. If they go without treatment, or self-medicate, they'll probably end up even sicker and in the long run cost the system—which means the rest of us—more.

Further, reducing what employers pay for health insurance and creating a tax-favored account for discretionary health spending will leave people more vulnerable to health emergencies. Instead of having their employers pay for emergency treatment when it's needed, individuals might well spend the money in their health savings accounts on health spas or other health-related peripherals and thus have no money to pay for essential care. At the other end of the range of possibilities are those individuals who remain healthy. Since 50 percent of the population accounts for only 2 percent of the nation's health costs, many of those individuals would undoubtedly end up with excess money in their accounts, which could then be rolled over into IRAs, giving the healthy well-to-do yet another way to avoid taxes.

A proponent of health savings accounts came to visit me in the Senate in the late 1980s. After he made his case, I told him my view—that such accounts were just another tax loophole and that most people with no private health insurance wouldn't be able to put enough money in such accounts to pay for even one episode of hospitalization. The people who most likely would opt for them would be those with means and good health.

When I learned, from a September 2005 report by the Kaiser Foundation, that 20 percent of all employers were offering their employees health savings accounts as an option, it was clear to me that our health care system is headed in the same direction as the pension system took when defined-contribution plans succeeded defined-benefit plans. In both cases, the individual gets less certainty and security. Rather than a way to ensure necessary benefits, the health-savings-account option is another way for employers to shed responsibility for a major part of their workers' fundamental well-being. As of now, some 3 million people have these employer-based health savings accounts. It's hard to see how such accounts are the answer for 300 million of us. They are an insignificant response to a very big problem.

Another disadvantage of health savings accounts is that, in an effort to save money, consumers who aren't sick will jettison their regular checkups, even though regular checkups are the most likely way to detect a serious illness. By getting early treatment, people save the system the cost of emergency treatment later on.

The story assumes that as individuals bear a greater proportion of their health costs, they will eliminate unnecessary doctor visits (such as those regular checkups), thus saving the system the cost of the billing. But 80 percent of America's health care costs are run up by 20 percent of its population—people who need serious procedures such as coronary bypass operations, cancer surgery, or chemotherapy or who suffer from chronic diseases, such as hypertension or diabetes. Research for the Congressional Budget Office shows that the 20 percent usually suffer from three chronic diseases at once, see an average of twelve doctors a year, are hospitalized at least once a year, and fill an average of fifty prescriptions annually. The story we're told does nothing to manage these patients better. A large part of health care costs comes in the last six months of life; cutting back on doctor visits will do little to reduce them.

The story also assumes a high degree of what might be called health literacy on the part of individuals. While improving health literacy is a good thing, it is reckless to create a system in which people are left on their own to decide whether or not to get treatment or what form of treatment to get. Many of them do not have enough knowledge to make informed judgments about their health. The National Academy of Sciences' Institute of Medicine recently estimated that at least 90 million Americans have trouble understanding some degree of health care information. To cast these individuals, many of whom have no access to the Internet, out into the world with only health savings accounts that have little money in them, and an exhortation to investigate the various health plans, doctors, hospitals, and treatment options on the Internet, seems harsh.

But the major flaw in the story we are told about health care is the failure to acknowledge that systemic problems require systemic, not piecemeal, remedies. For example, elimination of the same mistakes made over and over in hospitals by medical personnel requires a systematic way of collecting the information, documenting what went wrong, and then correcting it. Health savings accounts alone won't get rid of those errors. Another problem calling for a systemic solution concerns the need to treat a patient over the full treatment cycle. Today hospitals charge specific amounts for treating particular ailments. Emphasis should be on quality and outcomes throughout the system and across various specialties, not simply on performing a particular procedure or ordering a particular test. What is needed is coordination of care from the acute stage to long-term management of the disease. A third such problem relates to keeping patients informed about hospital and doctor performance. We need systemwide standards and information systems. Since hospitals are not required to report results, patients are forced to make life-and-death decisions about doctors and hospitals with little knowledge about their track records on delivering quality care. Because they don't have the information to decide where they can get the best care, they decide only whether or not they can afford any care at all. The changes that will solve our health care crisis must be systemic.

The Uninsured

American technology has given us the best health care in the world, but we don't have the best health care *system*. We spend nearly twice as much per capita on health care as Germany and Canada do. Health costs went up 7.4 percent in 2005, and health care expenditures are expected to reach 20 percent of GDP between 2015 and 2020. Yet we rank seventeenth in infant mortality among all the countries of the world, fortieth in life expectancy, and near the top in obesity, which afflicts more than a third of American women and more than a fourth of American men.

The biggest indictment of the American health care system is that 46 million of our citizens still have no health insurance. For that many people to live without health insurance is a betrayal of the Founders' promise of life, liberty, and the pursuit of happiness. Forty-six million sounds abstract, but it is more than all the people living in the following states combined: Mississippi, Iowa, Missouri, Arkansas, Louisiana, Oklahoma, Kansas, Nebraska, South Dakota, North Dakota, Montana, Wyoming, Colorado, Utah, and Arizona. If none of the people living in those states had health insurance, would we turn our backs on them? I don't think so. For one thing, their senators and representatives wouldn't stand for it. But the uninsured are not in one place. They don't have their own congressmen. They are spread out among us.

If we gave it a moment's thought, we would know who they are: the cabdrivers, the waiters and waitresses, the workers who clean our office buildings, the young people who give up health coverage because they can't imagine being sick and want to have the money to rent an apartment. They are the people who care for our elderly parents and oversee our children while we work. They are laid-off workers who can't get insurance between jobs because their child has diabetes. They are, by and large, hardworking people who can't afford to buy insurance themselves. Many of them work for small businesses that cannot afford to provide it.

I know people who stay in jobs they don't like simply because, if they left, they'd lose their health insurance. I've met elderly women who cut their pills in half to make them last longer because they would rather be insufficiently medicated than not have money for food. I have spoken with middle-aged men who describe all the symptoms of colon cancer but won't go to a doctor, because if it were cancer and they got treatment, they would be bankrupt. How do these stories make America strong? They don't.

I remember a young mother in New Hampshire whose husband was laid off from his job and lost his health insurance. One of their three kids got sick, and she took him to the doctor's office. As she was leaving, she stopped at the receptionist's desk, took out her wallet, and paid for the visit in cash. The young boy, who knew how tough economic times were for the family, looked at his mother and said, "I'm sorry, Mom." "Why?" she said. "I'm sorry I got sick," he replied. No child in America should have to apologize for getting sick just because the family can't afford health care.

The High Cost of Health Care

In America, to a greater degree than in any other country, health insurance is provided in the workplace as part of the employment contract. One hundred seventy-five million of us get our health coverage that way. During World War II, wages were frozen briefly, but companies still needed talented workers, so they started offering health insurance as a part of the compensation package. Between 1940 and 1950, workers covered by employers went from 7 percent of the workforce to nearly 20 percent. By 1980 it was 40 percent of all workers. The government subsidized employer-provided insurance in two ways: First, the cost was not counted as income for the worker and thus not taxed as income; second, the company could deduct the cost from its own income.

For many years, this system seemed like a good deal for everyone. But as health costs started to increase, as a result of the aging of the population and the rising cost of medical technology, company earnings were squeezed and health care policy became a boardroom issue. In 2005, whereas inflation was 3.4 percent, the increase in health costs was more than double that level. In some companies, the cost of employee health care has become prohibitive. General Motors estimates that its health care costs are responsible for $1,400 of the selling price of each new car it produces. Many small businesses are dropping coverage, and many large companies are raising the portion that must be paid by the employee—so much so that many employees are opting to go without insurance.* At Wal-Mart, the nation's largest employer, an internal memo leaked in 2005 proposed reducing costs by hiring more part-time workers, requiring people to pay more for coverage for their spouses, reducing company contributions for life insurance, and discouraging unhealthy job applicants from pursuing employment with the company. Other companies have noticed, and some will surely follow Wal-Mart's example.

Hardly anyone is happy with the current health care arrangements. According to the National Coalition on Health Care, every thirty seconds someone in the United States files for bankruptcy because of a serious health problem. Health care costs were the number-one cause of U.S. bankruptcies in 2005. Doctors increasingly leave medicine rather than continually fight with insurance companies over the treatment they feel their patients need. They spend billions just trying to get paid, and insurance companies spend the same amount trying not to pay. Doctors also spend too much time on the phone with nonmedical bureaucrats, explaining a decision or inquiring about reimbursement. Malpractice insurance pushes them to the brink of financial ruin. For many, the joy of practicing medicine is gone; some say that if they had known the system would be what it is today, they would never have gone to medical school. The quality of nursing is also down, as the system's regulators restrict what a caring nurse can do. A surprising number of nurses admit that nursing has become just a job, not a calling.

---

*Indeed, employees now pay 73 percent more in health-insurance premiums than they did in 2000.

When mistakes are made—by anyone: doctor, nurse, pharmacist—there is no incentive to admit them and take remedial action. The fear of lawsuits promotes a lack of transparency and accountability that trumps common sense. Because of the threat of litigation, 79 percent of physicians order more tests than necessary and 41 percent prescribe unnecessary antibiotics. Ten cents of every health care dollar paid by individuals and companies goes for litigation and defensive medicine.

Some estimates have put total annual administrative costs in our health system as high as $300 billion. Patients get some idea about unnecessary administrative costs when they have to fill out three or four marginally different forms asking for the same information whenever they go to a new doctor or even the old one.

Medicaid patients, our poorest citizens, often get third-class care. Many of them take a bus to go across town to see a doctor, only to find that the doctor doesn't accept Medicaid patients. More than a third of all doctors refuse to take Medicaid patients, because the reimbursement rates are too low. Under pressure of state budget cuts, Medicaid services and eligibility have been cut drastically. In 2003, twenty-seven states reported narrowing eligibility. That year, twenty-five states reduced benefits, seventeen increased copayments, and thirty-seven reduced provider payments. Still, states spend more money on Medicaid than they do on K–12 education. Medicare, the health care program for the elderly, is in general a success, but its costs are open-ended and unsustainable.

Most players in the health care debate want to solve only their own difficulties. Doctors want malpractice reform. Health plans want more subscribers. Teaching hospitals want capital-construction tax breaks and subsidies for medical schools. Insurance companies want to accumulate premiums and deny coverage to patients with costly illnesses. Businesses want relief from the ever-increasing cost of health insurance and in the current system seek to get it through deep discounts from hospitals. The poor want higher doctor participation in Medicaid. The elderly want more Medicare benefits at no additional cost. The problem is that each group's objectives are only a part of the health care story. Their narrow focus limits their vision. They fail to see the national interest.

Holistic Reform

There will never be a partial solution to America's health care crisis. If you fix only one part of the system, health care players will simply shift the costs to other parts. It's like a glob of honey: You block it on one side, it comes out on the other. Insurance companies shift costs to consumers in the form of higher rates. Hospitals reduce what they pay doctors, and health plans cut back on what they pay hospitals. Hospitals merge to get better bargaining power against health plans. Hospitals boost prices for various procedures and treatments in anticipation of Medicare asking for large group discounts. When companies want to avoid the cost of drug benefits for their retirees, they support Medicare coverage of drug costs. When unions talk about the rising cost of health care, they want employers to pick it up. When state governments complain about Medicaid costs, they try to lay these costs off on the federal Medicare program. Each group wants cost control to be someone else's problem. Only reform of the whole can contain costs over the long term.

Bill Clinton proposed health care reform in 1993, and he should get credit for at least trying, but he and his wife were naïve. I never will forget a weekend retreat with Democratic senators after Clinton showcased the program in his first State of the Union address. Those in attendance had many years of legislative experience; some had undertaken big reforms before and had an idea of what they required. The first lady, her favorite pollster, and the administration's substantive point man for health reform attended the retreat. Sitting on a stage, they explained how they proposed to get the legislation enacted. They wanted to get it passed by the July 4 recess, they said, or certainly by the August recess. One senator asked what their strategy would be if the legislation hadn't passed by then. "You don't understand," Mrs. Clinton replied. "We will demonize those who are blocking this legislation, and it will pass." Unfortunately, the reform attempt collapsed. When I saw the TV ads, paid for by the insurance industry, demonizing Mrs. Clinton and the White House legislation, I thought about the ironies of high-stakes reform in Washington.

The debate over health care reform in America usually reduces, sooner or later, to a question of socialized medicine. The term was conjured up as a scare tactic by the American Medical Association when Harry Truman proposed universal coverage in 1945, and it is perpetuated by politicians now whose purpose is at least to maintain the status quo. Some want to go further: end Medicare and Medicaid, and turn all of health care over to the private sector. Since more than half of all health care spending today comes from the government through Medicare, Medicaid, veterans' coverage, government employee coverage, and tax subsidies to the private sector, proponents of no government involvement in health care must be seen as truly radical. In such a polarized atmosphere, the politics of fear and distortion usually trumps the best of intentions, particularly if the charges are repeated often enough—witness the fate of the Clinton plan.

The optimal reform in health care will always be complicated. When I ran for the Democratic presidential nomination in 2000, I put health care at the center of my campaign. The proposal I offered had a lot of moving parts, but the basic thrust was correct. It provided universal access but didn't mandate that people sign up. It allowed the private sector to do what it does best, which is offer a variety of health plans, each with different benefits and costs, from which an individual could pick. It allowed the government to do what it does best, which is help people pay for their plans with government subsidies based on the participants' income. Finally, it allowed local communities, through community health centers and neighborhood clinics, to do what they do best, which is focus on health education, preventive medicine, and delivery of care to particularly difficult-to-reach ethnic populations. At this 30,000-foot level, the program was understandable, and audiences would nod their heads in approval. When I went into the actual complexity, people often didn't follow the details, which made the proposal prey to artful distortion. The opposing campaign took our best-estimate numbers for government payments to the individual at a particular time and implied that they were inadequate, particularly as costs inevitably went up. They exaggerated the program's overall costs and claimed that, by providing insufficient subsidies, the plan over time would hurt the most vulnerable citizens. I failed to find a concise way to refute the charge.

The plan I offered during that campaign also replaced Medicaid, by giving poor people the same basic care as rich people, bringing them into a health care program like that enjoyed by federal employees (including senators). There would have been no third-class health care anymore—but the prospect of replacing Medicaid with something new was a hard sell to the poor. They feared that if they gave it up, they'd have nothing. They didn't trust politicians. For these poor Americans, a terrible system was better than nothing. Medicaid recipients couldn't imagine anything better than the status quo. The irony was that any universal health coverage proposal that creates one system will require the poor to give up Medicaid and the elderly to give up Medicare so that a better system can be established. In a world in which voters get only sound bites of the candidates and their ideas, being comprehensive and specific has its downside. But politicians must take the risk, for too many American lives are at stake.

The New Story

The new story on health care states that we are a rich country, blessed with a working democracy and citizens who, because of ethical or religious convictions, know that we ought to help the poor and vulnerable. Remember the Good Samaritan? Given these facts, we can, in the words of the health analyst Leif Wellington Haase, "improve the overall health of the population; encourage medical innovation that will make future generations healthier; offer hope for individuals to survive unexpected illness, injury, and trauma; and allow the terminally ill to die with as much dignity and comfort as possible." Part of our shared humanity is to make sure that the sick among us are not abandoned. Our attitude toward those who need medical help will also power our attempts to reduce the big killer diseases, such as heart disease and cancer, and the quiet killers, such as diabetes, obesity, and asthma. It will strengthen our determination to curb infant mortality and intensify our outrage when foreign royalty come to one of our best hospitals for the latest medical treatment while three blocks away a pregnant woman can't afford a doctor.

Health care should be a right. But rights come with responsibilities attached. Individuals must take responsibility for their own health by how they behave. Two-thirds of adults in America are overweight, in large part because they consume too much sugar and too many trans fats and don't exercise. In the new story, your employer tries to keep you healthy, because your health affects the firm's productivity. Employers discourage unhealthy lifestyles and reward people who exercise, get annual checkups, and lose excess weight. Schools do away with vending machines that sell junk food, require physical conditioning classes, and develop detailed health education courses, including anti-drug education from the sixth grade on. Learning the food groups is the beginning, but not the end, of health instruction. If you still insist on unhealthy behavior, then you'll be charged more for health insurance. Otherwise, the rest of us pay more because of your bad habits.

The biggest driver of costs in American health care is advances in medical technology.* Pharmaceutical companies create markets for expensive drugs, some of which are breakthrough drugs but many of which are not. The same goes for medical devices, such as heart stents or artificial knees. The marketing of devices, drugs, advanced treatments, and even hospitals directly to the consumer often confuses people. You used to leave it to your doctor to sort through these claims, but now, because of the increase in malpractice suits, doctors are often hesitant to respond to patients' inquiries. What is needed is a quasi-federal agency, perhaps the National Academy of Sciences' Institute of Medicine, that will determine which drugs, medical devices, and new treatments are cost-effective. These items would have to be covered in a minimum policy, but insurance companies could always augment that coverage.

To make our new story a reality requires acceptance of several simple principles. First, the focus of the system should be on quality of care for the patient. Second, it must be mandatory for all Ameri-

---

*From 1975 to 1995, these accounted for 50 percent of the annual increase in costs.

cans to have health insurance; low income cannot be an acceptable barrier. Third, individuals must do their part to stay well and not overutilize the system. Fourth, individuals should retain some choice over the kind of coverage they receive. Fifth, recurring costs should be reduced, not shifted. Sixth, specific national goals should be set that improve health outcomes, such as slashing the number of medical errors in hospitals, reducing infant mortality, lowering the number of sick days at work, combatting obesity and diabetes, filing fewer lawsuits, and providing better information to prospective patients about which doctors and hospitals do what well and where they are.

The new story says that once we are all covered by the same system—one that assures quality and offers many choices—costs can be controlled. If we add electronic record keeping and electronic prescribing, annual costs, according to a 2003 study sponsored by the Markle Foundation, can be reduced by $125 billion.* If we add to that a reduction in medical errors, such as administering the wrong doses, failing to sterilize equipment, or getting billing wrong, costs can be reduced even further. If we then implement a personal health system consisting of sensors and computers that monitor the self-sufficient and ambulatory elderly in their homes—instead of forcing them into nursing facilities, which cost ten times as much—we can reduce costs even more. If we then give patients the latest scientific information about prevention, we can cut costs still more. With everyone covered and a systemwide information setup in place, fewer workers will lose days of work and fewer students will lose days of school. Fewer babies will die in childbirth. Fewer children will die of asthma. Fewer teenagers will die of drug overdoses. Fewer adults will die of AIDS. Fewer people will commit suicide. America will finally be able to claim that, as in sixteen other advanced democracies, everyone who gets sick can afford to see a doctor.

The most important initial step we should take to improve the quality of our health care is to adopt a goal of zero medical errors. Medical errors annually cost all of us billions of dollars in corrective

---

*The average cost per doctor to set up a system of electronic records is $33,000, or $1,375 per month for two years, but only 20 percent of doctors have done so.

health costs, higher insurance premiums, and unnecessary human suffering. The number of people dying in American hospitals from medical errors is the equivalent of a 747 airplane crashing every day of the year.* The system catches only 1 percent of medication errors, and the hospital infection rate has been growing for decades, to the point where it now affects one out of twelve people admitted to U.S. hospitals. As a nation, we should regard such a situation as intolerable. To ameliorate it, we should start by holding hospital CEOs and heads of medicine responsible for developing data collection that will reveal the patterns of mistakes in their hospitals; only then can a system be developed that will prevent such errors from recurring.

A pioneer in this area is Paul H. O'Neill, who, before he was President Bush's first treasury secretary, oversaw the near elimination of workplace injuries while he was chairman and CEO of Alcoa. In the late 1990s he ran the Pittsburgh Regional Healthcare Initiative, and he has recently formed the Value Capture Policy Institute, which studies ways to improve health care. "Health care organizations to date have reacted to cost pressures by driving themselves by goals unrelated to the quality of their care," he stated in testimony in March 2006 before the Senate Finance Committee. "Measures derived from perverse financial incentives, such as 'average length of stay,' dominate the industry but are not rooted in human biology and healing. . . . The health care workforce is much less motivated by cost savings than they are by improving care for patients and by their own safety."

From these premises, O'Neill recommends four changes: First, end the billing process in which, he says, hospitals overbill insurance companies by some 70 percent in order to end up collecting what they're owed. The current billing process is a dishonest, time-consuming dance in which hospitals in effect keep two sets of books. O'Neill argues for transparency and rapid reimbursement.

Next, since 75 percent of health care costs (according to the Insti-

---

*A study issued in the summer of 2004 by HealthGrades, Inc., a leading health care ratings organization, reported that in each of the years 2000, 2001, and 2002, an average of 195,000 Medicare patients died in hospitals because of medical errors. According to one estimate, a person is almost 2,000 times likelier to die because of hospital medical errors than in an airplane crash.

tute of Medicine and the Centers for Disease Control and Prevention) arise from chronic diseases, the emphasis should be on prevention and primary care, instead of paying billions of dollars annually to treat people after they're already very sick. While health care costs rose 50 percent nationally in the first five years of the decade, the Veterans Benefits Administration held them constant, and improved quality as well, by emphasizing primary and preventive care and electronic case monitoring. To achieve optimum care we'll need more preventive-medicine specialists; in 2002 we had fewer than there were in 1970. A greater emphasis on preventive medicine could, according to some estimates, save us $26 billion per year systemwide.

Third, O'Neill argues, we need a health care system of truth telling, in which errors are "exposed and learned from, immediately, so that they won't be repeated." Congress established a rudimentary data collection system in 2005. The key to its success is not simply the collection of data on medical errors but the dispersal of that information to the widest possible audience. Through its oversight of the regulations that will implement the law, Congress should guarantee that every player in the system—doctors, nurses, administrative personnel, as well as the public—can examine the data. If all health care personnel have access to relevant information, they can see how their efforts are improving the outcomes for patients and their own safety.

Finally, O'Neill recommends that doctors and staff members report errors in the first twenty-four hours and take steps within a week to prevent them from recurring. Then there could be some malpractice relief for the doctors and the hospitals. If they don't report in timely fashion, there would be no limits on amounts obtainable by plaintiffs.

O'Neill estimates, based on his experience with hospitals he's worked with, that such a deliberate attempt to reduce errors and waste could save between 30 and 50 percent of the $2 trillion we now spend annually on health care. If he's anywhere close, it will then be easy to cover everyone with insurance and still have money left over for other improvements.

Another step toward quality would be to institute transparent outcomes in all hospitals. At the Cleveland Clinic, every department, from cardiology to orthopedics, has to define a successful outcome for every procedure or surgery and then report to the public how well it performed according to its established standards. We ought to have national quality standards, so someone who needs a heart operation, say, can go to various hospital Web sites and see how many heart operations a hospital has performed in the last several years, how experienced the heart surgeons are, what methods were used, what the outcomes were, what each operation cost the hospital, what it cost the patient, and the level of patient satisfaction with the results.

Michael E. Porter and Elizabeth Olmsted Teisberg, two leading management thinkers, go a step further in their book, *Redefining Health Care.* They argue for value-based medicine, or health care designed to achieve the highest value for patients. Value, defined as the medical outcomes per dollar spent, is the purpose of health care. The key to driving improvements in value is to measure the outcomes of the care and not try to dictate the process.

Medical outcomes start with survival but include completeness of recovery, time required to return to normal activity, pain, and errors and complications in the treatment process. Medical outcomes must be compared with costs to determine value. Today, most providers think of costs in terms of charges rather than isolating the total cost of a given patient's care.

Value-based competition in health care would trigger major changes in how care delivery is organized. Care would be integrated for a medical condition (e.g., diabetes, heart disease, joint disease). Patients would no longer be passed from specialist to specialist but would receive coordinated care over the full care cycle for their condition, from screening to ongoing disease management. Providers would compete in each care cycle to deliver the best medical outcome per dollar spent compared with other systems.

Porter and Teisberg see an important role for the government in catalyzing and enabling value-based health care: "Government should establish and oversee a process of defining and ratifying a minimum set of outcome measures for each medical condition."

The National Academy of Sciences' Institute of Medicine might take on the job of coordinating the various medical disciplines and their societies in this effort. As with the Bureau of Labor Statistics, the objective should be a set of generally agreed upon standards, monitored annually and widely distributed. Porter and Teisberg insist that no health care provider

> should have the right to practice medicine without measuring and providing evidence of outcomes and ultimately value, as charges [prices] are combined with outcomes. . . . Mandatory reporting is justified by pressing public need for such information in health care delivery. Just as the SEC has strict, detailed reporting requirements for public companies, designed to protect investors, the same is needed for health care providers. The social benefits of results information will be even greater in health care than in financial markets, because the physical well-being of Americans is at stake.

With such information widely available, hospitals and doctors would compete on value. Innovation would flourish, as it does in other industries, and Americans would get better care with improving efficiency.

Hospitals would no longer attempt to offer all services to their local communities. Instead, they would compete regionally based on excellence in addressing particular medical conditions. Patients and their doctors would seek providers with a track record of success in addressing their medical circumstances, in the region or in some cases nationally. Value, not artificial health plan restrictions, should determine the choice of treatment and provider for a particular disease. Insurance companies should help people get the information, advice, and support they need to enable excellent care, not ration services, issue incomprehensible payment statements, and dispute their liability. Prices for care should be transparent and, once set by physicians and hospitals, the same for all patients, regardless of whether they work for a big corporation or are self-employed.

Medicare could jump-start value-based medicine by starting to act like a health plan, not just a bill payer. For example, Medicare should require outcome and cost reporting; move reimbursement to payments for full care cycles rather than discrete visits, tests, procedures, and treatments; and offer prevention, screening, and disease management services for beneficiaries to minimize their need for expensive acute care.

Universal Coverage

When I was a boy, I realized that my father was different from other fathers, because he never drove a car, threw a ball, or walked farther than several blocks. Today we would call him disabled. He had calcified arthritis of the lower spine. He ate health food before it became the rage and sought treatment from the Mayo Clinic. He could afford to pay for it. Today there are many fathers in similar difficulties who can't. They retire on disability and live reduced lives. I want everyone in America to have the same chance as my father had to get good health care.

With all that said, I can see at least two potential approaches to establishing universal health care.

The simplest would be Medicare for All. It could be phased in by first establishing Medicare for children, followed by Medicare for people with incomes under $50,000, and then Medicare for everyone else who remained uncovered. Once everyone was in this single-payer system, the aforementioned cost shifts would end. All citizens would have the same benefits and payment schedule. Advertising and marketing costs, which now amount to about 5 percent of health care costs, could be eliminated. Duplicate hospital facilities could be eliminated. Administrative costs would be slashed. The 15 percent administrative costs of the current private system, resulting from the bureaucratic tug-of-war between hospitals and doctors on one side and insurance companies on the other, would come to match the 1.5 percent administrative costs of Medicare. Doctors would spend less time battling insurance companies and more time treating patients. The coverage would be easy for people to understand. Businesses would no longer be burdened with paying open-ended health care costs for their workers; they could then hire more workers at better pay and become more competitive internationally. People would no longer have to stay in jobs they didn't like just to keep health coverage for their families. Government would have leverage in bargaining for lower costs with doctors, hospitals, and pharmaceutical companies. The crazy quilt of government tax subsidies, aimed at getting the private sector to serve the public interest through employer-paid health care, could be redirected to paying the health care bills for those who need help. Medicare for All would complete what everyone from Harry Truman to Bill Clinton has tried to do.

The second path would be to use conservative means (vouchers) to achieve liberal ends (universal coverage). Under this approach, everyone would be required to have health insurance. The government would promote value-based medicine, design a minimum policy, ensure the consistency of information about quality and price, provide subsidies to individuals below a certain income level, and regulate the insurance industry so as to ensure that it spreads risk over the sick as well as the healthy population and avoids discrimination against any consumer group (such as those below a certain income level or with a particular health history). The private sector would offer people a choice of health plans, each of which would be paid for in part by the government and in part by the employer or individual, the individual's share depending on income. New health service companies or even community organizations would be the delivery points for preventive care, nutrition education, and health counselling.

Under such a system, individuals, rather than their employers, would be in charge of their health care, but they would be embedded in a supportive network that would help them to utilize better what the health care system offered. With about half of the nation's health care costs attributable to ailments related to smoking, drinking, drugs, diet, and lack of exercise, an ongoing national communication campaign could persuade people that an important part of health care costs derives from their own behavior. Individual responsibility could be emphasized by increasing the cost of policies for those who continue their bad habits. When individual and community, public sector and private sector, are brought together, with assigned responsibilities for each, everyone would have a role in making us all healthier.

These government vouchers would have to be generous enough to allow every citizen to buy an adequate plan. People who have more money and want special nurses, private rooms, or other luxury items could always supplement their plans. Health histories and genetic markers would play no role in insurance companies' deciding what to charge; only age and gender would be considered—as they are under the current system. With an adequate subsidy awarded to each individual, insurance companies would compete to provide the best coverage. The plans would be modelled on the federal employees' health plan. The money for individual subsidies could come in part from eliminating the $40 billion annual federal reimbursement to hospitals who give uncompensated care (since everyone would now have compensated care), from cutting back on the $150 billion tax exclusion for private health insurance that flows now to employer-paid health care no matter how expensive, and from reducing Medicaid costs by better case management. Another proposal is to have the federal government cover the state share of what is now Medicaid in exchange for the states picking up the federal portion of disability benefits.

The single-payer system, in which the government pays for everyone to have a basic health care plan, seems simplest and most effective to me, but a hybrid approach that uses conservative means to achieve liberal goals and embraces value-based medicine has the best chance to become law and assures the most innovation. While neither political party has enough votes to pass its version of national health care insurance, each party has sufficient clout to stop a proposal by the other. As Matt Miller points out in *The 2% Solution*, successful compromise depends on whether Democrats can accept the private sector as a creative force in achieving universal coverage and whether Republicans will spend enough money to ensure that everyone has adequate health care. The issue of universal coverage has been so polarized for so long that the major obstacle to success is trust between the two political parties.

But legislators led by an administration willing to listen and committed to the principle of universal coverage can reach an agreement. They could lock themselves in a room and emerge only when they have a deal. There are plenty of precedents for just such an approach.

Republicans in particular have reason to compromise. Health care costs are now overburdening business, and it is only a matter of time until big business asks the federal government to take over the whole responsibility. If Republicans want to retain a role for the private sector in health care and avoid turning over control to the government, this hybrid approach offers them their best bet.

Here are some specific policy changes:

1. Enact Medicare for All or make health insurance mandatory for all Americans with tax-credit or voucher subsidies based on income.

2. Encourage adoption of electronic record keeping and prescriptions by making Medicaid and Medicare payments to providers contingent (after a transition period) on their implementing the necessary changes.

3. Require a medical-error reduction strategy for all hospitals, in exchange for limiting liability in malpractice lawsuits. Annual evaluation of performance on medical errors will determine whether the limits on liability will remain in place the following year.

4. Establish a federal agency that weighs costs and outcomes of new medical technology and then compiles a list of cost-effective drugs, medical devices, and new treatments.

5. Use Medicare to promote value-based medicine and require providers to supply information on diseases and treatments pursuant to standards established by doctors' societies working with the National Academy of Sciences' Institute of Medicine or other quasi-government agencies that would provide objective information similar to that amassed by the Bureau of Labor Statistics.

6. Charge more for the health insurance policies of people who

refuse to correct their self-destructive behavior, such as smoking or excessive eating that leads to obesity.

7. Ban trans fats, which kill 30,000 people in this country annually and may cause as many as 228,000 heart attacks.*

8. Emphasize preventive and primary care.

Again, it is our choice.

---

*See, for instance, Nicholas Kristof's column on "killer" Girl Scout cookies in *The New York Times*, May 21, 2006.

Chapter 8.

EDUCATION

The story we are told about education says that the use of vouchers for private and parochial schools, or turning public schools over to private corporations, will break an educational monopoly that has failed to challenge students effectively. Vouchers will also subject public education to market forces, which will bring improvement. Standardized tests in the public schools should measure educational achievement, but there should be no national standards in testing or curriculum — local control remains inviolate. Parents trust their school districts more than they trust some "Big Brother knows best" federal system. The story also says that while urban public education is in bad shape, suburban and small-town public schools are doing just fine.

The trouble with vouchers as a solution to the problems of public education is that the numbers don't add up. Every year, over $80 billion is invested in the physical infrastructure of public education, and $475 billion is spent annually in public education overall. Eighty-eight percent of the children in this country — 48.6 million of them — attend public schools. There are only 6.4 million children in private and parochial schools. These are totally different kinds of institutions doing different jobs: Public schools must take everyone; private and parochial schools can select their students. School vouchers may be a sliver of the answer in urban areas where parents have no alternative for their children except a dysfunctional public school—indeed, when I was in the Senate, I supported them on a test basis for some urban areas—but they are not a general answer. No matter how much we spend on vouchers, there will never be a private education system that can duplicate the investment in plant, equipment, and personnel that already exists in the public school system. The question is not how to create a parallel system but how to transform the public one.

In arguing for local control, the story ignores the fact that many school boards are simply not up to the task of running a twenty-first-century school. Many are not professionally staffed. School board members, while often well-meaning, are also often unqualified to determine the best chemistry textbook or the newest best practice in teaching or the school design that best fits our technological age. Too many boards are politicized and become places for grand-standing. In larger urban districts, there is scant talent in finance, procurement, information systems, or human resources. And the school boards are no match for the unions—just look at their re-spective presences in Washington, DC. The National Education Association has 550 employees, and the National School Boards Association has 140. The budget of the National School Board Asso-ciation is $27.2 million, whereas the NEA and the AFT (American Federation of Teachers) get hundreds of millions in membership dues, which fuel their efforts at the state and federal levels. More-over, there is no place for school boards to go for expert, impartial advice. That frequently leaves them the victim of the latest textbook company with a good sales force, or the most aggressive educational consultants promoting a new fad. Finally, many school boards don't appreciate the seriousness of the educational challenges from China, India, Russia, and other countries. Education has become a national security issue. Rigid local control doesn't make sense in a globalized world.

Ensuring that our students receive a quality education requires us to measure their progress. Standardized testing, while necessary, is not sufficient. Many successful people have scored badly on stan-dardized tests even as they reached mastery in their chosen fields.

Every child learns differently. One often hears about students who drill incessantly and score well on tests but haven't learned to think critically. What our students need is the creativity to invent the new new thing, not just the expertise to manufacture it efficiently.

The "No Child Left Behind" legislation relies on the predictive powers of tests, although no test can gauge the spirit of a child whose character or imagination will produce a high degree of achievement. The states determine the content of the tests that measure proficiency, so there are wide variations. Because multiple-choice questions are cheaper to grade, many states stay away from essay questions; what is measured is the ability to recall facts, not to structure and use information. And without national standards, test scores do not provide a relevant measure of how we are doing as a nation. The noted education expert Diane Ravitch has compared test scores on standardized state tests of fourth- and eighth-grade math and reading skills with how the same students did on the federally administered National Assessment of Educational Progress tests. Whether it was Georgia, New York, Texas, North Carolina, or Idaho, students scored far lower on the federal tests than they did on the state tests. Idaho, for example, reported that on the state math test, 90 percent of its fourth-grade students were proficient, but on the federal test they achieved only a 41 percent proficiency rating. Georgia reported that 87 percent of its students did well in the fourth-grade reading test; the federal test concluded that only 26 percent were proficient. The NAEP tests were developed over the years by a bipartisan independent board. Many of the state tests had lower standards, in part because, in Ravitch's words, they responded to "the demands of parents, school officials and taxpayers for good news."

The answers offered by our current story on education are very small answers to a very big problem.

It's Not Just the Inner Cities

While urban public schools do face serious difficulties, the problems with our educational system go far beyond them. In New York State and in South Carolina, there are schools in which not one student passes the state math exam, let alone the federal test. From 1992 until 2003, the percentage of fourth-graders nationwide who performed "below basic," the lowest category in reading, on the National Assessment of Educational Progress test remained virtually unchanged at 37 percent.

The best public schools in the United States are in the wealthiest districts—and most suburban schools aren't wealthy. Parents who fled the cities for the suburbs in the 1970s generally couldn't afford to buy houses in the richest districts. They had to settle for districts with a less robust local tax base. Many of the schools their children attend today don't have all the academic offerings of a public school in a wealthy district: They have fewer language courses and less sophisticated science and computer labs—and, just as serious, they aren't aware of what they don't have. They become insular. They fail to see the larger world and thereby fail to prepare their students to compete in it.

Parents in much of suburbia ought to hear the truth about their children's education. Someone ought to tell them that we're falling behind internationally. The rest of the world is hungry, while we sit here fat and happy and increasingly ignorant. Nicholas Kristof, of *The New York Times*, reports that "one-fifth of all Americans still believe the Sun goes around the Earth, instead of the other way around. And only about half know that humans did not live at the same time as dinosaurs." Only 10 percent know what radiation is. A Princeton University survey found that only 22 percent of students at elite universities knew that the words "government of the people, by the people, for the people" came from the Gettysburg Address, and in the same survey, a quarter of the respondents said that the Pilgrims signed the Magna Carta aboard the *Mayflower*. A friend of mine told me recently that his car broke down, and while he was waiting in the repair shop for it to be fixed he heard one mechanic ask another, "What's six times seven?" "I think it's thirty-five," came the answer.

American Students in the World

In a world where the Internet has levelled the playing field, today's American students will face more competition when they enter the workforce than any previous generation. Today's corporations have their workforces spread all over the world. The high-technology jobs that were monopolized by Americans in the 1990s are now routinely outsourced to India and China. As a result, our student performance must be measured by worldwide standards. And the data show that the student who spends more time in school and does more homework will win. A 2005 study by Tom Loveless of the Brookings Institution reported that the average American grade school student between nine and twelve years old does, on average, four hours of homework per week and watches thirteen and a half hours of TV. Kristof, in a column entitled "Math and Science Education in a Global Age," reports that U.S. children spend 900 hours a year in classes and 1,023 hours in front of the television. God knows how many hours are spent on mindless video games. Kids are programmed into social and sports activities after school as if they were robots, but often their parents can't seem to inspire them to do much home study.

American kids go to school about six and a half hours a day, for 180 days a year. If you subtract the days devoted to parent-teacher conferences, professional development, field trips, and testing, that leaves (in the instance of one case study involving a California middle school) only 119 days for instruction, a part of which includes activities such as study hall. Meanwhile, in Germany, China, Japan, and Sweden, schools operate for as much as 220 days a year, and in China students attend school nine and a half hours a day. Our kids go to pep rallies and driver's education. Their kids study a second foreign language and more science. Nearly all Chinese high school students complete a national curriculum that includes advanced biology and calculus. In the United States, only 13 percent of high school students learn calculus, and fewer than 18 percent study advanced biology. Who do you think will be ahead in the economic competition thirty years from now?

In some areas, China and India are already ahead of us. Combined, these two countries graduate close to half a million engineers a year. In the United States, the number is 137,000. The McKinsey Global Institute predicts that, in the life sciences, the number of young Chinese and Indian researchers will increase by 35 percent, to 1.6 million, by 2008, while in the United States that category will decline by 11 percent, to 760,000. The innovation coming out of these two countries, in everything from software and medicine to industrial processes, has just begun.

The rivalry that other nations feel with the United States should never be underestimated. Everyone likes to see the big guy stumble. China and France are particularly ethnocentric, but India, Japan, and Germany are not far behind. They are doubtless tired of having heard so long about American "know-how." The nationalism of the Chinese is particularly strong. China needs us today. They continue to bolster our economy with their capital investment and to avail themselves of our system of higher education. More than 60,000 Chinese students attend American universities and have done so in increasing numbers since they first arrived in 1978. The day may come when they don't need us anymore, and by then we might well need them. With China holding almost a trillion dollars in dollar-denominated financial assets, graduating 350,000 engineers a year, building multiple university systems, and offering U.S. science professors million-dollar-a-year contracts to move their labs to Chinese universities, what seems impossible to imagine today could be a reality tomorrow.

When I was a kid and left food on my plate, my mother would say, "Bill, remember the starving kids in India and China." Today, in a world in which the Internet potentially gives every child a giant library and access to the world's best minds, Thomas Friedman, in *The World Is Flat*, reminds us that parents should be saying, "Mary, do your homework. Remember that the kids in India and China are spending nearly twice as much time in school as you do."

Urban Education

People of economic means have left the public school system and created their own parallel system. They are so convinced that public schools cannot provide a decent education that they often voluntarily pay over $20,000 per child per year, on top of the share of their taxes going to the public schools. It is easy to ignore this as a phenomenon pertaining only to a minority of the population; however, it is these very students who will disproportionately go to the best colleges, get the best jobs, and produce offspring who are also unlikely to go to public schools. Here we are seeing another kind of segregation, one that exacerbates the problem of the "haves" and the "have-nots."

When it comes to public education in our major cities, the old story is correct in pointing out that public education there is a disaster. Fifteen million American children are trapped in mostly segregated, abysmally performing urban schools. That's more than the population of Norway and Sweden combined. The U.S. Supreme Court desegregated public schools in *Brown v. Board of Education* because, in the words of the ruling, "Separate educational facilities are inherently unequal." Today America has gone back on the promise of that decision. Many urban school districts are rigidly segregated. In Chicago, half the public school students are black. In Atlanta, it's 88 percent. In Boston, it's 46 percent. In Los Angeles, three-quarters of the public school students are Hispanic. (Ironically, many of these schools are named for Martin Luther King Jr.) Fifty years after *Brown v. Board of Education*, many black children never encounter a white classmate or teacher. One high school social studies teacher I know, in a school that doesn't have one white student, often asks her class what percent of the population of Americans they believe is black. They usually guess between 80 and 90 percent. They live in an isolated society, a segregated society, a society of color in which it's difficult for them to imagine a wider world. "That's why they can't understand," the teacher says, "why most of the nation's leaders are white." Ten years ago, the columnist Jack White, writing in *Time* magazine, lamented, "Before we gave up on integration, we should have tried it."

There is much about this story of resegregation that is infuriating. Jonathan Kozol, in his latest book, *The Shame of the Nation: The Restoration of Apartheid Schooling in America*, quotes Theodore M. Shaw, the head of the NAACP Legal Defense and Education Fund, who takes the pessimism of many today to the next level: "If schools are going to continue to be separate in most cities, then we have to ask if we can get at least the 'equal' part." But that isn't happening either; if anything, things are going the other way. Kozol points out that "[t]hirty-five out of 48 states spend less on students in school districts with the highest number of minority children than on students in the districts with the fewest children of minorities." The achievement gap between black and white students narrowed for a while, but by the 1990s it had started to widen again. By the time many black and Hispanic students reach the twelfth grade, passed along by "social promotions," they are still reading at a seventh-grade level or worse.

In twenty schools in Philadelphia, no more than 11.4 percent of the students are proficient in math at their grade level. Fewer than 30.0 percent of the black male students in Chicago and New York City schools graduate with their class. The dropout rate in 48 of the 100 largest urban schools is more than 50.0 percent; these kids are forever condemned to lower income, poorer health, more brushes with the law, and shorter life expectancy than those who complete high school. Their failure creates a burden on all of us, in the form of taxes that go to expenditures ranging from the prison system to unemployment compensation. Indeed, more young African American men are in prison today than in college, compared with 1980, when they were three times more likely to go to college than to jail.

A Nation at Risk

The erosion of quality in American elementary and secondary education has been invisible to most people, even though it has been going on for years. The problem is systemwide: Whether it's in suburban, rural, small-town, or urban America, low standards are a common problem. A 2003 study by the Organization for Economic Cooperation and Development put American tenth-graders twenty-fourth out of twenty-nine nations in educational performance, with U.S. students scoring below average in science and far below average in problem solving and practical math. In short, too many schools have become comfortable with mediocrity. The lowered expectations are like termites eating away at the foundation of our future. The deterioration that results represents a bigger threat to our national security than *Sputnik* did in 1957. Yet we do almost nothing about it.

The first major national study of America's public education system was issued in 1983 by the National Commission on Excellence in Education. It was called *A Nation at Risk*, and it stated: "If an unfriendly foreign power had attempted to impose on America the mediocre educational performance that exists today, we might have viewed it as an act of war. As it stands, we have allowed this to happen to ourselves. . . . We have, in effect, been committing an act of unthinking, unilateral educational disarmament." It went on to stress the importance of education not just for the nation's future economic growth and prosperity but also for the enrichment of the human spirit, the development of informed citizens in a democracy, and as a way to see diverse neighbors through the lens of our common humanity. It laid out specific recommendations on how to improve the public school system, such as longer school days, better teacher pay, and greater teacher accountability. In the last twenty years, few of these recommendations, including national standards, have been adopted.

Principals and Teachers

At the center of the decline are our public school principals and teachers.

Principals are supposed to be the leaders of their schools. Too often, they are not. Hamstrung by state and federal regulations, they often have no real say in the recruitment, hiring, or pay of quality teachers. They are shackled by the collectively bargained work rules of the National Education Association or the American Federation of Teachers. They are rarely well paid. Few have trained specifically for the job. Even fewer are held accountable for the performance of their schools. Many resent the refusal of a teacher-dominated bureaucracy to give them performance bonuses without corresponding raises for teachers and other educational personnel. In New York City, one of the two places in the nation where principals are unionized, many feel undermined, even within their own union, by the more numerous assistant principals, who won't vote for principals' raises unless they get them, too.

For many years, American public schools had great teachers. I remember when I was a child that, on a couple of occasions, middle-aged men knocked on our front door in Crystal City and asked if this was where Miss Crowe (my mother), their fourth-grade teacher, lived. They said they just wanted to thank her for being a positive influence in their lives. My guess is that there were a lot of children like me who witnessed such visits.

Then the school system changed. Intelligent and well-educated women, who had formed the heart of the teacher corps, began to have other career opportunities, and many left. The problems of the society at large found their way into the schools. For many school officials, concerns about drugs, violence, and the poor health and broken families of their students became greater preoccupations than education itself. Many two-earner families, stressed by work demands, depended on schools to play a larger and larger role in raising their children. More and more mandates were loaded on schools. Special education classes exploded. Mainstreaming left talented students unchallenged. Additional funding brought additional paperwork. Layer upon layer of bureaucracy smothered the creativity of our schools and swallowed up more and more funding. Fewer people assumed responsibility for results. Performance lagged. Standards were lowered. The students left without the basic skills needed to function in the modern workplace. It is remarkable that a country whose economy is built on innovation, whose technology has changed the world, has in effect allowed the computer revolution to skip over the classroom, where ways of doing things haven't changed much since 1900. One apologist for the current system recently remarked in all seriousness that although we were fourteenth in the world in math and science, we were number one in self-esteem. Therein lies the nub of the problem.

One fact remains: The key to learning is the teacher. A student's family or life circumstances are relevant but not determinative. There are plenty of stories, even now, about what the inspiration of one teacher can do. I know a writing teacher in the Bronx who was assigned as her advisee a ninth-grader who was repeating the grade for the third time. She gave him the inspiration he needed, and he completed all his credits for that year, but he was absent once again at the beginning of the tenth grade. The writing teacher went to his apartment in the projects and asked him why he wasn't in school. He told her he couldn't afford the right shoes for school. She took him to a store and bought him a pair for $100. Several weeks later he brought in $100 to repay the teacher, whom he referred to as an "angel." The teacher wouldn't accept the money and never told the principal what she had done. The student hasn't been absent since.

Thousands of teachers would nod their heads to this story. They are the ones who spend long hours preparing for class and devising unique ways to reach their students on an individual basis. For these teachers, job satisfaction comes from the smiles and lit-up eyes of a student who gets excited about learning.

Our kids deserve the best teachers, but today in many places they're not getting them. Nearly a third of the math and science teachers in our public schools had neither a major nor a minor in the subject they're teaching. They are often only one week ahead of the class—or just coasting on last year's preparation. That isn't good enough.

Inexperience is a serious problem. Young teachers stay in the profession, on average, only about five years. Forty-two percent of the nation's 2.9 million public school teachers are near retirement, which means that over a million replacements will be necessary in the next few years. If we don't find good ones, we will not fare well in the global economic competition and we will narrow the range of our children's capacity for joy, wonder, and active citizenship.

Our public schools are further hobbled by fear of lawsuits. School boards refuse to keep schools open after hours for special programs that could keep kids off the streets, because they want to avoid legal liability. Seesaws and jungle gyms can no longer be found on most school playgrounds, for fear of lawsuits if a child falls off. In one Los Angeles school playground there is a sign that says, "No running." In New York City, sixty-six separate steps are required to suspend an unruly student and eighty-three steps, which could take more than a year to complete, to get rid of an incompetent teacher. A teacher in New York City schools can, in some cases, be legally liable for correcting or disciplining a kid out of the classroom. That means that if the teacher stops a fight in the halls, he or she could be sued by the combatants. Philip K. Howard, founder of Common Good, a bipartisan organization dedicated to legal reform, has explained how our legal system hamstrings our schools. "In America today, teachers will not put an arm around a crying child for fear of being sued for unwanted sexual touching. Principals who want to instill pride in students by insisting that they dress neatly can't demand the same thing of teachers. Common sense in schools has been shoved aside by bureaucracy, union rules, and fear of being dragged into a legal proceeding."

Teaching is one of the very few professions I know of that only rarely rewards improved performance. When I was a basketball player, I knew that if I improved and we won the championship, I'd be paid more. That's also true of lawyers, bankers, and countless other professionals, including college professors. But it's not true for K–12 teachers. They advance according to seniority.

Teachers are paid not because they're good but because they're there. And sometimes they aren't even that. The newest teaching dysfunction is the prevalence of substitute teachers. At Palo Alto High School in California, with 120 full-time teachers, substitutes were called in—sometimes several in one day—for 1,322 full days last year. In all my years of school, from first grade through high school, there were two days a year devoted to teachers' meetings, during which time the school closed, and something like five days of substitute teachers over my entire twelve-year public education. School boards tolerate this absenteeism because in school board elections the turnout is so small that a well-organized group, such as the teachers' union, can ensure the election of friendly board members.

Too many administrators in American school districts have jobs, not missions. Too many people get paid too much for setting policy for sporting events, filling out paperwork, processing applications for grants, or establishing unnecessary regulations that manage the school day in excruciating detail—in other words, not teaching. Too many school improvement plans fail to get any input from teachers, parents, and community members before they're announced. Then everyone is surprised when the plans don't produce better results. Part of the problem is that the state and federal bureaucrats who write the nit-picking regulations are just implementing the legislative intent of politicians to micromanage the schools.

The unions argue that it's impossible to hold a teacher accountable for student performance. After all, they say, so many things happen outside the classroom that teachers cannot control. How can I teach kids who are violent or on drugs? How can I teach someone to read if his peers make fun of him for trying? How can I teach a child whose parents neglect their responsibilities for her education? How can I, in my one-hour class, change the habits of a lifetime, or counter the messages the child gets at home or from TV? There are thousands of excuses, but that's all they are—excuses.

Plenty of principals and teachers are better than their union leadership. A young principal in New York City wrote me recently about her commitment to education:

Life makes most sense to me when I am able to see and feel how much we all are dependent upon and tied to one another. When I can see this, the future isn't just my personal future, or families' future, but humanity's future. My spirit isn't just my spirit. It is a part of a collective spirit that some of us call belief and others God and still others hope. Those of us who invest in schools are investing in our children but by doing so we're investing in ourselves and in the idea that we can live now and forever in each other.

Plenty of people want to help improve the public schools. An organization called Donors Choose was started in 2000 by a young high school teacher in New York, who was inspired by a sad fact: Teachers can't always get the materials needed to do their jobs. Donors Choose (www.DonorsChoose.com) is a Web site where public school teachers post requests for financing of specific projects that will make them more effective in the classroom. The projects include "Where did all the pencils go" ($60), "Dictionaries for At-Home Use" ($259), and "Geological Field Trip" ($200). Most proposals are for far more than microscopes and other materials. They are creative ideas for helping students learn. "Cooking Across the Curriculum" asks for cookbooks, mixers, bowls, and a mini-refrigerator for a third-grade class. The teacher writes that "cooking incorporates curriculum areas in an engaging and memorable way," for example, experiencing how matter changes when you bake a cake (science), or how an apple gets from the tree to the pie (social studies), or how recipes require you to know fractions (math). Donors select what project they'd like to fund and send their money to Donors Choose, which pays the bills the teacher submits. Donors Choose sends each teacher a thank-you notes kit, and the kids tell their benefactors how they feel about getting the book or the microscope. Today Donors Choose serves over 4,745 schools in ten states and has received over 37,000 donations from all fifty states; the $9 million raised has helped more than half a million kids. It is this kind of idealism that can turn teaching into the mission of a generation.

National Leadership

Nearly 90 percent of funding for elementary and secondary public education comes from state and local taxes. Yet it takes a president to effect nationwide change. Without a president who recognizes the failure of our educational system and declares it a national emergency, the American people are likely to remain unaware of how serious the situation is. No president since Lyndon Johnson, who signed into law sixty education bills, has put the effort, attention, and resources into making our grade school and high school students the best educated in the world. The bipartisan "No Child Left Behind" education initiative headed in the right direction of greater accountability, but the program was too narrow in scope and Congress didn't fund it adequately. It certainly doesn't approach the ambition of President Johnson, who told aides hours after he assumed the presidency that he wanted "every boy and girl in this country to get all the education they can take."

We need an educational system that challenges our brightest students to realize their potential; otherwise, we will no longer be a superpower. But we also need to ensure a high-quality education for every child. Even though many of them won't become inventors or theorists or seminal thinkers, they will be competent in the basics and they will know how and where to find the information they need. Mastering the basics seems like a modest aspiration, but it is crucial. Without a competent workforce, the new ideas and technological breakthroughs will languish—or be taken up in some other country, one with a competent, well-educated labor force.

I remember October 4, 1957, as if it were yesterday. The school principal came into our ninth-grade math class and announced that the Soviet Union had just put the first satellite into Earth orbit. We were shocked and more than a little alarmed about what it meant for our national security. *Sputnik* shook the country out of its postwar lethargy. Suddenly, in the middle of a cold war, America was behind in space technology. To meet the Soviet challenge, Congress passed the National Defense Education Act. Thousands of engineering scholarships became available. President Eisenhower called on young people to meet this challenge. Several of my high school friends decided they would become engineers, and a few did. The nation had a purpose that motivated a generation, and the ambitions of those young engineers matched the need.

The national need today is even more pressing than it was in 1957. While other countries can produce products more cheaply than we can in the United States, we must out-think, out-invent, and out-synthesize them. Everything from the technology of our weapons to the quality of our environment depends on education. Even the maintenance of democracy itself is at stake. Yet today we deny reality. Our schools are trapped in inertia. There has been no external shock—no burning building—to wake us up. We drift, while other nations gain on us.

THE NEW STORY

We don't have to accept an obsolete educational system with underperforming principals and teachers, unchallenged students, and educational mediocrity. We can tell a new story about education, one that makes education so exciting that kids don't want to leave at the end of the school day; one in which a child's imagination and capacity to dream are encouraged along with a facility in algebra; one in which talented teachers with the best technology tailor instruction individually to produce knowledgeable and creative students; one in which principals are allowed to impose high intellectual standards and rewarded generously when they succeed; one in which teachers are well-paid, held accountable for results, and given the respect they deserve.

To realize this new story's promise, we have to reevaluate the mind-sets that keep us trapped in the past: the agrarian society's nine-month school year, the six-and-a-half-hour school day, the uniformity of classroom periods, the lack of time afforded students for independent scholastic work. In the new story, the creation of new school designs, thanks to greater federal attention to research and development, will become a national goal. We want high scores on math tests, but we don't want to turn our children into robots who haven't learned enough about government to understand how to work together in our democracy. We want students who can show their mastery of a subject to their peers, to parents, and the community at science fairs, school assemblies, and community meetings. We will give prizes for creativity in all subjects.

In the new story, teachers know the names of all their students and form collaborative relationships with parents—relationships that might be as simple as regular phone contact or as complex as Internet monitoring of each student's performance against a set of criteria measuring skills, attitude, and overall progress. The wide-eyed openness to learning we see in the young in first and second grade should continue into middle school and high school. Motivating students to learn is a top priority. School districts ensure that their teachers have the latest technology. Students learn the math drills via computer, allowing teachers to do what only they can do, which is deal with the unique learning style of each student. By reading, writing, researching, and exploring on computers, students can learn a lot more on their own than they do now. Teachers thus freed up can function as coaches, creating an atmosphere of high expectations without the debilitating anxiety that impedes the risk taking necessary for real learning. Beyond schools, technology can create communities of learning that extend from local to global and from young to old.

In the new story, the federal Department of Education becomes an action-oriented organization that deploys SWAT teams of experts to districts that request help on a wide range of issues: the introduction of innovative curricula, the creation of a self-motivated school culture, response to the unique challenges faced by a majority of non-English-speaking students. The employees of this reconstituted Department of Education are less like bureaucrats and more like Marines. To buttress efforts at the federal level, regional consortiums of schools will be established, so that schools can share their experience and best practices with one another. If we can put men on the moon, surely by the seventh grade our students ought to be technologically savvy, sound in math, reading, and science, proficient in at least one foreign language, aware of our history, and motivated to broaden their knowledge and skills in high school.

In the new story, teaching will become one of the nation's most popular professions. With more freedom to do what they really want to do, teachers will thrive. College graduates will see elementary and secondary school teaching as a rewarding career, with sufficient pay—one in which they can have a profound impact on other people's lives. Teaching will become a prestigious profession of meaning once again.

To bring this new story into existence will take a huge effort over many years. There is tremendous inertia, and there are tremendous pressures that work to keep the status quo in public education. To shake up the public school system will unsettle many special interests. It will force those who assumed they had all the answers to consider other legitimate points of view. It will demand accountability for how the taxpayers' money has been spent.

• • •

What policies will it take to implement the new story?

1. Establishment of national standards for testing and curriculum, especially in math, science, reading, and foreign languages, is essential for American students to be able to

compete in a global economy. Rigid local control makes no sense in our interconnected world.

2. Talented young people need to be attracted into the teaching profession. There is already a palpable thirst for service among young people; 12 percent of 2005's graduating class at Yale, for example, applied to Teach for America, an organization that sends recently graduated college students to teach in poor urban and rural school districts. Unfortunately, after three years only 34 percent are still teaching. Money is one reason. Matt Miller reports in *The 2% Solution* that, according to the former New York City schools chancellor Harold Levy, the difference in 1970 between what a first-year lawyer was paid at a prestigious Manhattan firm and what a first-year teacher was paid in the city school system was $2,000, whereas the differential today is $103,000. Teacher salaries should be as much as doubled and allocated based on student performance against standards developed in part by teachers themselves. Math and science teachers should be paid even more. A pedagogical hierarchy should be established, with a required minimum number of years of experience at each level. The federal government should subsidize teacher salaries for the biggest urban and poorest rural and suburban systems and then reduce Title I funding that doesn't go to teachers. The best students should be challenged to advance as rigorously as the worst students are. Mainstreaming should not hold back those with the greatest potential and ability. With regard to performance, perhaps it is the schools that should be judged, not individual teachers. When teachers know they will be rewarded if their school makes substantial progress or retains a high rating, they will have an incentive to build a better school. A lot of bad teachers will be identified and weeded out by the teachers themselves.

3. Responsibility for overall school performance, however, will lie with the principal, who should be involved in the recruitment of teachers and the measurement of their performance in accordance with standards set in part by the teachers themselves. Principals should be given new authority, in cooperation

with enlightened unions, to eliminate bad teachers. Cutting the costs of administration, which include the costs of state bureaucracy and amount to more than a tenth of today's public education budget, will allow more money for principal and teacher salaries. Principals will be judged on the performance of their schools—which will be measured against other schools with the same proportion of poor, minority, special education, and non-English-speaking students. As the New York City schools chancellor Joel Klein has proposed, the important criteria are "English and math test scores and school safety and attendance for elementary and middle schools, the principal's leadership skills, parental involvement, and how effectively schools use data to monitor students."

4. Elementary and secondary school teachers need continuing education. We expect doctors to keep up with their field, and airline pilots are required to take fresh training and competency tests at regular intervals. Teachers should be no different. A high school physics teacher who is fifty years old can't coast on what he learned thirty years earlier. When I was a visiting professor at Notre Dame in 1998, an inner-city junior high school class from Benton Harbor, Michigan, attended my public lecture on education policy. After I spoke, one student asked me why, if he and his classmates had to take tests to make sure they knew their subject, teachers shouldn't have to do the same. He got a good laugh from the young audience, but he had a point. Teachers should be required to attend classes in the latest teaching innovations, and they should be periodically required to pass a test in their subject. One month every three years should be added to the teachers' work year, during which they would have to take a special, upgraded, and federally financed continuing education course in their chosen field.

5. Children need more school and smaller classes. A five-year demonstration should be set up in some sizable district, or even in an entire state, in which kids go to school for 220 days out of the year and for eight hours a day. Delaware, with its 121,000 public school children in nineteen districts, would

be a good test case. Teacher pay, performance, and class size are key factors here: If teachers are incompetent and poorly paid, with thirty-five kids in a class, then putting children in classrooms for eight hours a day instead of six will not improve the quality of their education. Classes should be much smaller. Each child deserves more attention. With two additional hours each day, a school could offer more science and math but also more opportunity for creative learning in music, painting, creative writing, and dance. Proficiency in these subjects may not be measurable by test scores, but it pays off in areas where there is no less need: cooperation, tolerance, discipline, and dedication to a calling. The easiest way to achieve smaller classes is by simply requiring that funds under No Child Left Behind go to a school only if it has a three-year plan to achieve class sizes of eighteen students in grades K–2, twenty-two in grades 3–8, and twenty-four in high school. An alternative way to meet the requirement would be to increase the number of teachers in the classroom.

6. The federal government should give out 1,000 teaching prizes annually. The awards would be for teacher proposals showing innovation and excellence in teaching; winning proposals would be funded and each winning teacher would receive a $50,000 stipend.

7. Children need to start learning early. A national prekindergarten program should be available for any student whose parents want it. Those early years make all the difference in children's readiness to learn once they enter elementary school. According to experts, in the last twenty years, 70 percent of the children of college graduates attended prekindergarten programs, but only 38 percent of the children of high school dropouts did so. The federal government should spend $7 to $10 billion per year on such a program if the state and local governments will spend the other $9 to $17 billion in additional funding necessary to make it universal.

8. More money should be spent on education research. Of the

$475 billion spent annually on public school education in this country, only 0.1 percent goes to research and development. A comparable private company would spend anywhere from 3 to 5 percent of its annual budget on research and development. Christopher Whittle, the founder and CEO of Edison Schools Inc.—which now oversees 330,000 students at 136 schools in 25 states, the District of Columbia, and the United Kingdom—advocates the establishment of a national education research institute comparable to the National Institutes of Health (NIH) or the Defense Advanced Research Projects Agency (DARPA). Such an institute would be a fertile source of ideas, designs, and intellectual standards. Health care is a $2 trillion industry, and the NIH spends $27 billion annually on health-related research. If the same proportion of money were to be spent on education research, it would amount to $6.5 billion per year. It would take only a small fraction of that amount to reconceive our school systems totally. Some will say we already know what to do to improve our schools and the problem is that we don't spend enough money to do it. But surely we haven't thought of all the ways to improve a system designed 100 years ago.

Whittle has suggested that the federal government sponsor a competition for the development of the best school designs—including curriculum, structure of the school day, forms of compensation, and nonacademic school organization. Entries in the contest could come from all three sectors: the private, the nonprofit, and the public; the only limitation would be that a proposal ought to represent no more than a 10 percent increase over current spending on the public school system. The top three designs would be funded for three years each and then evaluated, with the results distributed to the states and championed by the president. The innovations could be startling. Among them might be experimenting with 100 kids in a lecture class, as happens in college, or 15 kids per math class; or organizing a high school like an office, with a computer at each workstation; or requiring teachers and principals to make student motivation a major emphasis; or tailoring subjects to make them relevant to the wider world.

9. The newly created National Institute of Education should take a close look at our graduate schools of education. Graduate work in every discipline requires a unique, innovative contribution to that discipline. A PhD degree in microbiology, for example, requires a novel experiment, peer review, and defense. In the end, the candidate earns his or her doctorate by contributing to the field of study. Our graduate schools of education do not put such a premium on original thought. They should. New education PhDs should shake the system up and bring innovation to it.

10. To guarantee accountability in the fifty largest school districts in America, ultimate responsibility for school performance must fall to an elected leader—the mayor. While there is always the danger of patronage jobs in a school system, the teachers' union, as watchdog of administrative expenses, could become a check on that tendency. After all, any dollar wasted on a mayoral no-show job is a dollar that could have gone to a teacher. In New York and Chicago, and recently to a lesser degree in Los Angeles, the mayors have already taken over the school systems. Joel Klein and Arne Duncan, his Chicago counterpart, oversee these reforms with the enthusiasm of men who want to change the world. They and their mayoral bosses meet regularly with parents (read, voters) on school organization and performance. Mayors are likely to lose reelection if, after assuming responsibility for results, they neglect their schools. That's accountability, too.

11. Finally, we must counter the reemergence of segregation in urban school districts. One way to attract white students to schools that are predominantly black is to make those schools the best schools in the area. It starts with an all-out effort to recruit excellent principals, pay them a salary commensurate with their responsibility, and hold them accountable. Instead of attracting the least competent and most inexperienced teachers to these inner-city districts, it should be national pol-

icy to attract the best teachers there by paying them bonuses that could double their salaries and maybe even offer housing allowances. The federal government should use the leverage of Title I funding to support differential pay structures. The effort could begin with the young and idealistic who want to correct one of America's most flagrant social wrongs.

With the right principal and teachers, any child can be reached eventually. To say otherwise smacks of racism. To those who argue that we have to eliminate poverty before we can improve the urban public schools, I say go to a classroom of eager third-graders in the Bronx or South Atlanta or Houston and look into their eyes; see if you don't care that by the time they're sixth-graders many of them—because of over-crowded classes, a peer culture of indifference, and an environment that is too often violent—will have tuned out of education altogether. We cannot allow the 5 percent of kids who don't want to learn to make it impossible for the 95 percent who do.

The civil rights movement was an effort to overcome injustice. Today there is no greater injustice than in our failing, segregated urban schools. At least let us have equal funding for urban schools, as well as teachers and principals who are leaders and have the freedom to lead and the ability to inspire.

Once we are serious about making our worst schools into our best schools, drastic action is needed. In addition to prekindergarten classes, smaller classes, and support for increasing teacher and principal salaries, we will need to give parents a choice of public schools. We will need to give every child a per capita amount of education funding, which travels with him or her to the public school of choice and which, when it arrives, becomes money for the principal to spend in whatever way he or she chooses that will improve the school, including security. Every district that adopts this kind of choice plan will get a bonus payment from the federal government. We also need the elimination of federal barriers to the establishment of charter schools; assistance to districts in the areas of transportation, finance management, and procurement; and a reduction in bureaucracy and patronage jobs. When all this is done, white suburban families will pay to send their kids to the urban school, because it has a higher percentage than the suburban schools of graduates accepted by prestigious colleges.

Our largest untapped national resource is the great number of Latino and black children stuck in impoverished urban and rural schools. Putting the effort and money into getting these kids interested in science and math early, and giving them teachers who will expect them to succeed against tough standards and provide them with loving support, will make America a stronger and more just country.

Today there is a convergence between our moral imperatives as a nation and what we have to do to keep our technological edge. America needs the talents of all its children. To write off the millions in impoverished urban and rural districts and allow the drift in our suburban and small-town schools to continue is to admit defeat, squander our potential, increase the costs of crime and illiteracy, and renege on the promises made by the Founders. We're a better people than that!

But it's our choice.

Summary

THE NEW AMERICAN STORY

For a reasonable amount of money we can make sure that every child in America has a great education, that all Americans have health insurance, and that all our workers have secure pensions. With a reorientation of our tax system we can do what we want to do on education, health, and pensions, as well as reduce our dependence on foreign oil, clean up the environment, increase national savings, encourage employment, and allow Americans to keep more of each additional dollar they earn. Outlined here are all the elements of the New American Story that have federal tax and spending implications. As you see, there are more savings than there is spending. The difference could be used to reduce the budget deficit or cut taxes. My purpose is to demonstrate how easily in terms of the budget the New American Story can be realized. The numbers are approximate based on solid evidence, but as with all projections, they are just informed estimates. The important thing is to show that there is more than enough to do what we want to do for the country. As with all family budgets, it's just a matter of allocation and income.

What We Get (What It Costs the Federal Government)

I. Economy and Oil

- Reduce employment taxes (Social Security, Medicare, or unemployment insurance) ($100 billion)—see pages 83–84
- Increase investment in basic and applied research at universities and government institutes ($5 billion)—see pages 71–74
- Increase the earned income tax credit ($16 billion)—see pages 80–82
- Provide rebates to those who purchase fuel-efficient vehicles ($20 billion)—see page 110

II. Pensions

- Make the Social Security system good for seventy-five years—see pages 78–80, 123–28
- Create a new federal program matching annual individual pension contributions up to $20,000 per year (up to $140 billion)—see pages 129–30
- Infuse capital into the Pension Benefit Guaranty Corporation ($23 billion per year for three years)—see pages 116–19, 128
- Establish a birthright grant of $5,000 for every child born in America after 2008 ($20 billion)—see page 130

III. Health Care

- Provide health care for all Americans: single-payer option ($300 billion initially, much less over time) or mandatory coverage for all Americans with subsidies for people of moderate incomes ($100 billion)—see pages 150–52
- Establish a federal institute to determine the cost-effectiveness of drugs, medical devices, and medical technology ($500 million)—see page 144

IV. EDUCATION

- Increase teacher and principal salaries in hard-pressed urban, rural, and suburban areas to as much as twice current salaries in exchange for differentiated pay for teachers and the measuring of teacher performance against a set of standards developed in part by the teachers themselves ($60 billion)—see pages 163–68, 172

- Require one month every three years of summer continuing education in their chosen field for all 2.9 million teachers ($2.7 billion)—see page 173

- Establish 1,000 teaching prizes annually that fund proposals showing innovation and excellence in teaching and give each winning teacher a stipend of $50,000 ($100 million)—see page 174

- Establish universal prekindergarten with an offer of a federal government annual contribution of $10 billion—see page 174

- Set up an NIH-type education research and development agency and create a competition for the best school design—including curriculum, structure of the school day, forms of compensation, and nonacademic school organization, with the three winners getting funding for three years ($1 billion)—see pages 174–76

- Encourage public school choice ($5 billion)—see page 177

- Provide assistance in finance, human resources, and transportation to large urban school districts ($1 billion)—see pages 177–78

- Provide free college tuition and fees up to $12,000 per student for academic high school seniors in the top third of their classes and more for math, science, engineering, and graduate study ($30 billion in year five)—see pages 71–74, 85

V. OTHER

- Support creation of an international environmental lending institution to help poor countries reduce global warming ($1 billion)—see page 53

- Publicly fund congressional and presidential campaigns ($2 billion)—see pages 209–12, 219–20

- Pay the U.S. share of the $10 to $15 billion necessary to assure pri-

mary education for children living in poor countries ($3 billion)—
see pages 52–53

TOTAL: $540 to $740 billion depending on health care choice

How We Pay for It

- Make Social Security solvent for seventy-five years: new state and
  local government employees join the Social Security system;
  upper-income Americans pay Social Security taxes on more income; the elderly get slightly lower cost-of-living adjustments;
  workers have to work three years longer—phased in fully by 2099;
  eligibility for disability is narrowly liberalized between sixty-seven
  and seventy—see pages 78–80, 123–28
- Cut defense spending 10 percent ($50 billion)—see pages 76–77
- Cut corporate welfare 30 percent ($30 billion)—see pages 84, 100
- Cut earmarked appropriations ($20 billion)—see page 79
- Reduce oil subsidies by 30 percent ($21 billion)—see pages
  110–11
- Cut farm subsidies for the wealthiest farmers ($7 billion)—see
  page 84
- Reduce medical errors and costs that flow from them ($125 bil-
  lion)—see pages 145–50, 153
- Make greater use of preventive medicine ($10 billion)—see page 147
- Reap savings from electronic records in health care ($40 billion;
  the Markle Foundation says $125 billion in total is possible)—see
  pages 145, 153
- Limit the health tax exclusion for employer-paid health insurance
  ($50 billion) or eliminate it in the context of moving to a single-
  payer system ($150 billion)—see pages 150–54
- End hospital subsidies for treating the uninsured ($40 billion)—
  see page 152
- Shift from Title I education to higher teacher and principal
  salaries ($5 billion)—see page 172
- Raise the income tax progressively in the context of tax reform,
  which lowers tax rates and eliminates loopholes ($140 billion)—
  see pages 80–82

- Eliminate the deduction for defined-contribution pension plans ($140 billion)—see pages 129–30
- Increase IRS collection of taxes by adding more agents and technology ($9 billion)—see page 82
- Impose a $1 per gallon gas tax or carbon tax or equivalent tax on natural resources and/or pollution ($100 billion)—see page 83
- Adopt a fee-rebate system that assesses a fee on fuel-inefficient vehicles ($20 billion)—see page 110

TOTAL: $807 to $907 billion depending on health care choice

Part III.

THE POLITICAL LANDSCAPE

Chapter 9.

POLITICS

In the second part of this book, I discussed what needs to be done. In this third part, I want to explore the tools at our disposal and the obstacles built into any attempts to effect large-scale change in this country. This means confronting our politics: how it works and how it could be improved; why the Republican Party, as now constituted, can't realize the New American Story; and why the Democrats have chosen not to take it up. The answers to these questions lie buried in each party's history and in the lessons politicians have drawn from our recent past. Yet power in our democracy rests not with the elected but with the people. Citizens banding together are still the most potent force for change, and when they come together in a profound way, what was considered political death to attempt becomes good politics. Which of our political parties will most effectively carry out the new story? Are they, as currently constituted, up to this enormous task?

Politics helps democracy answer two questions: What rules do we have to abide by, and who gets what? Politics is how democracy takes ideas and turns them into action. The former Republican senator Alan Simpson has said, "In politics there are no right answers, only a continuing series of compromises among groups resulting in a changing, cloudy, and ambiguous series of public decisions, where appetite and ambition compete openly with knowledge and wisdom."

Often, it is a messy business. The cynical and the idealistic operate side by side. But it's important to remember that politics replaces violence or oppression as a way to organize the life of the state. And there are moments when politics produces beautiful music that leads to greater liberty or social advancement. Elections historically have been less than pure: Sometimes they were stolen; often economic power dominated them; almost always, they were predicated on promises that could never be kept. But in the end, more times than not, the people have had their say.

When I was in the U.S. Senate, I kept two framed prints on my office wall. One was a series of four etchings about British democracy by the eighteenth-century artist William Hogarth; the other was a print of the nineteenth-century Missourian George Caleb Bingham's *The County Election*. Both depicted what Election Day looked like in their respective eras: politicians making speeches; petitioners seeking jobs and favors; neighbors engaging in animated conversation; men of means lording it over the crowd; party officials presiding over the vote; suspicious characters lurking in the shadows; children excited by the commotion; much food, liquor, and even money changing hands; and finally, a few sad souls sitting by the side of the road begging for help.

I always felt that something very human emanated from those works of art. They showed you how politics mixes the mighty and the weak and puts them on equal footing: Each person has only one vote. If you boil politics down to its essence, it is about people in all their shapes and sizes. It is about their fears and anxieties as well as their hopes and dreams. It is a profession in which personal will, persistence, hard work, intelligence, and a sense of humor can carry you a long way. To people on the outside, it seems crass, even dirty, full of vain, preening politicians and ambitious, self-seeking supporters. Yet among practitioners of the art, there are clear standards of what is acceptable and what is not.

The overwhelming number of officeholders are squeaky clean. They can be power-driven and honest simultaneously, and the drive for power itself can be admirable. The question is, What do you do with power once it is attained? Do you help only those you know or who can benefit you, or do you help strangers, too?

There are official ethics rules in many professions, including political places such as the U.S. Senate, but they aren't as influential as the generally agreed upon customs. Your honor is at stake when a clear code of conduct is policed by others whom you respect. In the Senate, in my time, you could get away with embellishing your position on an issue, but breaking your word was a sure path to failure.

In my last year there, I offered an amendment to an appropriations bill dealing with the safety of natural gas pipelines in heavily populated areas such as New Jersey. All amendments are supposed to be germane to the appropriation. If the bill deals with defense, you aren't supposed to offer an amendment dealing with transportation. From time to time, senators would offer amendments that weren't germane, and if the amendments were popular, they sometimes passed. The risk that day in 1996 was that my amendment was not germane. If it passed, it could lead to other amendments that might sink the bill if they were adopted. The Senate majority leader at the time was Trent Lott (R.–Miss.), whom I did not know well. He came to me on the Senate floor and asked me to withdraw my amendment. I said no. He asked twice again, over the course of several hours. Finally, he told me that if I withdrew the amendment, he would assure me that, as majority leader, with power to set the schedule and a pocket full of chits, he would get it passed on another bill. He gave me his word. I then pulled the amendment down. A few months later I left the Senate and the amendment had still not been placed on another bill. I went into private life. One day the following fall, when I was teaching at Stanford, I got a phone call from Trent Lott's office. It was his chief of staff, who told me that the amendment I had withdrawn the previous year had just passed the Senate. I was floored. I was no longer in the Senate; I certainly couldn't help Trent Lott anymore. Yet as an honorable man he had kept his word.

Besides being a better way than violence for a society to make decisions, politics can be a pressure valve for frustration and anger. If you're a politician, you're the target of those feelings; it comes with the territory. I frequently felt the sting of people's anger about circumstances far beyond my control. In those moments, I said to my-self, "There's nothing I can do about the source of their anger, so relax and enjoy being the piñata."

In August 1983, the Soviet Union shot down Korean Air Lines 007, which had strayed into Soviet airspace. Two days later, I was moving up the beaches of New Jersey, conducting my annual four-day walking town meeting with thousands of New Jerseyans. Out-rage over the Soviet act swelled up from the beachgoers like the surge of a nor'easter. They wanted to strike back. They demanded that the U.S. government do something—now! It was in moments such as this that I appreciated the Founders' wisdom in making the Senate term six years and not the two-year cycle of a representative, with its vulnerability to the emotion of the moment.

The constant collision of power and principle, human folly and human nobility, produces hundreds of stories. Some of them are sad: bright people with vision who faltered because of a blindness to ethical nuance; experienced and competent officeholders who lost elections because time had passed them by; idealistic politicians who allowed incumbency and comfort to erode their convictions bit by bit, until there was nothing left but self-promotion. Sometimes the stories are comical. A Democratic New Jersey pol who was the boss of part of a county was very interested in who controlled county government and the governor's office, for these posts had prosecutor appointments and money to bestow. Congress seemed far removed from his sphere, yet he needed to fill the federal slot on the primary ballot with someone who wouldn't give him trouble, so he selected his lieutenant—call him Joe—who wasn't the smartest guy in the world. Joe wouldn't have much of a chance against the Republican incumbent, but he was conscientious. After he won the primary (whose outcome was predetermined by the boss's machine), he went to the boss and asked, "What should we do now?" The boss looked at him and said, "Joe, we're going to follow the Winnebago strategy."

"What's that?" Joe asked.

"Starting tomorrow," the boss replied, "I want you to get into the Winnebago and not come out until after the election."

What It Demands

New Jersey politics was a long way from life in the small town in Missouri I grew up in. I didn't have a political childhood. Rarely was conversation around the dinner table about politics. Although my father was Republican, I don't know to this day which party my mother supported. My interest in the wider world of politics came from sitting in our basement reading *Life* magazines about World War II and the diplomacy leading up to it, feeling the excitement of my aunt's campaign for the office of county assessor as a Republican in an overwhelmingly Democratic county, listening to Edward R. Murrow's *I Can Hear It Now* records, over and over, and sitting in silence with my father as he listened to the radio news each night at 6:00 p.m.

When I was a senior in high school, I wrote a term paper about the presidential contest of 1896 between William Jennings Bryan and William McKinley. I can still smell the old library books I used for my research. I marvelled at the campaign and became a fan of McKinley's campaign manager, Mark Hanna. Once, after a high school basketball game, a reporter asked me whom I most admired. I named the evangelist Billy Graham, the basketball player Bob Pettit, and Mark Hanna. But politics didn't become personal to me until the civil rights revolution. It was then that I saw firsthand how politics could make America a better place. With my appetite whetted, I read Ted Sorensen's memoir of JFK and Teddy White's *The Making of the President, 1960*. It occurred to me that I'd rather be a politician than the State Department diplomat I had thought I wanted to become when I was reading those *Life* magazines in the basement. And then Robert Kennedy sealed the deal for me. I heard him speak in the summer of 1964, when I was a college intern in Washington. He talked about politics as a noble profession and said that there was no higher calling; he talked about the joys of making the world a better place; about the need for all people to be treated equally before the law; about struggling on in dark days, against the odds, because you believed in something larger than yourself; and about the country—its history, its promise, and what it meant to the world. As he spoke, I realized that politics was my calling. It would take years of experimentation and soul searching before I arrived as a candidate in 1978, but the seed was planted in 1964.

As I looked more closely at American history, I saw how integral politics was to the great decisions of our country's life, bringing the politician and the moment together to transform the nation for the better. John Adams and Thomas Jefferson effected change through politics. From the founding of the country on, and especially in the presidential race of 1800, their conflict was epochal, personal, even vicious, but as old men they became close friends, having shared the basic convictions about democracy that led to the formation of the country and the establishment of the two-party system. Abraham Lincoln was acting as a master politician when he brought his rivals into the cabinet and made them as responsible as he was for the fate of his administration. Teddy Roosevelt and Woodrow Wilson ran the ideal political campaign in 1912, full of unequivocal differences beautifully expressed with a confidence that the people could be trusted with the truth as the candidates saw it.

Franklin Delano Roosevelt enjoyed the game of politics. He loved the performance of his speeches, the human interactions through which his persuasive powers flowed, the improvisation that kept hope alive and conditions improving for average people. He insisted, for instance, that every person in America get a Social Security card. When an actuary from the Social Security Administration protested that it wasn't actuarially sound to suggest that each person have his or her own personal account, FDR threw his head back laughing and said he knew that, but the card, by giving all Americans tangible evidence of their stake in the system, would keep those SOBs on Capitol Hill from repealing the law. He sometimes changed his positions on issues the way a man changes his tie. Having run in 1932 on a platform that included a balanced budget, he became the first deliberate deficit spender—because that was what the country needed and that was what gave him the people's support. As the economist John Maynard Keynes once replied in answer to a question about why he had changed his position on an issue, "When circumstances change, I change my views. What do you do, sir?"

Sometimes American politics can be bipartisan, as with Harry Truman's foreign policy at the end of World War II or Lyndon Johnson's civil rights legislation of the 1960s or Richard Nixon's and Gerald Ford's environmental laws of the 1970s. Other times you draw the line in the sand and mobilize your base, as Ronald Reagan did with his Supreme Court appointments and Bill Clinton did on his first budget.

For every Woodrow Wilson, there was a Colonel Edward House and Joseph P. Tumulty, who constantly thought of politics—what was possible, how to get it done, how to pass a law, how to win an election. FDR had James Farley. Truman had Clark Clifford and his former colleagues in the U.S. Senate. Dwight Eisenhower had Sherman Adams and Leonard Hall. JFK had Robert Kennedy and Lawrence O'Brien. Lyndon Johnson had many advisers but no political confidants, and maybe that is why he stumbled; Richard Nixon had H. R. Haldeman and John Ehrlichman, which may have been why *he* stumbled. Jimmy Carter had Jody Powell and Hamilton Jordan. Ronald Reagan had Michael Deaver, James Baker, and Edwin Meese. George H. W. Bush had John Sununu and Lee Atwater. Bill Clinton had Hillary Clinton and a cast of political courtiers, each of whom postured as the president's man or woman. And George W. Bush has Karl Rove, who sees himself as another Mark Hanna. What such advisers do is help a president turn his agenda into reality. Nothing gets done if you simply make great speeches. Someone has to crack the whip, figure out how to get a majority in Congress, and most important, understand what at least 50 percent of the electorate will support. Policy without politics is just talk; politics without policy is wasted energy.

When I ran for the Senate in 1978, I knew very little about practical politics. I had never run for office before, but I had made appearances for office seekers since 1972. I cared about policy, liked to campaign, and enjoyed people. I ran against the New Jersey Democratic political machine of the time, which was on its last legs. People felt they knew me because I had been on their living room televisions twice a week for ten years as a professional basketball player in New York. They had seen me in pressure situations. My celebrity put two hundred people instead of fifty in a room to hear me speak, which meant I could fail or succeed before four times as many voters as my opponents.

One thing I learned from that campaign was to respect the professional politicians who had worked in the party and in various government jobs for decades. They may not have had advanced degrees in economics, but they understood life, the illusory aspects of power, and what made people tick. I was an outsider, but they knew and liked me. My job—since virtually the whole political establishment, from the governor to the lowliest of mayors, had endorsed my opponent—was to make sure they didn't have a pretext to work hard against me. Even though they weren't supporting me, I talked with many of them on a regular basis. It was my way of telling them that I understood their importance in our democracy and realized that they had to support my opponent because the governor had asked them to. The subtext was that I knew, if they could have decided for themselves, they would have been with me. I had coffee with one big-city mayor, a basketball fan, once a week in his office, hoping he could fulfill his obligation to the governor without pulling out all the stops to beat me. He managed to keep that balance, and I won the primary handily and then the general election.

Three years later, the New Jersey governorship went to a Republican. Many Democrats wanted me to become, in effect, the state party's hands-on leader. I couldn't do that and be a U.S. senator, too, so I said no. Each of us has to decide where we can best serve. I felt if I spent my time selecting who got the party endorsement for each county post, I wouldn't have enough time left to do the job the people elected me to do. Besides, at the time my most important bond was with the people, not the politicians. As long as I maintained that relationship, raised a lot of money, and won big, I figured that the politicians would give me their respect.

But going directly to the people takes on new meaning when you run for president of the United States. The politics of running for that office dwarf any other kind of politics. I ran in 2000 and got knocked out early. Even though my loss in New Hampshire was the narrowest in the state's presidential primary history and the delegate count after Iowa and New Hampshire stood at only 42 delegates for

Al Gore and 27 for me out of a total of 2,169 needed for the nomination, the press declared it over. My long-shot race against an
incumbent vice president had missed.

Thinking about those eighteen months I spent running for president brings back a rush of memories: of the campaign kickoff before
my family and childhood friends in my hometown of Crystal City,
Missouri; of decorous gatherings in people's living rooms or back-
yards; of raucous town meetings full of unpredictability, and
speeches before thousands of supporters; of interest groups mar-
shalling their power and making their threats; of an event at Madison Square Garden in which my former teammates and opponents
returned to the Garden court to offer their testimonials of support;
of flying in small planes across Iowa in summer, with the farms and
their rows of newly sprouted corn stretching as far as the eye could
see; of New Hampshire in the fall, with its subtle vistas and changing leaves in all their colorful grandeur; of motel rooms in small
Iowa towns in winter that had no thermostats, so you either kept the
heat off and froze or turned it on and sweated the night through; of
bumper stickers in New England that read, "Another Celtic Fan
for Bradley"; of driving through snow with my three staunchest
supporters—Senator Bob Kerrey, Senator Paul Wellstone, and Professor Cornel West—on the eve of the New Hampshire primary; of
urban communities across the country crackling with energy and
grasping for some reason to hope; of gatherings along the Texas-
Mexico border, where some Mexican Americans had lived for five
generations and the musical rhythms of the Spanish language reminded you that America was changing; of so many meetings with
local officials and party members and potential volunteers that
places and faces blurred; of sixteen-hour days at fairs and festivals
and football games; of enlisting fund-raisers who had never raised
political money before but were committed to me, undaunted by
political threats, and willing to give it a try; of the unique pressures
before a big debate and the spin afterward that often determined the
"winner"; of the relentless investigation of your personal background by press and opponents, so that nothing in your life up to
that time was private and every shortcoming was trumpeted; of people's eyes filled with hope when they looked at you and saw a poten-

tial president; of the vastness of this land from sea to sea and the magnificent diversity and goodness of its people.

Several years after he lost the presidential race, Walter Mondale is said to have asked George McGovern, another defeated presidential candidate, "George, when do you get over it?" To which McGovern replied, "Never." Although my defeat was only in the primaries, I identify with the sentiment.

The politics of a presidential primary race is similar to conducting a 5,000-person orchestra—it's hard to get it to do exactly what you want. The race is in part a guerrilla war of organizing new people outside the political culture; in this sense it is more like attracting customers to an entirely new product than running a new national ad campaign for Coca-Cola. But it is also a classic land war of getting the big tanks of politics—the county and state parties, the unions, the large interest groups—to endorse your candidacy. And all of it has to be packaged so as to get the attention of the press, whose appetite is unquenchable. The press, not the political bosses, now determine the victor in a presidential primary. They know it, and you know it. Depending on their collective judgment, a candidate's strength one month can become a fatal weakness the following month: Authenticity can be praised as honesty or criticized as lacking in political sophistication. Independence can be called acting from strength or not being a team player. Passion can explain why people flock to your candidacy or why you seem inflexible and stubborn. The list goes on and on. The naïve candidate thinks the game can be controlled, and some manage to do that—for a while. But inevitably, the iron rule of celebrity takes effect: The faster and higher you go up, the sooner and stronger will forces be set in motion to bring you down. It's a cycle as sure as the seasons. Timing is everything. You want your peak to come on Election Day.

A presidential campaign highlights the problems with our politics from the vantage point of only one office. The same difficulties crop up in congressional, state, and local races. To understand these problems, you have to understand their context: In America today, politics emphasizes conflict. Compromise is out and confrontation is in. Never mind how the American people really feel.

The Red and the Blue

The biggest political lie perpetrated on the American people in the last half century is that the country is irrevocably polarized between those who are conservative and live in "red states" in the heartland and those who are liberal and live in "blue states" along the two coasts. The consensus among pundits, amplified by the media, is that the old economic divisions have given way to a deep schism on morality, religion, and sexuality. After the 2004 presidential election, exit polls revealed that 22 percent of voters let "moral values" determine how they voted—the next highest category being jobs and the economy, close behind at 20 percent. In *The Age of Anxiety: McCarthyism to Terrorism*, Haynes Johnson, one of America's great journalists, raises the issue of "moral values" in a political context and asks,

> Which morals, which values? Yours or mine? The morality taught by Jesus, Moses, Mohammed, Buddha, Confucius, or agnostics and atheists? The morality of sanctioning torture, of imprisoning innocents, of lying about the reasons for launching a pre-emptive war, trampling on civil rights and liberties, or helping the powerful at the expense of the powerless?

The media do not ask these kinds of questions or demand this kind of clarity. Instead, there is talk of the moral abyss yawning between red states and blue states. As Terry Mattingly of the *Knoxville News Sentinel* wrote of the 2000 election, it's "Hollywood vs. Nashville . . . National Public Radio vs. talk radio . . . *The New York Times* vs. *National Review Online*, Dan Rather vs. Rush Limbaugh, Rosie O'Donnell vs. Dr. Laura, Barbra Streisand vs. Dr. James Dobson." David Broder, the dean of national political writers, wrote in *The Washington Post* of the 2000 presidential race, "The divide went deeper than politics. It reached into the nation's psyche. . . . It was the moral dimension that kept Bush in the race." In October 2003, George W. Bush's campaign strategist Matthew Dowd told Ronald Brownstein of the *Los Angeles Times*, "You've got 80% to 90% of the country that look at each other like they are on separate planets."

On the eve of the last presidential election, *The Economist* observed that "America is more bitterly divided than it has been for a generation."

Morris Fiorina, a political science professor at Stanford University who has collected these assertions, effectively demolishes them in his remarkable little book *Culture War? The Myth of a Polarized America.* He goes back through the National Election Studies, compiled at the University of Michigan under a National Science Foundation grant, which ask people postelection whether and how they voted. After reviewing all national elections since 1972, he concludes:

> The myth of a culture war rests on misinterpretation of election returns, lack of hard examination of polling data, systematic and self-serving misrepresentation by issue activists, and selective coverage by an uncritical media more concerned with news value than with getting the story right. There is little evidence that Americans' ideological or policy *positions* are more polarized today than they were two or three decades ago, although their *choices* often seem to be. The explanation is that the political figures Americans evaluate are more polarized. A polarized political class makes the citizenry appear polarized, but it is only that—an appearance.

What Fiorina shows is that people have a lot in common and that their positions, views, and beliefs, rather than shifting radically in the last thirty years, have remained remarkably the same. The center holds, with ferocious tenacity. Over the last several decades (except on the issue of abortion), those who classify themselves as liberals or conservatives haven't gotten any further apart. Polling data on controlling immigration, choosing the environment over jobs, believing the moral climate is wrong, supporting women's rights, school vouchers, English as the official language, and tolerance of others' moral views show a remarkable absence of disagreement in the country. In the postelection 2000 survey, only 14 percent of the respondents, in red and blue states alike, thought the Clinton budget surplus should be used to cut taxes. Paying off the national debt and increasing domestic spending scored higher, and between 35 and 38 percent of respondents, in red and blue states alike, felt the surplus should be used to bolster Social Security and Medicare.

Neither red nor blue states are "all" anything, even on hot-button issues. The 2000 National Election Study shows that 52 percent of red-state voters want gun control, 70 percent of people in the blue states favor the death penalty, and 62 percent of red-state voters say there should be no job discrimination against gays. The analyses show further that 63 percent of red-state voters approved of President Clinton's foreign policy, and 74 percent approved of his handling of the economy. The larger role that moral issues played in the elections of 1992 and 2000 was more the result of media interest in Bill Clinton's sex life than of any permanent shift in the importance of religion in politics. Indeed, in 1996, when Clinton's peccadilloes were no longer in the news and Republicans nominated Bob Dole, who was not a fire-breathing social conservative, the issue of morals played a minor role in the election outcome.

All the talk about red and blue states ignores the fact that, in twenty-three states in 2004, the minority party got at least 45 percent of the vote. And the election of 2006 showed that even in red states such as Bob Dole's Kansas there were sufficient numbers of moderate citizens to elect two moderate Democratic congresspeople and reelect a Democratic governor. The forces that bring us together as Americans are stronger than those that divide us. We have not become so polarized that neighbors of different parties can't root together for their favorite team, worship at the same church, set up a block party, work together at a local level and outside government to make our communities better places to raise our children. We share more than the political pundits, political consultants, and even some politicians acknowledge.

So how do you account for all the headlines and breathless debates on cable TV news shows about the fact that the country has never been more polarized? In part, the conflict story exists because the media like it; in part, because the political elites in each party confirm it. Each party goes for the other's jugular, egged on by consultants and political operatives who make a living out of electoral politics. Each party takes extreme positions on narrow issues and then attacks the other side; the media then amplify the conflict. The Washington press corps seems to have bought into the polarization story, partly because it shares the Washington-based culture with the political elites. The two groups socialize regularly. They read the same newspapers and newsmagazines; they send their kids to the same schools; they shop in the same supermarkets. They talk, talk, talk to one another, and in Washington there is one dominant topic of conversation: politics. Is it any wonder that the media reflect the views of the polarized elites, who continually solicit media attention? The loser here is the public, the vast majority of which does not share the extreme views of the Washington-based special interests that form the core of the two party coalitions.

The Special Interests

In the Democratic Party, the dominant interest groups are abortion activists, gay-rights activists, environmentalists, supporters of gun control, labor unionists, and trial lawyers. Only labor unionists have a broad-based agenda. In the Republican Party, the dominant groups are those who support the diametrically opposed positions, except in the case of the environment, a multifaceted issue on which some Republicans speak for a stewardship that is widely accepted by the public. Interest groups in both parties have strengthened over the years. Today they wield clout far beyond their numbers. Old-line party organizations have eroded, because there are fewer patronage jobs, so fewer citizens have a direct employment stake in the outcome of an election. After 1968, the Democratic Party changed its rules, such as those governing selection of delegates to the national convention. Since the reforms, the strength of the old barons of the party has eroded. Easier access to ballot positions for non-machine candidates, the drying up of money that came in brown paper bags, increased media scrutiny of candidates and congressional hearings, and the party rules that opened up delegate selection to grassroots supporters all put the kibosh on the old machine way of doing things.

Into this vacuum came what the political scientist Aaron Wildavsky called "purists." These are activists who devote most of their time to the political process, raise money from like-minded citizens, maintain lists of members filed by congressional districts, set up shop in Washington, DC, and try to influence Congress and the Executive Branch to adopt their view on a single specific issue. It doesn't matter how many Americans care about the issue, because *they* care about it, and they do their very best to impose this view on others. They activate their members in party primaries, which have much lower turnout than general elections. They get a disproportionate share of media coverage because their strident rhetoric makes for good TV. Because they're fervent, even relentless, they bully candidates. And as more and more purists become active, they begin to influence the candidates' positions.

On no issue do interest groups play a bigger role than abortion. Abortion opponents believe that life begins at conception—therefore all abortions, at whatever stage in the pregnancy, take the life of a child and should be prohibited. Many abortion supporters believe there should be no regulation of abortion beyond what the Supreme Court has established. The two sides promote their views with equal intensity and tend to demonize their opponents. They express no interest in the plight of the poor or those with no health insurance, or in the state of public education. They care only about their issue—abortion—and they judge all candidates on that basis.

During my first campaign for the Senate, I supported a woman's right to choose, but I didn't parade my support and therefore was more or less left alone by those voters who opposed abortion. I had been no more than a week in the Senate when the annual March for Life took place in Washington. On January 22, the date of the *Roe v. Wade* decision legalizing abortion, thousands of Right-to-Life advocates descended on the city, chanting, carrying banners, and buttonholing members of Congress. Some 300 of them showed up outside my temporary quarters in the Russell Senate Office Building. I still hadn't assembled a staff, but my secretary got a hearing room and I told them I'd be there in an hour. I showed up, and an uproar broke out. One adult pushed a boy who couldn't have been much more than ten years old toward me. He was carrying a jar filled with something. "When does life begin?" they shouted. I attempted to explain the rationale behind *Roe v. Wade*'s restrictions on abortion in the third trimester. To no avail. "Look! Look at what's in that jar! It's an aborted fetus, Senator! How does it feel to support murder?" After a long forty-five minutes, a little shell-shocked, I made it back to my office.

On the other side are the pro-choice supporters, who want no additional limitations on abortion whatsoever. They have reasons for opposing any regulation at all related to the issue. You can't require parental notification, because if you did, a father might beat his daughter when he found out she was pregnant. You can't require a waiting period, because the woman might have a more difficult abortion two weeks later, and that wouldn't be humane or fair. When pro-choice adherents are challenged on the specifics of their positions and forced to admit that a particular regulation isn't all that heinous, they fall back on the camel's-nose-in-the-tent argument: One regulation leads to another and then another, until abortion has been prohibited for all women, under all circumstances. The message they deliver to elected officials is "Our way or no way." Not once, in eighteen years in the Senate, did I hear a lobbyist or constituent on either side of the abortion debate express any sympathy for or understanding of the other side.

What I experienced on the abortion issue was the fire of true believers—but the public doesn't share it. The American people haven't changed their position on abortion since 1974, one year after it became a legal procedure in America. Although polls fluctuate in a particular moment, the underlying continuity of views is clear. The vast majority of Americans think abortion should be legal but are troubled by it. Neither party reflects this nuanced view. Republicans are (or profess to be) so deeply troubled by legalized abortion that they think it should be illegal once again, and Democrats don't seem troubled by legalized abortion at all. Neither party has identified with the millions of women and their partners who want abortion preserved as an option even as they experience deep anguish in reaching their decisions to abort. Yet each party has made the extreme view the litmus test for candidate endorsements.

But why are candidates so easily dominated by this and other special interests? One reason is gerrymandering, the drawing of congressional district lines so that a particular party has a commanding advantage. Over the last twenty-five years, increased precision from computer modelling, efforts to create black districts in order to comply with the Voting Rights Act, and the natural tendency of incumbents to improve their prospects have created a House of Representatives in which barely more than 10 percent of the 435 seats are regularly contested. The effect of this is profound. If a candidate runs in a district where 52 percent of the registered voters belong to one party and 48 percent to the other, that candidate has to pay attention to the views of constituents in the other party. He or she needs their votes. The effect of this process is to moderate extreme positions. The political skill required is consensus building. By contrast, if the candidate is in a district that is divided 60–40, he or she doesn't even have to acknowledge the existence of people in the other party, much less pay attention to their views. The general election in such districts is guaranteed for the candidate by the disparity in registered voters; the worry is the primary. If the candidate is a moderate, a primary challenge may erupt from one of the rabid interest-group purists. In a primary with a small turnout (and most of them are), the purists can mobilize enough votes to give any candidate heartburn and in some cases enough to defeat him or her. To avoid that outcome, candidates bow to the most extreme elements in their coalition.

These days even presidents play to the extremists. George W. Bush, aware of the primary challenge that sapped his father's reelection effort in 1992, played slavishly to his base for four years. Whenever there was a decision between doing what the majority of Americans wanted and appealing to his base, he chose the latter. Avoiding a primary appeared to become his obsession. Whether it was abortion, a constitutional amendment banning gay marriage, tax cuts, end-of-life issues, giving business a virtual blank check to exploit the natural world, or selling out to the oil, tobacco, or gun lobbies, he chose the most extreme position. When Ronald Reagan did that, you knew it was mostly politics; when Bush did it, his eyes were on fire. Perhaps he is just the better actor—but his appointment of radicals to positions of responsibility in his administration suggests that there was indeed more here than politics. If the president of the United States adheres to the dictates of his party's most extreme elements, imagine how quickly a moderate congressperson will fold. The House of Representatives sometimes reminds me of a gang of kids in a chorus, each trying to sing louder than the next so that he or she will get the most applause — in this case, from extreme special interests.

Elected officials also accommodate interest groups, because it's easier now for activists to make a politician's life miserable. On one level, that's good. Open hearings and recorded votes give activists the access and information enabling them to push their views and monitor an elected official's performance. *The Austin* (Texas) *Chronicle* reports that at one city council meeting there were so many people who wanted to register their opinions on a local environmental issue, the meeting didn't end until just before sunrise the next day, even though speakers were limited to five minutes each. On another level, though, greater transparency makes the smallest disagreement into a big issue, with partisans on each side screaming at one another and demanding adherence to the most extreme positions. There is no venue in which politicians of opposite parties can make substantial moves toward compromise outside the purview of those who would polarize.

Interest groups can hound a candidate at every appearance. They can dominate every public meeting. Sometimes other voters get angry at the purists and try to keep them quiet; more often, the average voters leave frustrated. Having made the effort to come out to a town meeting, they can't even get their issues addressed by the candidate, because the question period has been hogged by the purists. In such a charged atmosphere, compromise and progress become nearly impossible.

The presidential nominating process, with its emphasis on the Iowa caucus, also puts a premium on the role of activists. I believe it's important for the process of selecting the most powerful person in the world to begin in a state like Iowa or New Hampshire, because doing so requires the candidates to meet people in small gatherings, even in living rooms, where the voters can look them in the eye and take their measure. At least in Iowa and New Hampshire — before the giant media campaigns, the arrival of Secret Service protection, the rope lines and security screenings that block access to the crowd—a candidate has to deal with the unpredictability of individual voters, who may well demand straight answers to their questions before they decide to give you their vote. But there is an important difference between these two early-voting states: One has a secret ballot and the other doesn't.

Iowans are some of the best people in America—generous, fair, well-informed—but the caucus system is essentially undemocratic. The Iowa voter has to go to a local hall on a cold January night and at the appointed moment, after a series of brief speeches, vote by walking to the corner of the room in which his or her candidate's supporters are standing. Not surprisingly, very few people attend. The highest turnout ever at the Iowa caucuses was in 1988, when Republicans and Democrats combined brought out a total of 12 percent of the voting-age population. In 2004, only 120,000 people showed up at the Democratic caucus, even though 700,000 had voted for Al Gore in the 2000 general election. Since there is no secret ballot, interest groups can openly intimidate caucus goers. When I ran for president in 2000, I had union members come to me in tears and say they were for me even though their union had endorsed Gore. They could not go to my corner in the caucus, they said, because if their shop steward saw them, they might lose their jobs. New Hampshire, by contrast, always surprises—in part because the voters in this small state are nothing if not independent-minded. Families go from candidate speech to candidate speech to arrive at their choice. They take the process seriously and accord it the respect often missing in the general-election electorate. Most important, on Election Day in the New Hampshire primary, the ballot keeps each person's verdict a secret.

If you see fire in the eyes of some purists, you see dollar signs in those of others. A candidate's need to raise more and more money in each election gives additional clout to interest groups. Candidates increasingly have to raise all their money on their own. Parties can make meaningful contributions, but no candidate depends on their largesse. If there are 435 House elections every two years, there are 435 fund-raising operations. In such an environment, interest groups with their own fund-raising bases can easily direct them toward a particular candidate. Other groups collect large numbers of contributions from purists, bundle them, and give them to a candidate. Candidates try to bring the interest groups into their fund-raising operations. Tom DeLay, former House majority leader, turned milking the corporate special interests into an art form, one that eventually skidded toward a grand jury indictment and resignation from the House.

The interest groups know how to exact a price for their generosity. The result is that more and more winners at least listen to the advice of groups that see the world through a narrow prism and ignore the panoramic view of the American political landscape. Ironically, interest groups, whose money pays for the polls and focus groups that tell a candidate how to find the way to the voters' hearts, use the same techniques to find the language that will most influence the candidate once he or she is in office. The process becomes an exercise in duplicity, fuelled by seemingly endless amounts of money. The only people who benefit in this environment are the consultants.

Increasingly, candidates themselves must be very wealthy and fund their own campaigns, or else they will be forced to depend on special-interest money. Sometimes candidates raise money for their campaigns from ordinary people and use special interests to fund independent committees that attack their opponents in ways that would backfire if the candidates tried them directly.

As the late social scientist Mancur Olson argued in *The Rise and Decline of Nations*, the increasing power of interest groups is harmful to economic growth, full employment, coherent government, and social mobility. Because their agendas dominate, what rarely gets addressed comprehensively is what most people want: affordable health care, excellent schools, adequate pensions, a clean environment, and an economy that generates more and more well-paying jobs. Instead, an inordinate amount of attention goes to issues such as abortion, gay rights, gun control, medical marijuana, the display of the Ten Commandments, the wording of the Pledge of Allegiance, or the subsidy desires of a particular corporation or industry—issues that don't motivate the majority but are all-important to the activists.

It doesn't have to be this way.

Out of this context of conflict and self-pleading come the fundamental problems with our political system today. In their campaign coverage, the media go for the sensational and the superficial, tending to discourage the thoughtful, detailed, or nuanced expression of a candidate's beliefs. Moreover, not enough politicians speak from their core convictions. And there is way too much money in politics. The end result is that fewer and fewer Americans even bother to vote.

Voter Turnout

The most discouraging thing about our current politics is that fewer than half the people who were eligible to vote did so in 1996 and 2000, and only 61 percent voted in the heavily contested presidential election of 2004. Off-year congressional election turnout ranges from 35 to 40 percent. The International Institute for Democracy and Electoral Assistance compared voter turnout in national elections from 1945 to 1998 in 140 countries. Italy was first, with 92 percent, whereas the United States was 139th, with an average turnout of 48 percent. Why is voter turnout so low here?

When it comes to campaigns—whether for president, Congress, or governor—the American electorate is frustrated. The litany of complaints grows every day. "I don't even bother to vote—both parties are the same." "Why can't candidates just tell me what they believe?" "Why don't candidates talk to me about what I care about instead of what their pollster told them to care about?" "Why do both candidates have to be so negative?" "All politics is corrupt." "A pox on both parties." "When I vote, I vote against someone, not for someone." And on and on.

The way campaigns are conducted in America today helps explain the disaffection of voters. To many practitioners, politics these days is fundamentally war. If the other party takes over, they believe the country will go down the drain. The rules in this war are few or none: Too often, people will do anything to win. Political consultants are the generals. Candidates are the soldiers. Through polling and focus groups, consultants find the most effective language to persuade voters to support their candidate or party. Explaining complex issues is a real loser in politics today. Don't even bother. The assumption is that the public wants entertainment, not information. Just make sure your side has a great talking head on TV who can pound the opponent with simplistic epithets: "flip-flopper," for example, is a proven winner, used successfully against George Bush I, John Kerry, and any number of candidates for the U.S. Senate. Above all, attack your opponent viciously to show you really want the job. The smaller the number of people who vote, the easier it will be for your predictable base to determine the election. The result of all this is to depress turnout.

I used to tell constituents that if they didn't vote they lost their right to complain. Politicians want to get reelected. They pay attention to the voters. They also know who doesn't vote, and the tragedy is that they therefore address few of the issues important to nonvoters, who are disproportionately young, poor, and minority. When the nonvoters do tune in, they hear politicians talking about things that don't concern them, so they become even more disaffected, even more likely not to vote. It's a downward spiral.

There are also practical reasons for the low turnout. Tuesday is an inconvenient day for voting. Imagine men or women who have to be at work by 8:00 a.m. and get docked or possibly fired if they're late. They get up an hour early to get to the polls, which open at 7:00 a.m. Upon arrival, they find a long line. It moves slowly. They have to leave to get to work before they reach the voting booth. By the time they come back at the end of the day, if they make it through the traffic in time or manage to arrange for someone to pick up the kids from after-school activities, there are even longer lines of people just like them who are trying to vote after work.

Why do we make a citizen's most sacred democratic duty so inconvenient to fulfill? Why Tuesday? I'll bet you can't tell me. Be honest. It was established back in 1845, so that all Americans could vote on the same day; before that, states had set their own dates. So, why Tuesday? Saturday was a workday. Sunday was the Sabbath. It could take a whole day to travel to the polls in the horse-and-buggy age of 1845, so Monday was out. That left Tuesday or Wednesday. Wednesday in many places was market day, so by default it became Tuesday.

Today, over 150 years later, it's still Tuesday, but the horse and buggy are gone and the two-earner family has arrived, juggling professional and family responsibilities in an ever more stressed environment. While 94 percent of the people in a survey conducted jointly by the Tarrance Group and Lake, Snell, Perry, Mermin/ Decision Research in the fall of 2005 said that "voting is an important civic duty that everyone should do," more than a third of those who usually don't vote said that the reason was "too busy/didn't have time/working."

Money

Money in politics is like ants in your kitchen. If you don't block all the holes, some will find a way in.* In 2004, a total of nearly $4.0 billion was spent on the congressional and presidential election campaigns, up from $2.2 billion in 1996. In 1978, when I ran for the Senate for the first time, my expenses in the primary and general elections combined amounted to about $1.3 million. In 2000, Jon Corzine, the winning Senate candidate in New Jersey, spent nearly $63 million.

In order to amass that kind of money, you either have to be very wealthy and fund the campaign yourself or spend time every single day raising money. A candidate's most important qualification is often his or her fund-raising ability. Money buys the requisite TV and radio ads, direct mail, campaign manpower, targeted outreach. Money bolsters the party organization and the people who live on its payrolls. On Election Day, it brings people out to the polls. The prevailing ethos says if you're unknown, unconventional, or poor, don't bother to run. The average cost of running for a seat in the House of Representatives is now over $1 million, which means the candidate must raise at least $2,000 every weekday for two years. It used to be

---

*See my book *Time Present, Time Past* (Knopf, 1996).

that when someone was elected to a six-year senatorial term, he or she was able to spend the first four years being a senator and the last two being a candidate. Now senators are candidates for reelection the day after they've won. Every hour that elected officials spend dialing for dollars—calling people they have never met and asking them for money—is time not spent on issue mastering or interaction with constituents.

And who are the people contributing the money? Fund-raisers come from many sources. They may be family members, or friends, or colleagues who grew to respect the candidate's abilities in his or her former profession. Then there are the lobbyists wanting access and the individuals wanting special favors. Some contributors are even betting that the candidate's abilities will best serve the national interest. But all of them want to give money to someone who will win.

In an essay about money in politics in the April 1, 2006, *Washington Spectator*—an essay that every American should read—the veteran political commentator Bill Moyers noted: "Less than one-half of one percent of all Americans made a political contribution of $200 or more to a federal candidate in 2004." Political giving is a game for the few and the well-to-do. When George W. Bush ran in 2000, he said, "It's time to clean up the toxic environment of Washington, DC." And he promised that the standards of his administration would be "not only what is legal, but what is right, not what lawyers allow but what the public deserves." He said this at the same time he was raising $67 million, much of it from corporate interests, in his Republican primary race. When he won, idealistic language fell by the wayside and payoff time arrived. House Majority Leader Tom DeLay's "K Street Project" opened the inner sanctum of Congress to lobbyists, who wrote bills that blatantly pushed their self-interest and killed those that worked against it.

Wherever there is easy money to be made—whether in Silicon Valley in the late 1990s or in the nation's capital today—the locusts swarm. Moyers points out that, since Bush took office, the number of lobbyists has more than doubled: from 16,342 in 2000 to 34,785 in 2005. That's 65 lobbyists for each member of Congress. When I was in the Senate, I used to think the money that corporations spent on lobbying was excessive compared with what they got for it, but today the amount of corporate money spent on lobbying is mind-boggling. Jeffrey H. Birnbaum, in a June 2005 story in *The Washington Post* ("The Road to Riches Is Called K Street"), reported that Republican lobbyists were charging their new corporate clients between $25,000 and $40,000 per month. Moyers wrote that special interests now spend nearly $200 million per month "wining, dining, and seducing federal officials." The federal budget has become a trough at which corporations feed with no shame. The news is out—Washington is open for business.

When I was on the Senate Finance Committee, there were always lobbyists seeking special favors on tax bills for their clients, but they were astute enough to offer some rationale relating to the public interest. When their argument was sound, you sometimes supported their proposal. When it wasn't, you said no. Today all that's necessary to attract the attention of an elected official—and it *is* a necessary condition—is a sizable amount of money contributed to the official's campaign. While Democrats like the former House majority whip Tony Coelho and the former Democratic National Committee chairman Terry McAuliffe used the "pay to play" routine in unsavory ways, they could never match Tom DeLay in his blatant appeal to special interests, his total blindness to the public good, his insistence that K Street lobbyists hire his former staff members, his ruthlessness in punishing those who crossed him, and his generosity in rewarding those who kept writing the checks, funding his party, bankrolling his junkets, hiring his family. In the nineteenth century, there were senators on the payrolls of railroad companies and trusts. They were small potatoes compared with the crowd in power today.

Is it any wonder that the public distrusts its representatives? In a speech entitled "Saving Our Democracy" and posted on the Internet (www.alternet.org/story/32750/), the estimable Bill Moyers cited a recent CBS News/*New York Times* poll showing that 70 percent of the American people believe that lobbyists bribing federal officials is just the way it works in Washington, and 57 percent believe that half the Congress allows bribes to affect their votes.

Moyers puts it this way:

If a player sliding into home plate reached into his pocket and handed the umpire $1000 before he made the call, what would we call that? A bribe. And if a lawyer handed a judge $1000 before he issued a ruling, what do we call that? A bribe. But when a lobbyist or CEO sidles up to a member of Congress at a fundraiser or in a skybox and hands him a check for $1000, what do we call that? A campaign contribution.

And he quotes Representative Barney Frank (D.–Mass.) on Congress: "We are the only people in the world required by law to take large amounts of money from strangers and then act as if it had no effect on our behavior." Cynics say that nothing will change—but something has already changed. Since 1995, when I announced that I was leaving the Senate, saying, "Politics is broken," the corrosive power of money has only gotten worse. What is at stake is our democracy itself.

Media and Spin

The media are also part of the problem, and Americans are not blind to their destructiveness in pulling apart our common bonds and bombarding us with trivia and trash. Entertainment often trumps serious journalism, especially on TV. Nicholas Kristof pointed out in a July 2005 column in *The New York Times* that in the preceding year ABC had covered the genocide in Darfur for a total of eighteen minutes. "If only Michael Jackson's trial had been held in Darfur," he mourned. "Last month, CNN, Fox News, NBC, MSNBC, ABC and CBS collectively ran fifty-five times as many stories about Michael Jackson as they ran about genocide in Darfur." Foreign policy issues, outside a shooting war, seldom reach the American television viewer. Rarely does thoughtful analysis replace spin in the videotaped reactions to a breaking news story, and there is very little continuity or follow-up on stories and few follow-up questions in television interviews.

Each political party thinks the other gets too much of a break from the media. Neither thinks its viewpoint receives fair coverage. More and more people watch the cable channel that confirms their predispositions. Few news programs—outside the Sunday morning shows, such as *Meet the Press*—give an honest shake to both parties. Comedians—Jon Stewart of *The Daily Show*, Stephen Colbert of *The Colbert Report*, and the late-night talk-show hosts—are fast becoming the nation's most influential providers of political commentary.

Without vigilant news media, the party in power has no real check. But just as the media can be ruthless, so can the White House. Its occupants can control coverage by denying access to reporters or practicing a more overt intimidation by having their political allies call the employers of offending reporters to imply retaliation or retribution if coverage doesn't change. Since vast media conglomerates usually have some issue pending before government, such threats can have an impact and can even lead to self-censorship. On a more benign level, a White House, knowing the media's predilections, can manipulate them easily. By revealing a story that can be covered as a headline, such as an orange terror alert or the announcement of the breakup of some potential terrorist cell, it can hide an embarrassing report that requires more explanation than just a headline and that is being issued simultaneously—say, about our deteriorating schools or the dangerous levels of risk in the economy. And the White House isn't the only problem. A TV program or newspaper that offends some vocal group has to be ready for a barrage of calls. If these callers are fanatic or insistent enough, many journalists will begin to shy away from the pain next time.

Public relations techniques have come to dominate the nexus of public policy and politics. As a lobbyist I know once said, "My job is not to tell the truth, it's to tell my client's story. It's the press's job to determine if it's true." To the masters of spin, it doesn't make a difference what the truth is; they can create their own truth. If something is unpleasant, just deny it or muddy the waters. If you get pushed to the wall, just lie. The press will report the lie anyway, because they need opposing views on every issue. For example, as Paul Krugman pointed out in his July 28, 2006, *New York Times* column, Edward Lazear, the chairman of the Council of Economic Advisers, said the following about the Bush tax cuts: "The tax cuts have made the tax code more progressive and reduced income inequality." The opposite is true. By simply reporting a lie often enough, you create an impression of truth, especially in the absence of a countervailing story. But many point-counterpoint television shows simply result in shouting matches. Fairness and truth go out the window. Often it is two on one—the moderator and the conservative against the liberal, or vice versa, depending on the cable channel. Given the twenty-four-hour news cycle and cable television's need for ever more material, having two politicians yelling at each other is a cheap way to fill airtime.

Political spin has gotten so bad that many people can't tell what the truth is. They eventually decide that both sides are lying, and they begin to think of the media simply as the pipe through which the lies flow. In *The Age of Anxiety*, Haynes Johnson writes that the press too often

> has operated under a specious standard of objectivity that treats conflicting political claims as equal by "balancing" polemical assertions—giving each side the same weight without attempting to determine the truth of either and without calling attention to often flagrant misstatements and outright lies. It's "he says/she says," and thank you viewers/readers for letting us give you their contrary and often false opinions without any assessment of their accuracy.

This is one reason why, as I said in Chapter 5, 53 percent of the news reports about global warming reflect doubt that human actions cause it, whereas no—repeat, no—peer-reviewed scientific studies do. No one holds the spin artists accountable. When narrow special-interest groups dominate a news program, journalists could be asking, "How many members does your organization have?" or "Who appointed you to speak out on this issue?" but they don't. They could be making a distinction between activist and crackpot, but they don't. They could be seeking the truth in all its human complexity, but they don't. Conflict is too good a story.

Candidate Conviction

Not enough politicians speak from their core convictions. For politicians to do that, they must be willing to take on their consultants and often their fund-raisers. Such politicians must also be strong enough to stand before an angry group of constituents and explain their course of action with a clarity and strength that at least gains respect, even at the cost of votes.

Political consultants have an encyclopedic knowledge of a narrow area of human behavior; they don't address the whole. They're simply working for their clients and doing their jobs in a messed-up game. Just as academics and other experts know a great deal about a single subject, political consultants know a great deal about how to win elections. But the way they win elections makes governing more difficult.

Often candidates run for office because they really do want to make the world a better place. They enter the process with a desire to do bold things. They remember when they were first inspired by politics, and they want to reclaim that feeling. Some have planned their pursuit of public office for years, and then they hit the stone wall of political reality: In order to run, they need consultants and money—a lot of money.

Consultants know that, to win, you need 15 percent of the voters in the middle, dispersed among multiple demographic subgroups. The job of the consultant is to design very narrow, targeted messages to reach each of these subgroups. The candidate then repeats those targeted messages, over and over. This system has squeezed nuance and spontaneity out of politics.

The consultants tell the fund-raisers that, in order to win, the candidate has to stay on message with the poll-tested answer, and often that he or she has to go for the opponent's jugular, in television ads or in televised debates. The fund-raiser in turn encourages the candidate to do exactly what the consultant tells him or her—after all, the consultant is the specialist who knows how to win. To borrow a metaphor from my years in professional basketball: the fund-raiser is the owner, the consultant is the coach, and the candidate is the player. One is reminded of Robert Redford's character in the 1972 movie *The Candidate*, who on winning a U.S. Senate seat, asks his campaign manager, "What do we do now?"

Too many candidates agree to this strategy—often against their better judgment. On the stump and in the debates and the town hall meetings and the electorate's living rooms, and even in discussions with the editorial boards of newspapers, they don't talk about what they really want to do if they're elected. They offer little in the way of specifics. They rarely take a principled stand. Instead, they talk mostly about what the consultant tells them it is essential to do in order to move the poll numbers. Then, when they win, they don't have a mandate to do the big and difficult things that in their heart of hearts were the reasons for entering politics in the first place.

The public needs to see the candidate's conviction, from which will flow the candidate's leadership. But the consultant will argue that a big idea can be distorted, so keep it small and simple. The result: Nothing of importance is said, and frustration among the body politic grows. If a candidate rejects this narrow approach and loses, the fund-raisers say, "I told you so! If you'd listened to your consultant, you would have won. What value are your big ideas if you're out of office?" And, of course, they have a point.

A notable exception to this rule of candidate timidity is Senator Russ Feingold (D.–Wis.). In 1998, he ran for a second term. In his first term, he was a major advocate of campaign finance reform and coauthor of the McCain-Feingold bill, which among other things banned national political parties from accepting or spending soft-money contributions (large donations to parties in excess of what can legally be contributed to a candidate) but which had not yet been enacted. Feingold decided that since soft money was abolished in his legislation, he would not accept soft-money contributions that benefited his own campaign. The national Democratic Party disagreed with him but went along. Feingold had a sixteen-point lead in September. His Republican opponent took all the soft money he could get and began to close the gap. By early October, the gap had narrowed to six points. The national party urged Feingold to take soft money now. Feingold refused. The week before the election, the race became nearly a dead heat. National Democrats told Feingold that if he didn't take soft money to finance the final TV blitz, he could lose. Feingold refused. This campaign story has a happy ending, because Senator Feingold squeaked through, but the bigger story was that he ran his race guided by a set of principles he refused to relinquish despite the advice of the pros. What politics needs is more Russ Feingolds.

Consultants know how to manipulate the electorate by tapping into its collective subconscious and steering it up to one point— Election Day. But for the voters, there is a hangover effect. They often don't feel satisfied with their decisions. The negative ads and the character assassination are foreign to the day-to-day experiences of most people. On the job and in their personal lives, being reasonable pays dividends. In politics, being reasonable is a liability. So even as they vote—a vote promoted by the consultant's strategy— citizens become disaffected and sometimes disgusted. The politician becomes someone with a set of values and a code of behavior utterly foreign to them.

When I ran for president in 2000, I had a standard line in my stump speech, which I must have given 1,000 times. It went something like this: "The premise of my campaign is that you can tell people exactly what you believe and win." Well . . . Maybe the problem was me. I still believe that political candor is both possible and productive, and that because this is fundamentally an imitative profession, when a candidate comes along and wins that way, other candidates will begin to say what they truly believe because they see it as the new path to victory.

THE NEW STORY

The new story says that we can end gerrymandering, increase voter turnout, reduce the role of money in our politics, lead media to support a new kind of politics, and have candidates who run on their convictions rather than the advice of their consultants.

The specifics?

1. Congressional district lines should be drawn by nonpartisan commissions with representatives appointed by the state legis-

lature, the governor, and various civic organizations, such as the League of Women Voters. The charge to the commissions should be to draw lines that cross as few township or city lines as possible and produce districts that, if possible, have roughly equal numbers of Republicans and Democrats. Instead of the new district plan being ratified by the state legislature, it should be submitted to the electorate as a whole for approval. A second possibility would be to submit it to a panel of three federal judges.

2. The antidote to nonvoting is to make voting easier. Election Day should be moved from Tuesday to Saturday and Sunday. If we give people two days on a weekend, turnout should increase. Many people vote in schools; weekend voting would not disrupt the school day. On weekends, people could take their children to the polls with them, thereby inculcating in them the importance of voting. Finally, the groups who told the Tarrance Group et al. survey that they were more likely to vote on a weekend are the largest of the nonvoter groups—African Americans, eighteen- to thirty-four-year-olds, Hispanics, singles, and working women.

Other suggestions to make voting easier include allowing drop-by voting, in which people can come for three weeks before the election to cast their votes at certain secure polling places, as they do in California, or making it simpler for people to vote by mail, as they do in Oregon, or giving voters the right to register even on Election Day, as they do in Minnesota. All these changes will allow more Americans to decide our collective destiny.

The answer to the problem of democracy is more democracy, not less democracy. As Morris Fiorina says, "If the presidential electorate were to double and the off-year electorate to nearly triple, it is likely that parties and candidates would make different appeals to capture the support of new voters who would now be showing up at the polls." Increasing the size of the electorate to 80 percent of the eligible voters would have as big an impact on our democracy as enfranchising women and blacks did. If democracy is about all of us, then as close to all of us as possible must vote. Otherwise democracy functions only for some of us.

3. The cleanest and clearest way to reform the campaign finance system is for the public to finance campaigns. In doing so, we would be taking our future out of the hands of those who want something for their money besides good government. We spend almost $1.4 billion a year to promote democracy abroad. Given the gross abuses of the last decade, the best investment of taxpayer dollars would be to spend roughly the same amount each year ($3.6 billion per two-year cycle) on publicly financed congressional races. While doing so won't stop the billionaire candidates from opting out of the public finance system and spending more than the amount allotted by Congress, it will at least ensure that all the candidates have enough to make their case. If we can champion democracy abroad, why can't we ensure its integrity at home? The answer is, we can.

Another possibility would be to handle the corrosive power of money the way we have handled other issues that have impeded the functioning of our democracy. Constitutional amendments have long been our way to improve democracy, whether it was expanding the right to vote or directly electing senators. If you believe that money does not distort our democracy—and some people I respect still don't, arguing (however speciously, in my opinion) that since companies spend much more money advertising drugs ($13.8 billion per year), spending on political ads has a long way to go—then you will oppose a constitutional amendment declaring that "federal, state, and local governments may limit the total amount of money spent in a political campaign." But if you think our democracy is at risk of being offered to the highest bidder, then the constitutional route offers the only certain way of limiting money in politics. The Supreme Court in *Buckley v. Valeo*, a shortsighted 1976 decision, ruled that money spent on a campaign is equivalent to speech and so cannot be limited under the Constitution. The result is that a rich man has a microphone on a cable channel reaching millions and a poor man is left with a megaphone on his front porch reaching his neighbor. And our democracy suffers.

At this time, I believe that, of the two options, public financing has a better chance of becoming law than a constitutional amendment. If it passes, the special interests that block health care reform, water down pension reform, continue to demand oil subsidies, and exploit our environment will have considerably less access to the inner sanctums of government, and our elected representatives can get back to dealing with the people's business.

4. What we can do about the failure of the media to play a constructive role in our democracy is reinstate the fairness doctrine, break up the concentration of media power, realize the potential of the Internet (the citizens' medium) through social-political networking, require that a specific amount of time be devoted to public issues and campaigns in exchange for a federal broadcast license, find the economic leverage to do the same thing for cable TV, and (however unlikely this may seem) expect the CEOs of media companies occasionally to put their role as citizens on a par with their role as moguls—that is, increase the public's understanding of national issues as well as single-mindedly maximize the bottom line.

5. With regard to candidates' running on their core convictions: Like many democratic reforms, everyone considers it impossible until it happens—and then people wonder why it didn't happen sooner. If enough political candidates ran candid and courageous races (as Russ Feingold did), it would be an important beginning even in the absence of campaign finance reform. Ultimately it will take many such candidates, who possess a fire in their bellies for reform, to revive America's politics. In politics, a clear and visionary program stands a chance of attracting candidates of courage—people who want to be a part of shaping their nation's destiny rather than sim-

ply exercise power for its own sake or on behalf of corrupt patrons. It is that hope that led me to offer the New American Story.

Surely there are more than enough talented citizens, wealthy patriots, and politically committed ordinary Americans to make this happen. All that's necessary is to realize it's truly possible.

The choice is ours.

Chapter 10.

WHY REPUBLICANS CAN'T

I grew up in Crystal City, Missouri, in a nominally Republican family. My father, a banker, was an elector for New York's Governor Thomas E. Dewey in his run against Missouri's native son, Harry Truman, in 1948. I remember seeing, the morning after the election, the champagne bottle from the night before, sitting, still corked, atop our big RCA radio in the living room.

I was taught that Republicans were prudent, like my father. They were careful with the taxpayers' money, but they had a heart as well. My father always said that what he was proudest of in his banking career was that during the Great Depression he hadn't foreclosed on a single home. He was a Robert Taft man in the 1952 Republican primary, sure that Senator Taft of Ohio, who did not hesitate to counter Democratic spending plans in the Senate, understood a small-town banker's concerns better than General Dwight D. Eisenhower, the commander of the Allied forces in Europe during World War II, did.

All my friends—the sons and daughters of workers in Crystal City's glass factory—were Democrats. But I was my father's son. Over the years, Republicans had been tolerant on race, skeptical of federal spending, even for the military, and committed to the belief that the free-enterprise system was America's gift to the world and that its best exemplar was Main Street in small-town America. Republicans were defenders of the status quo—dull, but dependably dull.

When Richard Nixon ran against John Kennedy in 1960, I wore a Nixon button to my high school, just as I had worn an "I like Ike" button four years before. But between 1960 and 1964, the civil rights revolution and a more thorough reading of American history swept me into the Democratic Party. I crossed the line from Republican to Democrat when, as a college intern in the summer of 1964, I sat in the Senate gallery watching the roll call on the landmark Civil Rights Act, which among other things, desegregated public facilities in America. When the soon to be Republican presidential nominee, Barry Goldwater, voted no, that served as the final push for me. I was from then on a Democrat, and I cast my first presidential election ballot that fall for Lyndon Johnson.

The Grand Old Party

Abraham Lincoln, perhaps our greatest president, was a Republican, but no Republican president since has approached his genius or courage or the magnitude of his accomplishments. Republicans continue to call themselves the party of Lincoln, but they are not. The party of Lincoln died with Lincoln, whose compassionate boldness has rarely reappeared in its ranks.

In the decade after his death, the most significant Republican was Rutherford B. Hayes, who in the 1876 election cut a deal with the white South that would have horrified Lincoln. In exchange for the support of white Southerners in the Electoral College, President Hayes removed federal troops from the South and returned power to the white elite, who proceeded to pass what came to be known as Jim Crow laws, thereby imposing a new servitude on black Americans.

At the end of the nineteenth century, the Republicans became the party of William McKinley and his political guru, Mark Hanna, a man deeply admired by George W. Bush's chief political strategist, Karl Rove. Rove was fond of saying that the model for the 2000 presidential election was 1896, the year McKinley defeated the populist Democrat William Jennings Bryan. McKinley and Hanna won in 1896 by agreeing to turn the party over to business. Economic power became more and more concentrated. Lip service was paid to those who worked in the mines and factories, but little was done to balance the clout of private capital. In the American West during that era, these business interests violated vast areas of land, cutting down forests, extracting minerals, and draining rivers for irrigation. In the East, industrial and financial powers exploited their workers with impunity: Child labor, thirteen-hour days, dangerous workplaces, and meager pay were the rule.

When McKinley was assassinated, in 1901, his vice president, Theodore Roosevelt, took over. Roosevelt was cut from a different cloth. Energetic, bold, unflinching in the face of opposition, he transformed the government. To counter the increasing concentration of corporate power, he used government to break up Standard Oil and attack the wealthy patricians who, he believed, had a stranglehold on the country. A generation of progressive thought informed his actions; writers, thinkers, and social scientists had seen the excesses of the Gilded Age and reacted to them in a creative burst of energy that produced influential books such as Henry George's *Progress and Poverty*, Henry Adams's *Democracy*, William Dean Howells's *The Rise of Silas Lapham*, and Upton Sinclair's *The Jungle*. Journalists such as Lincoln Steffens and Ida M. Tarbell exposed the worst excesses of corporate power. Artists such as John Sloan and George Bellows painted slums, chambermaids, and boxers in an attempt to champion real people and promote social equality. Daughters of privilege, such as Jane Addams, lived among the poor, reported on their desperate plight, and demanded government action. Religious leaders, such as Walter Rauschenbusch and Washington Gladden, took the gospel of Jesus Christ, which preached personal salvation, and applied it to righting social wrongs by seeking to create a kingdom of God on Earth. The plight of the less fortunate had to be improved; the value of a human life was the same no matter whether it was the life of a tenement dweller or a member of the New York Social Register; the charge to citizens was not simply to make money but to serve their fellow human beings; the challenge of democracy was to reform itself from time to time, so as to guarantee the most direct expression of the people's will. When Roosevelt broke with the Republican Party's reactionary past, he had an existing body of thought with which to construct a social program.

From western Republicans of a progressive bent, with their emphasis on popular democracy, came proposals such as the direct election of U.S. senators, who had until then been selected by increasingly corrupt state legislatures; women's suffrage, which began in the western territories; the short ballot, an improvement over the complexity of boss-rigged ballots; initiative, referendum, and recall, which injected direct democracy into our representative government; the progressive income tax to replace tariffs and sales taxes; limitations on campaign contributions; and a graduated inheritance tax. From their eastern counterparts of a more federalist bent, who were more comfortable with a strong central government, came proposals for a national health service, regulation of interstate corporations, and clear legal guidelines for business that would create a stable economy with steady investment and growing prosperity.

Theodore Roosevelt's seven years of progressive government ended when he chose not to run again in 1908. He anointed his secretary of war, William Howard Taft, who promised Roosevelt that he would carry on the progressive cause. Roosevelt then absented himself from the country for Taft's first year, so as not to overshadow his successor. Once in office, Taft essentially tilted the Republican Party back into the hands of the corporate and financial elite, although not as far back as desired by the old McKinley-Hanna crowd. When Roosevelt returned and saw the direction of the party and the nation, he started his own party, the Progressive, or Bull Moose, Party, and ran against Taft in the 1912 election. The Democrat, Woodrow Wilson, won, but T.R. came in second, with 27.4 percent of the vote.

Wilson continued Roosevelt's progressive agenda by creating the Federal Reserve System and the Federal Trade Commission, supporting women's suffrage, and maneuvering a graduated federal income tax through Congress. He fought for the economic well-being of small business and the farmer. But after eight years in office, the president who saw us through World War I but lost the peace lay unpopular and sick, and in 1921 the Republicans were back—the same old Republicans—with Warren G. Harding as president. The Republican Party, except for Herbert Hoover's creation of an antitrust division at the Justice Department and the reduction of taxes on low income earners, would remain in tune with the interests of big business for the next thirty-two years.

Then Republican economic mismanagement brought on the Depression, and Democrats ascended to power. They took Theodore Roosevelt's progressivism as their own and extended it. His distant cousin, Franklin Delano Roosevelt, came to the rescue of the country by turning on his own class and telling a nation in deep economic distress that he stood with the farmers, workers, and immigrants, and not with the "economic royalists." He ran against the rich, who amounted to just a sliver of America in the 1930s, and reached out to the poor and unemployed, who numbered in the millions in the fall of 1932, when FDR was elected.

Republicans, meanwhile, kept on insisting that business should have great influence in the halls of government. The best government was the least government. They wanted the freedom to do as they liked with their employees, with nature, and with their money. They reflexively opposed everything Roosevelt did. They voted against the Social Security Act. They voted against the National Industrial Recovery Act, an effort to help small businesses by giving the president greater power to regulate commerce. They voted against the creation of the Securities and Exchange Commission and the Federal Communications Commission, both of which attempted to assure honesty, fairness, and competition in the economy. They voted against the Works Progress Administration and the Civilian Conservation Corps, both of which generated jobs for the unemployed. They voted against the Wagner Act, which created the modern labor movement. They became the "No" party—they weren't for much of anything. The party of Theodore Roosevelt was long dead.

In 1952, there was a race for the Republican nomination between Senator Robert Taft of Ohio, son of the former president, and General Dwight Eisenhower, the hero of World War II. Taft represented the section of the party opposed to government. He was for a balanced budget, and he was skeptical of foreign involvement. Eisenhower represented a more cosmopolitan view. He was the nominee of the eastern establishment, a benign version of the old-money Republicans of half a century before—bankers and lawyers who had come out of World War II with confidence that they could manage the new international order. Having seen war up close, President Eisenhower ended the Korean conflict, rejected the advice of his generals to wage a preventive war against the Soviet Union, refused to send U.S. troops (as opposed to advisers) to Vietnam, and turned a cold shoulder to Israel when it invaded the Sinai Peninsula at the time of seizure of the Suez Canal by Britain and France. During his second presidential campaign, he refused to advocate the dismantling of the welfare state, which he said was "here to stay"—he just wanted to manage it better by installing corporate leaders as cabinet officers. He championed the interstate highway system, enforced the desegregation of our public schools, signed the Civil Rights Act of 1957, made four outstanding appointments to the Supreme Court, and, in response to the Soviet Union's launch of *Sputnik*, signed the National Defense Education Act to encourage young Americans to become scientists and engineers. In many ways, he is one of our most successful presidents.

The natural inheritor of the Eisenhower brand of Republicanism was Richard Nixon, his vice president. Nixon ran for president in 1960 as a moderate; the hawk was his Democratic opponent, John F. Kennedy. Kennedy was the cold warrior who would close the "missile gap" that Eisenhower had supposedly allowed to develop with the Soviet Union. Nixon got 32 percent of the black vote; he was the last Republican to get above 15 percent.

When Nixon lost, the Republican Party began to change. There was a new kind of Republican—not primarily eastern now but increasingly western. Fervently anticommunist (no Democrat would out-defense them again) and radically against the federal government (in favor of repealing Social Security, against civil rights legislation), they were fervent conservative ideologues rather than tools of the Fortune 500. They were deeply suspicious on a cultural level of those who had controlled the Republican Party for the previous seventy years and who, according to the informal westerners, "put on airs." This new Republican Party found its standard-bearer in

Senator Barry Goldwater of Arizona. His book *The Conscience of a Conservative* (1960) became a bible for the movement. When he lost disastrously in 1964 to Lyndon B. Johnson, the right wing of the Republican Party simply redoubled its efforts and increased in ideological intensity.

The turmoil of the 1960s, with the civil rights movement and Vietnam protests, created a new context for Republican strategists. Richard Nixon, ever vigilant in response to the political winds, took advantage of the Democrats' embrace of civil rights and opposition to Vietnam. Granted, not all Democrats opposed Vietnam; in fact, the war was being waged by a Democratic president. But the television news made sure the country knew that the "long-haired, pot-smoking" protesters were Democrats. As for civil rights, Lyndon Johnson, acting out of moral conviction, had sponsored the Civil Rights Act of 1964. After he signed it, he reportedly remarked to an aide that "we have lost the South for a generation."

Nixon—a graduate of the moderate Eisenhower establishment, a westerner who got to the Senate by running an anticommunist smear campaign against his opponent, Helen Gahagan Douglas, in 1950, and a smart political survivor who, in the face of corruption charges during the 1952 presidential campaign, stared down even Eisenhower, who wanted him off the ticket—skillfully played the hand he had been dealt. He never forgot that the liberal Republican Nelson Rockefeller of New York was booed by conservative delegates at the 1964 Republican National Convention; he knew he needed ultraconservative support.

In 1968, Nixon, as Eisenhower had during the Korean War, implied that he could end the Vietnam War. Meanwhile, he was secretly interfering with President Johnson's peace negotiations. He also played shamelessly to prejudice against blacks with his so-called Southern strategy, which consisted chiefly of speaking in code so that white racists would know he was on their side. A third-party candidate, Governor George Wallace of Alabama, who was a populist and archsegregationist, drained working-class votes in the North from the Democratic nominee, Hubert Humphrey, by appealing both to racial fears and the "little guy's" anger with the economic establishment. Nixon won enough of the South to put him over.

Once in office, he reverted to a governing style that denied a blank check to the ultraright and the racists; he had just used them to get elected. During the Nixon years, great efforts were made to let science and rational, open inquiry determine policy. During his tenure and that of his successor, Gerald Ford, the environmental movement was strengthened and significant pieces of legislation became law: the Clean Air Act, the Clean Water Act, and the Solid Waste Disposal Act. Nixon proposed comprehensive health insurance and a minimum income for all Americans. He increased aid to higher education.

After Watergate, Ford did his best to reclaim the Eisenhower touch, but even with a senior administration consisting of the then moderates Dick Cheney, Donald Rumsfeld, and Henry Kissinger, he failed. Ford was challenged in the 1976 primaries by the former governor of California, Ronald Reagan, who in late October 1964, in support of Goldwater, had electrified conservatives with his televised speech "A Time for Choosing." Reagan could not dislodge the incumbent, but the Democratic nominee did. Former governor Jimmy Carter of Georgia—honest, religious, a former submarine officer, and a candidate who wanted a government "as good as the American people"—was the perfect antidote for the disgrace the country had suffered because of Watergate and Ford's pardon of Nixon. He won a close election and then faced a crippling oil-supply disruption, spiralling inflation, high interest rates, and the Iranian hostage crisis. His thoughtfulness and honesty were turned into weaknesses by his Republican opponents, setting the stage for Reagan's victory in 1980.

Underestimated throughout his career, Reagan ran a campaign that appealed to conservatives, and he added a new idea to the Republican arsenal: tax cuts. He proposed cutting income taxes 30 percent across the board. The so-called supply-side argument was that cutting taxes would not reduce government revenue but increase it. He also wanted to get rid of government regulations, reduce non-defense spending, and increase military spending. When he won, he kept all four of these campaign promises—although, as far as non-defense spending was concerned, he simply limited its expansion. New York's Democratic senator Daniel P. Moynihan characterized the Reagan tax cuts as a way of exerting maximum pressure to cut the programs of the welfare state. That's exactly what happened, but the increased military spending and the tax cuts dwarfed the reining in of non-defense spending. The result was a mushrooming deficit. Reagan also turned over stewardship of the public lands to James Watt, a radical antigovernment westerner, and appointed Anne Gorsuch, a pro-development activist, to direct the Environmental Protection Agency. (Democrats and environmentalist Republicans suspected she was there to weaken environmental protection; they were right.)

By then, the '68 Nixon Southern strategy of playing to the racial prejudice of some Southerners had been established in the Republican Party playbook. Reagan kicked off his 1980 campaign with a visit to Philadelphia, Mississippi, the site of the murders of three civil rights workers in 1964. He never mentioned them, and this omission, along with his very presence in that place, won the hearts of the anti-black South. The racist strategy played out most often in the schools; after all, it was *Brown v. Board of Education* that had ignited the civil rights revolution in 1954. After the picture of young African Americans in Little Rock being escorted to class by soldiers from the 101st Airborne had appeared in the news, and after the country had been moved by the eloquence of Martin Luther King Jr. calling on America to live up to its professed ideals, overt resegregation became a losing strategy. The code word was "anti-busing," which pandered to the legitimate desires of many parents for their children to attend neighborhood schools.

The Reagan campaign team also proposed financial aid for students in private schools. In the South, that meant white academies populated by children whose parents didn't want them mingling with blacks. In the North, paradoxically, the targeted recipients of this largesse were Catholic parochial schools, many of which were predominantly minority and significantly non-Catholic. In this way, the Republicans could cater to the prejudices of their white base in the South while simultaneously appealing to the economic interests of a large bloc of non-racist voters in the North.

At the core of Reagan's campaign strategy was what he felt most deeply about: ending communism. He issued patriotic calls about

America's role as leader of the free world and the danger posed by the "evil empire" of the Soviet Union, a message that appealed to many of the Democrats who had supported the war in Vietnam. These Democrats were often urban ethnic voters, who also benefited from aid to parochial schools and who felt doubly betrayed by their party for not spending enough on defense and for "giving everything away" to minorities. When the California governor emphasized work, family, and neighborhood, he attracted even more Democrats. And no one could fault his geniality.

In such a stew of emotions, the religious right was born. By the late 1970s, they had joined the Catholic opposition to abortion. Over the next several years, they demonized AIDS sufferers, used the pornography issue to stigmatize defenders of free speech as moral retrogrades, and sought to end sex education in the public schools. They proposed constitutional amendments to overturn the Supreme Court decisions prohibiting prayer in the schools and allowing women the right to an abortion.

The Rise of Republican Factions

But even as the Republicans controlled the political dialogue after 1980, fissures began to creep into the party structure. Having been mostly in the minority for fifty years, they began to see that creating a majority required assembling Republicans who held a variety of views. Managing a diverse coalition would demand rigid party discipline. (Not for nothing was House Majority Leader Tom DeLay nicknamed "The Hammer.")

By 1988 the Republican Party was composed of a dozen factions: the corporatists, the anticommunists, the realists, the messianists, the fundamentalists, the Main Streeters, the libertarians, the subsidists, the liberals, the racemongers, the crime busters, and the supply-siders.

The *corporatists* felt, as they had since McKinley, that they could more easily have their way with government in a Republican administration. These corporate leaders had been interested in protective tariffs in the early twentieth century; by the late 1970s their main objective was to reduce their own taxes. They supported the federal government when it gave them money and opposed it when it attempted to impose regulations. Free trade and Eisenhower-style internationalism ranked high on their agenda. They didn't fear government; they just wanted to control it.

The *anticommunists* were xenophobes who emerged from the McCarthy era obsessed with communists at home and abroad. Their best-known organization was the John Birch Society. They cared little about civil liberties. They wanted to destroy the Soviet Union, warning in apocalyptic language that it was getting stronger and stronger. They made free use of the word "treason" in criticizing their opponents. They wanted more money for defense, and their foreign policy was one of confrontation. By 1988, the Soviet Union was falling apart, but to its very end they characterized it as having fearsome power. Finally they turned their paranoia on China, the last large communist nation, and warned that it, too, operated from a ruthless design to dominate the world.

The *realists* combined a post–World War II optimism with a post-Vietnam pessimism. Above all, they were rational and calculating. Balance of power was their guiding principle in foreign policy, as it had been among statesmen as far back as Metternich and Bismarck. Wilsonian idealism, with its international focus, made them nervous. They were hesitant to commit troops abroad and doubted that government, even the military, could build nations out of warring tribal or ethnic groups. Before America went to war, they wanted an exit strategy, and when America went to war, they wanted a large enough deployment of troops to win. In domestic policy, they felt (as noted by Pat Moynihan, then working in the Nixon White House) that the answer to bad social-scientific solutions to crime or race or poverty was better social science, not the ideological posturing that today would be called political correctness.

The *messianist* Republicans, a.k.a. neocons, believed in America's destiny. They took John Winthrop's noble description of Puritan New England as "a city upon a hill" and turned it into a form of self-conscious chauvinism derived from a sense of America's divine mission to liberate the world for democracy. Our system of governance was the best in the world and our economy the most vital. Other nations offered us little to learn about the human spirit. The patriotism of the messianists took the form of imposing on other nations our system and our way of looking at things. They wanted a strong military that we wouldn't hesitate to use in pursuing our goals. International opinion didn't interest them, but they cared a great deal about what a majority of Americans thought. Only the consent of the governed was relevant, and that was expressed in U.S. elections, not international popularity contests. They had the confident cold-bloodedness of muggers and the conviction of missionaries.

The *fundamentalist* Republicans were Christians who believed in the literal truth of the Bible. They saw the world in terms of black and white, good and evil. Either you were saved or you went to Hell. They harbored deep suspicions about science and about government in general. They regarded anyone who disagreed with them as ignorant and quite possibly evil, making negotiation or cooperation difficult. Yet they wanted to take control of government and use it to impose their conservative morality on the rest of society. Many of them believed that women shouldn't work and that children should be home-schooled. They fulminated against the coarsening of our culture, the bias of the liberal media, the self-indulgent hedonism of Hollywood. Jimmy Carter, an evangelical Southern Baptist who believes in the authority and teaching of the Bible every bit as much as these fundamentalists do, has characterized them with three words: "rigidity, domination, and exclusion."

The *Main Streeters* were like my father. They believed in small-town virtues—Babbitt without the small-mindedness. Their word was their bond. They were church members but not self-consciously religious. They supported local civic organizations, gave to the United Way, served on the school board. They didn't seek federal subsidies. Who the mayor was wasn't as important to them as the health of their businesses. Above all, they wanted less government spending and a balanced budget.

The *libertarian* Republicans, like the splinter party of that name, wanted to abolish government interference in the private and economic lives of Americans. They were strongly pro-choice on abortion, against military interventions, for lower taxes and free trade, and championed the First Amendment, which guarantees the right to free speech. They were worried about their privacy in an age of large computer databases. They doubted the efficiency of grand government designs and of any sort of social engineering, whether here or abroad. Above all, they believed in the free market.

The *subsidists* were primarily westerners who had grown up with the federal government owning as much as 90 percent of the land in their part of the United States. They had a love-hate relationship with Washington, DC. They wanted to end most federal regulation and oversight of their use of public resources. At the same time, they wanted to increase federal subsidies to the timber, mining, grazing, and irrigated agriculture industries. They were slow in adapting to the increased urbanization of the West and its changing economic base. They failed to see that the limiting factor for development was availability of water, not the federal government.

The Republican *liberals*, who overwhelmingly came from the two coasts, had been in decline since the Goldwater revolution. They looked outward to engage the world. They believed, like Theodore Roosevelt, that government had a role in regulating the economy and helping the poor. They eagerly sought bipartisan solutions. They listened well and rarely engaged in demagoguery. They showed courage by standing up to Senator Joseph R. McCarthy in the early 1950s. They joined the civil rights revolution in the 1960s and the environmental movement in the 1970s. They produced great senators, such as Jacob Javits of New York, Mark Hatfield and Bob Packwood of Oregon, Thomas Kuchel of California, Lowell Weicker of Connecticut, John Chafee of Rhode Island, and Susan Collins and Olympia Snowe of Maine.

The *racemongers* expressed prejudice that wouldn't die. They continued to play the race card in elections and actively sought to limit black aspirations. Throughout the 1960s, they railed at the Supreme Court and Chief Justice Earl Warren by wearing "Impeach Earl Warren" buttons. They called heroes such as Martin Luther King Jr. "rabble-rousers" and opposed a national holiday in his name. They demonized "welfare queens" but voted against the child-care and job bills that would help women get off welfare. They took an extreme social-Darwinist approach, suggesting that minorities should pull themselves up by their bootstraps. They denied the existence of racism. They opposed affirmative action and most programs for the poor. They wanted to cut public education dollars for schools that were largely black or Hispanic. They ignored the problems of Medicaid. They formed an early part of the anti-immigration movement.

The *crime busters* believed that the death penalty was an all-purpose answer to the violence and pathology of our society. They wanted to give more authority to the police. They felt the Supreme Court had made an error in establishing the right to counsel before police questioning. They equated drugs with licentiousness and wanted to send drug users and pushers away for long prison time. They supported sentencing guidelines that gave no flexibility to judges, whom they suspected of being too liberal. Rehabilitation didn't interest them. Punishment did—the stricter the better.

Finally, the *supply-siders* believed that tax cuts could solve everything from urban decay and economic downturns to third-world development. Deficits were unimportant. Economic growth was the Holy Grail, and tax cuts were the way to effect it. They took John Kennedy's dictum that "a rising tide lifts all boats" as their movement's slogan. They had little interest in defense policy or foreign policy. On race, some of them were liberal, but on issues of the economy they were doctrinaire.

Few Republicans held all these views, but whoever was the party's standard-bearer had to give the impression that he did.

In recent years, under George W. Bush, certain elements of the coalition have become ascendant. The fundamentalists have defeated the libertarians on all social issues. The supply-siders and the subsidists have defeated the Main Streeters on tax cuts, the deficit, and government subsidies. The messianists came to the fore in the run-up to the war in Iraq; the realists remained silent. The crime busters have made surprisingly little noise, and the liberals have all but disappeared. The racemongers, aware of the growing Hispanic population of potential voters, beat a tactical retreat until 2006, when they once again played the race card against the Democrats' African American U.S. Senate candidate Harold Ford of Tennessee.

But the big winners of the Bush years are the corporatists, who have indeed had their way with government, getting special deals unrequested—and undreamed of—by the corporate supporters of Eisenhower.

The only way these disparate elements in the Republican Party can be brought together is by projecting outward against some foe. If you can identify an "other" to demonize, you can mask the intramural differences. For years, anticommunism held the coalition together, but by the early 1990s the communist threat had evaporated, and as a motivating ideology anywhere, communism was dead. Now the challenge was to say what you were for, not what you were against. With accelerating globalization and technological advance sweeping across a unipolar world, the Republicans had to find a new approach.

From 1992 until 2001, the Republican Party would struggle to define what it was for. Each element of the party had its own agenda, but when they were all put together, it was a laundry list, not a philosophy. The internal contradictions of their agenda led to simmering discontent. For example, the Main Streeters were disenchanted with the party's slavish adherence to the supply-side idea that the answer to every economic problem was tax cuts. They fretted publicly that the deficit would soar as it had in the 1980s after the Reagan tax cuts. Some of the old anticommunists were auditioning China for the role of villain, but to do so they'd have to wage a frontal assault on the corporatists, who wanted to do business in China, and on the realists, who saw China not in an ideological but in a geopolitical context. Things were not looking good for Republicans, even after the Supreme Court handed them a presidential victory in 2000. Then, after September 11, 2001, the opportunity for party unity arose once again—we had a new foreign enemy.

Antiterrorism replaced anticommunism. The prospect of an aggressive Islamic caliphate, a Muslim Empire stretching from Indonesia to Europe, replaced the threat of communism conquering the world. The fear of radical Bolsheviks morphed into the fear of radical Muslims. The party could overcome its internal divisions by rallying around the banner of an all-out battle against a real threat. In the 2004 presidential race, Republicans made the election about the war on terror—a strategy that Karl Rove had decided on as early as 2002. Bush would run for reelection as a wartime president.

The administration implemented Rove's reelection strategy in many ways. There were six orange alerts between 2002 and the 2004 election. Since the election, and as of this writing, there have been two. Frequent speeches and briefings by administration officials attacked Osama bin Laden, and when it seemed that he had been driven to ground, and perhaps killed, they shifted the focus of public attention to Saddam Hussein. Bush prepared for that shift by telling Secretary of Defense Donald Rumsfeld seventy-two days after September 11 to begin secret planning for an invasion of Iraq. The Iraq War put Bush in command of an army fighting a country whose leader was easy to characterize as the personification of evil. The quick victory on the field of traditional war was followed by Bush's aircraft-carrier landing and cocky assertion of "Mission accomplished." The president often spoke to cheering military audiences, while the White House made sure that the press was not allowed to photograph the coffins of dead soldiers. All this fed into creating the image that Karl Rove wanted in 2004. The Bush campaign put out a very simple message: "We will protect you better than the other guy." Short, sweet, and entirely nonresponsive to the problems looming on the domestic front.

Such a message, besides being manipulative, dealt with only one of the problems threatening Americans. It said nothing about the economy, in a time of globalization and technological change; nothing about education, in a time when inventiveness had become America's most important strategic asset; nothing about health care, in a time when more than 45 million Americans didn't have health insurance and costs were out of control; nothing on pensions, when Americans who thought they had a secure retirement were arriving at it empty-handed; nothing on the environment, in a time of dangerous global climate change and massive migration to the water-constrained American West; nothing about our oil addiction, at a time of rising oil prices; nothing on the giant budget deficit, at a time when burgeoning national indebtedness threatened a lower standard of living for our children; nothing on political corruption, when more and more Americans considered bribery a way of life in

Washington; nothing on the power of the media, when every day their trivialization of these issues left the citizenry more and more unprepared to exercise its role in informed self-government.

The Republican campaign itself was malicious and despicable, charging John Kerry with padding his war record and accusing him of having shown contempt for American soldiers under fire when he opposed the war on his return from Vietnam. It was the same tactic Republicans had used in 2002 in defeating Georgia's Senator Max Cleland, a quadriplegic Vietnam veteran they charged with being soft on defense. The worst attacks on Kerry came from a committee set up by erstwhile colleagues of Karl Rove and associates of the Bush family, who were now acting in a structure that made it possible for the Bush campaign to deny that it was responsible. Intimations of treason filled the air once again, and the strategy worked.

The 2004 Republican campaign was a blatant attempt to frighten the American people. When a leader appeals to fear, he touches one of our deepest collective nerves. Just as individuals often make poor decisions in life out of fear, so do nations. Witness the internment of Japanese Americans during World War II and the mass deportation of Mexican Americans during the Great Depression, or the character assassination of the McCarthy era. Presidents should lead the citizenry beyond fear, as Franklin Delano Roosevelt did in the depths of the Depression. Contrast FDR's "The only thing we have to fear is fear itself" with the first Bush term, whose messages were hardly designed to reassure the public that whatever threat we faced as a nation, we were up to dealing with. (If we defeated Hitler, who is Osama bin Laden?) Instead, Bush kept the focus on Bin Laden and then on Saddam and, in doing so, made them into giants ever more menacing to average Americans. We were going to avenge 9/11. We were going to get Osama bin Laden "dead or alive." FDR never talked that way after Pearl Harbor. After declaring December 7, 1941, "a date which will live in infamy," he went on to instill in us a conviction that we would win because of our strengths and that it was important to the world that we win. He bucked people up, urging them to sacrifice for the troops. He gave each American, even children, something to do to help the country win. Maybe it was collecting scrap iron, or planting a victory garden, or enduring the hardships of rationing. Maybe it was buying U.S. savings bonds. Surely it was sending sons and husbands to fight the just war. Every American knew the stakes—and the sacrifices required.

Such breadth of leadership in the face of a real threat was not what Bush was interested in. Certainly he wanted to win the war, and he saw things in stark terms of good and evil. But too much of the effort was stage-managed to bring about his reelection. The more afraid Americans were, the better his chances. Because he failed to ask for sacrifices from everyone, he allowed people to feel that Iraq and the war on terrorism were apart from their daily lives and let the terrible burden of war fall on a small number of young people in the armed forces and National Guard. Because of the way he led, he left people fearful instead of rallying them.

Limited Government

If there is something other than antiterrorism that unites all Republicans today (at least rhetorically), it is limited government. But when Republicans say "limited government," they never define what they mean. Do they want to repeal the welfare measures that sprang from the New Deal? That was what Taft and Goldwater wanted to do. Or are they like Ike, who accepted the welfare state? If not, what would they eliminate: Medicare, Social Security, aid for highways, education, college loans? Would they close the national parks? Would they disband the regulatory agencies? They don't say.

"Limited government" is a hollow concept unless you can be specific, and most of them aren't. They will pick here and there at certain government programs to cut but rarely touch a constituency they might need in the next election, especially the clientele of their K Street lobbyist fund-raisers. The most striking fact of the first Bush term was that the president didn't veto a single appropriations bill, even as spending rose sharply. The last time that happened during a full-term presidency was in that of John Quincy Adams, from 1825 to 1829. My father would have resigned from the party because of such Republican profligacy.

Hostility toward government is deep-seated in the hearts of Republicans. Most rank-and-file Republicans want government out of their lives. They want no interference with the way they run their businesses. They demean government every chance they get. Remember Reagan saying, "Government is the problem"? They don't want to pay taxes; they resent the regulations of the Environmental Protection Agency; they see less need than Democrats do for the Food and Drug Administration, the Federal Trade Commission, the Securities and Exchange Commission, and other regulatory agencies. They want things left to the private sector and to individuals.

With this mind-set, it's understandable why, when they control government, they appoint cronies instead of competent professionals to head government agencies—one prominent example being FEMA, the Federal Emergency Management Agency, in charge of responding to natural disasters such as hurricanes. To Republicans, who have very little respect for government, these jobs connote patronage, not responsibility. Unable to abolish government agencies, they often turn them over to advocates of the very industries they are supposed to regulate. The current administration is loaded with lobbyists who now "regulate" the industries for which they formerly lobbied and for which they will lobby once again, after they're out of government. One imagines that, when they return to their old jobs, bonuses will await them for their loyal work on the inside.

The pattern during the Bush II years has been to use a public purpose as a way to enrich your friends but with no oversight to assure that the public purpose is being achieved. No-bid contracts occur routinely and are awarded to favored companies, whose executives have personal ties to administration officials and disproportionately to Republican politicians in red states. This is considered just good politics. Not surprisingly, some of the companies who got the no-bid contracts in Iraq did scandalously lousy jobs. One company got $243 million to build 150 health clinics; two years later the money was gone but only 20 clinics have been constructed. Who was watching that company? Not its friends in the administration.

Excessive politicizing of public policy had its best example in the early days after deposing Saddam in Iraq. Then, as Rajiv Chandrasekaran recounts in his new book, *Imperial Life in the Emerald City: Inside Iraq's Green Zone*, political loyalty and political connections were more important than talent. The choke point for hiring was in the Defense Department, where nearly all significant employees had to get by Jim O'Beirne, a political appointee, who screened out those insufficiently loyal to the Republican cause. Having voted for George Bush, or supporting his version of the war on terror or his vision for Iraq, even agreeing with the Republican position on *Roe v. Wade*, became more important in the hiring decisions than fluency in Arabic or experience in postwar reconstruction. As one loyalist told Chandrasekaran, "I'm not here for Iraqis. I'm here for George Bush."

The result, of course, was colossal incompetence. Chandrasekaran writes:

> Endowed with $18 billion in U.S. reconstruction funds and a comparatively quiescent environment in the immediate aftermath of the U.S. invasion, the CPA [Coalition Provisional Authority, run by America's viceroy, L. Paul Bremer] was the U.S. government's first and best hope to resuscitate Iraq—to establish order, promote rebuilding and assemble a viable government, all of which, experts believe, would have constricted the insurgency and mitigated the chances of civil war. . . . But many CPA staff members were more interested in other things: in instituting a flat tax, in selling off government assets, in ending food rations and otherwise fashioning a new nation that looked a lot like the United States. Many of them spent their days cloistered in the Green Zone, a walled-off enclave in central Baghdad with towering palms, posh villas, well-stocked bars, and resort-size swimming pools.

An example of this cronyism was the hiring of James Haveman, who was charged with reviving the Iraqi health care system. He had been recommended to Deputy Secretary of Defense Paul Wolfowitz by the former Republican governor of Michigan, John Engler, under whom he had served as community health director. Haveman, a social worker by training, possessed few obvious qualifications for the job. Running a Christian adoption agency in Michigan that worked to discourage women from having abortions and travelling abroad as director of a faith-based relief organization that delivered health care in the developing world were his two most notable achievements at the time of his appointment. One of Haveman's strongly held views was that health care in Iraq should not be free, and that Iraqis henceforth should pay a small fee for care. He allocated a sizable portion of the Iraqi health ministry's $793 million to maternity hospitals and community medical clinics, in preference—his critics charge—to emergency rooms that were treating the victims of insurgents' attacks. Although proud of his record in Iraq (he points to raises in salaries for health care workers, as well as money allocated for vaccinations), Haveman left the country in just under a year, having accomplished virtually nothing of lasting importance.

Even homeland security has turned into a giant pork barrel, as retired ambassador Charles Freeman pointed out to new members of Congress in January 2007. The Department of Homeland Security identified 160 places as potential terrorist sites in 2003. Then, after the big money was appropriated for homeland security, the definition of potential targets was loosened, and suddenly there were 1,849 sites. Today, there are more than 77,000 potential terrorist sites in America, including the Apple and Pork Festival in Illinois.

Neglect of government leads to ineffective government. Unqualified people run its agencies; unworthy companies are enriched; civil-service professionals are cut out of the policy process in favor of political appointees; budgets are reduced, so laws cannot be adequately enforced; and responsibilities are reorganized, so politics, not substance, will dictate decisions. Those are all the things you do when you don't like government. The result: The nation suffers.

Individuals acting on their own can't solve the problems of the world. The nonprofit sector doesn't have enough resources (for example, foundations give public schools about $1.2 billion annually, out of the $475.0 billion spent for public education), and the purpose of business is to make a profit, not to solve public problems. Only government has the reach and the authority to accomplish big things. In a dynamic capitalist economy, government not only helps those who have fallen by the wayside but also establishes the rules and the stability which allow that economy to thrive. The one thing every developing country desperately needs is what we have: a stable governmental apparatus capable of honesty and competence. Yet too often Republicans demean its very existence.

Systems Approaches

Fewer and fewer Republicans see the need for a systems approach; they seem satisfied with a string of positions on various issues. The health care crisis, they say, can be solved by health savings accounts. The pension crisis can be solved by the privatization of Social Security and defined-contribution plans. The education crisis can be solved by vouchers and state standardized tests. The oil crisis is not a crisis at all, but if it were to become one, it could be solved by $100 rebates and greater subsidies to oil companies. The environmental crisis is dealt with by denying it exists. And on the economy, the answer is always and ever the same: tax cuts.

The key insight of systems analysis is the interrelation of the parts. It recognizes that we are all individuals living in a social whole, and when the whole unravels, the individual suffers. A system is holistic—greater than the sum of its parts. The current Republican ideology of hyperindividualism has no understanding of the whole and thus cannot really fathom the importance of taking the whole, interrelated system into account in making policy.

When Dwight Eisenhower promoted the interstate highway system, he was seeing the country whole. If you want to move people around the country effectively, you can't have a crazy quilt of roads; you need a road *system*. When FDR instituted the Securities and Exchange Commission, he did so to give financial markets the confidence that someone was representing all of us, vouching for the safety of the financial *system*, so that crooks and fast-buck artists would be less likely to steal investors' money. When Congress passed the Colorado River compacts, it took charge not of a part of the river in one state but of the entire river *system* in seven states and Mexico, assuring equitable use and clear rules. We need to embrace systems approaches and make the necessary investment in their research and development, instead of running from them and constraining investment so that governmental failure is guaranteed. Ironically, when it comes to the military, Republicans admit that effectiveness depends on a systems approach and adequate resources. Indeed, the military has done a good job on systems. That's what you need when you run a big enterprise like the Pentagon. The rest of government has not, and given current Republican thinking, it never will.

The Role of a President

A party is shaped by a president, and President Bush appears only to react to events. September 11 isn't the only example. Planning is an integrative task, and he's not good at it. Reacting, by contrast, is generally black and white, and for that he is very well suited. In that mode, you get to intuit an answer, as opposed to thinking your way through to it. Such a mind sees the world as either-or. Either you're for him or against him. Either Islam is bad or it is good. Either Democrats are patriotic (as Bush defines patriotism) or they are unpatriotic. If someone wins, somebody else loses. Bush does not understand that you can think through a problem such as health care and come up with answers that open new questions—which, when solved, bring added benefit. You can get a group of people working on an issue, and as long as egos are left at the door, you can devise a solution that could have arisen only because of the group's interaction. This is creative thinking. Using this kind of approach, you can have a win-win situation. Economic growth, properly managed and buttressed by effective social programs, can be good for everyone. Trade agreements that take into account the needs of the poorest in society can be a net plus. United States military power legitimized by international support can prevent genocide, defeat terrorism, and deter nuclear proliferation. Averting disastrous climate change isn't a trade-off between jobs and clean air, as President Bush would have us believe. We can generate economic growth by cleaning up the environment. Government doesn't have to burden an economy; it can liberate it. The president and most of his administration seem stuck in zero-sum thinking, when the country's possibilities are far brighter and far more expansive than that.

No administration in modern history has been as undemocratic as the current Bush team. From the beginning, there has been a deep suspicion of anyone outside the inner circle. The motivating ethos seems to be one not of substance but of holding power for power's sake—as if government existed to serve the party, not the other way around. In their single-mindedness, Republicans threw principles—even those their own party once stood for—out the window. The case can be made that George Bush has destroyed the Republican Party by his profligacy, his arrogance, his stubborn machismo, and his absolute conviction that whatever he does is right. As a result, some factions of the party may become so alienated that they will join the Democrats or form a third party.

When Congress was drafting legislation for Medicare drug coverage, the administration did not allow its bureaucracy to divulge the true cost even to Republican congressmen. A key civil servant was threatened with job loss if he did his job of giving Congress the facts. The administration was evidently afraid that, if the true amount were known, Republicans who were fiscally conservative Main Streeters or antigovernment libertarians would not vote for such a gigantic expansion of an entitlement program, so they lied, saying the prescription-drug benefit would cost $400 billion over ten years, when their estimates showed that the true cost was $534 billion—$134 billion, or 33 percent, higher. When the final vote was called in the Republican-controlled House, a majority voted against the bill. As if withholding the true figures were not bad enough, the administration then violated House standards by keeping the vote open for nearly three hours instead of the customary fifteen minutes. During those three hours, Tom DeLay and the rest of the House Republican leadership put heavy pressure on Main Streeters and libertarians to switch their votes, even, depending on whose version of the story you believe, offering one of them a DeLay endorsement of his son's congressional bid to succeed his father or threatening him with the defeat of his son. Such extreme tactics are unusual even in the bare-knuckle game of congressional politics.

Ultimately, the prescription-drug bill passed in a form so mind-bogglingly complex that most congresspeople didn't have the faintest idea of all its provisions. You can bet that certain lobbyists did. They helped write the bill. Complexity is the habitat of special interests—a little date change in one place, a little formula tweak here, a little phase-in there, none of it explained clearly to Congress, let alone the voters. Special-interest provisions weren't invented by Republicans, of course, but under the DeLay-Bush leadership, clandestine manipulation and legislative payoffs became a governing style.

Why was there such a gross violation of the political norms of the House? Why did the president tell such a lie to his own party? Perhaps the answer is because the Bush White House operates by placing a shroud of secrecy over vast areas of government—not just health care but also national security and the environment. Some argue that Bush is simply determined to protect the prerogatives of executive power. But the real reason for the prescription-drug fiasco was more mundane: It was pure politics.

In the 1990s, Bill Clinton, in an act of political genius, defanged nearly the whole Republican coalition by co-opting issues they had used against the Democrats. He trumped the Main Streeters by running a budget surplus, the racemongers by instituting welfare reform, the crime busters by increasing aid to local police and supporting the death penalty, the realists by holding defense spending steady, the messianists by going into Kosovo, the libertarians by opposing government interference with abortion rights, the subsidists by leaving their sweetheart deals intact, the liberals by asking them to join him in a streamlined government constituted to solve problems, and the corporatists by pushing free trade and allowing an unprecedented consolidation of corporate power through massive mergers and acquisitions. Republicans—with the exception of the now ascendant fundamentalists and supply-siders—had little to criticize, because Clinton was doing what they had long advocated, but in his own way.

Karl Rove and company followed the same strategy in 2004, intent on removing issues from the Democrats' attack portfolio. First, they passed an education bill (No Child Left Behind) that caved in on requiring national standards, and then they failed to provide adequate funding for the bill's provisions. However, politically, it allowed the president and other Republicans to look good on the education issue. Likewise, with regard to the drug benefit, they managed to inoculate themselves from Democratic accusations that they were heartless to seniors and at the same time reward their corporate cronies. (To spend $534 billion in order to counter one potential political vulnerability gives new meaning to the phrase "big spender.") The clearest indication of the drug-benefit bill's political purpose is the provision that forbids Medicare to use the leverage of its 40 million eligible seniors to negotiate lower drug prices. The biggest winners were private insurance companies, drug companies, and the Bush reelection campaign. The substance wasn't important; the politics was what counted.

Iraq

The only political issue of the Bush presidency that will cost more than the prescription-drug benefit is Iraq. The same self-righteousness and swagger that played fast and loose with the facts on Medicare misled Congress and the public and got us into this terrible war. The central lie was not the nonexistent weapons of mass destruction or the prediction that Iraqis would greet American "liberators" with flowers or the notion that Iraq could immediately finance its own economic development with its oil revenues or the prospect that Iraq would give us permanent military bases to project our power in the region or that a democratic Iraq would be Israel's friend. These false assessments were as much evidence of incompetence as they were lies. The central lie was, rather, the espoused view that Iraq was linked to Al Qaeda—and Saddam Hussein to Osama bin Laden—and therefore to September 11, 2001. As I said in Chapter 3, in the summer of 2006, 64 percent of the American public still believed that Saddam had a relationship with Al Qaeda.

In pushing ahead with both the Iraq War and the Medicare drug benefit, the Republicans rejected their own people: their Main Streeters, who believed in restraining government spending, as well as their realists, who agreed with Colin Powell's doctrine as chairman of the Joint Chiefs that military force should be deployed abroad only as a last resort, only when you can see an exit strategy, and only if the force is massive enough to assure success within a reasonable time period. The war on terrorism is serious business, but it ought to consist of intelligence operations, police actions, and targeted military strikes, not the full-scale invasion of another country that harbors no Al Qaeda training center or Taliban theocracy.

The Iraq War is a war of choice—and no war should be chosen. It should be a last resort, when all else fails.

Clearly Bush was determined to avoid the fatal mistake of his father's presidency, in which the elder Bush successfully waged war only to lose at home because he had no domestic policy of consequence and no enthusiasm for developing one. Bush II went for guns *and* butter, which is why government spending went up 33 percent in just four years. When you add up the $67 billion annually for earmarked projects in favored congressional districts, the $534 billion over ten years for the Medicare drug benefit (in February 2005 it was adjusted to $724 billion), the $218 billion of lost revenue annually from the tax cuts, and the $300 billion and growing for Iraq, you see that the cost of the White House agenda made the reelection effort of 2004 the most expensive in history.

Bush and the Environment

Another aspect of the Bush presidency different from past Republican administrations is its deep distrust of environmental science. In June 2002, when the Environmental Protection Agency released a report warning of the effects of fossil fuels on global warming, Bush dismissed it as a "report put out by the bureaucracy." In other words, he disowned his own administration's work. In the EPA's annual air-pollution report that year, the White House cut the entire climate-change section. A year later, the EPA's comprehensive review of the environment contained this sentence: "Climate change has global consequences for human health and the environment." According to *The New Republic*'s editor Franklin Foer, the White House cut the sentence and then implied that global cooling was as serious a threat. Throughout the draft report, the White House inserted "may," "potentially," and other words to indicate doubt when, in the mainstream scientific community, there was none. Tom Hamburger and Alan C. Miller of the *Los Angeles Times* reported in March 2004 that when the administration watered down the regulations for mercury emissions, "EPA staffers say they were told not to undertake the normal scientific and economic studies called for under a standing executive order." The EPA administrator, the former New Jersey governor Christine Todd Whitman, who had a good environmental record in environmentally conscious New Jersey, had an impossible assignment, given the priorities of the White House. She left the administration in the summer of 2003 in order to spend more time with her family, but surely she also must have been tired of losing policy fights and being vilified by liberal and conservative activists alike.

After she departed the EPA, Governor Whitman wrote a book in praise of moderate Republicanism—particularly on social issues, such as abortion rights. Yet when her pro-environmental views were being ignored by the White House, she remained silent, choosing to be a team player whose political future would be served by going along with things she didn't believe in, instead of a leader who chose to resign on principle.

And yet there are Republican exceptions to this example of timidity. Bill Owens, the Republican governor of Colorado, was instrumental in modifying a state provision that required state surpluses to be refunded to taxpayers and voter approval to be given for tax increases. He felt that the change was essential because the deteriorating roads of Colorado deserved more money. Grover Norquist, a far-right Republican political activist whose whole world is Washington spin, said of Owens, "His national political career is over" and "Being on the wrong side of this issue is a career-ender." It would seem that Governor Owens put the future of his state above conventional ambition or party ideology. Another Republican, former New Jersey Republican governor Tom Kean, also consistently acted in the nation's interest as the head of the National Commission on Terrorist Attacks upon the United States (the 9/11 Commission), building a bipartisan consensus and openly challenging the administration when it refused to produce the necessary documents. He made few friends in the White House, but in remaining steadfast to the mission of telling the American people the truth, he provided the best example of Republican leadership in a generation.

Whereas the EPA administrator Whitman simply adjusted her sense of the possible in silence, the interior secretary Gale Norton was proactively destructive. In the 1980s, Norton's counterpart was

James Watt, a nice man personally, who spoke exclusively for the fundamentalists and the subsidists, often sayings things that embarrassed the Reagan administration. He elicited fervent opposition from environmentalists of both parties. His confrontational, macho style ignited support for environmental organizations from the grass roots to the seats of power in Washington. The result was that very little of the conservative environmental agenda got done—Watt had made its consequences too clear.

Gale Norton was different. She said soothing things to Congress and avoided statements that put her in the headlines. She rarely asked Congress to act. She seemed happiest in the absence of any environmental legislation—even efforts to repeal the laws with which she disagreed. She preferred to do her damage quietly, through appointment, regulation, and interpretation. It was the stealth way, hidden from view. A department with the right political appointees can find many reasons not to enforce the law. They can frustrate the law's intent by issuing contradictory regulations, thereby precipitating a legal battle that can go on for years and prevent the law from being implemented (as happened to California's Central Valley Project in 1992). In her more than six years on the job, Norton elicited little attention, even though she presided over a department whose key posts were occupied by former Republican lobbyists from the mining, ranching, energy, and water industries. And then there is the use of language, almost Orwellian in effect. As Robert F. Kennedy Jr. says about the administration's environmental record in his hard-hitting book *Crimes Against Nature*,

> Bush's "Healthy Forests" initiative promotes destructive logging of old-growth forests. His "Clear Skies" program suggests repealing key provisions of the Clean Air Act. The administration talks about "streamlining" and "reforming" regulations when it means weakening them, and "thinning" when it means logging or clear-cutting. Cloaked in this meticulously crafted language that is designed to deceive the public, the administration—often unwittingly abetted by a toothless and negligent press—intends to effectively eliminate the nation's most important environmental laws by the end of its term.

Although most CEOs are corporatist Republicans, not all are hostile to the environment. Some feel a strong concern for the fragility of our planet. When a national government cuts the budget for research and rejects the science that industry depends on for its competitive edge, more and more CEOs will eventually part ways with the governing party. Because they have to think globally, CEOs of multinational corporations increasingly will understand why green is good business and stewardship is common sense. Environmental issues such as climate change or water allocation will become a part of their own self-interested, long-term planning process. British Petroleum ads are announcing that BP stands for "Beyond Petroleum." Royal Dutch/Shell has invested over a billion dollars in alternative energy research and development. It is far ahead of some elements of the Republican coalition. But individual companies, no matter how clearly they see the issues, cannot have a lasting effect. Only a concerted government effort can protect our planet.

Stem-Cell Research

Bush's support, in deference to his Christian fundamentalist base, for teaching the theory of "intelligent design" alongside the theory of evolution in high school biology classes arguably does little lasting harm. However, the administration's position on stem-cell research, another target of the Christian right, could cost lives. One of Bush's most tortured positions, it allowed federal dollars to be used for research into existing stem-cell lines but not for the creation of new lines. All the hoopla about how the president wrestled with the issue was an obvious attempt to appease both the fundamentalists, who believe that life begins at conception and thus want no such research at all, and the liberals and corporatists (to say nothing of Nancy Reagan), who believe that stem-cell research, besides facilitating job creation and technological breakthroughs, will hasten the development of cures for deadly afflictions such as Alzheimer's and Parkinson's disease.

In an op-ed piece in *The New York Times* in March 2005, the former Republican senator John C. Danforth, an ordained Episcopal minister who understands the shortsightedness of such an approach, wrote:

> It is not evident to many of us that cells in a petri dish are equivalent to identifiable people suffering from terrible diseases. I am and have always been pro-life. But the only explanation for legislators comparing cells in a petri dish to babies in the womb is the extension of religious doctrine into statutory law. . . .
>
> The problem is not with people or churches that are politically active. It is with a party that has gone so far in adopting a sectarian agenda that it has become the political extension of a religious movement. . . .
>
> Take stem cell research. Criminalizing the work of scientists doing such research would give strong support to one religious doctrine, and it would punish people who believe it is their religious duty to use science to heal the sick. . . .
>
> As a senator, I worried every day about the size of the federal deficit. I did not spend a single minute worrying about the effect of gays on the institution of marriage. Today it seems to be the other way around.

To which I say, "Amen!"

The Mistrust of Experts

There is within the Republican Party a deep suspicion of the empirical basis of science in general, and when government is called upon to get involved, many Republicans see only a liberal political agenda. In 1993, some of them founded an organization called the Advancement of Sound Science Coalition. Stanton Glantz and Elisa Ong, of the Institute for Health Policy Studies at the University of California, San Francisco, describe it thus: "The 'sound science' movement is not an indigenous effort from within the profession to improve the quality of scientific discourse, but reflects sophisticated public relations campaigns controlled by industry executives and lawyers whose aim is to manipulate the standards of scientific proof to serve the corporate interests of their clients." Gale Norton advised the group before joining the administration. As usual, Republicans use words that are chosen to hide what they mean. "Intelligent design" used to be called creationism; "sound science" means corporate science; "reasoned inquiry" leads to extreme results.

For a while, the administration considered prohibiting scientists who received government support from engaging in peer review of any scientific research done by the agency from which they received the support. When that proposal fell of its own weight, the administration shifted responsibility for agency decision making from government experts, who might actually know something about the subject, to political appointees, who do what the White House tells them to do. Republican members of Congress participate in this sort of intimidation, too. In June 2005, Joe Barton (R.–Tex.), then chairman of the House Energy and Commerce Committee and a longtime friend of oil interests, didn't like what several eminent climatologists had to say about global warming. David Ignatius, writing in *The Washington Post*, reports that Barton sent letters to three of these scientists

> demanding information about what he claimed were methodological flaws and data errors in their studies of global warming. Barton's letters to the scientists had a peremptory, when-did-you-stop-beating-your-wife tone. [One scientist] was told that within less than three weeks, he must list "all financial support you have received related to your research," provide "the location of all data archives relating to each published study for which you were an author," "provide all agreements relating to . . . underlying grants or funding," and deliver similarly detailed information in five other categories.

Such behavior is a long way from that of Republicans under Eisenhower, or even Nixon, both of whom supported science. These days the answers seem to come from God—or from corporate cronies who know the right answer (or at least the politically expedient one) before the research is done.

Franklin Foer, the editor of *The New Republic*, wrote in July 2004 that the Bush administration "takes the radically postmodern view that 'science,' 'objectivity,' and 'truth' are guises for an ulterior, leftist agenda; that experts are so incapable of dispassionate and disinterested analysis that their work doesn't even merit a hearing." That "postmodern view" applies in spades to the administration's attitude toward the intelligence community. The CIA is full of experts. During my years in government, I thought that it had, person for person, the best talent in government. From its founding, its purpose was to gather information and tell policy makers the facts. But the Defense Department of the Bush administration, driven by the zeal of the political appointees Paul Wolfowitz and Douglas Feith, so distrusted the CIA that they reportedly prevented Defense Department employees from engaging in interagency reviews about worst-case scenarios in Iraq. A Policy Counterterrorism Evaluation Group was set up in the Defense Department under Feith for the purpose of, in Foer's words, "reanalyzing the CIA's raw intelligence and scouring for instances of Iraqi sponsorship of terrorism that the Agency had been too biased to catch." Foer goes on to write that Richard Perle, Iraq war advocate, occasional adviser to Israel's Likud Party, old cold warrior, and former chairman of the administration's Defense Policy Board, described the justification for the reanalysis group in a July 2003 interview with PBS's *Frontline* as follows: "If you're walking down the street, [and] you're not looking for hidden treasure, you won't find it. If you're looking for it, you may find something. In this case, the CIA hadn't been looking."

Foer notes further:

Perle's metaphor, however, crumbles almost instantly. For starters, it's not like the CIA hadn't spent thousands of man-hours searching for an Al Qaeda–Iraq nexus. . . . The CIA searched intensely and found little significant evidence. And that's the problem with Perle's analysis. He wanted foregone conclusions built into the intelligence analysts' assumptions. (The treasure must be hidden!) This methodology led the Bush administration to look past the CIA's caveat-riddled assessment of Saddam's WMD programs, overrule the Agency's doubts about whether Iraqi agents had tried to buy Nigerian yellowcake, and uncritically swallow testimony from defectors provided by the Iraqi National Congress.

Faith-based Economics

The Bush administration's antipathy for experts extends even to tax policy. When you propose a tax cut, you have to determine its impact on the budget. Ever since tax cuts were added to the Republican political arsenal in 1980 by Ronald Reagan, some supply-side Republicans have insisted on a so-called dynamic analysis of the proposed tax cut. A dynamic analysis means not simply calculating the amount of revenue lost from a tax cut but also showing how the cut will stimulate economic growth, raising incomes and therefore resulting in more tax revenues. The deficit is then the difference between what is lost in tax revenue from a particular tax cut and what is gained in economic growth.

Until the Bush administration, such analyses were rejected in official policy circles, because they involved so many assumptions that you could make them say anything. The government bodies that deal with tax policy—the Joint Tax Committee, the Congressional Budget Office, and the Office of Management and Budget—gave an objective but static analysis, concluding, for example, that a tax cut of $100 billion would result in roughly $100 billion less in government revenue, which would increase the deficit by roughly $100 billion.

In the Bush White House, this approach—the one used by the ultimate supply-sider, Ronald Reagan, and by George Bush's father—no longer sufficed. It produced inconvenient facts, such as that tax cuts increase the deficit. The Bush administration prefers the faith-based economics of "dynamic analysis." The Council of Economic Advisers, the president's economists, promote dynamic analysis with very few caveats and without explaining a convincing methodology—that is, they attempt to justify the theory that tax cuts create more growth and more government revenue.

The amazing thing is that the media don't hold supply-siders accountable. If the economy grows and the budget deficit drops, the supply-siders assert that it was because of tax cuts—not low interest rates or spending cuts or technological innovation or the sinking value of the dollar, which promotes exports. If the deficit goes up and the economy sinks, few in the media ever revisit the supply-siders' predictions. In the face of evidence that the premise isn't working, supply-siders simply continue to invoke dynamic analysis and advocate further tax cuts.

What Do the Republicans Stand For?

So what *do* Republicans stand for? The Medicare drug entitlement has denied them the platform of "limited government." A first term without one presidential veto even as federal spending increased 33 percent has denied them the platform of "fiscal responsibility." The Iraq War has destroyed the idea that they are advocates of a sober, limited foreign policy. The demeaning of government belies the convictions of liberal Republicans, who presumably still believe that the federal government, if it is managed well, can solve national problems. The total capitulation to the fundamentalist right on everything from stem-cell research to demonizing gays to U.S. policy on the Israeli-Palestinian conflict has eliminated the word "moderate" from the Republican lexicon and flouted everything the libertarian Republicans stood for. The Patriot Act has extended the long arm of government into the private lives of citizens, allowing for everything from reading your medical records and taking note of your bookstore purchases to searching your house or business premises without your knowledge. Robert Taft, Everett Dirksen, Howard Baker Jr. — even Barry Goldwater — would never have stood for it. The opening up of government coffers to industry special interests by granting them obscenely generous special favors has embarrassed those Republicans who believe that the market, not Congress, is the most efficient allocator of resources. The refusal even to jawbone oil companies into returning a portion of the billions they got from government errors in writing oil leases in the Gulf of Mexico, and the reduction of what tobacco companies will have to pay in the national tobacco settlement to fund stop-smoking programs (from $130 billion over twenty-five years to $10 billion over five years), along with legislation that makes it nearly impossible to sue the gun industry, have removed any doubt that, under this administration, government has been for sale. The result of all this could be to destroy the Republican Party as we have known it. Only ambition for power holds the current Republican coalition together. All this is the work of one Republican president in just six years.

Given the contradictions that exist within that coalition, and the rigidity of its elements, Republicans can't begin to solve the problems facing America. They offer simplistic and ideological answers, require lockstep adherence to narrow party positions (in order to hold their various factions together), proclaim the absoluteness of their version of morality, and serve whoever has the biggest bankroll. They can issue no clear call to the nation without appealing to fear, greed, nostalgia, or prejudice.

Conservative Republican ideology flows from a premise that human beings are inherently evil or sinful. Only religion can save us from our true natures. Paradoxically, this ideology champions the individual (and places all responsibility on the individual), because its adherents doubt that people can unselfishly join in a national effort to make their collective lives better. Human nature, these ideologues say, makes such cooperation impossible. Our sense of commonality gives way before the power of our individuality. So government, which is the expression of our collective efforts and views, can only be flawed and corrupt. The irony is that these Republican naysayers, who control eighteen of the fifty state Republican parties and have large minorities in another twenty-six, are pessimistic about what we can do together in spite of their membership in churches whose congregations continually work together for the common good.

A greater irony is that their pessimism about what we can do together gives way to an unjustified optimism when it comes to what the individual can do. Together we can't develop a health care system that is affordable and comprehensive, they say—but all of us as individuals, aware that no one will be there to take care of us, can produce enough money from somewhere or other to cover our own doctor bills and can learn enough over the Internet to make complex choices on treatment and health plans. They are confident that individuals will amass enough money for health care and decent pensions by relying on the performance of the stock market, even though 51 percent of Americans own no stocks. If you can believe that individuals who don't save will now save if they are given a tax incentive, or that individuals who have little medical knowledge will suddenly acquire it, why can't you believe that a group of people with the right incentives and inspiration can act unselfishly? That is what happens in America when we are at our best.

At its heart, the Republican message limits the human spirit's ability to soar. Each of us, like the grasshopper in Aesop's fable, should suffer the consequences of our individual actions and not be redeemed by collective action. Too often the Republicans currently in power seem to want only retribution, not salvation, and least of all justice. I have been inspired too often by collective action that transforms lives for the better to accept such a pinched view of our possibilities as a people.

When it comes to the rules of our democracy, the Republicans usually start with a reasonable premise—such as that people shouldn't vote twice or illegal immigrants should not be able to vote. Who could object to that? They then prescribe actions that are undemocratic. For example, the House recently passed a bill stipulating that by 2008 you can't vote if you don't have a passport, driver's license, or some other enhanced governmental identification (whatever that is). Bank statements mailed to your house, or university ID cards, won't suffice. The effect of these prescriptions will be to disenfranchise voters who are likely to vote Democratic—those people too poor to have a passport, say, or too old to drive a car. In Missouri, Republican legislators recently pushed through a law requiring a government-issued ID—a law that could disqualify as many as 200,000 Missourians: To get the proper documentation often requires showing a birth certificate, which many people don't have and in some cases cannot afford to get. In Texas, it's a crime to carry someone else's filled-out absentee ballot to a mailbox unless you're a family member or designated in writing by the voter. So much for helping the disabled to vote. Republicans try to manipulate even the mechanical aspects of voting. In Florida, once paper ballots have been counted by machine, it is illegal to tally them by hand. Throughout the country, Republicans advocate touch-screen electronic voting, which is vulnerable to hackers, implemented by private companies with little public oversight, and, best of all to Republicans, cannot be re-counted if the machine malfunctions. While these approaches are more subtle than having off-duty police stand in black precincts to intimidate voters, as Republicans did in the 1980s, they have the same effect—to reduce the Democratic turnout.

I have a friend who knows one of the Republican Party's most prodigious fund-raisers. In a candid moment one night over dinner, the fund-raiser confided to my friend that Republicans didn't have the issues to reach the majority of Americans and get their votes. To win, he said, they ran smarter campaigns than the Democrats: They raised more money, exerted more discipline on their candidates, conveyed a clearer message. They used the most advanced private-sector data-mining skills to target their messages at the precinct level and built grassroots organizations that pulled those voters to the polls. He cited the example of the fundamentalist Christians in southern Ohio, who dramatically increased their turnout between 2000 and 2004. Republicans also use state referenda in election years to get out their vote. In November 2004, eleven states (including Ohio) put state constitutional amendments opposing gay marriage on the ballot. The action served two purposes: It was a skillful diversionary tactic—let's talk about gays, not about jobs or health care—and a way to get out the vote, since those who trooped to the polls to vote against gay marriage would doubtless also vote Republican. Republicans have become masters at using culture as a wedge, by raising emotional but peripheral issues such as the death penalty, gun control, gay marriage, the Pledge of Allegiance, the Ten Commandments—all in an attempt to draw a contrast between themselves and Democrats that favors them with targeted populations. All of these techniques explain why Republicans, according to political analyst Michael Barone, have dominated 97 of the 100 fastest-growing counties in the country, and they are also why many of the party's big fund-raisers believe the debacle of 2006 was just an anomaly.

The Republican Pyramid

How did this political machine develop?

In the late sixties, the streets were full of people protesting the war in Vietnam. In 1970 students demonstrating against the war were shot at Kent State by young National Guardsmen. The Weatherman faction of the Students for a Democratic Society was openly calling for revolution while the mainline SDS called for organized resistance to the draft. The Black Panthers were charging the society with racist exploitation. The media gave each group's actions much attention. Radical became chic. In this context, Lewis Powell, a distinguished Virginia lawyer soon to become a Supreme Court justice, wrote a memo in August 1971 to a member of the board of directors of the U.S. Chamber of Commerce laying out what he saw as the threat to the free-enterprise system posed by liberal professors, television commentators, college students, journalists, war protesters, and the new left. Powell proposed a comprehensive set of countermeasures. He argued that Republicans should dominate and control the debate in venues he called "the respectable elements of society": the media, university campuses, intellectual journals, the arts and sciences. He urged conservatives to make support of the free-enterprise agenda the only possible choice for politicians. Such an effort, he said, should be massively funded. He urged funding conservative scholars in universities and closely monitoring textbooks to assess whether they treated free enterprise fairly. He recommended the establishment of conservative education programs in high schools. Finally, he wanted to place the right's views in scholarly journals and pursue an activist strategy in local, state, and federal courts.

The Republican structure that emerged from Powell's blueprint looks like a pyramid. The first level consists of the funders. In 2004, the National Committee for Responsive Philanthropy put out a report by Jeff Krehely, Meaghan House, and Emily Kernan entitled *Axis of Ideology: Conservative Foundations and Public Policy*. In it we learn that conservative foundations such as the Sarah Scaife Foundation of Pittsburgh, the Lynde and Harry Bradley Foundation of Milwaukee, the John M. Olin Foundation of New York, and the Koch Family Foundations of Kansas and Washington, DC, have given hundreds of millions of dollars to conservative think tanks. Recipients include groups such as the Manhattan Institute for Policy Research (which attacks the philosophical basis of social welfare programs), the National Center for Policy Analysis (which supports Social Security privatization), the Center for Security Policy (which advocates withdrawing from the Anti-Ballistic Missile Treaty), the Heritage Foundation, the Cato Institute, the Intercollegiate Studies Institute, and the American Enterprise Institute. In addition, conservative money went to private, state-based think tanks who try to influence the thinking of state legislatures.

In 1989, there were only twelve state-based, free-enterprise-oriented think tanks; now that number is forty. *Axis of Ideology* reports that total conservative giving from Pennsylvania foundations between 1999 and 2001 was $60 million. New York foundations gave $48 million in grants to conservative public policy organizations, with California, Wisconsin, and Kansas all doing likewise in double figures, ranging from $10 million to $40 million. Some conservative organizations put out expansive mission statements, such as the American Legislative Exchange Council's declared intent "to promote the principles of federalism by developing and promoting policies that reflect the Jeffersonian principles that the powers of government are derived from, and assigned to, first the People, then the States, and finally the National Government." They produce publications, such as the Heritage Foundation's "Support and Defend: How Congress Can Save the Constitution from the Supreme Court" or another from the same foundation, a "WebMemo" entitled simply "In Defense of Marriage."

After developing their ideas, the think tanks make sure the ideas get on television even if some Republicans disagree with them (and they do). The Heritage Foundation's 2002 annual report revealed that Heritage scholars had made more television appearances that year than throughout the 1990s. In that year alone, they logged 600 national and international television programs, 1,000 radio broadcasts, and 8,000 newspaper and magazine articles and editorials. Heritage seizes every chance it gets to proselytize. It provides to its college interns an "intense" exposure to conservative ideas, themes, and principles. It devotes more than 40 percent of its budget to government relations, media, and education programs.

At the American Enterprise Institute, a new program aims to study, according to *Axis of Ideology*, not only "economic prosperity, technological prowess and social equity" but also "family breakdown, poor schools, high levels of crime, coarsening of popular culture, the ethical dilemmas of bioengineering and the threat of mass terrorism." (These subjects are a long way from Lewis Powell's free-enterprise focus.) Heritage and AEI agree that success depends on affirmative ideas (conservatives can't just be naysayers but must present a positive alternative), bipartisanship (they reach out to Democrats, who often are willing to cosponsor a proposal they think will moderate their image), and above all long-term general funding.

The think tanks hire the intellectuals who generate ideas (health savings accounts, privatization of Social Security, school vouchers, estate-tax elimination) that are passed on up to the next level of the pyramid, which is the political level. Here the gurus (Karl Rove, Ken Mehlman, Ed Gillespie) take the ideas and, through focus groups and sophisticated polling, turn them into slogans—reverse discrimination, limousine liberals, death tax, compassionate conservatism. The slogans go on up to the next level of the pyramid, which is the media level. Rush Limbaugh, Ann Coulter, and others repeat the slogans, over and over. In time, the slogans condition an electorate to believe that Democrats are "big spenders," "soft on crime," and "weak on defense." Because Democrats want the Bush tax cuts to benefit the middle class more than the wealthy, they are said to be "conducting class warfare." They are "blind" to the power of religious faith, or "trapped" in the 1960s paradigm of pot-smoking protest, or "committed to high taxes" and "spendthrift" government and willing to waste money on the "undeserving" poor. Above all, they fail to understand that "Americans are overtaxed."

At the top of the Republican pyramid sits the president. Before a Republican presidential candidate runs, he has a body of conservative think-tank work, assembled over the years, from which to draw his economic and social program. It is conceptual and programmatic, with the winning political language and slogans attached. It has powerful appeal to the right wing. The monetary investment in talent and ideas has paid off. In this sense, Bush has outdone his Republican predecessor Theodore Roosevelt, who built on the intellectual ferment of the progressive tradition. All a conservative Republican presidential candidate has to do is repeat the tested phrases and concentrate on how to tar the opponent. Moderate Republicans have been shouted off the stage, like Nelson Rockefeller at the 1964 Republican convention.

The battle of ideas has, by design, infiltrated college campuses. At the time of the *Axis of Ideology* report, the Young Republicans had more than 120,000 members in 1,148 chapters, while Democrats listed only 500 college chapters. These college Republican organizations try to influence the thinking and teaching on U.S. campuses. For example, they fund conservative student newspapers. The Intercollegiate Studies Institute, whose goal is to "educate for liberty," supports 900 representatives on college campuses nationwide and counts 50,000 students and faculty as members. The 300 conferences that the ISI annually mounts promote limited government, personal liberty, the free-enterprise system, and traditional morality. Conservative students keep an eye on their professors for "liberal bias." At the University of Texas at Austin, a conservative student published a watch list of liberal professors. A book by the right-wing activist David Horowitz called *The Professors: The 101 Most Dangerous Academics in America* was published in early 2006. College professors are being attacked, according to *Axis of Ideology*, for pushing a "far left interpretation of American history" and "criticizing American foreign policy and the Bush administration."

One of the biggest education investments by conservative think tanks is in the area of school choice. The Bradley Foundation has spent $21 million on programs promoting private and parochial school vouchers in Milwaukee alone and has pledged another $20 million. By far the most controversial legal organization funded by conservative money is Judicial Watch, which claims to oversee the ethical conduct of public life. Nearly all of its 107 cases (as of the 2004 publication of *Axis of Ideology*) were brought against Bill Clinton, Hillary Clinton, or Clinton administration officials—though early in the Bush II presidency it also started going after Tom DeLay.

In the social area, almost a quarter of the $17,664,633 spent by conservative foundations between 1999 and 2001, according to Krehely, House, and Kernan, went for organizations working to defeat feminist issues. These organizations, such as the Independent Women's Forum and the Clare Boothe Luce Policy Institute, consider feminism an extreme ideology. They want to roll back Title IX (which gave women, among other things, equal access to sports in school programs), eliminate a battlefield role for women in the military, and reconsider policies against sexual harassment. They don't see a gender bias in society, and they think the women's movement has damaged women, families, and society.

In the environmental area, the most prominent organization is the Foundation for Research on Economics & the Environment (FREE), whose members describe themselves as "intellectual entrepreneurs, explaining how economic incentives, secure property rights, the rule of law, and responsible prosperity can foster a healthy environment." With funding from conservative foundations and companies such as ExxonMobil, Merck, and General Motors, they conduct all-expenses-paid seminars for federal judges. They assert that current environmental laws harm economic efficiency and should be modified and that judges should reinterpret the Constitution to undermine existing environmental laws and uphold the property rights of corporations and landowners. Krehely, House, and Kernan reveal that between 1992 and 1998, 137 federal judges took 194 trips to FREE seminars, largely in Montana and Wisconsin, and if you add those judges who expressed an interest in attending, this amounts to nearly a third of the federal judiciary. Finally, money from conservative foundations went to the conservative media watchdog groups, such as the Media Research Center and Accuracy in Media, for the purpose of exposing and neutralizing what these groups consider liberal media bias. Accuracy in Media publishes its results in a bimonthly newsletter, has established a speakers' bureau, and sponsors syndicated weekly newspaper columns.

This conservative Republican pyramid has become a structure that is very difficult for Democrats to duplicate in a short time. It has been built up for more than thirty years. Some characteristics of the effort stand out. Republican groups generally allow the recipients of their money great flexibility by giving general operating funds, not funds tied to specific projects. They invest for the long term—not just years but decades, recognizing that ideas such as Social Security privatization take time to develop and that organizations need time to mature. They stay with their grantees, allowing them to work toward a common conservative goal at a leisurely pace. They invest in efforts to communicate the ideas—to get them into the public policy debate and the broader public awareness. By reaching agreement on broader political goals, they don't have to micromanage or coordinate action; it's left to the grantees to organize their service to the larger cause.

The pyramid of money, ideas, political research, and media has allowed conservative Republicans to have some vague idea of their brand. With increasing conflict among the party factions, the prospect of continued acquiescence becomes less likely. In presidential elections, Republicans are able to define the brand more clearly and more neutrally. In 2004 the Bush brand was that George W. Bush would do a better job protecting America from terrorism than John Kerry would. It was the one brand that could cover up the deep divisions in the party.

Up to now, political campaign skills and the pyramid structure have allowed conservative Republicans to win races that otherwise might have gone to Democrats. Even when polls showed that most of the participants agreed with a Democratic agenda, and even when to vote Republican was to vote against their own self-interest, people voted Republican. That is why the election of 2006 came as such a shock to many congressional Republicans. They failed to see how others perceived their excesses in everything from Iraq to earmarks to fund-raising to moral hypocrisy. The result of the election said that moderate Americans of all political persuasions had had enough extremism and lying.

The free-enterprise system that Lewis Powell wanted to defend against the 1960s radicals is in no danger (if it ever was), but the values of several of the factions in the Republican Party are. Given the current animosity between the realists and the messianists on foreign policy, and between the fundamentalists and the liberals, libertarians, and corporatists on the role of science, the Republican pyramid is in some danger of crumbling. That would be the ultimate irony: The very success and dominance of the current Republican Party's narrow agenda, even within the party, leads to splintering of the unity that the pyramid is supposed to facilitate.

Republican rule leaves the country with no answers to our most pressing questions. You get the feeling that Republicans want office only to deny Democrats the chance to solve problems by way of government. Since government in our everyday world is crucial to the resolution of our problems, these problems only worsen. Just look at the budget surplus in 2000 and the budget deficit today.

Republicans have drifted a long way from the party of Abraham Lincoln or the party of Teddy Roosevelt or even the party of Dwight Eisenhower. They resemble what they sought to be—the party of William McKinley. Nothing happened in his term except a jingoistic war, narrowed constitutional rights, unsafe workplaces, destruction of the environment, massive wealth creation for a few, and the further worsening of the average American's economic and social conditions. Sound familiar? They delivered what they promised, after all.

Chapter 11.

WHY DEMOCRATS DON'T

The Democratic Party traces its origin back to Thomas Jefferson, even though Jefferson called himself a Republican. The author of the Declaration of Independence represented the empowerment of average people and a challenge to the established order. He believed in science, distrusted commerce, and championed self-reliant farmers. As a slaveholder, he saw the inherent conflict between slavery and the principles he had written into the Declaration of Independence. By the time Andrew Jackson of Tennessee became president, the Federalists that Jefferson defeated in 1800 had melted away and the "Republicans" had split into the Democratic Party and the new Whig Party.

As a Democrat, Jackson won the popular vote in 1824 but lost the election. When the Electoral College deadlocked, the outcome was determined by Congress, where the Whig Henry Clay cut a deal with John Quincy Adams, the son of the second president. Adams won the presidency over Jackson, but when Clay was appointed secretary of state, the arrangement became obvious, and Jackson's successful challenge in 1828 was more or less foreordained. Jackson broke the hold of Massachusetts and Virginia on the White House, becoming the first "westerner" to win the presidency. He had a few rough edges, and he made some terrible decisions (such as the forced removal of the Cherokees from Georgia and Alabama to Oklahoma), but he was very much a man of the people. Encouraged by his victory, citizens took a more active role in shaping their government. In state constitutional conventions across America, ordinary people took over from the elites. Jackson opened the White House to any of his supporters, however poor, who were in town for the inauguration. He opposed the reauthorization of the Second Bank of the United States, preferring, in the Jeffersonian tradition, to put his faith in local enterprises and not in a national institution he felt was the captive of eastern capital.

James K. Polk was the next Democrat to make significant decisions for America's future. He went to war with Mexico and, with victory, annexed vast areas of what is now the American Southwest. He bought California, settled the Oregon Territory boundary dispute, achieved tariff reduction, and reestablished an independent treasury. Once he had accomplished those four objectives, which he had laid out at the beginning of his term, he chose not to run for reelection. After Polk, even though three more Democrats became president, it would be nearly seventy years before the emergence of another Democrat of historical importance. During this long, dry spell, Democrats made fateful mistakes—the largest of which was becoming the party of racial bigotry in the South. The Radical Republicans—those Northern politicians dedicated to destroying the vestiges of a slave culture—failed to reconstruct the South during the ten years after Appomattox. The old habits and customs persisted, and the Democratic Party served as their political expression, challenging the Republicans who held power in the South thanks to the votes of the newly enfranchised former slaves. The Democratic Party became the party of entrenched states' rights. The election of the Republican Rutherford B. Hayes in 1876 led to the removal of federal troops from the South. Earlier that year the Supreme Court, in *United States v. Cruikshank*, ruled that the states, not the federal government, were responsible for protecting African Americans from anti-black violence. After the *Cruikshank* decision, the Democrats, to their everlasting discredit, presided over the systematic disenfranchisement of black voters and the establishment of laws that kept the races separate, with whites in a legal and practical position of dominance.

The next Democrat after Polk to change the course of the country was Governor Woodrow Wilson of New Jersey. The late nineteenth century had been a time of rapacious industrialization. The United States had become a continental power, but at the expense of the frightful exploitation of average people by the robber barons. The progressive movement was a response to this exploitation. Wilson built on the intellectual work of the progressives and brought his own considerable mental skills to the job of taking America in a new direction. He broke up the big concentrations of private power and spread it among smaller business entities. He also broadened democratic participation by supporting the right of women to vote. Having seen the economic busts of the previous century and witnessed their destructive impact on millions of Americans, he reversed Andrew Jackson's position and created the Federal Reserve System of twelve regional banks in order to stabilize the economy. He led Americans into World War I to "make the world safe for democracy." After the war, Wilson laid out the postwar strategy at Versailles; its core element was a League of Nations, whose deliberations, he argued, would prevent future wars.

Wilson's legacy is significant, and many of the substantive ideas realized over the next forty years came from his inspiration and insight. He was a brilliant congressional strategist in the early part of his first term, but he was not a party man. As governor, he had rejected the New Jersey Democratic machine, and as president he left much of the national politics to his confidants, Joseph Patrick Tumulty and "Colonel" Edward House, while he focused on policy and the broader sweep of history. Beyond magnificent speeches that eloquently laid out where the country was and where it should go, he had little taste for negotiation, haggling, or assembling a political coalition.

The 1920s saw Democrats in retreat. The party, with unmemorable candidates, lost three presidential elections in ten years. Even though Republicans such as Warren Harding, Calvin Coolidge, and Herbert Hoover were not political giants, Democrats couldn't penetrate the euphoric hedonism of the Jazz Age. "A chicken in every pot" became the Republican slogan, and the Democrats had no alternative.

The father of the modern Democratic Party was Franklin Delano Roosevelt. In the tragedy of the Depression, most Americans were struggling. Millions were poor. People were afraid and ready to listen to a national leader who offered real solutions. FDR had a teachable moment. He responded in word and deed. People gathered around their radios to listen to his fireside chats because they believed he was there to help them. The political calculation was clear. If you can make life better for the majority, the majority will give you their votes. If you can give them a story of how they got to where they are, they will understand how it happened and how you can make their lives better. Theodore Roosevelt had blamed "the malefactors of great wealth." Likewise, FDR implicated the "economic royalists," asserting that the speculation of the 1920s had been driven by the rich wanting to get richer and allowing their greed to overcome their judgment. He asked the people to give him the authority to act in their interests. Government should be for the average Joe and Jane, not just for the wealthy.

After FDR won in 1932, the forces of reaction that had shaped the Republican Party to a greater or lesser extent since 1896 rose up against him. But the more they protested, the more they made FDR's point. The result was a Roosevelt sweep of the election of 1936. He had created a new majority, a Democratic coalition whose components were Southerners who had been ruined economically by the Depression and saw the need for national action; working people in the North, who desperately needed help and had begun to organize themselves in labor unions; big-city machines, with their immigrants, particularly from Ireland and Southern and Eastern Europe; intellectuals, who generated new ideas to deal with the national crisis; the remnants of the progressive movement in the West; and farmers, who had seen their livelihood snuffed out by falling prices and economic dislocation.

FDR organized an active government response to the hard times of the Depression. As I said in Chapter 10, he established the Works Progress Administration, which gave people jobs building schools and other public structures, and the Civilian Conservation Corps, which employed Americans to protect our natural heritage. He created the Agricultural Adjustment Administration, which provided help for farmers, and signed the Wagner Act, which recognized labor unions and enabled them to organize. He established the Securities and Exchange Commission, which rid the financial system of its worst excesses and gave investors confidence that some entity was overseeing the market. Even with all these efforts, unemployment remained unacceptably high. It was World War II that created the jobs, but at the price of greater government involvement in the economy.

In the aftermath of the war, families saw their living standards rise. The GI Bill of Rights, which FDR had signed in 1944 and Harry Truman implemented, created a wider college-educated population than had existed before the war and guaranteed a generation of well-qualified workers. Government regulation kept interest rates low and stable. The savings-and-loan industry financed millions of first-time home purchases. Price supports gave farmers predictable income. The transformed war industries created millions of new jobs. Industrial labor unions bargained for good packages that included health care and pensions for their workers.

While the presidential runs of Governor Adlai Stevenson of Illinois in 1952 and 1956 inspired many Democrats, he failed to win. During one of his campaigns, a woman is reputed to have come up to him and exclaimed, "Governor Stevenson, all the thinking people of America are for you"—to which Stevenson responded, "I know, madame, but we need a majority." Dwight Eisenhower's common touch and tortured syntax trumped Stevenson's intellectual sensibilities and verbal eloquence. Eisenhower was an elusive target for the Democrats. He did not question the larger government that FDR and Truman had left him; he just wanted its managers to come from large corporations. Americans liked Ike. They also felt comfortable with a general as leader of the country at the height of the cold war.

That lesson was not lost on John F. Kennedy, who in the presidential race against Richard Nixon in 1960 took the harder line, asserting (erroneously) that under Eisenhower the Soviets had surpassed us in the production of missiles, resulting in a "missile gap" we needed to close by increased defense spending. Eisenhower fumed, but the young senator kept repeating the charge. Kennedy's understanding of the media, his eloquence and sense of humor, and the nation's infatuation with his telegenic image combined to maximum effect. His youth softened his patrician background, and he inspired a generation with his inaugural words "Ask not what your country can do for you; ask what you can do for your country." His most memorable legislative achievement was the creation of the Peace Corps.

Kennedy made mistakes—approving the attempt by Cuban exiles to overthrow Fidel Castro at the Bay of Pigs and escalating our involvement in Vietnam—but there were also moments of great statecraft, such as his handling of the Cuban missile crisis in 1962. However, far beyond what he did in life, it was Kennedy's death that made the biggest impact on his country. There was the majestic funeral and then the endless TV reruns of his speeches, the reflections of his stalwarts and friends, the universal grief—all combined to create something close to a legend. The nation's heart went out to the president's wife and family. Who will ever forget the picture of three-year-old John saluting? Camelot was dead. The sense of lost possibilities was palpable.

After the trauma of the assassination, people once again looked to a president for leadership. Lyndon Johnson was there and ready. He seized his own teachable moment and realized much of the potential of the progressive dream. Under Johnson, the federal government would speak with its most authoritative voice since the New Deal. The passage of Medicare provided the elderly with health care, and Medicaid gave health coverage to the poor. The federal government furnished significant new aid to public schools. The civil rights acts banished the stench of de jure racism and guaranteed the vote to African Americans. Johnson vowed to end air pollution in our cities and protected vast areas of public land from development. Against the Republican view that the best government was local government, Democrats did not hesitate to use the federal government in new ways to improve the lot of average Americans. Johnson's Great Society programs targeted poverty. He argued that it was good politics to make the poor into taxpayers. By financing community organizations directly through his Community Action Programs, he enraged big-city mayors but gave a generation of

African Americans, Latinos, and Native Americans a role in the larger society. Idealism inspired these government efforts, and optimism accompanied each new program. Democrats knew they were working on big things. They allowed themselves to dream of a better day, and they worked to realize it.

But in dealing with the Vietnam War, it was as if all Johnson's genius had deserted him. He had no real understanding of the forces of Vietnamese nationalism or the complexity of fighting a guerrilla war. He had inherited the war from JFK. He trusted friends in the Senate who backed the war. His cabinet officers, also inherited from JFK, said it could be won. His sons-in-law were fighting in the jungles of Southeast Asia. LBJ was torn between the death he witnessed and the national duty he felt. (I will always remember a photograph of him after sleepless nights, his coat off, sleeves rolled up, head in the palms of his hands, sitting at a conference table in the White House. It caught the loneliness of a president in time of war.) Suspicious of the media and the so-called eastern establishment, LBJ persevered even more adamantly when public protests against the war broke out. He continued on the path until it disappeared in front of him. In the 1968 presidential primaries, even though he wasn't on the ballot, the people of New Hampshire had given him a win over Senator Eugene McCarthy by write-in votes, but it was not enough to allow him to escape the pull of his own discouragement. The light at the end of the tunnel never came, and he chose not to run for reelection.

In many ways, the Great Society was the culmination of the New Deal. By the time the Vietnam War had sapped his physical strength and political capital, Johnson had achieved much, but when Richard Nixon assumed office, the era of progressive achievement was over.

Almost a decade would pass before another Democrat won the presidency. This time it was Jimmy Carter, a man of shining honesty and personal integrity. In the post-Watergate world of 1976, his character, more than his platform, secured his victory. For four years he tried to move the party toward a responsible center. The peace treaty between Israel and Egypt was a crowning achievement, and his Alaska lands bill locked up millions of pristine acres for the enjoyment of our children's children. In the middle of an oil-supply disruption, he told the people the truth about their own responsibility as citizens in dealing with the skyrocketing prices and our dangerous dependence on insecure sources of foreign oil.

Carter's main initiatives were in foreign policy, energy, and the environment. Democrats squealed whenever he attempted to cut nondefense programs, and because of his proper prudence, he even suffered a primary challenge from the nation's best-known liberal, Edward Kennedy. Although Carter's rural origins and evangelical Baptist background had contributed to his winning the South in 1976, they meant little to the ethnically diverse urban electorate of the Northeast. A decade of robust inflation and the Iranian hostage crisis combined to defeat him.

New social issues were at the fore in the 1976 campaign. I remember Senator Henry Jackson's deer-in-the-headlights look on *Meet the Press* during the primary, when for the first time in his long career he was asked about gay rights. Feminism hadn't hardened into orthodoxy yet, but plenty of women were adding careers to the traditional roles of wife and mother. Affirmative action now applied to women as well as minorities, and in 1973 the Supreme Court had broadened the concept of individual rights to include the right to privacy. The anti-abortion counterrevolution was just getting organized.

All this political ferment gave rise to the chill of political correctness. It most likely began in 1965, when Daniel Patrick Moynihan, then an assistant secretary of labor in the Johnson administration, was attacked for pointing out that single parenthood was an epidemic in the black community and that it diminished life chances for millions of children. A guaranteed minimum income, an idea that he crafted while he was an aide to Richard Nixon on domestic policy, was fiercely rejected. Southern Democrats felt it offered too much, and Democratic interest groups and liberal members of Congress believed it was not enough, even though Democratic liberals had been advocating such a program for a generation. It appeared to many observers that Democrats were at cross-purposes with their own beliefs, simply because the president offering the proposals was Republican. It was a time of 100-percent-or-nothing Democrats, who wouldn't compromise.

The Democratic Party's presidential nominees since 1948—Truman, Stevenson, Kennedy, Johnson, Humphrey, McGovern, and Carter— were all, in one way or another, the political children of FDR. They would refer to him whenever they sought to confirm their Democratic pedigree. Whether it was Truman's Fair Deal, Kennedy's New Frontier, or Johnson's Great Society, they tried to echo FDR's program and even his language. They wanted to use the federal government to make the world a better place.

Franklin Roosevelt's response to a Great Depression could not be Jimmy Carter's response to an oil crisis. Accustomed to comfortable majorities in the House and Senate, Democrats didn't have to think creatively; they could just continue asserting the traditional wisdom and playing "Happy Days Are Here Again." The only problem was that by Carter's presidency the country was changing. Because Democrats never spent any time determining the effectiveness of government programs, they became identified with those programs that didn't work—and with the taxes required to pay for them. The more targeted or obscure the program, the more the public felt its money was being wasted. In 1978, there was a tax revolt in California, a state once willing to pay the necessary taxes for the best elementary and secondary education in the country and the freeways that defined the American future. Using the ballot initiative, an innovation of progressive reform, a group of citizens managed to put a cap on property taxes. When Proposition 13 passed, it announced to the country that there was a limit to what people would pay in taxes. Republicans heard the message. Democrats didn't.

The Second Father

The modern Democratic Party has, in effect, a second father. He was a Republican—Ronald Reagan. Reagan cast a broad shadow, and many Democrats ran from it. His political journey was a long one: In the 1940s he was an FDR Democrat; in the 1960s he became a Goldwater conservative and advocated a smaller federal government. Still, Reagan often alluded to FDR in his speeches and, in a unique bit of political jujitsu, claimed the Roosevelt mantle even as he tried to destroy the New Deal's achievements.

After Reagan won in 1980 and nine Democratic senators were defeated, giving control of the Senate to the Republicans, Democrats lost not just their confidence but some of their convictions as well. Indeed, their pro-government stance of the previous forty-eight years was said to be the cause of the party's defeat. Ronald Reagan had tapped into the anxiety that many taxpayers felt about the nature of the federal bureaucracy, portraying it as too big, too intrusive, and too wasteful. A kind of Democratic panic ensued. It was as if "government" had become a bad word. Republicans had successfully defined the political moment, and we Democrats increasingly sought to be Republican lite. At the time, few of us seemed to understand the depth of our party's problem. "In politics," the late political scientist David Green wrote in *The Language of Politics in America: Shaping Political Consciousness from McKinley to Reagan*, "real intellectual victory is achieved not by transmitting one's language to supporters but by transmitting it to critics." When you adopt your opponents' definition of the situation, including their premises and even some of their substantive analysis, effective opposition becomes difficult. By 1984, when former vice president Walter Mondale ran, Democrats were no longer in control of the dialogue.*

The Democratic Party's reaction to Ronald Reagan shaped a generation of Democratic politicians, as we sought to differentiate ourselves from both Reagan and FDR—Reagan because he was a Republican and FDR because he was a "big spender." Instead of creating something new that was true to our origins, we tried to split the difference between the legacy of FDR and the political potency of Reagan. The key to doing this was public relations—managing and targeting the message. We became the party of intentions, not results—intent on proclaiming that one or another initiative would improve people's lives; whether it actually did or not was never determined. If you couldn't admit the importance of government,

*See my book *Time Present, Time Past* (Knopf, 1996).

then you couldn't talk about the big things government could do—just talk about a lot of small things important to different segments of the electorate, but don't risk talking to the electorate as a whole.

One of the early efforts to distance ourselves from the FDR legacy was the Democratic Leadership Council, formed out of discontent with the Democratic National Committee and the perceived necessity to move to the middle—far away from FDR. It started with only a few people. Its activities consisted primarily of holding conferences that gave politicians a platform to espouse middle-of-the-road positions and generating research papers that sought to bridge the gap between FDR and Reagan. The DLC solicited Democratic officeholders as members and rich, business-friendly Democrats as contributors.

The organization has been run for some twenty years by the same man, Al From, a bright, aggressive former Democratic staffer in the U.S. Senate and House of Representatives. From its beginning, he positioned the organization as the anti-DNC and its members as the new Democratic conservatives. Above all, the DLC has sought to move the party to more eclectic policies that embody modest aspirations. That way, Republicans couldn't attack us as big spenders. The DLC attempted to ingratiate itself with business by supporting deregulation in areas of the economy, such as utilities, that had been under government regulation since the 1930s. It advocated welfare reform, along with an assortment of experimental policies that wouldn't cost much. These new Democrats took positions on Social Security and Medicare, on pension policy and health care, elementary and secondary education, and tax reform, but most shied away from using government as a tool to make the country stronger and more just. Sometimes the DLC seemed more anti-liberal than anti-Republican. It was a haven for younger politicians who wished to distinguish themselves from the Old Democrats of the DNC, the custodian of what remained of the old coalition.

The Clinton Years

Throughout the 1980s, one of the more active members of the Democratic Leadership Council was Governor Bill Clinton of Arkansas, who in 1992 became the Democratic nominee for president. Clinton had adopted the splitting-the-difference lessons of the Reagan years, and more important, he was a son of the South and understood that principles straightforwardly expressed could be dangerous, particularly when it came to race or class.

Clinton's 1992 general election campaign was brilliant. He tapped into the economic anxiety of the middle class and came across as empathetic with the sufferings of people hard-hit by the brief recession of 1990–91. I spent a day with him on one of his early bus tours through Ohio and Pennsylvania, which he undertook immediately after the Democratic National Convention in New York. He was at the top of his game, but what was more interesting for me was the people: They lined the roads for a glimpse of the Democratic candidate; they waited hours to hear him speak. You could sense they believed that Clinton offered a solution to their problems, that he was the custodian of their hopes. He had promised to fix the economy and to provide everyone with health insurance. The campaign's competence and his own charisma and intellect made him a star, but they weren't enough for a long while. In the head-to-head against George Bush I, he was behind. Then, when Ross Perot entered the race, changing everything from debate strategy to Election Day operations, the Arkansas governor found his way to victory.

Clinton is the classic example of a politician of process, one who rejects drawing lines in the political sand based on principle and believes that what's important is to keep the game going. A man of great intelligence and sensitivity, he is also an inspiring political speaker, notwithstanding his bomb at the 1988 Democratic Convention. He has the common touch; people feel he cares about them. One of the regrettable aspects of his presidency was that all that talent never got spent on big issues. It was a success in one sense: The federal budget was handled responsibly, beginning with the key budget of 1993, which contributed to low interest rates and booming economic times. He kept his promise to revive the economy. But in many ways Clinton's tenure in the White House was a lost opportunity.

A president makes his mark not by basking in the glow of good times but by steering the ship of state through bad times. Those bad times are an opportunity to change the future. There was no such teachable moment on Clinton's watch. The first terrorist bombing of the World Trade Center had little national impact. His greatest chances to shape the future came in trade, health care, and education. When he urged Democrats to accept free trade, the industrial unions screamed, but Clinton never caved in. The North American Free Trade Agreement and completion of the Uruguay trade round, along with the 1993 budget, were his pinnacle achievements. His political dexterity allowed him to keep labor leaders onboard; after all, they had nowhere else to go. What he didn't do often enough beyond providing the metaphor of a "bridge to the future" was explain why an open, growing global economy was good for America. Ordinary Americans saw the jobs that were disappearing in their companies or their towns but not the jobs that were created in new industries such as biotech, information technology, and product design, or in redesigned sectors, such as retailing and marketing. Clinton didn't systematically address the legitimate fears of these people or talk about what the average worker had to do in order to prosper or how long the transition to a new economy would take. He didn't give people a vivid enough context or a bright enough picture of what was possible for them in a world economy.

On health care, Clinton started with the right ambition to do something large and worthy of his skills. Here he was hampered by the sharing of responsibility with an activist first lady. Health care belonged to her, and everyone knew it. You never got the feeling that his heart was as deeply invested in health care as it was in concocting a viable budget or passing a trade agreement. Hillary Clinton's political skills were not well honed, so mistakes were made—mistakes of conception, consultation, pace, and strategy. After the universal health care proposal stumbled and the Republicans swept Congress in 1994, Clinton concluded that, in his words, "The era of big government is over." He abandoned health care reform and proposed only small domestic initiatives (except for welfare reform, which was driven by Republicans) for the rest of his presidency. It was a clear admission that Republicans had won the battle of ideas.

On education, Clinton's record is a mystery. No president in our history has known more about elementary and secondary education in America. As governor of Arkansas, he had achieved education reform by requiring teachers to take competency tests and raising their pay. He knew what public education needed; he and his wife were both proof of its power to transform lives. He saw clearly its importance for our future economic competitiveness. But other than increasing the federal government's investment in education and training, establishing some college tuition programs, creating the modest beginnings of accountability in exchange for federal education aid, and starting a few minor efforts to support charter schools and provide more Internet access for public schools, there is nothing in his record to indicate national leadership in this area. It is the nation's loss, for although he had the bully pulpit and the federal budget surplus, he didn't deploy either in the service of bold educational initiatives.

Changing the performance of public education in America is a political minefield, but great presidents spend their political capital to do great things. Clinton spent the bulk of his time pointing out small distinctions between Republicans and himself and holding on to power. Maybe he was trapped by the conservative Republican political-media juggernaut that had developed since the 1970s. Maybe he felt the national moment limited him to promulgating trade agreements and balancing budgets. Maybe after 1994 the Republican Congress proved insurmountable. Maybe he lacked the courage to challenge entrenched power. Maybe he was only a process politician. Whatever the reason, the nation missed a golden opportunity. From 1994 to 1996, Clinton focused on his reelection; his second term was taken up with defending himself against a self-inflicted public relations disaster and a zealous prosecutor. Great projects took a backseat.

I suspect that the person most disappointed by the Clinton years is Clinton himself. There are plenty of things in his eight years to take credit for, in a laundry-list sense, not the least of which was rising incomes for African Americans and Hispanics, but there is no crowning achievement, no redefinition of his times, no law passed commensurate with his abilities or with what he must have dreamed of when he took the bus trip from Jefferson's Monticello to Washington for his first inauguration in 1993.

After Clinton came the presidential candidacies of Al Gore and John Kerry. Neither one connected emotionally with the American people. While each had political skills (which, in Gore's case, I can attest to firsthand), neither one appeared to enjoy campaigning. Both seemed detached; when they tried to express emotion, it was as if something inside them blocked the power of their feelings. Both were honest men and would have made competent presidents. Ironically, Gore's high point came when he conceded, after a hard-fought month of Florida recount. In that speech, he did everything right. He was statesmanlike, emotional, funny, honest, and patriotic in a very natural way. More than a few Democrats, over the next four years, remembered that moment and thought of what might have been and, as important, what might have been avoided.

What Do Democrats Stand For?

The 1994 midterm elections revealed the rot at the core of the old Democratic coalition. The South was lost. Labor couldn't produce enough votes. Blacks didn't turn out. Latinos weren't registered. Women fled the ranks. Suburban white ethnics voted against the party. Small business felt overtaxed, and the middle class felt unappreciated by the party. For the first time since 1952, the House of Representatives went Republican, and then in 2000 Republicans regained the presidency. In the aftermath of these defeats, there was the normal finger-pointing and the predictable but contradictory advice about changing the image of the party, communicating more effectively, getting a better candidate, moving to the center, reinvigorating the Democratic base—but there was no clear and comprehensive statement about what the party stood for.*

Unlike the Republican Party, which is rent with factions, the Democratic Party is relatively faction-free. There are aggressive interest groups organized around single issues, but these differ from factions, which are usually defined by more than one issue. Some Democrats are anti-abortion, more are pro-choice; some are pro–free trade, more are anti–trade agreement; some are for gay marriage,

---

*See my book *Time Present, Time Past* (Knopf, 1996).

more are for civil unions for gays; some want a single-payer health system, more want a hybrid of public and private approaches; some are for gun control, more are against it; some want tax cuts, more want money spent on education and health care and on protecting Social Security. Many Democrats are unpredictable combinations of these categories and therefore don't form factions. The Republican fundamentalists have a view of life that includes abortion, gays, stem-cell research; in the Democratic Party, those subjects are relegated to single-issue organizations such as NARAL Pro-Choice America on abortion or the Human Rights Campaign on gay rights. No one group covers an agenda that cuts across many issues.

The only element of the party that might qualify as a faction is organized labor, but they are less than 8 percent of the private workforce today, and they are split between the older industrial unions, who are just trying to hold on in a world of globalization and technological change and who feel that Democrats abandoned them when they were under the siege of foreign competition, and the service unions, the most powerful of which are the teachers, who couldn't care less about foreign competition. The movement splits further between the unions that want to organize workers aggressively and those that want to protect what they have. That divide manifested itself formally after 2004, when the largest union, the SEIU (the Service Employees International Union), left the AFL-CIO. If this wasn't fragmentation enough, there were always unions, such as the Teamsters, who regularly flirted with Republicans. The days when labor spoke with one voice seem to be over. Each union has become a separate special interest.

Perhaps there are factions in Republican politics because for thirty-five years conservative Republicans have been investing in ideas and Democrats have coasted on the intellectual work of the New Deal. What was lacking was a point of view that tied different issues together into one story. There is no philosophy that connects what Democrats care about, no rooting of positions in an ethical system. For Democrats, the real divide was and is between the children of Ronald Reagan and the children of FDR—between those who took the election of 1980 as a rejection of our party's past and those who still believe that active government has a role in our society, between those who think big ideas are easy targets and work toward tactical dexterity on small issues and those who try to develop a strategy on large issues, between those who think that one person's gain is another person's loss and those who see how we can work together to develop enough for everyone. In this situation, a party line becomes very difficult to define, much less enforce.

Just as FDR defined what it means to be a Democrat and LBJ put the capstone on the New Deal, Democrats today need to define our national moment, give people a narrative for our times, propose specific programs. To restore our party's recognizable character requires choices. What will Democrats stand for? What will we seek to convey to the voters? We should start with values such as opportunity and security, freedom and obligation, and follow them up with our convictions: that anyone in America who works hard should be able to support his or her family; that those who want to excel should have the chance to excel and be rewarded for it handsomely; that those who have fallen by the roadside of life should get a helping hand to pull them back up; that tolerance is required in a pluralistic society; that obligation to community must balance the freedom of the individual; that leading the world is a team effort. We should build on our values and convictions with specific, tangible recommendations.

I believe that the Democratic Party should become synonymous in people's minds with a good job at good pay, universal health care, superior public education, pension security, a safe environment, a strong military, and a conviction that the best way to lead the world is by example. The party's energy and clout should be directed primarily at those issues that affect the most people. If proponents of narrow interests want action on their issues (pro-choice, gun control, and the like), they must first support the big agenda—jobs, the environment, pensions, health care, and education—and understand that only after those issues have been addressed will the government turn to the narrower issues. In other words, Democrats should adopt the New American Story about what is possible. They should then get the fundamentals right on the economy: how best to reduce the deficit, how best to encourage savings so that we get the maximum economic growth that will allow us to meet our country's changing social needs.

Finally, Democrats need to connect emotionally with the voters. Ronald Reagan did that by looking back at America's greatness. Democrats should do it by looking forward to its future, as well as taking pride in what is being done today, in communities across this country. For example, I know a woman in suburban Chicago whose eleven-year-old son died of cancer. As a tribute to him, she wrote letters to twenty youngsters from the kids-with-cancer camp he'd attended during the previous summer, letters bucking them up. Within a short time, she heard from relatives and friends of the children she'd written to, asking her to write to other children they knew who had cancer. She got so many requests that she started an organization called Love Letters, and in the last two decades she has sent thousands of letters to kids with cancer. I also know a woman in Waco, Texas, whose group sits with the elderly who are alone and afraid. I know a musician in New York whose organization gets songs professionally written and recorded specifically for kids who have cancer. I know a woman in California who takes the abandoned bodies of dead babies and gives them a mass and a proper burial. I know a man who quit his job as head of business development for Microsoft China to open schools and libraries in Nepal, Cambodia, and Laos. I know an emergency room doctor in California who started an organization called Questbridge to help talented low-income high school students get access to America's best colleges. I know a young man in Illinois who formed a group that removes refuse from the Mississippi River and one in Portland, Oregon, who teaches disabled kids to be competitive bike riders. The list goes on and on.

Democrats should tell people what's good about America, share stories of extraordinary unknown Americans such as those I've just listed, and create a larger national narrative showing that American generosity and ingenuity are alive and well. We should tell people that the idealism and heroics we observe locally can also be realized nationally, through the collective action of the federal government and the commitment of all of us to build a better country. We should then educate people about the new economic world we're entering and prepare them for it. If Americans came to see this kind of Democratic Party, they would recognize it not as the party of FDR and "Happy Days Are Here Again" but as the party that, even as it celebrates the goodness of our common humanity, can speak to future economic success and current economic worries simultaneously, and in so doing regain their trust.

The Eight Democratic Curses

Why hasn't this happened? If Republicans *can't* solve our problems, Democrats have *chosen not* to solve them. To be able to lead again with authority, Democrats need to deal with our eight perennial curses.

• The first curse on the Democratic Party is its *fear of thinking big*. When Woodrow Wilson created the Federal Reserve, he was thinking big. When FDR established Social Security, he was thinking big. When LBJ set up Medicare, he was thinking big. We seem to live in a time when the smaller the idea, the bigger its hype. Ever since Clinton's health care proposal crashed and burned, Democrats have run from big ideas—but the problems that must be solved in our world can be solved only by big proposals. If Democrats limit their ambition and their political risk taking, they cannot lead America in a new direction. Only boldness captures the imagination, and only by capturing the public's imagination can we do what must be done. Reestablishing the preeminence of American elementary education cannot be done by requiring school uniforms. Breaking our oil addiction and resultant dependence on the volatile Persian Gulf will require more than a few tax credits for solar energy. Managing our economy for maximum long-term economic growth involves more than an earmarked appropriation for a bridge in a congressman's district. Making sure all Americans have health insurance takes more than a tax credit for health savings accounts.

We Democrats should not avoid doing what's right because we fear being misunderstood, or stigmatized, or even losing an election. When the opposition shrinks the playing field, we shouldn't agree to play on it—we should instead redefine the game. Democrats have bought the idea that we can't do what we really want to do because it costs too much. When the country went to war in Iraq, we suddenly found $400 billion (and counting) we didn't have before. Yet we can't come up with $50 billion to secure pensions and give everyone with talent the chance to go to college. When Hurricane Katrina hit, the federal coffers opened up. I ask you, is the tragedy of a family who lost all their possessions in a hurricane qualitatively different from the tragedy of a family who went bankrupt because of health care costs? There is no contradiction between thinking big and acting frugally. Accountability and constant reassessment are not incompatible with conceptual boldness.

It is time for Democrats to challenge the core Republican orthodoxy about tax cuts. Opinion polls show that in 2000 more people (in both red and blue states) wanted the budget surplus to be used to reduce the national debt or for domestic spending than wanted tax cuts. All we have to do in order to build support for tax increases is make sure that people recognize the services they get for their taxes. I can't tell you how many town meetings I've held in which the negative responses to government spending would make you think the entire budget was going for welfare and foreign aid, when in fact last year those represented just over $45 billion out of a budget of $2.6 trillion. I don't like to pay taxes. No one does. We do it because we have a responsibility to one another. But for the last twenty-seven years, tax cuts have been seen as a sure political winner. During the Reagan years, Congress passed the largest tax cut in American history up to that point, and then a year later, in 1982, passed one of the largest tax increases in history and followed that the next year with another tax increase. Democrats remember Walter Mondale's promise to raise taxes in his 1984 nomination acceptance speech, but they forget Bill Clinton's tax increase in his 1993 budget, which was the trigger for six years of a good to great economy. Until we Democrats return to our origins and speak to people's real needs in education, health care, and pension security, we will be given credit neither for going along with Republican tax cuts nor for helping chunks of our own constituency with insufficiently funded, narrowly targeted programs. We will remain pale imitations of our former selves and imitators of a Republican ethic of small national government.

I have learned from personal experience that you can raise taxes if you're clear enough about why you're doing it. In 1986, I was a chief sponsor of major tax reform legislation that cut the top tax rate from 50 percent to 28 percent. A part of the law eliminated the exclusion for capital gains, which had the effect of raising the rate for sale of capital assets from 20 percent to 28 percent. About the time the bill was being considered, I had a fund-raiser at the home of a major lawyer in California's Silicon Valley, and many of the technology elite were in attendance. One of the first questions was on capital gains, which formed the biggest part of their income. Each of them felt that capital gains were driving entrepreneurial energy in the valley's technological world. I told them bluntly that the rate was going up to compensate for lower rates on all income and to help simplify the system. They grumbled, but even today people who were there tell me I made a good impression because I was not pandering but telling them the reasons behind the position I had taken, even if they didn't like to hear it. As far as I know, I didn't lose one person's support over the issue. If we can muster the same conviction about health care or education or pensions, then we will carry the day with a tax increase that goes to pay for those essentials.

When the Louisiana Territory became available because Napoleon needed to finance his European wars, Thomas Jefferson didn't know where the money to buy it would come from. Fifteen million dollars seemed like a lot of money in those days. It was also a questionable constitutional decision. Jefferson could not agree to the purchase without congressional approval, but he had to sign the deal before Congress could act. He went ahead because his dreams for America were expansive. He believed we were a land of destiny, and by seizing this opportunity to turn America into a continental nation he would be serving the nation's long-term interests. Congress agreed in time to make the payment. Thinking big means taking political risks. It's easy to let fear dominate. Vision is a priceless attribute for a party and a politician. Without it, a nation can perish;

with it, national destiny can be realized. Today we Democrats can remain paralyzed by our fear or strike out on a new course full of hope and promise as well as risk. It's our choice.

• The second curse is our *capitulation in the face of the Republican charge that we are soft on defense*. The foundation of John Kerry's presidential campaign was that as a decorated Vietnam veteran he was immune from such a charge. The Swift Boat ads showed he wasn't. When it comes to defense, Democrats think we have to play on the Republican field. We don't. No president of either party would consciously leave America undefended. It was, after all, a Democrat—Harry Truman—who established the collective security arrangements of the post–World War II world. Democrats as well as Republicans kept America strong during the forty-year cold war. There is no evidence that our adversaries prefer dealing with a Democratic president.

While it is true that Ronald Reagan dramatically increased defense spending, it is not clear that what he bought with that money was what broke the Soviet will. Technology—and what it could unleash in the future, given its trajectory—was more important than another MX missile or Bradley Fighting Vehicle. Mikhail Gorbachev went home from the 1986 Reykjavik summit convinced that the United States might develop a missile defense shield that would make the Soviet nuclear arsenal obsolete. He was afraid of breakthroughs in strategic capability, both offensive and defensive, that we could afford because of the dynamism of our economy. This concern, along with his long-standing view that the Soviet Union's economy could not continue to support an empire, led him to throw in the towel.

Democrats need to be forceful in our defense of America, but starting a war doesn't necessarily mean you're stronger on defense. Unlike Republicans, Democrats believe that the best military is one you never have to use. How has the fiasco in Iraq, which gets worse with each day, helped our standing in the world? Part of being strong militarily is knowing enough not to squander young lives and vast amounts of money on such adventures. After Iraq, our threat to intervene anywhere in the world will be much less credible; we have revealed the limitations of our power. Without question, we can still destroy other countries, but no weapons system can guarantee the political result that war is supposed to achieve.

Democrats have to make clear why Republicans are wrong when it comes to national defense. Democrats will always support the troops—but that doesn't mean saying yes to every defense contractor's no-bid pipe dream or every defense planner's "brilliant" idea. Republicans have never met a weapons system they didn't like. The military-industrial complex that President Eisenhower talked about exists, but what it really represents is the inability of politicians to define what we want the military to do. Because there is no clarity, the military services compete for resources, and we end up funding unnecessary weapons systems that were built to fight the last war. That's even before we get to all the defense spending whose sole purpose is to continue providing jobs in powerful congressmen's districts.

Senator Harry Truman made no excuses when he revealed the profiteering abuses of defense contractors in World War II, and Democrats today should not hesitate to hold the Pentagon and its corporate contractors responsible for results. For example, there is no excuse for the companies who produced the F-22 Air Force fighter aircraft, which came in 42 percent above budget and twenty months late, to get an $849 million bonus. Democrats should say, "No performance, no bonus." In The 2% Solution, Matt Miller quotes President Eisenhower: "Every gun that is made, every warship launched, every rocket fired signifies, in the final sense, a theft from those who hunger and are not fed, those who are cold and not clothed." As Miller observes, "Being strong doesn't mean winking at corporate wish lists just because they wave a flag, or kowtowing to contractors peddling yesterday's arms for tomorrow's threats." I agree.

Another reason Democrats need to define our defense aims clearly and implement them rigorously is that our military deserves it. The U.S. military is a remarkable institution. It has developed officers of unimpeachable integrity and wide-ranging competence faced with figuring out how best to defend us all against a kaleidoscope of changing threats. They know history, foreign languages, mathematics, and psychology, among other things, and they are loyal to their country and its civilian leadership. More than thirty years ago, when the civilian leadership told them to go from a draftee army to an all-volunteer force, the generals saluted and made it happen. Thanks to the decades of cooperation with the soldiers of other countries in NATO and Japan, and with all the military missions and foreign military officers sent here for training, the U.S. military understands the importance of cooperation with our allies. The military today is the most diverse institution in our country. It takes young people of every racial, ethnic, and economic background and turns them into soldiers who are willing to die for all of us. Imagine that you are the one walking the streets of Fallujah or Baghdad. You might or might not believe in the war, but you do your duty. These men and women need political leadership worthy of them. They need a government that gives them clarity of direction, aggressive oversight, honest feedback, and the equipment to do their job.

• The third curse is our *inability to counter the persistent accusation that we waste people's hard-earned tax dollars.* This mantra has been repeated by Republicans for years. Some Democrats have responded by agreeing with Republican budget proposals, which often come down hard on veterans, the elderly, and the poor. Instead we should point out that getting spending under control doesn't always require deep budget cuts; often what is needed is only to limit the steady increase in government spending. The largest federal deficits of the last fifty years have all occurred on the Republicans' watch, especially those of Ronald Reagan and George W. Bush. Democrats should remind people of that.

Democrats should be fierce in preventing waste and inefficiency in the spending of taxpayer dollars. Why leave it to the Republicans to attack waste? The real "special interests" are not single mothers on welfare but wealthy agribusiness and real-estate investors and corporate miners and others who champion the free market until they are asked to do without their subsidies, tax loopholes, and favorable regulations. The sweetheart deals that pervade our laws and regulations should be purged, but once a special provision has lodged in the bowels of bureaucratic regulations, few politicians will take the time or exert the energy to find it, much less eliminate it, no matter how much it costs. Democrats should lead the purging.*

Democrats should be rigorous in analyzing three aspects of public spending: purpose, procedure, and outcome. We need to establish criteria for the functions and operations of the federal government and its myriad programs. Why must this or that amount of money be spent by the federal government, instead of the state or local government, or the private sector? Does this particular legislation serve many people or only a few? Does it further the ideals of the Founders? Will this legislation achieve its objectives? Can we change this program to make it better? What is needed is clarity about what a piece of legislation is meant to achieve and ways to measure whether or not it has been successful.

With regard to procedure, Democrats need to insist on new information systems; without them, there will always be waste. People from the private sector profess themselves continually astonished by government accounting procedures, overlapping jurisdictions, and the political micromanaging built into outdated information systems. The Heritage Foundation head, Edwin Feulner, in his book *Getting America Right*, points out that "buried in the Treasury Department's 2003 *Financial Report of the United States Government* is a short section titled 'Unreconciled Transactions Affecting the Change in Net Position.'" In it, we learn that the federal government can't account for the spending of $24.5 billion of taxpayer money. Feulner continues:

> The government knows it was spent by someone, somewhere, on something, but auditors do not know who spent it, where it was spent, or on what. The report says the discrepancy occurred because federal agencies failed to report their expenditures adequately, and it concludes mildly that locating the money is a "priority." It seems unlikely that all of this $24.5 billion was flat-out stolen, but who knows?

*See my book *Time Present, Time Past* (Knopf, 1996).

The conclusion the Heritage Foundation draws from this story is that government is hopelessly inefficient, or even corrupt, and must be cut back. Democrats cannot defend the described abuses; they need to propose a proactive strategy to improve government efficiency. Democrats should be angrier than Republicans about the lost $24.5 billion. After all, it impugns all of government, and Democrats know that government is essential to solve our national problems. Democrats should be hawks about this kind of egregious mismanagement. My guess is that a large part of the $24.5 billion went missing not because it was "flat-out stolen" but because of outdated information systems trying to cope with the federal budget, which is the equivalent of a $2.6 trillion business with divisions located worldwide. The money was probably lost in the bureaucratic tangle of inadequate software programs, insufficient space to store data, and too few people to enter information in databases, or in a hundred other ways that no corporation would tolerate from its information-technology and human-resources departments.

In an attempt to guarantee that federal revenues won't be stolen, the federal bureaucracy tries to micromanage how they are spent. The result is that well-intentioned federal agencies spend time on process instead of on their respective missions. We establish regulations of Lilliputian detail and amazing complexity to catch those who would abuse the public trust. For example, in many agencies you can't order a computer, a chair, a set of new lightbulbs, or anything else in the last few months of the fiscal year. And in some places in the federal government, if anything costs more than $1,000, Washington needs to approve it at any time in the year. Often, Washington doesn't get to it until the fourth quarter, which means that you don't receive it. At many federal agencies there are people who keep track by the hour of how much you work, no matter whether you're a senior bureaucrat or a janitor. The federal employees' unions have negotiated procedures that make it virtually impossible to fire a federal employee for anything but gross dereliction of duty. The regulations lay out a process to do so, but its implementation involves so many waiting periods and windows for action that in effect the employees are unfireable. Moreover, most of the reports that employees and recipients of government funds have to fill out are read by no one.

What's needed is not more "gotcha" rules and regulations but a little more common sense. When U.S. Senator Claire McCaskill was the auditor of the state of Missouri, she investigated the state's child-support system. Those who ran it told her how well they were doing according to the federal criteria of number of cases opened, paternity established, and hearing dates set. She asked why more cases weren't being closed and money delivered to the children who needed it. "Oh," came the reply, "that's not how the bureaucracy measures our success." In fact they had failed to use all the available address-location resources to track down parents both owing and waiting on payments. Democrats should argue for greater accountability, certainly, but also for more flexibility in how an agency accomplishes its mission and measures its success. By trusting people and making our information technology more robust, we might get more creativity and better results.

The third criterion by which spending ought to be judged is outcome. The most underdeveloped of Congress's powers is oversight. When Jimmy Carter became president, he advocated zero-based budgeting, whereby at specified intervals all government programs had to be rejustified. Democrats killed his idea. We shouldn't have been so quick. Taxpayers deserve a rigorous accounting of whether their money is being spent wisely and is accomplishing its stated purpose. As noted in Chapter 4, the federal budget should be on the Internet, so that if a citizen searches for, say, "federal budget, breast cancer," he or she can see the total amount being spent on breast cancer by the various departments and maybe a link to the bills that authorized and appropriated the spending and then a link to the floor debate on the bills and who ultimately voted for them. Such transparency would go a long way toward demystifying federal spending. If Democrats don't want to be hobbled by that kind of rigor, accountability, and frugality, then we deserve the "big spender" label Republicans have given us. Without idealism, government itself seems like just another special interest. But without accountability, idealism becomes softheaded talk.

• The fourth Democratic curse is the impression we have created of a *closed-minded devotion to the secular.* This is an unintended consequence of one of our deepest values—the separation of church and state—but it needs to be addressed. The Republicans, by appealing to the leadership of the most conservative Christians on issues such as abortion, euthanasia, gay marriage, prayer in schools, and stem-cell research, have presented themselves as the party most in tune with religious Americans. When George W. Bush speaks of how and why he became a Christian, millions of Americans applaud the forthrightness of his faith. The irony is that many parishioners in those churches are people who have lost their pensions, or live without health insurance, or fear losing their jobs, or oppose the war in Iraq. Yet Democrats don't reach them where they live their lives. Self-conscious secularism blocks our path.

Some elements of the Democratic Party are condescending to evangelical Christians, and the faithful sense it. To these elements, all Baptists look alike. But the difference between Jimmy Carter and Pat Robertson is as day is to night, even though both profess Jesus Christ as their personal savior and believe in the authority and teaching of the Bible. Secularists lump all evangelicals into the same category because most evangelicals oppose abortion. Opponents of abortion, no matter how progressive they are on other issues, are often seen as the foe, since most Democrats fervently support a woman's right to choose. But politics is about more than one litmus test. Democrats have to keep a dialogue going with those who oppose abortion, so that together we can find areas of common ground—perhaps through promoting adoption, birth control, or even the morning-after pill, which has been shown to reduce the incidence of abortion. While leaders of anti-abortion groups seem absolutely rigid, millions of pro-life citizens could very well be open to finding common ground. If you don't listen to people who hold views different from your own—if you've made your mind up about what kind of people they are before you've even talked with them—you will never win them over.

Democrats also need to think long and hard about the issue of abortion itself. We don't have to change our view that a woman ought to have the right to choose, but we need to recognize the horrible moral dilemma that legalized abortion poses for many people. One way to ameliorate the dilemma might be to set a national goal for reducing abortions, lay out steps to achieve it through education and example, and publicly monitor it. Democrats should be less doctrinaire about when in a pregnancy an abortion can be performed. The six-month standard set in *Roe v. Wade* in 1973, which was determined on the basis of viability (the ability of the fetus to live outside the womb), has been eroded by medical science. Yet Democrats remain rigidly opposed to any change in the *Roe* viability standard and so lose voters who support us on most other issues. Refusing to compromise on the position that abortion should be available anytime is unreasonable. The American people are conflicted on this subject, and Democrats should acknowledge that. We need to loosen up and reach out.

Since 1980, Democrats have been urging Americans to vote Democratic because a Republican president might appoint someone to the Supreme Court who would narrow or repeal the right to an abortion. The very inflexibility of our position has driven many Democrats into the Republican Party, and now, thanks to the votes of those former Democrats, we have a Republican president and two new Supreme Court justices who are the abortion-rights advocates' biggest nightmare, and until 2007 we had a Republican House and a Republican Senate. If we had been more flexible, shown our moral anguish over abortion, and supported a few exceptions to or regulations of its practice (such as banning abortions for children under sixteen without parental consent), we would not have lost those Democrats and might have kept a Republican president from appointing justices who will probably tip the majority against abortion.

Jesus said that people should help the poor. Jesus said, "Blessed are the peacemakers." Jesus advised us to turn the other cheek. He asked us to love all people, to care for the sick and the lame. Jesus said, "Inasmuch as ye have done it unto one of the least of these my brethren, ye have done it unto me." These admonitions sound very much like Democratic values to me. Democrats should not shy away from expressing the morality of our views. Shouldn't health care be a right for all Americans? Don't the poor deserve help from the government? Shouldn't war be a last resort? Isn't it wrong for government to lie to the people? Shouldn't we be good stewards of the land, water, and air? Democrats support the separation of church and state because religion should be personal and freely expressed. It is not the Founders' America in any sense when a particular sectarian faith captures the power of government and imposes its views on others. That's where Democrats should draw the line, but we can do so from the standpoint of a shared faith. Abraham Lincoln was said to have replied, when asked if God was on the side of the Union, that it would be better to pray that we were on God's side. In a country where nearly two-thirds of the people say religion plays an important role in their lives, Democrats have to be comfortable enough in our own spiritual skins to let people know that we understand them and respect them for their faith—and even that we share it. Above all, Democrats have to avoid condescension. Former president Jimmy Carter is the best example of someone who lived his faith in office but never forced it on other people.

• The fifth curse is *wealth bashing*. Ever since FDR, Democrats have seen themselves as the party of the little guy and the enemy of moneyed privilege. The label FDR applied to Republicans— "economic royalists"—set the tone. Attacking the wealthy was good politics for FDR, because he was president at a time when most of the nation was poor or struggling. Today we're in different circumstances.

A Democratic leader must let those in the shadows of life and those who work hard every day for middle-class wages know that the party is with them, that it will help them, that they are understood— but the well-off among us should be given to understand that the Democratic tent is for them, too. Many people of means think of themselves as Democrats but are put off when the party appears to attack success—their success. Yet Democrats continue reflexively to make the wealthy their whipping boys, forgetting that there are many different kinds of wealthy people. Some are walking advertisements for the meritocracy that Democrats champion; others have (like FDR) grown beyond their privileged background and seek justice and opportunities for all. Politicians sometimes talk about "two

Americas," one well-to-do and one poor. The analysis is right, but the tone is wrong. Many well-to-do people are working to make the world a better place. Democrats can help those in need, defend them against powerful private interests, give them tools to better their lives, and inspire them to believe in a better day. We can do all those things without demonizing the wealthy. In fact, we need to mobilize the righteous rich for our cause.

Republicans have played shamelessly to the wealthy. They know that Democrats will fault them for this, but they don't care, because they have polled the issue thoroughly. They know that most people who are poor or middle-class dream of being rich. When Democrats attack the rich, it says to poor and middle-class Americans that we don't understand their ambitions to better themselves, that we demean their hope that their children will one day enjoy a higher standard of living than theirs. This is a part of the American dream, after all. Democrats need to forget class divisions and remember what all Americans have in common: Everyone aspires to something—to be a major leaguer, a lawyer, an artist; to get rich, to climb a mountain, to repair a car, to play the piano, to win a blue ribbon at the state fair, to build a dream house, to graduate from college, to invent the next big thing. Democrats should identify with that aspirational spirit, for it is what makes America great. Our efforts should go toward helping individuals, not attacking their goals.

None of this means that the wealthy shouldn't pay more taxes. From those to whom much is given, much should be asked. We need to appeal to the patriotism of the wealthy. As it is, many of them have no quarrel with the progressive tax system. If government is honest, accountable, and effective—and it can be—paying taxes will strengthen the whole, which is good for everybody. A rising tide of economic growth should lift all boats.

Many of the wealthy are as angry as populists are with those Americans who get rich not because of their genius or hard work but because of their political connections or bloodlines. They feel such unearned advantage demeans the efforts of the self-made person who has built a career from scratch. Inherited wealth is not intrinsically evil; it depends on what you do with it. Some build on the previous generation's success and deserve our praise. More than a few good companies became great companies because a son or daughter took the parental vision to a new level. You should have the right to pass along what you've earned to your children and those you love, up to a point. Democrats should propose *reform* of the estate tax but not its repeal.

Through government's investment in the health and education of all citizens, Democrats can assure that all Americans have a fair chance to reach their full potential, so that they, too, can leave a legacy of invention, service, and material assets to their posterity. The question isn't whether to tax the rich to help the poor; rather it is, What do you owe your fellow human beings simply because they're human beings? The American ethic asks us to find the fairest way for all Americans to contribute to the national well-being and to recognize that we are all connected through our common humanity.

Democrats need to create a positive definition of wealth. It ought to be defined as consisting of whatever ensures a high quality of life—not just money but a livable pension, decent health care, a good education, and a clean environment. It always amazed me, in my years on the Senate Finance Committee, to see how taxing the rich returned only pocket change—$200 or $300 in redistributed taxes—to each middle-class taxpayer. If that money were used for improvements in health care and education and the pension system, by contrast, it would give the middle class and the poor a larger share in the American dream. If every working mother had access to prenatal screening and a good child-care system, her children would be better prepared for kindergarten. If every company that promised its workers a pension had to set aside the money to deliver on that promise, the pressure on government budgets would be less. If every child could go to quality schools and have access to quality health care, the next generation would grow up ready and able to join a flourishing economy.

There are many wealthy people who are poor—and many poor and middle-class people who are wealthy—in spirit, in talent, in wisdom, in honor, in loving friends and family. The wealth of America is not just its GDP but the health and well-being of its citizens. Democrats should work to increase the wealth of the whole—the factors that improve our quality of life and the chances that we'll realize our full potential. These improvements will cost us only money, and that money has to come in part from those of us who have it, because when no one is left behind, all of us advance together.

• The sixth curse is the curse of our *special friends*. It relates to certain members of the Democratic coalition itself: teachers, trial lawyers, and autoworkers. Many of them have supported the Democratic Party for more than a generation. They share its ideals. But we are now at a time when parts of their agendas hold us back from what must be done. It is time to assert the general interest over the special interest, however painful that message may be.

Democrats prize the nation's teachers. Teachers, after all, are articulate and well-organized and share Democratic views on many issues. The prevailing ethos is that you don't criticize your friends. But it is precisely because teachers are our friends that we Democrats can risk the truth. Too many of them defend the status quo in school organization, student performance, and teacher accountability—a status quo that has become indefensible. Teachers' unions have consistently opposed reforms to address these issues, in disregard of the national interest. Democrats must tell teachers and principals that they will be held accountable for results. Teachers should be required to upgrade their skills; those who do should be paid more, and those who don't should be paid less. Just as it took the conservative president Richard Nixon to open relations with China in 1972, it will take a liberal president to persuade the nation's teachers and principals to do their part in keeping America great.

Another group in the Democratic coalition in need of stern words are trial lawyers. I know a doctor in Florida—not a surgeon—who saw his malpractice insurance go up $234,000 in one year. The bill for malpractice claims at the Cleveland Clinic from 2001 through 2005 was $154,504,802. In 2002, nearly 44 percent of all hospitals in America experienced malpractice premium increases of more than 50 percent. The RAND Corporation reports that, in the area of asbestos litigation, more than 700,000 claims have been filed over thirty years, costing defendants more than $70 billion. Courts have awarded more than $49 billion in such cases, nearly $23 billion of which went to the lawyers. In addition, defense costs amounted to $21 billion. The purpose of plaintiff litigation is to obtain redress for injured parties, not largesse for trial lawyers. Even the most seasoned populist who wants ordinary citizens to have some clout in the courts would agree that lawyers are taking a disproportionate share of the money that could have gone to the families of asbestosis victims.

In a recent federal trial in Texas related to silicosis—a disease of, among others, producers of ceramics and glass, caused by inhaling silica dust—the defendants, instead of immediately settling, demanded to see the individual backups to the claims presented by the plaintiffs' lawyers. What they found was that more than half of the 10,000 claimants had also filed asbestosis claims. In hundreds of cases, they also found, a silicosis diagnosis had been made by the same doctor who had certified the patient's asbestosis claim years before. Some of the doctors involved admitted under oath that they hadn't even talked with all the patients whose X rays they examined. "It is apparent that truth and justice had very little to do with these diagnoses," the U.S. district judge in the case, who was appointed by a Democrat, declared. "Otherwise more effort would have been devoted to insuring they were accurate. These diagnoses were driven by neither health nor justice; they were manufactured for money. The record does not reveal who originally devised this scheme but it is clear that the lawyers, doctors, and screening companies were all willing participants."

Plaintiffs should have the right to sue. Enron and WorldCom remind us of that. Pensioners defrauded by reckless management, children hurt by unsafe toys, families injured by faulty car brakes—all ought to have recourse through the courts. Yet too often members of the plaintiffs' bar file cases of no merit, expecting the company to settle rather than pursue the case to the point where it can show that the charges are specious. Often companies agree to settlements as a price of doing business, not because they have done anything wrong. Sometimes all it takes to prompt a lawsuit is a drop in the stock price. The intimidation and harassment are supposed to produce the payoff. The cost to American companies of plaintiff litigation last year was $260 billion, nearly nine times that of our nearest rival, Germany, with $30 billion. It is a cost that companies in countries with less aggressive plaintiff bars don't incur. There's got to be a better way.

One result of all of this litigiousness in health care is higher costs, flight of doctors from their profession, and little improvement in health care delivery. But Democrats walk in lockstep in opposition to any kind of tort reform. We reject Paul O'Neill's sensible proposal to limit malpractice liability for hospital medical errors reported in the first twenty-four hours and corrected in the first week. Other reasonable ideas, such as Common Good's proposal to establish health courts—like the bankruptcy courts or the old Admiralty courts—in which specialist judges would hear cases relating to hospitals and doctors in a timely manner and decide them without a jury, are rejected. If we had health courts presided over by judges who were health experts, trial lawyers would be less likely to go on fishing expeditions and the nation's doctors could practice medicine again as they see fit, instead of covering themselves by overprescribing and overtesting. Doctors who make egregious mistakes would be punished, but frivolous lawsuits would be thrown out.

Democrats have not yet offered any real alternative to the status quo—and trial lawyers have rewarded Democrats by fealty to their cause. The lawyers have gotten rich and have thus become stalwarts of the Democratic fund-raising base—in other words, just another special interest. By empowering the trial bar and getting hooked on its generous contributions to our war chests, we Democrats have become less and less likely to oppose the trial bar's agenda, no matter how self-serving it might be.

Which brings us to the autoworkers. Historically, their union has been run by some of the most talented and idealistic leaders in the labor movement. Men such as Leonard Woodcock, Douglas Fraser, Owen Bieber, and Stephen Yokich have fought for their members in the best tradition of the UAW's longtime president Walter Reuther. Today, some of their interests conflict with the public interest. They have opposed higher mileage standards, which could reduce our dependence on foreign oil, because retooling the production line could lead to temporary unemployment for some workers. They have opposed requiring companies to shore up private pension systems, because if auto companies were to set aside more money for pensions, current earnings would be hurt and auto industry jobs jeopardized. Their interest seems to be in guaranteeing the pensions of current retirees, not protecting the future pensions of younger workers.

Autoworkers also have rejected new approaches to health care. Workers with incomes over a certain amount and health care plans worth more than a certain amount should be taxed on a portion of the cost of their benefits. In bipartisan negotiations to salvage the Clinton health plan in 1994, a consortium of unions fiercely opposed any taxation of their benefits, no matter how rich they were. While that attitude is understandable when the proposal is partial reform, it makes no sense in a world of universal national health insurance, in which the premise is that everyone should have excellent health care. A national health plan might not be quite as generous as their current health plans, but all Americans would be covered. "Solidarity" can no longer simply apply to the labor movement, which today represents only 7.8 percent of private-sector workers, but must be extended to the citizens at large. Solving problems for all of us will require some people to give up a part of the gains they fought so hard for, in order to help people with no health or pension benefits, so that everyone can have a better life in a cleaner environment under a government that won't have to go to war ever again for oil.

Democrats must summon the courage to challenge our political friends. When oil prices spiked in 2006, Bush would have won plaudits had he brought the oil companies in and greeted them with a few harsh words. He would have been taking on Republican special interests. Not surprisingly, he refused the opportunity. If we take on not just Republican special interests but also our own special interests, the public will once again have confidence that we see their plight clearly and are prepared to fight to make their lives better.

• The seventh curse is that Democrats have *ceased to take a strong stand on principle*. The abolitionists, the progressives, the civil rights activists, and even some of the early environmentalists were willing to take a public policy stand that was rooted in a moral view of the world and based on individual conviction. Politicians of principle don't always win, but they often influence the discourse. The norm is for politicians to focus on process more than principle. Ideas alienate as well as attract. Political principle is tart in many mouths, whereas vagueness tastes like honey. For Democrats, the common-sense result has too often been to avoid the clarity of conviction powerfully expressed. Even the mention of ideology, political philosophy, or principle has been discouraged: Just get the politicians together, divvy up the economic pie, and keep moving forward toward an undefined end.*

Martin Luther King Jr.'s power resided chiefly in the rightness of his cause. What is the Democrats' righteous cause today? King influenced people because he was unafraid to challenge the nation's entrenched injustices. Have Democrats done that lately? King never worried about what well-placed people would think about what he was saying. Which Democratic officeholder today doesn't calibrate most of his or her utterances with the next election in mind? King didn't compromise his ideals for money. Wouldn't acting that way impede political fund-raising today? He stood on a platform of principle and told the country what he thought it needed, not what he thought it wanted to hear. Nor did he hesitate to put his life on the line. His convictions showed through. Where are the Democrats' convictions?

The late Senator Paul Wellstone of Minnesota was a Democrat who had convictions. He stood up for the poor, the downtrodden, the struggling family farmer, the union member who'd been downsized or outsourced. No one doubted where he stood. He believed that the federal government could be a powerful force for good. He believed that the only way you beat big money is to outorganize it at the grassroots level. His trust in the people was profound, and his respect for his country inspiring. When he spoke, his cadences would build to a finale that had the crowd on its feet cheering and clapping. When you heard him, you felt that there was no limit to what

---

*See my book *Time Present, Time Past* (Knopf, 1996).

we could achieve. Diminutive in stature, combative in style, loving in nature. The last significant vote he cast before his death in a plane crash was against the Iraq War.

• The Democrats' final curse is that we are *hypnotized by charisma*. Ever since JFK's Camelot, Democrats have been looking for a leader whose very presence would ensure the nation's primacy. Over the years, we have paid more attention to the lost charisma of JFK than to the steady accomplishments of LBJ. Many of us are still waiting for another charismatic leader whom we can invest with powers more magical than real. We forget that you need bare-knuckled know-how to change people's lives for the better. And you also need a plan. Bill Clinton had charisma, and he controlled the White House for eight years, the first Democrat to do so since FDR. Yet at the end of that time there were fewer Democratic senators, representatives, governors, and state legislators, and the party itself was deep in debt. Charisma had failed to trump the Republican Party's structure.

To understand how the Democratic Party works today, invert the pyramid that Republicans have built for themselves. Imagine a Democratic pyramid balancing precariously on its point, which is the presidential candidate. Instead of presidential candidates sitting atop a layer of money, ideas, political language, and media outreach, we require our presidential candidates to generate their own pyramids. They can't rely on a coherent, larger structure.

But as I wrote in an op-ed piece for *The New York Times* in March 2005:

> There is no clearly identifiable funding base for Democratic policy organizations, and in the frantic campaign rush there is no time for patient, long-term development of new ideas or new ways to sell old ideas. Campaigns don't start thinking about a Democratic brand until halfway through the election year, by which time winning the daily news cycle takes precedence over building a consistent message. . . .
>
> Every four years the party splits and rallies around several different individuals at once. Opponents in the primaries then exaggerate their

differences and leave the public confused about what Democrats believe.

In such a system tactics trump strategy. Candidates don't risk talking about big ideas because the ideas have never been sufficiently tested. Instead they usually wind up arguing about minor issues and express few deep convictions. In the worst case, they embrace "Republican-lite" platforms—never realizing that in doing so they're allowing the Republicans to define the terms of the debate.

Democrats need to abandon the star system and build a pyramidal structure from the grass roots up, like that constructed by Republicans since 1971. Liberal-leaning foundations and wealthy Democratic individuals must make explicit, long-term financial commitments to building a series of think tanks to generate the ideas that will once again give Democrats the conceptual advantage. With fresh ideas that flow from our values and convictions and address tomorrow's problems, we can begin to assert real leadership—and we'd be fighting for something more substantial than simply preventing Republicans from doing anything.

At the political level of the pyramid, the place to begin is with the party itself. Over the last thirty years, it has become dysfunctional and even moribund in many states. Large numbers of Democrats have no enthusiasm for getting together as Democrats at the local level. Local Democratic clubs dry up. There is little money for local organizing, and less enthusiasm. The national party hasn't helped; instead, it promotes a connection directly between the national party and individual voters in targeted states—an idea hatched in the minds of Washington consultants (who will of course be paid for the TV ads and polls that establish such a connection). Political communication should not be limited to ads and raising money. (Watch one, send the other.) It's as if we viewed the electorate as spectators, to be entertained by some hot new TV show and asked to do nothing but decide which of the performers on this political version of *American Idol* deserves the nod. People who want to play a more direct role in politics become frustrated. The national party has not given them anything to do—except donate money and stay out of the way.

As a party, we need a much greater investment in the technical aspects of campaigning: database management, branding exercises, and other business practices that Republicans long ago mastered. We need to develop our own wedge issues to split the Republican camp, just as they used race, gay marriage, and abortion to split ours. Budgets for marketing must be as robust in off years as in election years. We need to respond to people's beliefs about themselves and their communities, not simply enter debates with the idea of showing that our candidate is the brightest kid in the classroom. We need to contest Republicans on the twinned issues of patriotism and personal freedom. We need to castigate them for what they've done to the deficit, to the environment, to our standing in the world.

A promising wedge issue could be something as ubiquitous as the weather. We should go into the Republican congressional districts that have been hard-hit by hurricanes, floods, or droughts. We should assert that climate change has contributed to these natural disasters. We should then dredge up all the Republican congressmen's statements denying the existence of climate change, reveal the campaign contributions they got from interests that benefit from our continued addiction to fossil fuels, and then ask them to explain how refusing to act on climate change serves the national interest. We should bring the global to the local.

Connecting locally as a party is the key to our grassroots future. What we need is engagement with voters on issues, organization, and service—all at the local level. But the way Democrats organize our grass roots differs from how Republicans do it, and the way we're doing it is destroying the idealism of a generation of young people who want to work for a progressive American future.

Republicans engage local groups, often conservative Christian churches, which have a broad outreach across many issues. They enlist local people, who know the local rhythms and the local history, to contact their neighbors in an effort to boost Republican turnout. In fact, they go further. They identify potential voters who share lifestyle choices about TV shows, cars, sports, church, music, tourist destinations, and much more. In *Applebee's America: How Successful Political, Business, and Religious Leaders Connect with the New American Community*, Doug Sosnik, Matt Dowd, and Ron

Fournier report, "Nearly every time a person takes out a loan, books a flight, or conducts any of hundreds of other business transactions, he or she leaves a data trail. The average consumer travels through life trailed by thousands of clues to future buying and voting habits, a veritable gold mine for any organization with the money and motivation to solve the mysteries of his or her political attitudes." By collating such consumer data with voting histories and in-depth political polling, Republicans can determine which individuals with which specific consumption habits are likely Republican voters. This allows them to target potential Republican voters by consumer preference, which allows them to identify potential supporters in geographic areas that are not overwhelmingly Republican and have them contacted by like-minded Republicans (as opposed to pulling voters to the polls only in the heavily Republican districts).

In a world where we are cynical about TV commercials and especially political TV, the best way to reach potential supporters is through other voters who share their life preferences. It is the ultimate tailored communication, far more effective than blasting out a TV commercial to a million people, of whom only a small fraction may be potential supporters. Better to find the potentials first, wherever they are, and then bring them home. Republicans understand this. Democrats haven't. We're still battling for the undecided voter in the middle, which is a group that shrinks with each election.

Republicans begin their turnout effort over a year before the election. National organizers come into an already robust local organization, bringing with them the latest expertise in this lifestyle-oriented canvassing. By contrast, Democrats—as well as the progressive interest groups that make up our constituencies (Clean Water Action, the Sierra Club, the Fair Trade Federation, NARAL Pro-Choice America, the Human Rights Campaign)—have outsourced grassroots efforts to third parties, such as the Fund for Public Interest Research.

The Columbia University sociologist Dana Fisher, in her excellent book *Activism, Inc.: How the Outsourcing of Grassroots Campaigns Is Strangling Progressive Politics in America*, points out that the Fund for Public Interest Research—which goes by the pseudonym the People's Project in the book—works for several groups in the progressive coalition simultaneously, going door to door or standing on street corners, trying to interest people in giving money to and/or joining the various groups. They recruit young college students who want to work for a progressive agenda and turn them into cogs in a machine. No broad issue involvement. No discussion of a progressive ethos. No hands-on help to people. No attempt to provide meaning. It's only about doing a repetitive job, not unlike a call-center organization whose purpose is to move product. The regimentation begins with the charge to memorize a rigid script. Recruits are asked to role-play; they are supplied with pat answers to FAQs (frequently asked questions); they have quotas for money raising; they work long hours a day for low pay. And after doing that for a summer, or possibly a year, many of them burn out. The organizers have to know this, but they also know a new batch of kids will be coming in tomorrow. They don't need to worry about the negative experience these kids might have had and its implications for their future involvement in progressive politics.

One might argue that issues, philosophy, and local involvement are all the job of the Democratic Party, but volunteer grassroots organizing by the party disappeared twenty years ago. Now it's outsourced to paid experts. On a national level the Democratic Party, in 2004, did exactly what the People's Project did. It sent groups into targeted states, for a door-to-door effort to pull Democrats— strangers to them—to the polls. Unlike the Republicans, whose teams of experts go into local organizations already segmented by lifestyle preferences, with locals doing the bulk of the canvassing among their like-minded neighbors, Democrats dispatch union members, paid organizers, and short-term volunteers several months before an election to states in which they don't reside with the charge to organize an Election Day effort.

Republicans go to places such as mega-churches where real human contact takes place. Mega-churches have ongoing discussion groups on issues that affect people's lives: work, children, finances, child care, aging. In addition, some have book groups, sports teams, fitness classes, day-care centers, and even schools. What happens in the smaller groups bonds the members to the church as much as the pastor's sermon does on Sunday morning. Republicans often use these gatherings as focus groups. More important, Republicans plug into the politically active elements of the congregation, who become the local foot soldiers of the party's voter contact. Their role comes out of their involvement with the church and the meaning they derive from that association. Many of these same individuals also participate in community projects through their churches. Democrats ignore the potential of mega-churches for Democratic organizing, rarely talk about issues in a collegial way at a structured place, almost never (beyond the candidate's campaign) engage real people outside a focus group, and never provide ways for volunteers directly to help another human being. As Fisher notes:

> Only through *meaningful membership* that involves conversations and lasting connections can social capital and social networks be harnessed to bring about political change. Like-minded progressive Americans have the ability to connect voters with similar values and mobilize them to participate politically, but creating a political infrastructure that links local groups to national political institutions takes time and commitment; it will require people at the national and grassroots levels working together to establish grassroots connections that are deep enough to bear fruit.

The Democratic Party needs to engage the hearts and heads of its supporters.

People need opportunities to make their world a better place where they are. Serving your fellow human beings resonates with many people, especially the young. There is no reason that Democrats can't have local party chapters joining in with nonprofits to do hands-on community work with children or seniors or neighborhood improvement projects. Why couldn't groups such as Teach for America or Donors Choose originate inside the Democratic Party? That's how the old party machines built loyalty—by taking care of people. That personal connection with the lives of real people is what has been missing in the grassroots approach of the Democratic

Party. The party needs to create tangible achievements, locally developed and contributing, grain by grain of sand, to the beach of national political effort.

The Democratic Party should also systematically engage the minds of its supporters by soliciting policy and political ideas from the grass roots. In 2005, the Service Employees International Union sponsored something called Since Sliced Bread, as in the old saying "The best thing since sliced bread." People were invited to submit their new ideas on how to make America better. SEIU was surprised when over 22,000 proposals arrived, from which a panel of 23 judges selected the top 21. Some of these ideas already have been introduced as bills in the Congress.

There is no reason why the new Democratic Speaker of the House, Nancy Pelosi, along with Senate Majority Leader Harry Reid and the chairman of the Democratic National Committee, Howard Dean, shouldn't sponsor a contest for good ideas. With the Internet it's easy to make people feel included in this way. It also says that Democrats seek ideas from the people as well as from elite policy institutes. The winners would have Democratic sponsorship for making the ideas reality. Who knows? Maybe some wealthy donor could even establish monetary prizes for the best 20 ideas. That's clearly a more creative way to give money to the party than funding yet another TV ad.

Above all, the national political level of the Democratic pyramid must explain what it means to be a Democrat. At its best, the national party would fashion a message of hope rooted in principle and programs. By making our positions on issues part of a larger political philosophy and view of life, we could refute the negativity of American politics with the clarity of our convictions. We could say to the elderly that we would be there for them in their twilight years but that we could not promise them what we cannot afford. We could say to the young that they need not give up their idealism in order to be successful. We could say to the middle class that we would be with them when sickness or tragedy struck, helping them to get back on their feet or when they needed some governmental clout to deal with corporate exploitation. We could say to the poor, "Help is on the way, so take hold of our hand and pull yourself up."

We could say to those who have fattened themselves on our collective generosity, "Your days are numbered!" We could say to all Americans that you can triumph over ignorance and spitefulness, corruption and greed, and that you can take the high road and succeed—if enough of you take it together. We could lead them to see that there's a wave building in the country, and when it breaks it will carry away the trappings of political privilege and the insidious bond between big money and public power. We can break the grip of political lies on our imagination. We can pierce the bubble of self-importance that engulfs too many politicians, and we can usher in a new day of honesty, humanity, and understanding.*

When these messages, fervently expressed, reach the media level of the pyramid, the negativity the media churn out will give way to the good news of what is possible. Our days in the wilderness of Republican-controlled dialogue will be over. We will manage our own destiny by being ourselves. Human nature will not change, but a media strategy that conveys an America that is less paranoid, more generous, more hopeful, and more human will reflect a more realistic picture of life for most people. When they see that their lives can be better—that our children can be better educated, our families healthier, our livelihoods more secure—the enthusiasm will quicken. The wave will crest.

The president or presidential candidate who sits at the top of this pyramid will not be advocating a return to a distant past but will be engaged with the emerging future. He or she will treat science as a promise, not a threat. He or she will not keep inconvenient but essential information from the people. He or she will be the steward of our best impulses, not the panderer to our worst fears. This president of our best selves will look out on the world with a sense of curiosity and inclusiveness. His modesty will remind us of how much other countries and cultures have to say to us. Her humanity will remind us of why we need one another. His awareness of what must be preserved will balance his conviction of what must be changed. Nature will inspire her with its enormous diversity and its age-old cycles of renewal. He will see our enemies clearly but never stop trying

*See my book *The Journey from Here* (Artisan, 2000).

to make them our friends. She will regard those who lived before our time with gratitude and those who will follow with loving concern. The president of our best selves will carry our dreams and fears and find the balance between them that will inspire us to realize who we are individually and collectively. The Democratic Party will then have more than just a brand worth selling—it will have a faith worth fighting for. When that time comes, the last curse will be lifted. It won't happen overnight, but a journey begins with one step. Now is the time for Democrats to take it.

Only if Democrats deal with our eight curses and build a more inclusive house can we muster the power and credibility necessary to solve our nation's problems. The new leadership that Democrats offer will reach out to Republicans and independents alike and build a new party coalition based on principle, vision, and candor. It will recognize that in a world of instant news, when a photo of Abu Ghraib can be transmitted to billions of people in a nanosecond and a global press corps analyzes every presidential speech, it is reckless to use foreign policy to pander to domestic political constituencies. A new kind of Democratic leadership will engage the world by listening before it talks. It will help people where they live their lives by guaranteeing them good health care, quality education, and pension security while promoting the dynamism of the economy. It will seek reform of the political structure when that structure blocks the free expression of the people's will. It will remind those who join the Democratic team that the party has a purpose and a lineage that touches virtually every big moment in American history. The American poet Vachel Lindsay once wrote, "The tragedy is not to die. The tragedy is to die with commitments undefined, convictions unexpressed, and service unfulfilled." We Democrats need to keep our commitments, restate our convictions, and fulfill our service. We still have decisions to make and actions to take and much good to do, before it's too late.

Part IV.

REALIZING THE DREAM

Chapter 12.

WHY THE NEW STORY IS GOOD POLITICS

Championing the New American Story is good politics because it contrasts with the cynical politics of the last few decades—a politics that has blatantly tried to manipulate the electorate rather than level with it. What the new story seeks to achieve will affect all Americans, and as numerous surveys have demonstrated, the great majority of them want what it embodies. It is a truthful story about what America must do to remain the preeminent nation in the world. It puts the United States in a position to lead from the power of our example as a pluralistic democracy whose growing economy takes more and more people to higher economic ground.

The best way to relate to voters is to show them that you understand what they're worried about and that you have answers that will help them. Underneath the issue of the moment, which is driven by the headlines, lie deeper and abiding concerns: jobs, family, health care, education, economic security, a purposeful life. A sense of one's circumstances is shaped by many things, including one's fears, and fear can lead to an erosion of community, leaving each of us on our own to deal with a rapidly changing economy and a culture that sometimes offends our sense of right and wrong. I believe that people hunger for a politics that addresses the diminishment of our sense of belonging and gives us all the chance to be part of an inspired national community.

The period in American history that seems most like our own is the early twentieth century. New technologies, such as the telegraph and the railroad, had created a national market for the first time. People from the farms streamed to the city, and a massive flow of foreign immigrants produced an ominous sense of disconnectedness with the nation's past. The dominance of virtually every facet of American life by big business made ordinary citizens feel powerless and disoriented in the midst of rapid change. People feared they were losing control of their lives. Democracy seemed impotent before private power. Senators were on the payrolls of railroad companies. Journalists were on the payrolls of politicians. Countless special interests wanted tariff protection. Self-government itself seemed in danger. Thomas Jefferson's prediction that commerce would threaten democracy seemed to be coming true.

The major question was what to do about the concentration of power and wealth in the hands of a few. Each of the four presidential candidates in the 1912 election had a clear but different answer. For William Howard Taft, the incumbent, it was staying with the status quo. For Eugene V. Debs, the socialist, it was the creation of a socialist state, which would take over the means of production. The Democrat Woodrow Wilson wanted to break up the business monopolies and give power back to small economic units more easily subject to local control. Theodore Roosevelt, however, argued that economic decentralization was impossible. Too much had already happened. Instead, what was needed was the balancing of big business by a more powerful government and the development of a new nationalism of patriotic service. Wilson won the election. Roosevelt won the future.

When Teddy Roosevelt's distant cousin Franklin came to power, in 1933, he reined in the laissez-faire economy of the 1920s (whose mismanagement had created the Depression), and he used government planning and national regulation of business to regain control of the economy. His actions underlined the Democratic belief that the economy should work for everyone and not just the privileged few. It was Franklin Delano Roosevelt's program, but it was Teddy Roosevelt's vision.

Today we live in a similar time. People feel a loss of control. The average citizen is fearful in a world of globalization, technological change, growing inequality, economic insecurity, huge trade and budget deficits, erosion of community, proliferation of entitlements without oversight, increasing immigration, sophisticated global crime, and the ever-present threat of terrorism.

The New American Story says that it is good politics to confront these worries directly. The politics of avoidance and division can no longer be tolerated. The problems that face our country loom too large. We cannot waste any more time on bad politics. When the people are upset, they deserve the truth. Let them reject it if they choose, but then it will be democracy's choice to deny reality. Political leaders should not arrogate to themselves, based on a desire to hold on to political power, the right to hide the truth from the people. Indeed, the basis of democracy is truth. So the biggest reason that the New American Story is good politics is that the American people are ready for the truth about the issues most important to them.

On September 11, 2001, terrorists seized four planes. Two crashed into the World Trade Center, and one hit the Pentagon. The fourth plane crashed in a field in Pennsylvania, and the story of that plane has relevance to the New American Story. When the terrorists seized the cockpit and took control of the flight, the people on the plane saw what had happened. Some made cell-phone calls and discovered that other planes had hit the World Trade Center. They knew that, if nothing were done, they would die and their plane would hit another American symbol. The passengers had a small town meeting, to decide what to do. They concluded that they would attempt to seize the plane from the terrorists. By doing so, they might save themselves or they might at least prevent the plane from hitting the White House or the Capitol or whatever the terrorists had selected as the next target. The result was that, although they failed to save their own lives, they did succeed in forcing the plane to crash short of its destination in Washington, DC.

These patriotic Americans faced the truth of their situation and dealt with it. They decided to give their lives for the country. If they had denied their plight, or refused to work together, there would have been no heroic action and the plane would have struck another American landmark.

The story of Flight 93 reveals a deeply American trait. It is the same can-do spirit that allowed us to build a continental nation dedicated to the liberty and welfare of each of its citizens. When people sailed across the Atlantic to the New World or crossed the Great Plains headed west, they didn't know exactly how they'd get to their destination, but they set out to reach it. The same is true today of the problems confronting America. If we face the truth about the perilously low rate of national savings, or the deficiencies in our health care and educational systems, or the precarious state of pensions, or the dangers posed by global warming, or our addiction to fossil fuels, or our international fall from grace, we can deal with them. Americans are made that way.

Today the truth doesn't ask us to give up our lives, as it did on Flight 93; it asks only that we save for the future, take better care of ourselves, study harder, pay a little more in taxes, make fuel-efficient purchases, and understand what it means to be a citizen of the world. All we need are leaders who will tell us what our real situation is and what steps can be taken to make it better. The New American Story offers one possible path, and I believe the American people are up to realizing it.

Shortsighted, short-term political self-interest deters Republicans and Democrats alike from adopting the new story. They seem trapped within the structure of our current politics and incapable of framing a new kind of politics. Many of them seem to believe that the only way to get things done is through their own party. Notwithstanding Karl Rove's or Speaker Nancy Pelosi's ambitions, a veto-proof, filibuster-proof congressional majority in our current political environment is fantasy.

I believe that the only way to achieve one-party dominance is to convince the American people that your party is the true exponent of a new story that, if adopted, would solve many of their problems. But even better—and still possible, I believe—both parties could put away the politics of personal destruction and support the new story, recognizing that any large and lasting changes, absent over-whelming majorities, need bipartisan agreement.

When I came to the Senate, in 1979, the first senator to pay a welcoming visit to my office was a Republican, Jack Danforth of Missouri. Over the years, I concluded that there was no finer sena-tor than Dick Lugar (R.–Ind.), who was thoughtful, measured, and often courageous, and there was no senator I liked more than Alan Simpson (R.–Wyo.). In the House of Representatives, Republicans such as Jim Leach of Iowa and Doug Bereuter of Nebraska became trusted colleagues. In those days, a group of freshman senators from both parties used to meet regularly and share their thoughts about issues and the institution. The majorities on the Senate Finance Committee, of which I was a member, were often bipartisan. In 1980 I persuaded the Republicans David Durenberger of Min-nesota, John Chafee of Rhode Island, and Jack Danforth of Missouri to vote with me against the oil senators (such as the committee's chairman, Democrat Russell Long of Louisiana) to establish a tax on oil company profits, which had soared because of geopolitical turmoil in Iran.

There were very few party-line votes back then. In 1986 Al Simp-son and I sat down without staff to talk about the complex immigra-tion bill, of which he was the sponsor. I asked him fifteen or twenty questions. At the end of our meeting, I told him I was with him. I didn't even know if there was a Democratic position on the bill.

Those days seem far from the mean-spirited, rigidly partisan poli-tics of today. The losers in an era of excessive partisanship are the American people. If you don't have respect for the other side, it's more difficult to cooperate with it in doing the people's business. The new story offers an opportunity to reconstitute honest dialogue, true bipartisanship. There are conservative and liberal ideas embod-ied within it. It is wrong to say that all Republicans are so unfeeling that they don't care about people living in poverty or whether a fam-ily has a doctor or a child goes to a good school. They can cry, too. Plenty of Republicans are dissatisfied with the state of our country. They tell me so every day. They are Main Streeters, appalled by the galloping deficit and what it is stealing from our children. They are realists, upset by a reckless war and an arrogant foreign policy. They are libertarians, and even some corporatists, aghast at the excesses of the government intrusion into the most private areas of our lives. They are Republican liberals, who remember the party's leadership on the environment and who still believe—in the tradition of Teddy Roosevelt and Dwight Eisenhower—that government has a legitimate role to play in our lives. A party of messianists, supply-siders, subsidists, racemongers, and fundamentalists is not the Republican Party of my father. Nor is it the Republican Party of many Republicans. The substantive Republicans, who have ideas and want progress, seem to have lost ground to the political Republicans, who just want power for power's sake. But what do those substantive Republicans do about it?

Republicans can hold their noses against the stench of corruption and avert their eyes from the extremist remedies that have become commonplace. They can protest within the councils of government and try to change the minds of people whose minds seem impervious to reasoned argument. They can posture publicly about all the things they disagree with while supporting the party down the line—trying to have it both ways in a blatant attempt to mislead voters about their true convictions. They can ignore the irrevocable change in the party's base and assume that the last six years are an aberration, with the hope that reasonable people will someday take power back from extremists. Or they can decide that the country is at too critical a juncture for business as usual.

Republicans can reassert their moderate character and join with Democrats in negotiating a new agenda on America's role in the world, the economy, oil and the environment, pensions, health care, and education. The only prerequisite to negotiation must be a clear commitment to realizing the agenda in some form within a few years. The presence of moderate Republicans at the table will certainly alter some of the details in the agenda's provisions, but it would be worth it for Democrats to yield in some areas in order to get the bipartisan support that will guarantee the reform's success.

But some Democrats may not yield. They may themselves be partisan purists going for a supermajority. If that's the case, the bipartisan-moderate middle must step forward and take over the agenda, not unlike what happened on the Senate Finance Committee during the reign of Russell Long; or on the Senate floor in 1978, when the Republican Howard Baker Jr. and the Democrat Robert Byrd, working with a Democratic president, arranged ratification of the Panama Canal Treaty; or when the Democratic majority leader Lyndon Johnson and the Republican minority leader William F. Knowland, working with a Republican president, produced bipartisan support for the Civil Rights Bill of 1957; or when the Democratic majority leader Mike Mansfield and the Republican minority leader Everett Dirksen, working with a Democratic president, passed the Voting Rights Act of 1965; or even when the Democratic chairman of the House Ways and Means Committee Dan Rostenkowski and the Republican chairman of the Senate Finance Committee Bob Packwood teamed up with Ronald Reagan to pass the 1986 Tax Reform Act. In each case, the country was more important than the party, and the trust between patriots of opposite parties moved America forward.

I believe that in a world in which activists and political consultants focus on peripheral issues—even in a world in which few elections are legitimately contested and money seems a necessary evil—the political party that emphasizes what 70 percent of the people care about will be in power for a generation. Imagine a campaign that got across the New American Story—a campaign that laid out what we have to do to restore America's role in the world, grow the economy, free ourselves from dependence on oil, protect the environment, secure pensions, provide universal health care, and improve public education. Imagine a campaign that told voters how it would prioritize these issues and how it would pay for them. The contrast between that approach and politics as usual, with all its narrow issues fervently expressed, would certainly get the public's attention. Such an approach would be risky, and it would require a disciplined campaign effort, but if you reached just the wider community of Democrats or Republicans who don't usually vote in primaries (and certainly if you motivated the 40 to 50 percent of the population who don't *ever* vote, period), you would have transformed American politics.

Pundits will say that such a campaign is political suicide: Stay with the poll-tested, focus-grouped, public relations–spun voter communication. What they ignore is the yearning of people to hear the truth. What they fail to understand is that honesty and boldness are essential to extricate us from the undertow of the peripheral and the corrupt, and to reconstruct our self-government as a vibrant republic. What they can't fathom is how the truth engenders trust between a politician and the people. Imagine if voters understood a road map of action that would transform America and allow it to thrive in the future. Imagine if they could see that they are a part of its realization. Such a campaign would reinvigorate American democracy with its clear articulation of a new agenda. As people began to flock to the candor and vision of one party, the other would be forced to respond, not with nit-picking or malicious attacks, but positively. Remember, politics is fundamentally an imitative profession. The country desperately needs such a campaign.

I believe that the American people not only want such a campaign but also want such a government, one that addresses their principal daily concerns in a way that gives them hope—and then delivers on its promise. Government can't replace the empty feeling in someone's life, but it can help someone's material circumstances, and on good days it can offer the inspiration of a caring, future-oriented, national community. The facts that too many politicians are out of touch with the people—more dedicated to the agenda of the dominant interest groups of their party than they are to the general interest of the whole—and that the media fan the flames of the most extreme views and glorify political combat only offer the citizen a bigger opportunity to demand reform.

As I said in Chapter 9, what must be done is clear: Change the way congressional district lines are drawn so that they will look more like contiguous states instead of strands of spaghetti; allow people to vote over a two-day period, on Saturday and Sunday, not just on Tuesday; make it easier for people to register to vote, so that universal registration becomes a reality; reduce the role of money in elections by adopting public financing of elections or a constitutional amendment that allows limits on spending; require TV stations to carry a designated amount of issue-specific and political programming in exchange for their licenses; find the economic leverage to do the same thing for cable TV; and encourage social networking on the Internet, which will make citizen involvement and action easier. Finally, this plan needs a few politicians who will put their careers on the line for the New American Story. Some of them can be incumbents from each party. Others can be public-spirited citizens who no longer want to sit on the sidelines. The only requirement is to have the courage of their convictions; they must see clearly the moment we're living in and understand the stakes and their role in the unfolding national drama.

It is reassuring that the American people are reasonable when confronted with the truth. We are not some hopelessly divided, polarized, angry nation. The feelings and attitudes we share are greater than those that divide us. Even if bipartisanship does not prevail, there's no reason why civility cannot. You state your case as a party, and the people decide, but when they do, it's over. No excuses for the loser. No attempt at personal destruction of the winner simply because you're the loser. In a democracy, the irony is that some things, such as elections, must be final because healthy dialogue and disagreement should never be.

The New American Story offers us an opportunity to celebrate what is best about our politics—the willingness and determination of a free people to change the direction of their country. All it takes is a few politicians who realize it's good politics to ride this wave of popular will and who choose to do so because they believe that "the truth shall set you free."

Chapter 13.

WHAT CITIZENS CAN DO

The New American Story doesn't start with government. It begins with you. You have to believe that your individual efforts can make a difference. You have to want to take positive steps to make America and the world a better place. Sometimes complaint and criticism are helpful, but they are not enough; we must all accept the creative responsibility inherent in citizenship. Acknowledge that change begins with yourself and that you won't sit on the sidelines anymore. Whether it's running for office, working on a campaign, organizing a petition drive, building a grassroots movement, starting a nonprofit enterprise, or volunteering in community service—when people reach a point where they believe in themselves and the worth of their goals, they can realize those goals. The fire of idealism burns first in an individual heart.

All of us can fulfill our obligations of citizenship in ways that best suit us. I may no longer be a U.S. senator, a presidential candidate, or even a practicing politician, but I am a citizen. Having spent all day every day for over twenty years thinking about public policy and politics and seeing our national and international moment today, I had to take action. This book represents my attempt to fulfill my own citizenship responsibility. It may or may not make an impact, but at least I've given it my best shot. I hope you give yours, too.

The most important thing to do, once you believe you can make a difference, is to stay informed. Self-government works only if citizens take the time to learn enough about their community, nation, and world to have informed opinions. If you've read this far, you've learned something about the ways in which our democratic process and dialogue have been undermined. Build on this knowledge. Read and listen to others. Think about it yourself. Without information, action is blind; with it, your path will be sure-footed and purposeful. David Hume, Adam Smith, and other thinkers of the Scottish Enlightenment who shaped the thinking of our country's Founders emphasized the need for the active awareness of citizens. George Washington, John Adams, Thomas Jefferson, Alexander Hamilton, and Benjamin Franklin all knew that a knowledgeable citizenry is essential to a democracy.

Like any other human activity, citizenship must be learned. In a recent poll commissioned by the American Bar Association, 45 percent of the respondents couldn't name the three branches of government. If close to a majority of Americans have no knowledge of the workings of our democracy and no desire to participate in it, self-government is endangered. To ensure that every citizen understands how our government works, we should require a civics course in every high school as a condition of graduation. We need to cultivate our democracy.

We're often told that new technologies are reshaping our civilization. To some extent that's true, but technologies come and go, whereas democracy is 2,500 years old. It's important to understand why this form of government has lasted, how it has changed, what version of it we have, and how it can be used to make a better life for the greatest number of Americans. Technology should not shape democracy; rather, democracy should shape technology. Democracy humanizes and controls what Adam Smith called the "selfish passions" of commerce. It allows all citizens to escape exploitation, develop their skills, and build their own lives. It legitimizes our collective effort and lends moral purpose to our individual achievements. The ethos of democracy focuses on the many, not the few; the citizen, not the marketplace; the long term, not the short term;

the general interest, not the special interest. Math and science are important to our economic future, but teaching our children how to work together in a democracy is what will guarantee our freedom.

Once you have a desire to make a difference and you've taken steps to be informed, the next step is to get involved, passionately. Socrates captured this spirit of involvement during his trial, when he was faced with the prospect of exile from Athens: "Perhaps some-one may say, 'But surely, Socrates, after you have left us you can spend the rest of your life in quietly minding your own business.' This is the hardest thing of all to make some of you understand. If I say that . . . I cannot 'mind my own business,' you will not believe that I am serious." Inherent in the job of being a citizen is a refusal to mind one's own business. As a citizen, you are the caretaker of the public good. You don't see yourself as a representative of a special interest, and you don't think democracy amounts only to a negotiation among special interests. You are *dis*interested; you act for the whole, not just for yourself.

Such engagement will not be easy. It goes against the prevailing idea of how things ought to be done. In *The Unconscious Civilization*, John Ralston Saul writes that being a citizen is "not a particularly pleasant or easy style of life. It is not profitable, efficient, competitive or rewarded. It often consists of being persistently annoying to others as well as being stubborn and repetitive." But when you keep at it, beautiful things can happen. Like Socrates, we need to challenge the public lies that too often pass without comment and explain what it means to be a democracy committed to humanism and globalization simultaneously. Our own philosophers, economists, political scientists, and sociologists should engage on the public issues of the day, not just hole up in their academic sanctuaries.* Democracy depends on citizens who make waves. When citizens abdicate their inherent democratic power, they turn the system over to those who often use it for personal enrichment, or worse. A true citizen doesn't retreat to his or her private pleasures when the

---

*The university has citizenship responsibilities, too. Harvard (for example) has the country's largest endowment—more than $25 billion at last count. It has been described as a giant mutual fund with a little college attached. Wouldn't it be good to take a sliver of that endowment and establish Harvard academies within the public school systems of our fifty largest cities?

price of public silence is that society's big decisions are made by fewer and fewer people.

To bring about the New American Story, we need to let Washington know we want government to take on the big challenges, such as universal health insurance or education reform or increasing the national savings rate. We need to recruit others to the cause and persuade them to take direct political action by voting, writing their elected representatives, and speaking out in support of a position that reflects the common good, whether through citizen groups, talk radio, or the Internet. We should reject politicians who can't see the whole, won't work for the public good, or offer excuses for inaction.

For those who doubt the power of citizen action, let me tell you about one woman from Vermont. In 1991 Jody Williams, a political activist drained emotionally by her efforts to stop the Central American wars of the 1980s yet still anxious to make the world a better place, joined Bobby Muller of the Vietnam Veterans of America Foundation and Thomas Gebauer of the German relief organization Medico International to work toward what seemed an impossible goal: a worldwide ban on land mines. At first they went to natural allies, such as Human Rights Watch, church groups, and land mine victims' groups. By October 1992 they had broadened their coalition to include the Mines Advisory Group in the United Kingdom, Handicap International in France, and Physicians for Human Rights, an international group based in the United States. These allied organizations began reaching out to other interested parties. They established a Web site. They travelled all over the world speaking for the cause, organizing everywhere they went.

Jody Williams went to see one of her senators, Patrick Leahy, along with another Vermonter who was working with land mine amputees in Cambodia. In an appropriations bill, Leahy inserted a provision establishing a moratorium on U.S. land mine exports for one year. The French member of the coalition then went to François Mitterrand and told Mitterrand what the United States had done. The French president wanted to top it and thereupon announced a three-year moratorium on French land mine exports. Over the next five years, the original coalition grew to 1,300 nongovernmental organizations from eighty-five countries. Governments began to compete with one another to take the lead on the issue, until finally, in March 1995, Belgium became the first country to support a land mine ban worldwide. The nongovernmental coalition drafted an international treaty to do that, and by 1997 the treaty was being negotiated by ninety governments. Shortly thereafter, the Ottawa Treaty banning land mines was signed by 154 countries. All the years of effort had paid off. Williams and her colleagues received the 1997 Nobel Peace Prize for their work.

A similar kind of energy and commitment can make the New American Story a reality. Such an effort starts with a few committed souls who refuse to "mind their own business" and press the cause relentlessly through every means available.

If the office of a member of Congress is flooded by phone calls and e-mails, he or she sits up and listens. Those calls and e-mails from constituents have impact—particularly if they are not all following the same script. During my time in the Senate, Supreme Court nominations always brought a deluge of mail. The largest number of letters I ever got on an issue—430,000—was prompted by pending legislation on something as mundane as withholding taxes from bank interest and corporate dividends. Even though the bulk of them were form letters opposing the withholding of these taxes, the sheer volume got my attention. For much of my Senate career, I had my staff give me what they considered to be the fifteen best letters of the week. Some of them offered specific policy ideas; others told moving stories. All affected me. If enough people take the time to tell Congress to pay less attention to the special interests and more to the agenda of the New American Story, they will move that agenda onto the congressional calendar.

In order to make citizenship a calling, all Americans should set aside three hours a week for public service in their personal lives. We schedule time for work, church, and Little League games. Why not public service? If only 25 percent of the adult population followed this suggestion, it would mean over 7 billion hours of citizen action annually, and the country would be better for it.

I know a man who started an organization to get teenagers involved in the betterment of their community. If a teenager volunteers four hours in a community project such as refurbishing a park or playground or painting a building, the organization gives the volunteer a ticket to a rock concert. The only people at the concert are other kids who have volunteered. The results: the community gets cleaned up, kids discover their penchant for service, and everyone has a good time—not a bad combination.

Activities such as this will expose people to the exhilaration of giving to a stranger with no expectation of return. They will also allow people to see that the action of one person alone—although important to whoever is being helped—is only a minute part of the solution. From their personal experiences with those who have no health insurance, or pension, or food to eat, or clothes to wear, or roof over their heads, people will come to see why government is essential in dealing with our big problems. A citizens group can clean up a neighborhood, tutor a child, and feed some hungry people, but only a government can ameliorate global warming or ensure plentiful and safe water, or guide an economy to produce good jobs at good pay, or guarantee that the health care system delivers quality care and public schools provide a quality education.

We should inculcate the idea of citizen service in people while they're still young. Acceptance of the role of citizen—of trying to make a difference in the lives of strangers, instead of minding your own business when you see things going wrong around you—should begin formally in high school, with a civic education, but there should also be a commitment of time to public service while one is young. It should not be left to the churches, synagogues, mosques, and other religious organizations to do this. In that spirit, I suggest that, for two years sometime before young people turn twenty-five, they should be encouraged to perform some kind of public service, whether in the military, in a state teachers' corps, or in some other public service organization. That way all citizens can have the experience of giving something back to the community and the nation—which is the essence of what living in a community means.

During my presidential campaign in 2000, what thrilled me most were the thousands of young Americans across the country who volunteered for my effort—a phenomenon, it must be said, of most presidential campaigns. Many parents have since told me that the experience gave their children something to believe in that was larger than themselves. It allowed them to see that there is honor in working for a better world; that it's not naïve to appeal to the better side of human nature; that it's all right to have faith in your neighbor, in the American people, in humankind. I think that most of those kids will always be good citizens, because the campaign experience showed them how it feels to join with others in working for something you believe in. They know you don't have to abandon your convictions so as not to offend power, for real power—the power to mobilize an army of citizens who want to change the world—lies within each of us.*

For example, a young woman who had never done anything in politics before volunteered for my presidential campaign because I was a family friend and she had played basketball in college. In fact the only time I had met her before the campaign was at her sister's outdoor wedding reception, when we went over to the family basketball court and played an impromptu game of two-on-two against her brothers. In the campaign, she was assigned to Iowa, where she went in at the lowest level and quickly moved to advance, a function that prepares each event before the candidate arrives. By the end of the campaign, she was in a very responsible position on the debate team. Her role, with one or two other team members, was to negotiate debate arrangements with the representatives of my opponent and the TV network hosting the event. When my campaign failed, she took it hard, but then she gathered herself up and engaged the world again, becoming a principal in a new high school in the South Bronx specializing in writing and literature. She had made of the campaign a learning experience that allowed her to find her truest self and to make a new contribution to the well-being of the country. The same thing will happen to other young people who learn to act on their dreams.

---

*See my book The Journey from Here (Artisan, 2000).

The New American Story asks that you assume the responsibility of citizenship, which means participating in the political process and fighting creatively for laws that mandate a clean environment, a secure pension, a strong military, or health care for everyone. But it also means well-informed and passionate engagement—organizing your community for action, integrating your life into the whole, and taking responsibility for your country. We can't just talk, we have to act. We can't just support some political action committee headquartered far away. We need to think globally, organize locally, and act personally.

Each of us can do something to make America better.

Sometimes our action can be as simple as taking responsibility for ourselves, which is the first way of asking others to respect us. For example, the New American Story envisions all Americans with access to quality health care. For it to be affordable over the long run, each of us must take responsibility for our own physical well-being; nearly half of all health care costs are incurred because of self-destructive behavior. Taking care of your body is not simply good sense, it's also good citizenship. If you chain-smoke, for instance, is it fair to the rest of us, since we may have to pay for your eventual chemotherapy? If you fill your body with junk food full of trans fats, is it fair to burden the rest of us with the bill for your heart disease? Part of getting the benefit of being a member of the American community must be balanced by the obligation to take care of yourself, so as not to overutilize the health care system.

I know of a company in which all the workers, including the part-timers, get health insurance. After health care costs rose, the company felt the pressure. It knew that those costs were unsustainable, endangering its most important employee benefit, and it decided to engage its employees in an effort to keep costs down. It began a program of educating its workforce. It told its employees candidly about the unsustainable cost path of health care and suggested what they could do to keep costs down and thereby preserve the company's benefit for everybody. The requests were simple: Stop smoking. Exercise. Eat nutritious foods. Don't see a doctor unless you really need to. Don't go to the emergency room when you can wait twelve hours to go to the doctor's office. Research your health problem before you see a doctor. Decide what questions you want to ask before you go for your appointment. In 2005, the result of this effort, in the face of a 7.4 percent increase in health care costs for the country that year, was a slight *reduction* in health care costs for the company. Admittedly, it's only one year, but the larger point is that there is power behind the company's idea that "we're all in this together." As citizens we need to develop that same spirit about our country.

The health of the environment depends on individual action, too. Government can pass laws that clean up the environment and protect it from further harm. Government can require higher fuel efficiency standards and establish a gasoline or carbon tax so that less oil is consumed. But individual citizens also have a role in breaking our dependence on oil and reducing the amount of carbon dioxide in our atmosphere.

The role of the individual with regard to oil and the environment got a bad name when President Jimmy Carter addressed the country at the height of skyrocketing oil prices in 1979. Seated by a fireplace and wearing a cardigan sweater, he asked people to turn down their thermostats in winter to sixty-five degrees. Carter was ridiculed for what seemed a simplistic answer to a complicated problem, and he may well have created the wrong setting for his message, but now, almost thirty years later, when the importance of personal responsibility for the environmental crisis is beginning to be acknowledged, he seems to have been prescient.

There is a place for individual action. If you drive a hybrid car that gets forty to fifty miles per gallon, you are part of the solution. If you drive a gas-guzzling SUV, you are part of the problem. By our individual choices, we shape our energy future. Almost a third of the carbon dioxide that the United States annually contributes to the atmosphere comes from energy use in the home, and 30 percent of household electricity use is for hot-water heaters. By simply going to a tankless hot-water heater, like those used throughout Europe, you will save money on your electric bill and help to bring about the New American Story on oil and the environment.

When you get your utility bill, read it and compare it with the same month the year before, when you probably used about the same amount of energy; then ask the utility why there is a difference in the cost. Demand an answer you understand. Ask the company if it has a green option, in which a certain percentage of the power it supplies is guaranteed to come from renewable sources. If it doesn't, suggest that it develop one or, if possible, switch utilities. When it comes time to replace your air-conditioning, heating, or refrigerator, go with the most energy-efficient model. And make sure that your local government offers incentives for its citizens to make these choices.

Even with regard to assuring a comfortable retirement for all Americans, there are individual actions that will make governmental measures more likely and less expensive. Social Security guarantees you a minimum retirement income, but it's a bare minimum. Your employer can provide more security by matching your contribution to your defined-contribution plan, but ultimately it's up to you to develop the discipline to save—to put away a little money every month against the day when you won't have a job.

There isn't enough money in corporate America to ensure that everyone will have a comfortable retirement income. Necessarily, some won't. There are many people who work two jobs just to pay the basic bills of everyday living. It's difficult for them to put money away, but even if it is only a few dollars a month, they should try.* There are many other Americans who could save if they chose not to buy a gadget they don't really need or kept the family car for one more year or went on vacation for two weeks instead of three. It's up to all of us. It's up to us, too, to pass on the importance of saving to our children. My father used to tell me, "If you put your money in the bank, it works while you sleep." Everyone should learn the power of compound interest (leaving money in an account and reinvesting the interest), which Albert Einstein called the greatest invention in the history of mankind. If you take care of your own savings, it will be easier for government to insure you against the possibility of pension catastrophe caused by corporate bankruptcy.

The world is changed by small numbers of people who are totally

---

*And if they do, the federal government should match them for each dollar they save up to $20,000.

committed to a cause. I don't mean just revolutionaries, such as Jefferson or Lenin or Mao or Martin Luther King Jr. Whenever change takes place in any setting, it's the result of someone's vision and the dedication of a few people—just ask anyone who has started a new church or a new bank. The one thing all agents of change possess is the conviction that whatever they seek to achieve can indeed happen when they work together and that, if it does, the world will be a better place.

The work of citizens in a democracy is similar to that of jurors on a jury. Each member of the group brings his or her own background and perspective, and in the process of deliberation the group reaches a verdict that reflects the collective view. The magic of the jury, like the magic of democracy, is the interaction of citizens. Without the spirited interaction of people speaking their minds, democracy dries up. In our current politics, as conformist and as dominated by money as it is, that kind of democratic vitality is sometimes hard to imagine. Yet the institutional machinery is there, awaiting the reforms of an awakened citizenry.

Today, with the help of the Internet, there are ways to express your opinion and find those who share your political beliefs. Chat rooms and blogs allow people to interact directly. As party organizations atrophy and activists fill the vacuum, one way for the moderate middle to organize on behalf of the vast majority—who care more about health insurance, education, pensions, and clean air than they do about abortion rights, gay marriage, or gun control—is through a Web site called Meetup. The theory behind Meetup, an Internet company on whose corporate board I sit, is that face-to-face meetings among people who share common interests can revitalize our civil society. Over 250,000 Meetups have been established so far, including Stay at Home Moms Meetup, Russian-language Meetup, *Investor's Business Daily* Meetup, and Elvis Meetup. This is how it works: You go to the Web site (www.meetup.com) and search for a Meetup in your community about your interest—for example, "New American Story." You check to see if a New American Story Meetup already exists. If no one has started one nearby, you can sign up to be notified when someone does. Or you can start one yourself. The Web site makes it easy to organize a Meetup at a local café. All those individuals nearby who have signed up are notified. The company gives self-selected organizers ideas about how to build a group, but it's up to the organizers to take responsibility for the events and the groups.

In the last presidential primary campaign, Howard Dean built an enormous following with this unique organizing tool. In late 2003 and early 2004, monthly Howard Dean Meetups sometimes took place at over a thousand separate locations with a minimum of forty people in attendance. These were probably the largest simultaneous multilocation meetings in American political history. People attended to show their opposition to Bush and their support for someone they perceived as speaking out. If there were hundreds of meetings each day on national health insurance or education reform or other aspects of the New American Story, imagine the impact they would have on the political process. Politicians would sit up and take notice. And if those political meetings followed through with action, they would become powerful forces for change. Meetup and other ideas like it offer the potential for a renaissance in self-government.

Another example of the use of the Internet in politics is what I like to call Kosworld. The lawyer and techie Markos Moulitsas Zúniga started www.dailykos.com in 2002, and now half a million people visit the site daily. They debate issues, critique journalists, raise money for certain candidates, and call unreported news stories to the attention of the mainstream media. Anyone can post a mini-essay (or "diary") on the site. Daily Kos ranks the essays based on when they were posted and reader recommendations, so visitors to the site can find the most popular essays in various categories. The site provides links to other political sites: some large, such as www.moveon.org, a strong antiwar voice that is putting together a broad and positive liberal agenda and in the 2006 election made nearly 9 million calls on behalf of candidates who shared its views; others smaller and more specialized, such as www.firedoglake.com, which provides daily news coverage of world events; www.huffingtonpost.com, which gives numerous pundits a platform for their views; and one called www.epluribusmedia.org, which encourages high standards of ethics in journalism. Through www.dailykos.com, a group got together spontaneously and came up with an energy plan that rivals, according to journalist Bill McKibben writing in *The New York Review of Books*, anything put out by the think tanks. Such a plan could be the basis for pressuring Congress to act now. There are also practical politics on the site: People share tips on how to recruit volunteers, build mailing lists, and breathe fresh air into local Democratic organizations around the country. When you see what is happening in Kosworld, you begin to understand the potential of the Internet to help transform our democracy.

A third example is Gather.com, another company on whose board I sit. Gather is a social media site, a kind of MySpace for grown-ups or an eBay for content, that allows engaged, informed people to connect and communicate with others who share their passions. In the Gather community, hundreds of thousands of adults publish their thoughts and explore everything from politics and art to education. The blogosphere has enabled the free expression of ideas more broadly, rapidly, and cheaply than ever before, but when tens of millions all speak at once, brilliant ideas get lost in the cacophony. Gather organizes content, pays bloggers for their participation, identifies the best thinking, and engages in a conversation about that thinking. At this writing, members have formed more than 6,000 Gather groups, among them groups on sustainability (sustainability.gather.com), Amnesty International's promotion of human rights (aiusa.gather.com), and leadership in business and government (leadership.gather.com)—and who knows, maybe someday soon TheNewAmericanStory.gather.com.

A fourth such example is Essembly.com. Unlike Facebook.com, which is essentially a social meeting place, Essembly connects people for political dialogue, putting like-minded people in touch with one another. Essembly's algorithm determines their ideological similarity on a scale of 0 to 100, with 100 meaning that they agree on practically everything. Ideological similarity is then broken down by topic, so that two people on opposite sides of the political spectrum might score a 30 on the Iraq War and a 22 on abortion but find they are a 95 on concern for the environment. Such a breakdown encourages people to find areas of similarity, things they can agree on. People can organize from the bottom up by starting with a statement of a position called a resolve (e.g., tax cuts sometimes hurt the economy), building support around it, and recruiting supporters through the social network.

Such processes, over the long term, should level the playing field in the contest between new grassroots efforts and established national and international organizations. In rapid order, as people engage in the debate, they can identify like-minded warriors. The result is an exponential growth of active political dialogue and a revitalization of political community and self-government. It's just a step from there to mustering the energy necessary to bring about the New American Story. But it must be remembered that Web sites are only tools. The values of those who use them will determine to what end they apply the tools. Henry David Thoreau once said about the telegraph, "It's an improved means to an unimproved end." The same applies to information technology, unless our values shape its impact. Being able to transmit massive amounts of information in nanoseconds will mean nothing if we lose our humanity in the process. Another sage, the nineteenth-century Jewish moralist Israel of Slant, tells us, "The greatest way to save your soul is to save someone else's body." Our burgeoning information economy exists alongside seemingly intractable social problems that are going to take personal contact to solve. The Internet cannot mentor a kid, serve as a surrogate parent, read to the elderly, nurse the sick, transport the handicapped, or start a dance troupe, a computer class, a Little League team, or a poetry reading group. Only committed individuals can touch the soul of another human being. The New American Story reflects that awareness and offers us a guide for the path ahead. It says that there is no substitute for informed and engaged citizens who refuse to mind their own business, who are disinterested enough to fight for what is important not just for some of us but for all of us.

· · ·

Making the New American Story a reality requires government and citizens alike to be at their best. It combines community service and individual freedom to achieve what the vast majority of Americans want. It says that we have obligations to one another that we fulfill by collective and individual action. It says that we can't realize the American dream alone—we need one another. At the same time, the one life we are in total control of is our own, and by our personal actions we either help or hurt the chances for collective advancement. It is our choice. If enough of us want the New American Story, we can transform America.

When the New American Story is finally achieved, it will produce an "of course" in hindsight. All it took was the courage to dream big dreams and renew the Founders' original promise. All it took was the determination to play to our better selves and remind one another what we can accomplish together. All it took was a willingness to look within ourselves, and outward to the world, for the shared meaning in our lives. With humility and confidence, we will have built a better country, and we will know it deep down and be proud.

At the beginning of this book I said that I wrote it because of my concern for the state of our country. I close it with the conviction that we are up to the challenge of our times. In recent years, we have headed down a dangerous path toward empire, environmental destruction, and a general blindness to the conditions of life for millions of Americans and billions of fellow human beings around the globe. But the future, with all its wondrous technology, increasing interdependence, and responsive democracy, can bring all of us a better life while reestablishing America's position of respect and power in the world. For that to happen, we must be bold enough in our leadership, generous enough with our neighbors, truthful enough with our citizens, and farsighted enough toward the world. I'd prefer a Democratic administration, but if it is a Republican administration that adopts the new story, I'll be almost as happy. My real concern is for the American people. The only things that can stop us are fear, ignorance, self-centeredness, and greed. Those are not traits historically associated with Americans. Today their presence in our lives is more like a temporary fever than a permanent condition.

There will arise, as there always has, a group of citizens who will find their leader and change the world. That's what Americans do. That's why we can be proud of our history and confident of our future. That's why we still are, in Abraham Lincoln's words, "the last best hope" of humankind.

THE ETHIC OF CONNECTEDNESS

You're probably familiar with that iconic picture of the earth as seen from space—a beautiful "blue pearl" alone in a vast cosmic darkness. In that image, you can't see barriers of nation, gender, ethnicity, language, culture, religion, sexual orientation, or race. It's just one fragile planet, which we all share.

When you look at the earth from that far away, you know without a doubt that we're all connected at the level of our planet's ecosystem. Today, for the first time in the history of our species, there is an emerging global awareness that we're all responsible, together, for the health of this ecosystem. This emerging understanding of our responsibility forms the basis of what could be called "an ethic of connectedness."

But when it comes to discussions of national politics and policies— health care, for example, or education—the ethic of connectedness seems to disappear, and in its place is an ongoing argument between what might be called "the ethic of caring," with its emphasis on collective action (typically, the Democrats' position), and "the ethic of responsibility," with its emphasis on individual action (typically, the Republican position).

What distinguishes the ethic of connectedness from either of these is that it refuses to accept that there has to be a conflict between caring and responsibility, or between collective and individual action. The ethic of connectedness requires both caring (universal health insurance, for example) and responsibility (an expectation that people will take steps to promote their own health). Without that combination of collective action and individual responsibility, we cannot solve our nation's most pressing problems. Only at the level of government, which exists to speak for all us, can we formulate a foreign policy, establish rules for commerce, clean up the environment, and make health care, education, and a good pension available to all. But achieving our goals also depends on our individual actions. If you study hard, you're more likely to have the skills that will allow you to get a good job, support your family, and make the economy grow for all of us. If you take care of your own health, you make the health care system more affordable for everyone. If you trade in your SUV for an electric hybrid, you help to make the world a safer, cleaner place.

This ethic of connectedness is at the core of *The New American Story*, which celebrates our individual potential but also recognizes that it can be realized only in the context of our relatedness to others.

There is nothing new about the concept of interconnectedness. Most of us grew up with the admonition that each of us is our brother's or sister's keeper and we are all stewards of the land. And then there is John Donne's poem reminding us that "no man is an island." In fact, most spiritual teachings emphasize our human interconnectedness. What I've attempted to do in *The New American Story* is to show not only that this familiar idea is the common ground of our political history, but that it can support a new politics that is both inspiring and deeply practical.

Because our interconnectedness is growing, it is imperative that our politics should reflect it. Whether the issue concerns America's role in the world (with its need for each of us to practice citizenship on the local, national, and global levels) or the role of politics in America (with each of us called upon to stay informed and participate in the democratic process), our world asks us to care about our neighbors and our planet. Looking beyond the barriers that separate us, we see that all human beings possess common yearnings for family, love, freedom, respect, and fulfillment. Once you realize how profoundly you're tied to the unemployed worker in Michigan, or the uninsured mother in Colorado, or the person in Africa with AIDS—or even the ozone layer above Antarctica—you can't help wanting to do something to improve the situation. But what?

The good news is that practical solutions exist for many of our problems if we act not only in our own self-interest but also in the interests of the whole—interests that, in the long run, coincide with our own.

That is the key point. It's not unlike the ethic that governs a winning basketball team—you can't serve only yourself and win the championship. You have to serve your teammates—sacrifice for them, complement their strengths, cover for their weaknesses, give them your best—in order to win.

The metaphor may be somewhat inexact, but we are all on the same team in this world, so together either all of us will win (that is, live with dignity and in good health) or we'll just survive (live shorter lives filled with greater conflict and pain). Even the rich suffer when the poor don't have enough, because everyone is forced to deal with the violence bred by resentment and alienation, the loss of creativity when educational opportunities are limited, and the consequences of pandemic illnesses. Your own happiness is furthered when you live in a country in which people have good jobs, good health care, a good education, and security in old age. The motivation to assure these things becomes self-evident with an ethic of connectedness. It is this ethic that *The New American Story* attempts to embody. A practical understanding of that ethic will surely move us one step closer to realizing the great American dream of "liberty and justice for all."

ACKNOWLEDGMENTS

In writing this book I owe much to others:

I thank my editors: Kate Medina, who believed in this project and whose enthusiasm and knowledgeable comments brought it home; Sara Lippincott, whose careful attention to the whole text raised its quality several levels and whose candor and sense of humor never faltered; and Betty Sue Flowers, who asked the tough questions that honed my thoughts about substance and structure.

I thank my first reader, my wife, Ernestine, who offered her encouragement and gave the book her insightful attention.

I thank my friends who read all or part of the manuscript and made helpful comments: Herbert Allen III, Ken Apfel, Marcia Aronoff, Terry Bracy, John Gearen, Paul Gould, Simon Head, Matt Henshon, Melody Hobson, Tom Jensen, Pentti Kouri, Jim Leach, Jon Lovelace, Jim Manzi, Jessica Mathews, Dan Okimoto, Sydney Pollack, John Roos, Betty Sapoch, Mark Schmitt, Barry Schuler, Tom Singer, Joan Sullivan, Mark Taylor, John Thornton, John Wideman, and Rick Wright.

As a marginalia writer, I thank my trusted assistant, Beth Montgomery Vincent, and especially Jennifer Meeker, who decoded my scribble and turned it into clean text that I proceeded to cover with more scribble.

I thank my fact checker, Boris Fishman, whose dedication to detail gave me great comfort.

I thank my agent, Art Klebanoff, for his counsel and friendship over thirty years.

Finally, I thank Allen & Company for giving me the time to do this book.

INDEX

ABOUT THE AUTHOR

BILL BRADLEY has been a three-time basketball All-American at Princeton, an Olympic gold medalist, a Rhodes scholar, and a professional player for ten years with the New York Knicks. Elected to the Senate from New Jersey in 1978, 1984, and 1990, he has authored extensive legislation, including the Tax Reform Act of 1986. Bradley is the author of five other books: *Time Present, Time Past*, a *New York Times* bestseller about his life as a senator and his travels throughout the country; *Values of the Game*, another *New York Times* bestseller; *The Journey from Here*; *The Fair Tax*; and *Life on the Run*. Bill Bradley is married and has one daughter; he is currently a managing director at Allen & Company LLC in New York.

Casement

In memory of
Seán G. Ronan (1924–2000)

Casement

Angus Mitchell

HAUS PUBLISHING · LONDON

First published in Great Britain in 2003 by
Haus Publishing Limited
32 Store Street
London WC1E 7BS

A CIP catalogue record of this work is available from the British Library

ISBN 1-904341-41-1

Typeset by Palimpsest Book Production Limited,
Polmont, Stirlingshire

Printed and bound by Graphicom in Vicenza, Italy

Cover Image: courtesy of National Library of Ireland
Back cover: courtesy of National Library of Ireland
Page iii: courtesy of National Library of Ireland

CONTENTS

Introduction

It is a cruel thing to die with all men misunderstanding – misapprehending – and to be silent forever.[1]

Roger Casement

In early May 1916, awaiting trial for high treason as a prisoner in the Tower of London, Roger Casement dictated a brief autobiography to his solicitor. It was little more than a sketch that left considerable gaps in the narrative of an altogether extraordinary career spanning 20 years in Africa and seven in South America. It would end with his execution for his role in Ireland's 1916 Easter Rising in the midst of the First World War. When Casement dropped through the scaffold behind closed doors at Pentonville prison on 3 August 1916, few contemporaries understood who he was or what he represented; those who did know preferred to forget. A biographical pamphlet, circulated before his execution, admitted that though Casement was 'in a certain sense the figurehead and original prime mover in the rebellion' of 1916, no one knew much about him.[2]

This misunderstanding was partly self-perpetuated and partly obscured by the culture of secrecy surrounding the two conflicting spheres that Casement had briefly dominated: British foreign diplomacy and Irish revolutionary activity. His intense involvement with both of these causes meant his life would remain shrouded by a veil of mystery and intrigue. While he was widely known for his humanitarian activities exposing the Imperial atrocities of Belgium's King Leopold II in the Congo, his consular work remained unknown beyond the level of his published reports and his treatment in the Imperial press. Although his pro-Irish views were public knowledge in England, they were considered an eccentric enthusiasm rather than a dangerous threat to the Empire that he served with distinction.

Following his resignation from the Foreign Office in 1913, Casement emerged as a pivotal figure in transforming the conversation amongst cultural nationalists in Ireland into a dialogue of colonial resistance. The Home Rule crisis, fomented by the founding of the Ulster Volunteers by Edward Carson and F E Smith, forced Ireland's nationalist community to respond. Casement became the catalyst in the initial recruitment drive for the Volunteers and subsequently acted as the international emissary for the Irish independence movement in the US and Germany.

Despite the well of subsequent writing on Casement, much about this enigmatic man remains ignored, suppressed or obscured behind heated speculation about his sexuality and secret revolutionary activity. Moreover, his incorporation into Ireland's modern historical consciousness has been even more problematic. Although the 1916 Rising is commemorated as the founding moment of the Irish state, its interpretation has remained hotly contested. Of all nationalist leaders, Casement has proved the most disquieting and his significance is still entangled in a knot of contradictions and ambiguities. His reputation has suffered greatly from the propaganda campaign set in motion in September 1914, once his 'treasonable' activities had been identified. In Ireland, his significance has been diminished by his long record of service for the Empire, which certainly involved 'intelligence' activities. In Britain, his alliance with Germany after the outbreak of the First World War stigmatized him for the rest of the century as a 'pro-Germanist'. His abortive return to Ireland to stop the Rising in the forlorn hope of avoiding further bloodshed contradicted the ideal of 'blood sacrifice' espoused by other nationalist leaders. The fact that Casement was a 'gun-runner' who espoused understanding and unification did not suit the sour political atmosphere in Ireland until the search for peace and reconciliation began in the 1990s.

In England, Casement's treason was a devastating shock to his colleagues in the Foreign Office, in academia, in government and the church. Previously he had been considered to be one of the exemplary figures of his generation, whose moral heroism had elevated him to a visibility and near mystical status comparable to that of Gordon of Khartoum or David Livingstone.[3] However, after the outbreak of hostilities in 1914, his political involvement in Ireland was deemed completely unacceptable by many of those who had once felt honoured to serve beside him.

Casement's reputation has suffered most from the use of the *Black Diaries* or 'alleged Casement diaries' (so-called by Michael Collins when he was shown them at the House of Lords, shortly after the signing of the Free State Treaty in February 1922). These shadowy documents were first rumoured to exist in 1916 but remained a closely guarded secret until their partial release by the Public Record Office in 1959. As they were deliberately deployed between Casement's trial and execution to destroy his contemporary standing, so they continue to obfuscate understanding of his life until today. Furthermore, the construction of Casement's historical legacy after his execution is a powerful metaphor not only for the course of Anglo-Irish relations and the violent road towards Ireland's independent sovereignty but equally for the complex political negotiations of Britain as it dismantled its Empire.

The unresolved questions surrounding the debates over both his reputation and his body can, for the sake of convenience, be divided into four identifiable periods. The initial years (1916–39) – stretching from his death to the outbreak of the Second World War – saw the diaries' controversy move into the public domain as a consequence of unauthorized published declarations by the man who 'discovered' them, Basil Thomson. Throughout the 1930s, Casement's reputation was pulled in several contradictory directions. He was adopted as a political mascot by the two main republican parties in Ireland: Sinn Féin and Fianna Fail. Efforts to make a film of his life were discreetly censored by Eamon de Valera who commented in 1934 that 'a further period of time must elapse before the full extent of Casement's sacrifice can be understood.'[4] In Germany, the anti-fascist intellectual, Balder Olden, forced into exile with the rise of Hitler, wrote a biography of Casement in order to convey the need for a more responsible attitude among European powers towards Africa and South America. In 1936, a rally was held in Hyde Park, led by the socialist feminist Hanna Sheehy Skeffington, demanding the repatriation of Casement's body to Ireland. In the same year, the Protestant rebel Jack White paid tribute to Casement before leaving to fight in the Spanish Civil War on behalf of the Connolly Column and the anarchists. The poets W B Yeats and Alfred Noyes locked horns in an extraordinary dispute in the pages of the *Irish Press* about his reputation. The invocation of Casement, by the Nazi sympathizer Francis Stuart as a victim of a British intelligence conspiracy did nothing to further his cause once that ignominious regime had been defeated.

In the post-war period (1940–65), Casement re-emerged as a figure in Ulster. In 1953, the Gaelic Athletic Association (GAA) ground in West Belfast was named in his honour and became the catalyst for resurgent civic nationalism. Its opening was followed a few weeks later by the remarkable gathering at Murlough Bay in County Antrim and the unprecedented appearance of both Eamon de Valera and Sean McBride in Northern Ireland, sharing a podium to deliver orations in honour of Casement's global achievement. Post-war unionist confidence, however, was high and the allies were still unforgiving of de Valera's decision to maintain Irish 'neutrality' throughout the war. As peace was restored,

Casement's name echoed through the chambers at Westminster with respect to the hard-fought debates on the abolition of capital punishment, reforms over access to public records and amendments to the Sexual Offences Act. Few volumes of memoirs or accounts of First World War intelligence failed to make some reference to Casement, however small and insignificant. The controversy over the diaries was well summarized by the joint under-secretary of state for the Home Department, Bill Deedes, in an adjournment debate in the Commons on 3 May 1956:

'Official papers are not normally disclosed until a considerable time has elapsed. The practice is now to deposit papers in the Public Record Office after fifty years, and those on capital cases are not open to inspection. It is asked, "Is this in the interest of historical truth?" It has often been necessary to allow a passage of time before uncovering the whole truth about historical events. That is a fact which genuine historians accept. Although the rule is at times very irksome, it has sound foundations, and one relevant to this case is that as time elapses and as generation succeeds generation, the passion goes out of political controversy. This convention was not invented by the Home Office for Casement. But the Casement case is a good example of the convention's soundness. The events are still a source of passionate partisanship. Whatever the truth, and however we were to reveal it, the inevitable consequences would be to stimulate and not to mollify those passions. Moreover, any disclosure about this tragedy, whether it be the diaries do or do not exist, are genuine or otherwise, must lead to renewed controversy about Casement's character and his part in the events which occurred.'[5]

Publication of *The Black Diaries* in Paris in 1959 forced the government to admit to their existence and newspapers in Britain and Ireland were once more flooded with angry exchanges and accusations of 'conspiracy' and 'forgery'. Controversy over the diaries was brought to a temporary halt in 1965 with an end to the 'corpse diplomacy' and the decision by the British government to repatriate Casement's body to Ireland. Since 1916, a lobby of his supporters had campaigned ceaselessly through both diplomatic channels and popular appeals for the return of his remains. The refusal of the authorities to bury him in consecrated ground led to the most fantastic litany of stories and conspiracy theories about what had happened to his bones. Many important politicians involved themselves in the matter, including Jan Smuts, Ramsay MacDonald and Duncan Sandys. In 1965, after almost half a century of negotiation, agreement was reached between Prime Minister Harold Wilson and the former IRA chief turned Minister of External Affairs, Frank Aiken, at 10 Downing Street, a few hours after Winston Churchill's state funeral. A few weeks later, three representatives of the Irish government observed his exhumation from an unmarked grave in Pentonville prison. On 1 March 1965, after lying in state in Arbour Hill in Dublin, Casement's coffin was conveyed by gun carriage to Glasnevin cemetery in Ireland's first televised state funeral, passing Irish women, men and children who thickly lined O'Connell Street, on a day of freezing sleet and thunderstorms. At the graveside de Valera paid great honour to Ireland's unknown patriot, lauding his work on behalf of the 'downtrodden and the oppressed' and reassuring the Irish people that Casement's 'soul' was now reposing in 'heaven'.[6]

With his bones securely buried, there were renewed diplomatic efforts to negotiate a middle way over his historical legacy. From 1966 to 1993, the debate over the diaries became a form of subjugated knowledge. Casement was discreetly edited out of the general narratives of Africa, South America and British imperial histories. He received similar treatment in Ireland. Now he was subjected to the fashionable Freudian psychoanalytic biography, with its overwhelming tendency to treat all human behaviour as a reflection of deep-seated sexual motivations. Historians were granted permission to see the diaries at the discretion of the Home Secretary. The sidelining of the controversy in the mainstream media and the inexorable reduction of Casement's historical meaning effectively combined to censor a central voice in the invention of modern Ireland. In the early 1990s, an increasingly brash and economically successful Ireland deliberately turned its back on the past, including the ideals of civic nationalism and inclusive republicanism espoused by its founders. Casement was all but forgotten. Equally Casement's position as the most critical witness against the excesses of the colonial projects in Africa and South America receded to a dimming memory. Instead Roger Casement had become the *Black Diaries* incarnate, and was heralded both popularly and privately as a 'gay icon'.

The fourth and final period of the Casement debate was inaugurated in 1993 as a consequence of Britain's Open Government Initiative implemented during the premiership of John Major. The rapid release of hundreds of Casement files reflected a desire in some circles to break the culture of secrecy and implement a greater degree of transparency as part of democratic accountability. The diaries were released unconditionally at the Public Record Office in March 1994. More Home Office and Police Commission files followed in October 1995, the Security Service Personal Files in 1999 and the Metropolitan Police Special Branch Files in 2001. The release of this vast amount of hitherto inaccessible material (complemented by documents in the National Archive of Ireland) allows for a more nuanced assessment of Casement's meaning.

This brief biography outlines an emerging narrative that reveals Casement on the one hand as a vital critic of colonialism in Africa, South America and India, and on the other hand as the forgotten founding father of the modern Irish nation-state. Whether we consider the condition of post-imperial Africa, the future of the Amazonian rainforest, the precariousness of the Northern Ireland peace process, or the history of sexual politics, Casement remains a figure of substance.

From the extensive but massively dispersed archive of documentation held in Britain, Ireland, Germany, Africa, and South and North America, a clearer understanding of Casement's life is as central to any accurate reading of the foundational periods of African and Amazon history as it is for Ireland's comprehension of its own struggle for independence. The retrieval of the buried Casement narrative can come to symbolise a new era of understanding. Reconciliation between the opposing perspectives on the Anglo-Irish issue is so hard because there are so few shared narratives that bind such oppositions together, or allow for a tolerance of cultural diversity. In understanding Casement, England might better understand Ireland and Ireland might better understand the role it played within the British Empire. His work and writings, based upon his direct and unique experience, remain valid to our deeper knowledge of the historical tragedy that continues to advantage one part of our world at the expense of another. The repetitive use of the diaries to block a broader understanding of Casement has distorted his interpretation. Casement's legacy cannot be exclusively claimed by any one political group or religious denomination. His achievement belongs to that universal understanding based on humanity, tolerance, justice, decency and respect for difference.

ANGUS MITCHELL
THE BELL TOWER
ST MICHAEL'S CHURCH
LIMERICK, 2003

Early Life

A generation before the birth of Roger Casement, the Young Ireland movement was born. Inspired by the Young Italy association of Giuseppe Mazzini, founded to fight for a unified and republican Italy, the Young Irelanders sought social justice and the right to mass education in pursuit of a new national identity.

Casement in his twenties

While Ireland's political stage was dominated by the repeal politics of Daniel O'Connell, 'the Liberator', the social and economic spheres were overwhelmed by a decimating famine. From this convergence of intellectual initiative and social tragedy emerged the vision for the spiritual rebirth of the people which pursued its ends by two methods: re-education and violence.

In October 1842, three of the founding intellectuals of the Young Ireland movement, Charles Gavan Duffy (1816–1903), Thomas Davis (1814–45) and John Blake Dillon (1814–66) began publishing *The Nation*, a newspaper that was the vehicle for propounding the philosophy of the movement: to unite 'all races and creeds, Protestant and Catholic, Milesian and Cromwellian' into one nation through the healing and development of a common spirit. It was defined by the hope of Thomas Davis: 'Educate that you may be free.'[7]

Behind the efforts of the Young Ireland movement, the spectre of famine loomed. In the 1840s and 1850s, millions fled starvation and misery aboard the transatlantic ships to find new lives in the US and wherever else labour was needed. The emergence of an Irish diaspora and the collective memory of famine changed the relationship between England and Ireland as no other event in recent history. From the ashes of desperation arose a phoenix. In 1858, the exiled revolutionary James Stephens (1824–1901) founded the Irish Republican Brotherhood or Fenians, a secret insurrectionary organization, whose ultimate aim was to liberate Ireland by physical force.

In later life, Roger Casement was openly resentful that his schooling in Ballymena included neither the Irish language nor Irish history. In his essay 'The Language of the Outlaw' he looked at how the historical relationship between England and Ireland had been based upon the English view of Irish as an *uncultivated, rude, peasant speech* – a view he came to dispute and consider wholly unrepresentative. He was also at odds with the prevailing idea that Irish history began with the implementation of Tudor administration and that what had occurred before then had been largely unrecorded and, therefore, was not history. Such a view ignored the vast archive of material in the Irish language held in libraries throughout Europe. This debate over the origins of Irish history continues to cause tensions within Irish historiography.

The Irish independence movement would pursue two courses of action. The intellectual wing sought liberation by peaceful means: the establishment of an Irish identity, the revival of the Irish language, assertion of a counter-history and demand for social justice and civil rights for all citizens. Equally, a militant wing sought liberation via violence. Ultimately, both movements fused in Roger Casement.

Little is recorded about Casement's birth on 1 September 1864 apart from the location in Sandycove, Dublin, the neighbourhood where James Joyce's *Ulysses* begins. Indeed, knowledge of his childhood and youth is sketchy. After his execution, various memoirs were written by family members: the most significant anecdotes are related by his elder sister, Agnes, and his devoted cousin, Gertrude Bannister. Their hagiographies contain fragments that help assemble a picture of his childhood.

The family life was itinerant and rootless, socially hindered by the fact that Casement was the result of a 'mixed' marriage: his mother was a devout Catholic and his father a rebel Protestant. Different branches of the Casement family were situated near Ballycastle in County Antrim and in County Wicklow. His mother, Anne (*née* Jephson) (1834–73), was by most accounts related to the Jephsons of Elizabethan planter stock, from Mallow in County Cork. She was quite possibly a love child – the result of

Roger Casement Senior (1819–77), Father of Roger Casement.

a liaison between a Jephson and a Catholic member of the household. Her father died during a hunting accident in the 1840s but her Catholicism was certainly profound enough for her to take the children to Wales where they were secretly baptized at Rhyl.

Casement's father, also named Roger (1819–77), had led a romantic career as a young captain serving in the Third Dragoon Guards in India. His views, however, were not always orthodox; among his surviving papers, a long essay on Hindu mysticism indicates an interest in the eternal nature of 'spirit'. Invariably, these views would have influenced his children but they were unlikely to curry favour with the respectable Darwinian world of Victorian Britain. His soldiering exploits captured his sons' imaginations, in particular his involvement in the movement for Hungarian independence. In 1849, he smuggled a letter across Europe to Lord Palmerston (1784–1865) from the Hungarian patriot, Kossuth. In 1870 he revealed his political leanings when he wrote a letter to Léon Gambetta, the French revolutionary, expressing support for the newly founded Third Republic, 'hailing universal republicanism' and outlining plans for the defence of the Paris Commune.[8]

Significantly, Roger Casement senior also expressed sympathy for the Fenian movement, a position probably fostered by the failed Fenian uprising of 1867 led by John Devoy and the public hanging of the Manchester martyrs – Allen, Larkin and O'Brien.

Ireland's earliest secret revolutionary societies might be traced back to Rory O'More (1620–52) the chief conspirator behind the Rising of 1641 and the 'Defenders', a precursor of the United Irish rebels of 1798 and 1803 and the Ribbonmen. The code of secrecy surrounding the Fenian movement was in direct opposition to the 'openness' espoused by the Young Irelanders.

Such views would not have been out of step with the liberal sympathies gaining prominence in Westminster. In 1868, the election of William Gladstone as prime minister heralded a new imperial attitude towards Ireland. Gladstone confidently exclaimed, 'My mission is to pacify Ireland,' and he set about implementing a series of legal reforms to realize this brave political undertaking. In 1869, the Protestant Episcopal Church was disestablished, and in 1870 the First Irish Land Act was passed.[9] In Ireland, political pressure was applied with the founding of the Home Rule League by the Dublin barrister, Isaac Butt (1813–79). In 1879, Michael Davitt (1846–1906) founded the Land League which demanded nationalization of the land, agitated for an end to landlordism and began a countrywide campaign better known as the Irish Land War. Agrarian violence led to a second Land Act of 1881, which enshrined in

Home Rule was the cornerstone of the political aspirations of Irish nationalism from 1870 to 1918. It was a form of devolution whereby Ireland would be governed through its own elected parliamentary assembly although questions of imperial/foreign policy would still be determined by representation at Westminster. Its initial advocate was Isaac Butt (1813-79), but it found its most significant political exponent in Charles Stewart Parnell (1846-91). In 1886, the Liberal Prime Minister William Gladstone introduced the first Home Rule Bill, which was defeated by an alliance led by Joseph Chamberlain. The second Home Rule Bill of 1893 was rejected by the House of Lords. Ultimately, the third Bill of 1912 was placed on the statute book at the outbreak of war on condition of Irish participation. It was rendered redundant by the Easter Rising of 1916, by the emergence of Sinn Féin, and, after the signing of the Anglo-Irish Treaty in 1921, by the establishment of an independent Irish state comprising 26 of the 32 counties of Ireland.

law fixity of tenure, fair rents and free sale of the tenant's interest in his holding – this legislation finally gave official status to the Irish tenant.

While Davitt's agitation work excelled, the most significant parliamentary leader to emerge at this time was Charles Stewart Parnell (1846–91). Helped by his Protestant background and unrivalled in his oratory, Parnell ran circles inside the lobby of Westminster with his powers of organization and mastery of procedure. At the general election of 1885, 80 nationalist members of parliament were returned and Parnell's power peaked, only to decline rapidly over the next six years due to diminishing health, and the damage to his reputation caused by an extra-marital affair.

While these events formed the political and social background to Casement's upbringing, his family struggled to remain a unit. For a few years, they lived near St Helier on Jersey. When he was nine years old, Roger's mother died in childbirth and four years later his father died in Ballymena under circumstances that have never been fully explained. As he entered his teenage years, Casement found himself orphaned along with his sister Agnes and their two brothers, Tom and Charlie. The children were made wards in chancery of their Uncle John, and moved to the Casement family farm of Magherintemple in the Antrim glens above Ballymena.

It was an austere household, secure and confident in its adherence to high Victorian principles, a home filled with the exploits and memories of Empire. In the privileged sanctuary of the big house, Casement developed an impression of Empire from the conversations at home and by observing the ships passing the strategic stretch of the Sea of Moyle separating Antrim and Ireland from Kintyre and Scotland.

Casement attended Ballymena High School and was taught by the principal, Reverend Robert King, a leading Irish scholar and Protestant preacher. He found some solace in his deepening attachment to Ulster and the Glens of Antrim where he gained much pleasure through contact with ordinary people and became conscious of the speaking of Irish.

Beyond the genteel, rural world of Antrim, the orphaned Casement children spent time with their mother's sister, Grace, in Stanley, a peaceful suburb of Liverpool. His uncle, Edward Bannister, was a serving British Consul and adopted a fatherly role towards Roger, talking to him of his experiences in Africa and the opportunities available to a young man in the emerging regions of Empire. Gertrude Bannister remembered the attic where he stayed during his holidays in Liverpool and how it was 'papered with cartoons cut out of the *Weekly Freeman*, showing the various Irish nationalists who had suffered imprisonment at English hands for the sake of their belief in Ireland as a Nation.'[10]

From very early on, Casement began to develop a strong attachment to the ideas and personalities of history. In later years he would be described as a 'philosopher of history'.[11] Throughout his life, Casement remained a voracious reader and in many photographs he is buried in a book. A favourite was James Fenimore Cooper's *The Last of the Mohicans* which quite possibly nurtured in him an instinctive and natural respect for the life-ways and culture of the native American Indian. Equally, he was shaped by the nationalist poetry of James Clarence Mangan (1803–49), who influenced his own adolescent experiments in writing verse and even inspired him to mimic some of Mangan's titles such as 'The Nameless One'.

The most significant surviving examples of Casement's poetry are from manuscript notebooks dated 1882 and 1883, and reveal that he scribbled poems, many of them historical and epic, throughout adolescence.[12] While the poetry does not place him in the pantheon of Ireland's great poets it is interesting for what it reveals of his own historical influences and Celticist affinities. In these words lie the first evidence of Casement's growing attachment to history and his identification with the heroes of Gaelic Ulster, as well as the United Irish rebels of 1798 and 1803. He begins to articulate themes that would emerge later in his life: the relationship between violence and colonialism; and how history is managed and suppressed for the purposes of the conqueror. Buried beneath the lyrical surface is Casement's inherent understanding of the ancient landscape and memory of Ireland: the resonance of the destiny of the Irish nation as well as his identification with the spirit of resistance of the Ulster chiefs, the ideals of the United Irishmen and the vision of the Young Irelanders to achieve a peaceful and lasting settlement.

Casement's social position demanded that he procure employment. On leaving school, he used family connections to find clerical work in the Elder Dempster shipping company in Liverpool. By this time, the city had become one of the great emporiums of the world with much of its trade generated through the

No other natural product had a greater influence in shaping the tropical environment in the last two centuries than rubber. Although initially extracted from the rainforests of tropical Africa and America, it was successfully transplanted to the British and Dutch colonies of South East Asia. The main technical advances included vulcanization by Charles Goodyear (1844), and the invention of the pneumatic wheel by John Dunlop (1888). In 1905, the mass production of Ford's Model T vehicle generated a sudden surge in demand that far outstripped supply until 1910-11 when the British and Dutch plantations became commercially competitive. Throughout this period, vast fortunes were made on the London and New York stock exchanges through speculation in rubber shares.

increasing demand for rubber, vital for a new era of global industrialization.

The Phoenix Park murders of 1882 ended any chance of a peaceful settlement in Ireland and caused a climate of suspicion between the two islands. The land and people were now spun into a vortex of conspiracies and counter-conspiracies embodied in the administration of the chief secretary, Arthur James Balfour, who responded to increased levels of civil disturbance with increased levels of secrecy and conspiracies.

Casement, like many other Irishmen, turned his back on the escalating domestic tragedy and embarked instead on a voyage to seek fame and fortune in the far-flung ends of Empire. In Casement's case the great theatre of his manhood would be the unknown interiors of sub-Saharan Africa where the white man, in his various guises, was now beginning to wander at will.

Africa

The overwhelming impact of the colonial scramble for sub-Saharan Africa has damaged the continent in ways that continue to mire its development. In the 15th century, Portuguese navigation of the west coast of the continent and the great age of Atlantic exploration led to a series of discoveries, ending and beginning in Christopher Columbus's 1492 landfall in the 'New World'.

Tragically, the clash of different worlds did not progress towards a better cultural understanding but instead to the exploitation of one society by another, and a long historical process of conquest and colonization fuelled by the greatest crime in human history: the transatlantic slave trade. Although Britain nominally abolished slavery in 1807, the 19th-century mapping and exploration of the interior of Africa opened a new chapter of abuse. Following the lead of the Scottish missionary, David Livingstone, muscular Christianity and muscular commerce arrived to find new souls and new markets. Ideas of 'humanity' and 'civilization' were preached as a way by which the 'primitive' might be rescued from his natural state of 'savagery'.

Of the many white men who went in search of those

Henry Morton Stanley pioneer of Leopold's Congo Free State

promised riches – ivory, gold and precious jewels – no individual rivalled Henry Morton Stanley. In 1874, Stanley spent 999 days crossing Africa, from Zanzibar to the mouth of the Congo. His heroics were broadcast across the Empire and his story spread out from the gilded chambers of Westminster to the most remote classroom in the Scottish Highlands. On his triumphal return to Europe he found a backer in the shape of King Leopold II of Belgium who had convened a conference in Brussels of explorers, geographers and scientists to divine a way whereby Africa could be opened up for the 'benefit' of its indigenous peoples.

In November 1884, the Prussian Chancellor Otto von Bismarck gathered the leading imperial powers for the West Africa Conference in Berlin. Though there was no African representation, it was decided that humanitarian intentions would guide any imperial project. The British representative Sir Edward Malet claimed that the founders were 'dominated by a purely philanthropic idea', while Bismarck mentioned the 'noble efforts' destined to 'render great services in the cause of humanity', and Belgium's Leopold promised 'the work of moral and material regeneration'.[13] High principles, it was expounded, would lead the African out of an ancient darkness into the sunlight of European civilization. Understandably many idealistic young men with a sense of adventure set out for Africa to try and realize those aims.

In 1883, Casement had resigned

Several different arguments have been developed trying to reason why the scramble for Africa took place. In *Africa and the Victorians: The Official Mind of Imperialism* (1961), Ronald Robinson and John Gallagher argued that the Home Rule discussion in Ireland and Britain's military commitment in Egypt were two direct causes. Certainly another was the economic potential of the region: the search for new markets and the potential to extract ivory and rubber. Leopold II wished for financial independence in order to extend his own royal authority and the Congo became the ideal outpost for him to realize his financial aspirations.

his post with the shipping company and become a purser on board the SS *Bonny*, an African trading vessel. In total, he made three round trips to Africa before he was employed in 1884 by the International Association, controlled directly by Leopold. Ironically, Casement's African career began on the eve of the Berlin Conference with the very regime that he would ultimately expose. Later, his critics would argue that this was evidence of an irrational perspective. In fact, it strengthened his authority: his direct experience of working practices from within made him an exceptional witness to its excesses and hypocrisies.

Two years later, Casement volunteered for the Sanford Exploring Expedition. Led by the American entrepreneur, Henry Sanford, and armed with a concession from Leopold, the expedition set out to develop trade and industry in the upper Congo. The main commodity would be ivory but there were also potential revenues from gum copal, rubber, copper and palm oil. The key requirement for the company was a steamer and the main problem was how to get it beyond the cataracts above Matadi, the main port at the mouth of the Congo. It

SPECIAL NUMBER OF THE ILLUSTRATED LONDON NEWS, FEBRUARY 6, 1878

was decided that the vessel would be manufactured and packed up in London, and assembled in the upper Congo. Casement was employed (along with several other overseers) to coordinate the

300 Africans needed to transport the boxes beyond the falls and rapids. In just over three months, the work was completed and the Sanford Expedition had a steamer named the *Florida*.[14]

Before being used for company activities, the *Florida* was commandeered by Henry Stanley for the Emin Pasha Relief Expedition – an effort to rally philanthropic support at home in a bid to relieve Emin Pasha (1840–92), the German-born physician who had succeeded General Gordon as governor of the southern Sudanese province of Equatoria. After the Mahdist rising (1885), Pasha found himself isolated and it was Stanley's hope to rescue him from the same fate that ended the life of Gordon. Casement declined to join the force, probably realizing that the real motive for the expedition was military, and on the day he was due to set out for his new appointment at the company's station in the Kasai region, apparently he had a difference of opinion with the company manager. On 27 August 1888, he wrote a long letter to Sanford confirming his resignation.

Casement's analysis showed a keen understanding not just of questions of labour but also of the prospects of the ambitious railway projects underway. From very early on in his African experience, Casement demonstrated a competence that set him apart from other white men. He was happy to express his concerns for what was happening while articulating a natural sympathy for the African: *No doubt, in time the people will learn the value of useful and diligent lives, and then something may be hoped from the Congo – but until that time I do not believe there is anything like sufficient produce to keep a railway going, and pay for its construction.*[15] What is clear from these surviving letters is that he still had a practical and genuine belief in the potential of European intervention while maintaining a healthy suspicion of commercial ambition in a region with so many natural resources. In other words, he was still a long way from condemning the colonial system and the civilizing project as a façade masking naked exploitation on a continental scale.[16]

Early on in his career, marked out by a unique combination of courage, stamina and integrity few other Europeans possessed, he was able to survive long periods alone in the heart of Africa. Though tall and thin, he was physically robust, a strong swimmer and able to withstand the relentless hardships of life in an in-hospitable environment, including the fevers that would kill many of his contemporaries. During these years, he established a number of longstanding friendships with other African adven-turers, including Herbert Ward, Edward Glave and Fred Pule-ston. In his memoirs, *African Drums* (dedicated to Stanley and Casement), Puleston remembered Casement as a 'lovable and charming man' who was revered in the African memory with the titles 'Swami Casement' and 'Monafuma Casement' – 'Woman's God' and 'Son of a King'.[17]

However, the most important figure in the development of Casement's colonial perspective was the missionary, T H Hoste. In late 1888, he helped Casement to find employment as a lay helper in the Baptist mission station at Wathen, on the upper Congo. According to the chief missionary, William Holman Bentley, Casement had been 'led to Christ' through his experi-ence of Christianity in Africa. During the following months he managed the transport, building, planting, accounts and corre-spondence of the station. The job did not offer a significant finan-cial gain but he performed well; in fact, the only complaint levelled against him was his generosity in measuring out cloth sold in the mission storehouse to the local African community.[18]

When he returned to England in 1889, he had spent almost five years in Africa but had a yearning for more. Over Christmas and New Year, he toured the US with Herbert Ward, delivering lectures on life in the Congo and publishing some articles on his African experiences before returning to Africa. Within a few weeks he had met a young Polish adventurer, Józef Korzeniowski – who would find fame a few years later as 'Joseph Conrad'. The opening

Joseph Conrad (1857–1924) *Heart of Darkness* was both influenced by, and influential to, Casement's vision of Empire

lines of Conrad's Africa diary record: 'Made the acquaintance of Mr Roger Casement, which I should consider as a great pleasure under any circumstances and now it becomes a positive piece of luck. Thinks, speaks well, most intelligent and very sympathetic.'[19]

For three weeks, Conrad and Casement shared a room at Matadi and there is little doubt that Casement had a formative impact on Conrad's perceptions of Africa. The author's imagining of the civilizing project appeared in his novella *Heart of Darkness* – a literary work that would resonate deeply in the formation of western perceptions of Africa. The book maps the metaphysical conflict of European expansion: Marlow, who journeyed upriver through time, in search of the moral heart of the civilizing project; and Kurtz, the exemplary company manager, who rejects the laws governing civilization and 'goes native'. Casement's gradual evolution from imperial servant to anti-colonial revolutionary would loosely configure with this identity conflict.

In 1904, Conrad wrote 'that some particle of Las Casas' soul had found refuge in [Casement's] indefatigable body,'[20] comparing the adventurer to Bartolomé de las Casas, the 16th-century Catholic bishop who was the first influential voice to record the destruction of native American culture by the Spanish conquest. However, 12 years later, Conrad recorded a uniform condemnation of Casement as 'a man, properly speaking, of no mind at all' inevitably associating him with the 'hollow man' Kurtz.[21]

By the early 1890s, however, Casement's integrity and fair-dealing with Africans marked him out as one of the most competent white men involved in the colonial enterprise and it was inevitable that he would find official employment. A surviving letter between Casement and Stanley dated 28 June 1890, written from Matadi and describing his views on the Congo after a long period of absence, indicates not only an intimacy between Casement and Stanley but also Casement's wish to promote English trade: *I think there is scope for an English trading company on the lower Congo on a fairly big scale, and with capable transport agents to manage the carriers any well conducted English house with a business chief at its head, could still do wonders on the Upper Congo – provided the State gave it fair play – in spite of the presence there of the big Belgian Company with which I am temporarily connected.*[22]

In 1892, the Foreign Office recognized Casement's potential and he was recruited to serve in the Oil Rivers Protectorate (Nigeria), at Old Calabar, where he wrote detailed reports on a series of exploratory map-making expeditions into the Cross River region. In these reports and in his correspondence with the Aborigines Protection Society, Casement displayed a natural sympathy with local efforts to fight the tyranny of colonial misgovernment. Reporting in January 1894 from Old Calabar, on an outbreak of rebellion in Cameroon by *natives of Dahomey*, Casement condemned the actions of the *German government* in their harsh, punitive reprisals against the rebels, including 27 hangings of both men and women: *Although the men were their soldiers, we all on earth have a commission and a right to defend the weak against the strong, and to protect against brutality in any shape or form. The opinion of every Englishman in this part of the world – they are not many – is strongly in favour of the soldiers and dead against the German government.*[23]

From this very early point in his career, Casement's consular work in Africa would be defined by a conscientious approach to any given problem and the unflinching assessment of the evidence. Although in many ways he fitted the stereotype of the imperial adventurer, Casement was still determined to maintain the vision of humanity at the heart of his own understanding of the civilizing project. As the race for rubber began and the economic potential of the region was realized, others began to compromise that position.

In the summer of 1895, his work so impressed his superiors that he was granted a special dispensation from sitting the exams demanded for entry into the consular service. His initiative and experience were enough to take him directly into the Foreign Office. While in England on leave he was informed that he had been assigned to the strategically significant port of Lourenço Marques (Maputo) in Delagoa Bay, Portuguese East Africa. The Foreign Office feared a threat to British interests in the region and they needed someone to spy and report on the movement of arms into the Boer republics – Transvaal and Orange Free State.

Lourenço Marques was a sickly, inhospitable place. Casement's health was worn down and he had two periods of sick leave in March 1897 and in January 1898 respectively, the first noticeable bouts of malaria that would incapacitate him until his death. The copious official dispatches surviving from this time are evidence of his scrupulous defence of British trading interests and showed a marked ability to grapple with the finer points of law in regions where justice was often difficult to apply. Consular work refined his skills in the taking down of depositions and primed him for handling other complex legal issues.

After passing the first quarter of 1898 between Ireland and England, he received a new posting to São Paulo de Loanda (Angola). The territories of this consulship included all Portuguese possessions in West Africa south of the Gulf of Guinea, as well as the Independent State of the Congo and the Gabon – an unmanageably large area. Once again, however, it was Casement's undercover skills that were immediately required. The

Foreign Office was anxious to know what munitions were passing through the Congo into the Sudan to the French force in Fashoda, south of Khartoum. In December, Casement supplied intelligence that *considerable numbers of French officers and men and large quantities of ammunition, said to be destined for the Bahr El Ghaza, have been recently despatched.*[24] By the time the FO received his memo, Lord Kitchener had defeated the Dervishes at Omdurman and forced the French to withdraw.

Another reason for sending Casement into the area was to investigate the atrocity stories beginning to percolate back to Europe about the methods imposed under Leopold II's colonial regime. There were growing concerns that concessions had been secretly granted in breach of the Berlin agreement, causing rapid deterioration in the condition of Africans. Several of Casement's colleagues from earlier days had submitted separate reports on abuses and widespread crimes, and the matter had been taken up by the spokesman in London for Aborigines Protec-

Leopold II, King of Belgium
After the Berlin conference, he took personal control of the Congo Free State

tion, H R Fox Bourne. There were immediate denials from Leopold's frontman, H M Stanley, who assured the public that matters were above board, and initially the British government seemed indifferent to the matter. Others aired concerns that while large shipments of natural products (mainly rubber and ivory) left the mouth of the Congo destined for Europe, little returned up river beyond guns and munitions.

All competing interests over the trading regime diminished with the declaration of war by Britain on the Boers at the end of 1899. Casement was ordered back to Lourenço Marques to report once more on the movement of arms. He arrived on 8 January 1900, and for a bribe of £500 he was allowed to inspect the import registers, which revealed nothing improper. Within a month, somewhat frustrated, he proposed that the best way to stop the movement of contraband was to mount a commando raid and blow up the main railway bridge on the line connecting the Transvaal and Delagoa Bay, between Lourenço Marques and Pretoria. Casement travelled to Cape Town to present his proposal to his superiors. At the end of March, Lords Kitchener, Roberts and Milner approved the plan, and two months later an operation of 540 men set off for Kosi Bay with Casement leading one of the assault parties. But before they had even reached their destination, the mission was aborted by Lord Milner because the bridge could be repaired quickly and the expense of the operation did not justify the potential gain.

Despite the intervention of war, Casement had addressed a

The daughter of a Church of Ireland archdeacon, Alice Stopford Green (1847–1929) was raised in an intellectual environment and in 1877 married the distinguished liberal historian, J R Green (1837–83). After his death, she gradually established her own reputation, increasingly influenced by radical politics. In London, she nurtured an intellectual circle that included the most prominent historians of the day such as John Morley, H A L Fisher, James Bryce and Winston Churchill. She actively opposed the Boer War through her campaign on behalf of Boer prisoners on St Helena, and she extended her work on Africa through participation in the Congo Reform Association, the Morel Testimonial and the Connemara Relief Fund. After Casement's execution, she returned to live in Dublin and her pioneering books had an enduring influence on the development on the Irish national consciousness.

letter on 30 April 1900 to the Foreign Office asking the government to join Germany *in putting an end to the veritable reign of terror which exists on the Congo.*[25] In July, while on leave in England, he became aware of newly emerging efforts to change attitudes towards Africa inspired by the life and work of the Victorian ethnographer, Mary Kingsley. One of the most influential and active of the group was the Irish humanitarian and historian, Alice Stopford Green. Besides her relief work on behalf of Boer prisoners on St Helena, Green was part of a significant political lobby openly opposed to the war in South Africa. In 1900, she founded The Mary Kingsley Society of West Africa intending to promote a fairer understanding of the region's culture in the public mind. Among the committee members were the future prime minister, H H Asquith, the anthropologist of magic, J G Frazer, and the Pro-Consul, Viscount Cromer. Certainly the Boer War unleashed deep frictions in both attitudes towards and perceptions of the British imperial role in Africa. In the manifesto of the society, Green argued that Africa was deserving of a different kind of representation, and that the public had a right to know the facts of what was happening. Otherwise the Africans 'like the Jews' would be 'turned into a landless and unhappy people'.[26]

For Casement, the Boer War was a watershed. In later years, he would describe the conflict as the moment when his own anti-British imperial feelings began to emerge even though, at an official level, he condemned the actions of the pro-Boer Irish Brigade led by Colonel John Blake, Major John MacBride and Arthur Lynch. For the time being, however, he still believed that the best means of changing the system was to work within it. Thus, later that year, he prepared to leave England to establish a new British consulate at Kinshasa, partly to investigate claims of atrocities being committed in King Leopold's colonial possessions. Concern was growing as to what was happening behind the mask of commerce, Christianity and civilization.

Commercial interests in the region were driven by the rising demand for rubber, a material which represented progress by enabling the electrification of cities. Moreover, forecasts of a mass-produced motor car industry saw the price of rubber shares rocket. But the unchecked efforts to meet European needs hastened the rapid decimation of tropical regions and the forest people as demand began to outstrip supply. Whether the colonial powers were aware of this fact or chose simply to ignore the evidence was unclear.

International demand for rubber sparked a resource war in the tropics

On his way to Africa, Casement travelled via Belgium for an audience on 18 October 1900 with Leopold II to converse directly with the man responsible for the colony. It says something of his stature that the king requested to see Casement and even tried to use the meeting to coax the Foreign Office to change its attitude towards his regime. In Casement's mind, the king was in denial of the atrocities and he sent a long memo to the new Foreign Secretary, Lord Lansdowne, reporting his conversation. If Leopold had hoped to win Casement over to his side, the strategy failed.

Over the next two years, as Casement worked to establish a British consulate on the Congo, his reports to the Foreign Office hinted at an increasing disillusionment with the system's capacities to work for the good of Africa. On 9 March 1901, while at Stanley Pool, on the Congo river above Leopoldville, looking for a possible location for the consular office, he heard the news of Queen Victoria's death six weeks earlier and wrote how he could not *think of an England without the Queen.*[27] In early 1902, having persuaded the Foreign Office to relocate his consular office to Boma, at the mouth of the river, he held a party for 400 *black brothers* to commemorate the coronation of Edward VII:

Yesterday we had our coronation festivities: first a religious service in the local mission (an American place) chapel which was well attended – and then all the British West African natives in Boma came along to pay their respects to H.M. Consul. About 400 names were taken – and fully 100 more came without giving their names. They ate and drank 'till they could no more – gave hearty cheers for the King and Queen (as also for your humble servant) and went away about 1.30 p.m. in the most orderly way. It was quite a pleasure to see them enjoy so nice a day. The entertaining of my 'Black brothers' is not cheap. They imbibed 360 bottles ginger beer @ 6d. per bottle and 200 bottles of lager at 1 franc and 30 bottles of portwine (for the health of the King & Queen), 300 cigars, 1500 cigarettes, 6 large hams, 120 loaves of bread, butter and jam in immense quantities, 50 tins of H&P desert biscuits, 1 case of cakes, 30 tins of plum puddings and 3 cases of chocolates (the latter a specially nice preparation for the wives and children). I expect my bill for yesterdays entertainment will come to £60 or £70, but I don't grudge it as it does good to keep them black folk in touch with their govt. and it is in marked contrast with the way the Congo govt. treats its own black people. The local govt. were very civil in the way of saying nice things, and they were officially represented at our religious service.[28] Some of his attitudes still configured with the standard language of the colonizer and dwelled on lurid stories of cannibalism, but encoded in his reports there is evidence that his attitudes were beginning to change.

Meanwhile, in Britain, matters were moving on the question of Congo reform. The influential imperial statesman, Sir Charles Dilke, had helped organize a meeting at the Mansion House on 15 May 1902 to demand a reconvening of the countries that had signed the Berlin agreement in order to discuss the 'evils' occurring in West Africa. Lansdowne, however, was guarded in involving

Pictures like this were evidence of the 'barbarous acts of repression' inflicted on the Congolese.

the government officially in any such campaign, despite mounting pressure from the press and the public for intervention.

None the less, on the evening of 20 May 1903, Herbert Samuel raised the issue of the Congo in the House of Commons. His motion asked the government 'to intervene in the affairs of the Congo Free State for the purpose of mitigating the evils under which the Congolese suffered at the hands of the Government'. He drew specific attention to how labour was organized in the collection of rubber which led to 'continuous resistance, smuggling, mutinies, wars, punitive expeditions, constant seething turmoil, and barbarous acts of repression'.[29] Samuel then produced a series of statements to consolidate his accusations. Chilling images of horror were used to get his point across, including evidence that baskets of amputated hands were used to 'strike terror' among the local population. He wondered what barbarism was if the Congo administration was considered to be civilization.

Other speakers were equally scathing, with Sir Charles Dilke proclaiming: 'The whole anti-slavery world had been swindled by the Administration of the Congo State.' Sir John Gorst referred to the 'lessons of history' and reminded the House of the 'enslavement and extermination of the natives' that occurred 'arising out of the desire for the acquisition of property' and the 'covetous desire for gold and furs'.[30]

The Foreign Office had no option but to act. Their position was compromised by the fact that they lacked any tangible evidence beyond press reports. Leopold had already published denials and rallied the press firmly in defence of his cause. Casement, on the spot in West Africa, was contacted by Lansdowne and ordered to gather 'authentic information'[31] about the administration. On 5 June 1903, he set out on a trip that he had been contemplating for some time. He travelled from Bolobo to Chumbiri on board the small river launch *Henry Read*, a steamer belonging to the American Baptist Missionary Union. He realized that it was vital to have independent transport and, once essential repairs had been carried out, he chartered the launch for the rest of his journey.

On 20 July he set out his intentions to provide *a faithful and accurate representation of the state of affairs prevailing in the country.*[32] In early August, from the shores of Lake Mantumba, he reported on good authority the view that the Commission for the Protection of the Natives was a *dead letter: The state of the country is deplorable, disease and bad government, and the dreadful excess of the past have swept away fully 60 per cent of the population . . . Whole villages and districts I knew well and visited as flourishing communities in 1887 are to-day without a human being; others are reduced to a handful of sick or harassed creatures who say of the Government: 'Are the white men never going home, is this to go on for ever?'*[33]

Subsequent dispatches described an *absolute reign of terror* in the areas of highest rubber production along the banks of the Lolongo and Lopori rivers, the territory of the Anglo-Belgian India Rubber Company. On 12 September 1903, Casement wrote to the Governor-General of the Congo Free State: *I am amazed and confounded at what I have both seen and heard; and if I in the enjoyment of all the resources and privileges of civilized existence know not where to turn to, or to whom to make appeal on behalf of these unhappy people whose sufferings I have witnessed and whose wrongs have burnt into my heart, how can they, poor panic-stricken fugitives . . . turn for justice to their oppressors.*[34]

Casement's intervention is significant because it is a position that he would invoke again on behalf of both the Amazon Indian and, eventually, the Irish – an intervention dependent on his absolute integrity as a witness and authentic voice of the dispossessed. After three months of travelling he telegraphed news of the completion of his investigation: *Have returned from Upper Congo today with convincing evidence of shocking misgovernment and full-scale oppression.*[35]

In early November, Casement began the journey back to England. He landed on 1 December, and 48 hours later met with Lansdowne at the Foreign Office, who encouraged him to write a report as quickly as possible. Newspapermen, too, were hungry for his story. Within eight days he had delivered a draft that, unlike many of the missives sent during the course of his investigative journey, adopted moderate language, was terse and dispassionate in style, and deliberately avoided hyperbole. He described the workings of the Congo administration, exposing cases of forced labour and slavery, accounting malpractice and cases of brutality. His choice of evidence was intended to shock – and it did exactly that.

Casement's sense of outrage fuelled his desire to exploit other non-official ways of throwing more public light on the issue. He had begun a correspondence from the Congo with a young Anglo-Frenchman, the Quaker, E D Morel, and was aware of his

E D Morel founded the Congo Reform Association with Casement in 1904

Born in Paris to a French father and English Quaker mother, E D Morel (1873–1924) began his association with Africa in Liverpool, working for the Elder Dempster shipping company and writing for local newspapers on West African affairs. In 1904, he founded the Congo Reform Association and over the next decade built it into the most radical humanitarian initiative in Britain. Following the Agadir crisis, Morel campaigned against secret diplomacy in an effort to make British foreign policy more democratically accountable. After the First World War, he defeated Winston Churchill in the bitterly fought general election of 1922, and in January 1924 he was strongly tipped to be Foreign Secretary in Britain's first Labour government. He died later that year whilst on a walk in Devon.

crusading endeavour on behalf of the Congolese. Soon after his return, they met in London and Casement realized that with Morel's determination he could motivate an influential public campaign to bring more concerted non-governmental pressure to bear on the situation. To prove his sincerity he subscribed the first £100 from his Foreign Office salary as seed funding for the Congo Reform Association (CRA). He then contacted Joseph Conrad, whose *Heart of Darkness* had just been published to widespread critical acclaim. Casement liked the work but Conrad declined to actively join the crusade, although he was happy to lend it his intellectual blessing. The two men exchanged letters over the Christmas period, and in the first days of 1904 Casement met Conrad at his home in Kent.

Casement deliberately absented himself from the launch of the Congo Reform Association at the Philharmonic Hall in Liverpool on 23 March 1904. The founding manifesto was preambled by an impressive list of names including the African businessman and entrepreneur, John Holt, the historian, John Morley, the Presbyterian Minister, Reverend R J Campbell and the Quaker philanthropist, W A Cadbury. Such public names were supported by four bishops and a dozen influential peers of the realm. The stated intentions of the CRA were to secure 'just and humane treatment' of the inhabitants of the Congo State territories including 'restoration of their rights in land' and restoration of their 'individual freedom'.[36] Its foundation met with some opposition from other humanitarian groups, in particular the Aborigines Protection Society, but the in-fighting was quickly forgotten in the cause for lasting reform.

At an official level, publication of Casement's report was certainly not a foregone conclusion. One clerk in the Foreign Office argued that it should be used as a working report for a more substantial international commission of inquiry. It was understood, however, that Casement's investigation had benefited from the element of surprise and any subsequent efforts to discover the state of things would be deliberately opposed. Lord Salisbury took the final decision from 10 Downing Street and resolved that the names of both perpetrators and victims would be excised from the published report and replaced by letters and symbols. Casement objected furiously but to no avail, and the carefully manipulated version for public consumption was published on 12 February as *Correspondence and Report from His Majesty's Consul at Boma Respecting the Administration of the Independent State of the Congo*. Beyond placing in the public domain an indictment of the regime of the Congo Free State, the report also brought an end to Casement's active consular career in Africa. His negotiations with the Foreign Office had at times been tempestuous and met with heated opposition from the British Minister in Brussels, Constantine Phipps, but his continued involvement would prove no easier.

In Belgium, Casement's reports had been received with widespread scepticism, and in July 1904 Leopold II decided to dispatch his own commission of inquiry. Although Morel and Casement both dismissed the intentions behind the gesture, the Foreign Office and the British press remained open-minded about not pronouncing judgement on the matter until other evidence had been evaluated. Over the coming months and years, however, what ensued was a vicious propaganda war with disturbing and far-reaching consequences. The Congo Reform Association motivated awareness across Britain and abroad. Missionaries of most Christian denominations with direct experience in Africa strode on to the platform to enlighten public discussion. Lantern lectures staged in church halls and local theatres added a vital visual component to the crusade and projected deeply disturbing images into the public imagination. In addition to editing the newspaper *West African Mail*, Morel published a series of controversial books including *King Leopold's Rule in Africa* (1904) and *Red Rubber – The Story of the Rubber Trade Flourishing on the Congo in the year of Grace 1906* (1906).

Arthur Conan Doyle was a prominent intellectual supporter of Congo reform.

Important international intellectuals lent their weight to the cause. From the US, Samuel Clemens (Mark Twain) was a powerful dissenting voice against all types of imperialism – including those of the US – and contributed a damning critique entitled

'King Leopold's Soliloquy' (1907). In Britain, Arthur Conan Doyle, the popular author and creator of Sherlock Holmes, became increasingly active after the publication of *The Crime of the Congo* (1909). Congo reform would become the 'largest sustained protest against imperialism in the decades before the Great War'.[37]

At the end of 1904, after a brief attempt to relocate to a post in Lisbon, Casement was seconded without pay and spent the next 18 months off the active service list. Nevertheless, he remained in touch with the Foreign Office throughout that time whenever issues of his investigation required clarification. On 30 June 1905, he was informed by the Duke of Argyll that he had been awarded the Companion of St Michael and St George. A mark of his changing allegiances can be discerned in his deliberate effort to avoid the investiture ceremony, using the somewhat feeble excuse that knee trouble prevented him from genuflecting before the king.

The report commissioned by Leopold II was eventually released in November 1905 and went a long way towards vindicating those agitating for reform. Although it praised many aspects of the Congo Free State regime, it objected to the brutality inflicted on the Africans, including the 'taking of hostages, detention of chiefs, and the employment of sentries'.[38]

At this point, Casement's African life was ostensibly over. The vast corpus of documentation which survives mainly in the official archive at the Public Record Office makes his experience a defining source for African history. If his writings from that period are ever collected and published, they will fill several large volumes and allow him to be understood as an unrivalled analyst of the European scramble. Casement never relinquished the 'humane' and perhaps 'utopian' vision promised by the European statesmen who gathered together in Berlin in 1884 to carve up the continent on behalf of 'civilization'. However, Casement's direct experience of the imperial project saw his initial ideals evolve into a direct condemnation of the system and the irreparable damage it had initiated for both the people and their environment. His narrative remains on record as a horrifying insight into the administrative mechanisms of colonial exploitation. His vivid denouncements of the employment of terror in the maintenance of law, his cold exposé of the economic realities of free trade for those dispossessed and without the protective signifiers of freedom still haunt informed western perceptions of Africa. As the British Empire reached its zenith at the dawn of the 20th century, it had given voice to a man who would prove to be its nemesis. Casement had started to use the system to investigate the system.

Much of his African work had 'special mission' written all over it: the mapping of interior regions; the gathering of intelligence on the movement of arms and munitions; his aborted plan to blow up communication lines; his anonymous press contributions as a 'special correspondent'. All of these dimensions were quietly priming him for his eventual role as a revolutionary. His direct experience of the devastation of sub-Saharan Africa and his inscription of that moment into the empirical monolith of official documentation granted him the moral authority that helped justify his later action.

Casement's significance as a founding father of African independence would not be lost on those who continued the fight against colonial occupation. In 1965, when his bleached bones were exhumed from Pentonville prison to be returned to Ireland, Kwame Nkrumah (1909–72), the President of Ghana, the first independent country in Africa, expressed the debt owed to Casement by all 'those who have fought for African freedom'.[39]

In those tempting realms of virtual history, some might wonder how different Anglo-Irish relations could have been if the second Home Rule Bill had been passed in 1893. The Tory administration tried hard to kill Home Rule by kindness by establishing the Congested Districts Board in 1891 and through further efforts to facilitate the purchase of land ending with the great Land Act of 1903. But legislation did not end aspirations for Irish independence.

Following the death of the Irish nationalist Charles Stewart Parnell in 1891, Ireland was already starting to imagine and rediscover its identity in different directions. Out of this a new sense of nationalism germinated around the Gaelic Athletics Association, founded in 1884 to encourage Irish sports, and the Gaelic League, founded in 1893, with aspirations to revive the Irish language. The Irish literary revival can be traced back to the 1870s, when the journalist Standish O'Grady (1846–1928) discovered a library which forced a revision of many established concepts and inspired

Following the introduction of the Roman alphabet, the Irish language developed as the earliest written vernacular outside of Greek and Latin. Cistercian reforms of the church saw the end of the use of Irish in monastic centres and the language flourished within the great bardic families. The start of the Anglo-Norman invasion (1167) brought about the secularization of usage and it was adopted as both a court and vernacular language until the disintegration of the Gaelic order after the battle of Kinsale (1601). With successive waves of conquest and the decimating impact of the Irish famine, English began to gradually displace Irish. Today, the language lives on most actively in the last pockets of the *Gaeltacht* and through the Irish radio and television channels.

a renewed interest in the ancient Irish myths of Ireland among such figures as W B Yeats and George Russell. From this, a free-thinking, experimental, and sometimes subversive literary generation emerged that was prepared to explore the cultural frontiers, including the complex Irish triumvirate of Yeats, Oscar Wilde and George Bernard Shaw. The exploration of Irish identity was expressed in many modernist mediums from education to experimental theatre, arts and crafts, language schools, publishing, theosophy and occultism. The old social order was being challenged and on the whole it disapproved.

Given his background and consular position, Casement might well have been expected to join the Home Rule party. However, he was neither impressed by its political leaders, inspired by its political philosophy nor convinced that Home Rule could be achieved through constitutional methods. Although he would later claim that it had been the death of Parnell that had ended his concern in Irish affairs, his interests were revived in 1898, through the popular commemoration of the centenary of the rebellion of the United Irishmen.

In September, as he sailed from England to take up his new appointment in Loanda, Casement began his epic poem 'The Dream of the Celt'. Framed by powerful imagery of the sea, it returns to the theme of his youthful efforts: English

The secret Society of United Irishmen, founded by a group of middle-class Ulster Presbyterians in 1791, was inspired by the ideologies of the American and French revolutions. Its radical philosophy, disseminated through the *Northern Star*, sought a unification of the Irish people and the end to English control in Ireland. The rebellion of 1798 saw the death of its two main leaders, Lord Edward Fitzgerald (1763–98) and Wolfe Tone (1763–98), and after a second unsuccessful rising in Dublin in 1803 the organization collapsed although its spirit lived on.

misrule in Ireland under the Tudors and Stuarts. Underlying the verse is Casement's emerging vision for a new Ireland.

Over the next 15 years, until his resignation from consular activity, Casement's image of Ireland was constructed mainly from outside the country, first from Africa and then from Brazil and the Amazon. Thus, it was inevitable that his contribution to the movement would be to internationalize the discourse of Irish nationalism. Like others in the Gaelic League, he believed that political separatism could only be successful if the process of mental de-colonization was first achieved.

In Ireland, the discussion was sparked by the founding of the National Literary Society by Douglas Hyde and W B Yeats and the delivery of Hyde's inaugural lecture: *The Necessity for De-Anglicizing the Irish People* (1892). Hyde appealed to both nationalists and unionists to arrest the gradual decay of Irish culture and encourage the use of the language, Irish names and place-names, the playing of Irish music and the wearing of Irish tweed and linen.

Elsewhere in the Empire, particularly in India and Egypt, similar national discourses were starting to subvert British hegemony. In the US, W E B Du Bois (1868–1963), the sociologist and black-rights leader, wrote of the duality of being both African and American, a duality that created a unique consciousness founded on different histories, values and beliefs from the white, American independence leaders. To these ends, the nationalisms of Africa, India and Ireland were linked by the experience of dual consciousness.

The need to disengage Irish identity from imperial identity lies at the very core of Casement's political and historical writings. From 1903, he engaged in a process to define a separate and united Irish position. To those who considered Empire as absolute and unassailable this discourse was subversive but it none the less thrived within the nationalist cultural movement. Through his experiences in Africa he was aware of many inter-cultural connections. Indeed, Casement perceived this internal change, and in 1907 wrote to Alice Stopford Green from Santos, Brazil, to explain the change in his consciousness of Ireland based on his years in Africa:

It is a mistake for an Irishman to mix himself up with the English. He is bound to do either one of two things — either go to the wall, if he remains Irish — or become an Englishman himself. You see I very nearly did become one once! At the Boer War time. I had been away from Ireland for years — out of touch with everything native to my heart & mind — trying hard to do my duty & every fresh act of duty made me appreciably nearer the ideal of the Englishman. I had accepted Imperialism — British rule was to be extended at all costs, because it was the best for everyone under the sun, and those who opposed that extension ought rightly to be 'smashed'. I was on the high road to being a regular Imperialist jingo — altho' at heart underneath all & unsuspected almost to myself I had remained an Irishman. Well, the war gave me qualms at the end — the concentration camps bigger ones — & finally when up in those lonely Congo forests where I found Leopold — I found also myself — the incorrigible Irishman. I was remonstrated there by British, highly respectable and religious missionaries. 'Why make such a bother' they said — 'the state represents Law & Order & after all these people are savages & must be repressed with a firm hand.' Every fresh discovery I made of the hellishness of the Leopold system threw me back on myself alone for guidance. I knew that the FO wouldn't understand the thing — or that if they did they would take no action, for I realized then that I was looking at this tragedy with the eyes of another race — of a people once hunted themselves, whose hearts were based on affection as the root principle of contact with their fellow men and whose estimate of life was not of something eternally to be appraised at its market 'price'. And I said to myself then, far up the Lulanga river, that I would do my part as an Irishman, wherever it might lead me personally.

Since that, each year has confirmed me in my faith in that point of view. I got back to Ireland early in 1904 — got to find the Gaelic League at once — and all the old hopes and longings of my boyhood have sprung to life again . . . [40]

In an effort to resettle his spirit after the haunting traumas of the Congo, in the summer of 1904 Casement set out on a walking tour of Donegal and Galway to deliberately reconnect himself to Ireland. At the Sligo Feis he made the acquaintance of Douglas Hyde and became involved with the Irish language movement. At the end of June, he delayed taking up his appointment in Lisbon, extended his leave with excuses of bad health and attended the *Feis na Gleann* (Festival of the Glens) in Antrim.

Francis Joseph Bigger (1863–1926) combined his life as a Belfast solicitor with a deep patriotism for Ireland and is remembered as the most significant Ulster antiquarian of the last century involved in cultural nationalism. His interests stretched to Irish folk music and language and in 1924 he edited *Ulster dialects: words and phrases*. When he died, he bequeathed his valuable library of 3,000 books to the Belfast Public Library.

The event was organized by F J Bigger, the Belfast solicitor, antiquarian and editor of the *Ulster Journal of Archaeology*, and the politician Sir Horace Plunkett (1854–1932), who travelled from London to open the event. Perhaps its most remarkable feature was its spirit of unification. Over 2,000 people attended, mostly from Ulster: Home Rulers, Orangemen, Irish scholars and Gaelic leaguers. Activities included story-telling in Irish, bag-piping, dancing, spinning, knitting, wood carving and much singing. The main event was a hurling match and the winning team was presented with a replica of an ancient bronze shield. The event was promoted as a flowering of cultural nationalism, defining a renewed and healthy interest in the Gaelic spirit.

Through the organization of this event, Casement met many of the men and women with whom he would communicate until his death. He initiated a conversation on politics and history with the young and radical Quaker, Bulmer Hobson (1883–1969), but he was equally at ease in the company of the writer and politician, Stephen Gwynn (1864–1950), who left one of the most evocative accounts of Casement's presence at the *Feis*: 'He came strolling down after dinner, in evening clothes but with a loose coat of grey Irish frieze thrown over them and a straw hat crowning his dark, handsome face with its pointed black beard. Figure and face, he seemed to me then one of the finest-looking creatures I have ever seen; and his countenance had charm and distinction and a high chivalry. Knight errant he was; clear-sighted, cool-headed, knowing as well as any that ever lived how to strengthen his case by temperate statement, yet always charged with passion.'[41] Several of the formidable women in Casement's life were also involved in the organization including Ada (Ide) McNeill, the scholar Margaret Dobbs, the poet Alice Milligan and the Irish language teacher Agnes O'Farrelly.

Stories about Casement's participation in the *Feis* became part of the history of the Glen and remain alive in the oral culture today. When a landlord refused at the last minute to grant permission for his land to be used for a hurling match, Casement himself cut the thistles and weeds of another available field so that a pitch was prepared for the competition. He was also determined that the Irish-speaking inhabitants

From 1904, Alice Stopford Green became a formative influence on Casement's views on Ireland and social history

of Rathlin island should partake in events and travelled to Belfast to charter a small steam tug to transport them to the mainland.

From 1904 onwards Casement became an active supporter of a range of Irish causes. Among the projects he generously funded were the Irish Language Colleges in Ballingeary (Cork) and another in Ulster at Cloghaneely in Donegal. In September 1904, he visited the Aran Islands and was introduced to the Tawin school project in Galway Bay through his friendship with the O'Beirns, a local family of doctors with a keen interest in Gaelic League activities. He wrote to Douglas Hyde describing his experiences and offering a prognosis on the state of the Irish language. Subsequently, his views were published in *An Claidheamh Solvis*, an Irish-language publication edited by the republican and public educator, Patrick Pearse. Casement was a highly attractive figure to have won to the cause and he devoted much energy to the work in terms of funds, moral support and, most importantly, with the pen.

In 1905, on his leave of absence from the Foreign Office, Casement began his second consolidated period of writing on Irish issues, if his youthful poetry is considered the first. In unravelling this knot of articles, letters and unsigned contributions spread across the pro-nationalist press of the time, historians are faced with the problem of authenticity: Casement wrote pseudonymously and his manuscripts have not survived. The fraction of Casement's political writings that have been positively identified indicate a profound and wide-ranging view of history, as well as a conscious wish to use that history for political ends. Several themes that would later emerge in a more recognizable form can be traced back to this time. They include his opposition to the recruitment of Irishmen into the British army, the potential for the press to deceive the public and suppress unwelcome information, and an almost spiritual concern for the Irish language as the essence of the nation's soul.

His most easily identifiable writings have survived in the *United Irishman*. On 28 January 1905, his poem 'The Irish Language' appeared under the pseudonym 'Glens of Antrim'. A month later, he penned an essay, 'Kossuth's Irish Courier', an account of his father's adventures in 1849 running an urgent message across Europe to Lord Palmerston for the Hungarian revolutionary Lajos Kossuth. These initial contributions bound him unequivocally to the emerging forces of cultural and political nationalism. In 1904, when Arthur Griffith (1871–1922) founded Sinn Féin, he launched the movement with a series of articles on 'The Resurrection of Hungary', that became something of a manifesto for the independence movement. Casement's direct family connection to that episode of history did much for his credibility.

On 11 March Casement published an article in the *United Irishman* examining the relationship between history and law. It analysed Ireland's attitude to the Act of Union (1800) and the Crown, condemning the Act as *illegal and unconstitutional*. On 29 April another contribution to the newspaper entitled 'A Forgotten Nationalist' traced the publication of a 17th-century pamphlet by a Jesuit priest in Lisbon advocating the separation of Ireland and England. The May issue of *Ulad,* a publication produced by the Ulster theatre, ran Casement's analysis on 'The Prosecution of Irish' in which he attacked the efforts to suppress the use of Irish by law while constructing a case to show that Irish had *for centuries after the Anglo-Norman invasion* [been] *the language of prince and peer and peasant.*[42]

On 18 May 1905, Casement attended a lecture by Louise Farquharson, the Scottish nationalist, at the Gaelic Society of London on 'Ireland's ideal'. He announced his resignation from his London club, the Wellington, an action taken in order to redivert his membership fees to the Munster Irish Training College in Ballingeary. That evening he met the radical journalist, W P Ryan, and began to mix openly in advanced nationalist circles in London. He also promised regular financial support for various publications, a lengthening list which included Arthur Griffith's *Sinn Féin*, W P Ryan's *Irish Nation* and Bulmer Hobson's *The Peasant*, and later on, *Bean na hEireann* (Woman of Ireland),

Irish Freedom and *The Irish Volunteer*. In all of these publications (protected by pseudonyms) Casement expressed his views on a range of issues including the Swadeshi movement of India, Egyptian nationalism, the Maoris of New Zealand, chivalry, sport, religion and history.

Casement's most contentious piece of writing from this time was *Irishmen and the English Army*, a pamphlet co-authored with Alice Stopford Green and Hobson that was privately circulated by the Dungannon Club.[43] It questioned the long relationship between the British army and the Irish people: *When the Irish had lost their freedom they were to be used to destroy the freedom of others.* The distribution of the pamphlet in Ulster led to the arrest of a local nationalist sympathizer, Stephen Clarke of Ballycastle and his prosecution for intending to 'stir up sedition'. Casement wrote in Clarke's defence, pouring scorn on the authorities and raising the necessary funds to cover his legal costs.

Foreign Secretary Sir Edward Grey worked closely with Casement on his humanitarian campaigns in the Congo and South America, but their collaboration disintegrated after the declaration of war in 1914

Throughout 1905 and early 1906, Casement worked tirelessly promoting the movements for cultural nationalism and reform in the Congo. Inevitably, both campaigns fed into each other and were mutually influential. At the same time, the routing of the Conservatives (Unionists) by the Liberal Party at the end of 1905 brought an important political sea-change. Sir Edward Grey succeeded Lord Lansdowne as Foreign Secretary. Although Grey was a vocal supporter of Congo reform, the West Africa question was initially ignored and priority given to his secret diplomatic negotiations arising from the dispute between France and Germany over Morocco. While the Liberal Party would remain in power for the next decade, the Unionists were destined for a long period in the political wilderness.

At the end of May 1906, the death of Michael Davitt robbed Ireland of its most significant radical voice in parliament. Davitt's view that the real independence of Ireland was tied up with the ownership of land was a philosophy quite clearly extended by Casement to his campaign on behalf of the Congo. In a letter to Gertrude Bannister he described Davitt as *one of the last of the chivalrous sons who dreamed of an independent Ireland and did not fear to work for it by all means*.[44] While Casement's identification with Davitt's thinking can be traced back to his adolescent notebooks, whether Davitt's death meant that he now covertly shouldered the responsibilities of Irish radicalism might be judged by his subsequent actions.

Increasingly, Casement's main practical concerns were financial. The various 'Irishisms' he was supporting, along with small handouts to his family, meant that he had to find employment and from early 1906 his return to consular duties became necessary. This return would define a number of conflicts that were now emerging as a result of Casement's complex dimensions. While his identifiable writings from this period form a cogent and clearly evolving case for separatism, it required the adoption of different voices to express different views. Thus, his diplomatic persona varied from the voice he expressed privately, and the views he declared to his English friends were couched in a different tone to what he said to those who sympathized with advanced Irish nationalism. In creating a separate Irish identity, Casement needed not merely to dissimulate but almost to negate his public self.

In several ways, the Irish Casement that would develop from 1903 was a composite of the various figures who had been involved in the independence movement. He inherited the anti-Englishness of Parnell, the asceticism of John O'Leary, the socialist sympathies of Michael Davitt, the anti-imperialism of John Mitchel, and the aspirations for a United Ireland rooted in the Presbyterian protest of 1798 and the life and example of Wolfe Tone. Splintered radical ideologies were starting to crystallize in Casement's writings. When he set sail for Brazil on 21 September 1906 to take up his new post in Santos, he read two books central to the Young Ireland movement: A M Sullivan's *New Ireland* and John Mitchel's *Jail Journal*. He realized that his months out of the Foreign Office had *moulded all my subsequent actions, and carried me so far on the road to Mitchel's aspirations that everything I have since done seems but the natural upgrowth from the seed then sown.* [45]

Brazil

There was a certain logic behind Casement's posting to Brazil. Besides his working knowledge of Portuguese and his experience of the rubber industry, there was also the tragic history of slavery that bound West Africa to the Americas.

Fifty years after the 'discovery' of Brazil in 1500, Africans were being imported *en masse* to work the sugar plantations and to defend the settler population against Indian resistance. Of a conservative total, of the 10 million slaves to leave Africa at least 4 million went to Brazil.[46] By the 17th century, the Brazilian economy was entirely dependent on slavery. The historic commercial alliance between England and Portugal governed the transatlantic trade, and Brazil played a lucrative economic role for Britain's informal empire in South America.

In 1888, Brazil abolished slavery in preparation for the peaceful transition to republican government. By 1906 the fledgling republic had survived less than two decades of intense factional politics. Much of the idealism behind the rhetoric of becoming a republic had been betrayed. Despite these acts of emancipation, Brazil remained an oversized and socially unstable society struggling to escape the legacy of centuries of slavery, savage capitalism and colonial mismanagement.

Casement's appointment as consul to the states of São Paulo and Paraná required that he was stationed near the unremarkable commercial port of Santos, a strategic coastal trading hub south of São Paulo. Coffee was the main commodity handled at Santos, a product which had usurped sugar as southern Brazil's most profitable export commodity.

Casement left Southampton on 19 September on the SS *Nile*,

arrived in Santos on 9 October and formally began his duties on 16 October 1906. The great Victorian explorer, translator and linguist, Richard Burton, was the most famous of his predecessors, and Casement would have been familiar with his widely read work *Exploration of the Highlands of Brazil* (1869).

Casement's first impressions were critical of the state of the consulate and its location in an old coffee store. (It was not unknown for pedestrians to walk in off the street and ask for refreshments.) His time was largely passed listening to the stream of drunken sailors who survived as vagrants on the city's streets. Casement, in his typically efficient and reforming way, set about putting this house in order. He fired off a series of dispatches about the inadequacies of stationery and the neglect of the archives, and the Foreign Office responded accordingly. His special duties included reporting on and photographing foreign warships for the Commercial Intelligence Branch of the Board of

Casement's Brazilian postings included Santos, Para and Rio de Janeiro

Trade, as Whitehall was especially concerned with the rise of German naval influence in the region.

Casement lived on Santo Amaro, an island at the mouth of Santos harbour, amongst a mainly expatriate community. His pedantic and long-winded dispatches, especially on the question of *lex loci* marriages, reveal Casement's frustration with a post that was mainly concerned with mundane affairs. His abilities far exceeded the responsibilities of the job. Nevertheless, he dutifully delivered the annual consular report, taking issue with the fact that British and Irish imports were lumped together as *Ingeleze* in the Brazilian customs returns. He felt that the large amount of Guinness consumed in Brazil alone justified a separation of that particular statistic.[47] In March 1907 he enjoyed a brief vacation in Buenos Aires to escape the long, humid coastal heat of summer. On the last day of June, he returned to England with the intention of leaving the public service to take up a job offer in East Africa.

The summer of 1907 was spent in Ulster between Ballycastle and Donegal. His private letters reflect his mounting anger at increasing civil disturbance, in particular a clash between striking workers and 4,000 troops in Belfast which resulted in three civilian deaths. He found some peace in the west of Ireland and wrote enthusiastically about the Irish language college in Cloghaneely and the great progress in the linguistic revival.

There was some excitement within cultural nationalist circles on the publication of *The Making of Ireland and Its Undoing* by Alice Stopford Green. Though it was ignored within conventional academic circles, it was lionized by those endeavouring to rediscover Ireland's identity through a revision of standard historical positions. His trip came to a memorable end with a motoring excursion with Agnes O'Farrelly and Hugh Duffy, the organizer of the Gaelic League, through the Donegal *Gaeltacht*.

While in Donegal he was informed that a vacancy had come

up as Consul-General of Haiti and Santo Domingo, a highly coveted post which Casement was prepared to accept. On returning to London, however, to receive his instructions, the FO were sending out a different message. The post had instead been given to a Boer War veteran; Casement would be given another Brazilian appointment at Santa Maria do Belém do Pará (Pará), the Atlantic port at the mouth of the Amazon river. Casement felt slighted and found some refuge in a series of angry, private letters. Before heading off, he spent Christmas with his sister at the Spa hotel in Lucan, on the outskirts of Dublin.

In February 1908 he boarded the Booth steamship the SS *Anselm* back to the south Atlantic. On board was the Peruvian rubber baron, Julio César Arana, in the process of negotiating the flotation of his rubber company on the London Stock Exchange. Although both men politely acknowledged each other as fellow passengers, within a few years they would be engaged on opposite sides of a scandal that would rock the foundations of international investment in South America.

On 1 March 1908, Casement officially took charge of the consulate at Pará. His consular territories were almost as large and unmanageable as they were in Portuguese West Africa and included the states of Grand Pará, Amazonas and Maranhão. Over the course of the previous century, this vast tract of unmapped rainforest had produced increasing amounts of rubber. The impenetrable forest contained a concentration of wild *Hevea braziliensis*, the mighty rubber tree from which top grade latex was milked. Pará had grown rich and confident on the back of the rubber industry. The flow of transatlantic steamships moving upriver to Manaus and Iquitos in Peru, the other great centres of rubber production, all anchored in Pará. For European adventurers, businessmen and travellers, Pará was the first port of call – an exotic location flanked by the river on one side and the green wall of forest on the other.

Urban prosperity peaked at the dawn of the 20th century. Tram lines, shaded by avenues of coconut trees, connected the commercial port with residential suburbs. The Park Goeldi contained an important botanical research centre visited by the greatest botanists and plant-hunters of the age. Parrots migrated over the rooftops of the city at dawn and dusk, flying to and from their feeding grounds. Commerce circulated around the elegant iron and stained-glass structure of the *Ver o Peso* market where marble slabs displayed lines of intricately patterned fish. Rich earthy smells of the humid water and vegetation percolated through the back streets. Market places filled with the exotic mix of African, Amerindian and Asian influences. Herbalists crowded the pavements selling miracle cures distilled from dark hued teas and magical tinctures.

Once again, Casement found the consulate in a pitiful state of neglect. He reported how the previous consul had allowed things to degenerate to a desperate level. Archives (including secret dispatches) were haphazardly stored in an outhouse. Within days of arriving he was threatening the Foreign Office with resignation, complaining of the inflated expense, and the women of easy virtue who frequented his hotel *by day for their meals and at night for their amusement.*[48] Pará's lifestyle was typical of the American frontier city in the throes of a boom. Once his initial concerns had been resolved, he found new premises for the consulate above the London and Brazilian Bank in the Rua 15 de Novembro in the heart of the commercial quarter.

At the end of April, he made his first journey upriver to Manaus in order to inspect progress on the Madeira-Mamoré railway project. Plans to build a railway around the rapids of the Madeira river, a tributary of the Amazon, to facilitate the transportation of rubber to Pará, had been part of the treaty settlement of Petropolis (1903). This extraordinary feat of engineering proved to be the most expensive railway project ever undertaken in South

America and countless lives lost during its construction were forgotten when the line was finally opened in 1912. Returning from the journey on 9 May, Casement drafted a considered report analysing both labour problems and potential health risks. On 4 June he sent a letter to the Foreign Office about atrocity reports from the Peruvian-Colombian frontier region, but the unhealthy humid climate and his old African agues had started to affect his health. In late July he was forced to travel to Barbados where he spent almost two months convalescing.

At the end of September he returned briefly to Pará, but on 4 November he informed the Foreign Office that he had been told to leave on medical advice. The publication of his consular report had caused some disquiet amongst the business community, especially his comments on the rubber industry. He had voiced his concerns about the 'claims' made to vast tracts of forest and the misrepresentative use of the word 'estate' to define such claims. He also cited statistics to highlight the failure to bring education into the areas where rubber was collected and questioned *whether the universal subjection of this population to the spell of rubber production is altogether good for the people or the future of their country.*[49] Encoded into this report were further concerns on questions such as deforestation, tourism, food shortages and how to combat famine – ideas that at the end of the century would be the concern of international aid agencies.

Casement's imaginings of Ireland did not end and at some point during his time in Pará he delivered a lecture on the Irish origins of Brazil. His argument, supported by compelling evidence, contested Alexander von Humboldt's definition of the word 'Brazil' as derived from the name for the red wood tree originally felled along the Atlantic coast of southern Brazil. Casement argued that its origins were more ancient and rooted in the early Irish search for the mythical land of Hy-Brasil, located in the Atlantic, which had inspired St Brendan's voyage.

Back in Ireland in December, he became further embroiled in historical controversy over the refusal by the Library Committee of the Royal Dublin Society to allow a copy of Alice Stopford Green's history to be placed on their shelves and in a rather Swiftian mood of satire he dismissed the committee members as *living ethnological curiosities.*[50] A long and equally controversial review of the book appeared in the *Freeman's Journal* on 18 December. Casement praised Green's work on several levels and applauded it as a social history of medieval Ireland that had strengthened *Irish national self-respect*. It had

The appearance of the 'Insula de Brexile' on an Italian map of 1325 is the earliest evidence of the mythical island of 'Hy-Brasil', just beyond the horizon off the south-west coast of Ireland. The search for Hy-Brasil, however, can be traced back to the voyages that inspired St Brendan to sail west in search of new lands in the 6th century. It is mentioned in the *Navigatio Brendani* as a utopia and is richly described in the ancient folkloric memory of western Ireland. Although the origins of the name Brazil are usually attributed to the German natural scientist, Alexander von Humboldt, who ascribed them to the red wood tree felled along the Atlantic rainforest, his argument lacked the evidence of the influence of medieval Ireland on Atlantic culture.

pierce[d] *through that cloud of calumny, to get at the real conditions of the Ireland of the thirteenth, fourteenth and fifteenth centuries*, and exploded the *gigantic myth*. Most controversially he accosted *the special correspondents* and historians as *later-day* [sic] *Pigottists* deliberately employed to misrepresent Ireland as *barbaric* in order to justify the process of conquest.[51]

On Christmas Day 1908, in the company of his sister, Nina, and his cousin, Gertrude, he visited the house in which he was born at Lawson Terrace, Sandycove. From Dublin he travelled to England for New Year which he spent with the Mortens at Denham and then passed a few days in Paris with a friend from his African days, Herbert Ward, who had found a new life as a sculptor. In early March 1909 he finally sailed on the Royal Mail

Rio de Janeiro, where Casement took up the position of Consul General. Despite the remarkable natural beauty of the city, Casement disliked his time there

SS *Amazon* to take up his new post in Rio de Janeiro as Consul-General of Brazil.

Despite its fantastic location, buttressed around a series of meandering bays by soaring mountains and tropical forests, Casement disliked this urban paradise. From the outset, he thought it a *sham city* and despised the efforts of the *cariocas* to mimic Parisian life. As soon as he arrived he was ill, and in a letter to his cousin Gertrude Bannister at the end of his first week he noted despondently: *No home; no privacy; no comfort; no friends, no social life or pleasant friendly intercourse simply a hot stuffy office in a noisy tropical heat . . . and then a small bedroom in a Brazilian hotel.*[52]

On 14 June, the President of Brazil, Affonso Penna, died suddenly. Casement attended the funeral *in my war paint* (a sarcastic reference to his official consular uniform) and was caught on film as he *left the palace to get into the motor.*[53] The following week his image was seen in all the cinematographs across Brazil. In July, he travelled by train north up the coast to Vitoria, capital of Espirito Santo and an important outlet for trade from the mineral rich state of Minas Gerais. He spent time reorganizing consular offices and appointed a fellow Irishman, Brian Barry, as vice-consul. The following month, he was in Rio when the Brazilian writer and intellectual, Euclydes da Cunha, was gunned down in broad daylight and wrote a long dispatch about the circumstances of his death. In August he relocated to a hotel in the diplomatic colony of Petropolis, preferring to commute daily the 56 miles by the extremely uncomfortable narrow gauge railways that shunted between the more temperate peaks of the Brazilian highlands and the central station in Rio de Janeiro. Under the last Brazilian emperor, Dom Pedro II, Petropolis had been designated a diplomatic capital for the specific purpose of creating a more amenable and temperate climate for the conduct of diplomatic affairs. In his new surroundings, Casement made friends with the German diplomatic mission in particular, Baron von Nordenflycht, and with the British Minister, Sir William Haggard.

Of all the intellectuals to emerge after the declaration of the Brazilian republic in 1889, the most revered was Euclydes da Cunha (1866–1909). Combining a career as an engineer with his writing, he travelled to the backlands of north-eastern Brazil (Canudos) to report on the conflict between the republican armies and the dispossessed peasant population led by the messianic religious leader Antonio Conselheiro. Out of this emerged his brilliant book *Os Sertões* (*Rebellion in the Backlands*), the bible of Brazilian nationalism. Its publication in 1902 propelled da Cunha to the heart of the intellectual establishment.

In the latter half of the year he reported on the financial crisis of the Lloyd Brazileiro company. Brazil, however, was in the midst of an economic boom and expansion schemes encouraged commercial rivalries between competing European countries. The Commercial Intelligence Branch of the Board of Trade was kept closely informed about the tender for the building of the new naval dockyards in the Ilha das Cobras in Guanabara Bay and on the various improvements to the Brazilian navy.

In November 1909, as the heat of summer began to take hold, Casement travelled back to Vitoria before returning to Petropolis for Christmas with Sir William and Lady Haggard. Despite delighting in the warm days and nights, the cooling afternoon rains and the magnificent tropical colours, his spirit was once more growing restless. On 4 February 1910 a new consular official arrived, and on 1 March Casement announced that he was departing Rio for a period of leave. Although he would nominally remain Consul-General of Brazil until his resignation from the Foreign Office in August 1913, Casement would never see the city again.

From São Paulo he journeyed briefly to Argentina on personal business, spending time in Buenos Aires and Mar del Plata before making another long transatlantic voyage back to Europe via Montevideo, Bahia and Tenerife, arriving in Liverpool on 1 May, a week before the death of King Edward VII. Towards the end of the month, he returned to Ireland for a holiday in and around Ballycastle, working with various members of the *Feis* committee and seeing a good deal of Ada McNeill, Margaret Dobbs and Agnes O'Farrelly. While peacefully on leave, Casement was informed by both the Anti-Slavery Society and Sir Edward Grey at the Foreign Office of his selection as the official candidate to investigate the activities of a British-owned rubber company in the disputed frontier region of the Putumayo, bordering Peru, Colombia, Brazil and Ecuador.

THE PUTUMAYO ATROCITIES

The Putumayo atrocities first entered the British public imagination in the autumn of 1909, about the time of the death of Leopold II. A young American railroad engineer, Walter Hardenburg, had arrived in London clutching a dossier of statements alleging widespread atrocities committed against Amerindian communities in the north-west Amazon. The Anti-Slavery and Aborigines Protection Society (ASAPS) took up the case and the weekly magazine *Truth* decided to run with the story. On 22 September 1909, under the headline 'The Devil's Paradise – A British-Owned Congo', it published the first of several articles: 'When the history of crime in the 20th century comes to be written, and when the historian comes to deal with that particular phase of his subject in which the animating motive of the crime is greed, not the least difficult part of his task will be to elucidate the absolute truth in regard to the crimes committed in remote parts of the earth at the expense of the helpless and uncivilized aborigines.'[54]

The idea that City of London money was financing a company that was committing atrocities comparable to the Congo horrors was difficult for the British imperial imagination to accept, nourished as it was on views of altruism and fair play. After several months of prevarication and increasing pressure from the ASAPS, Sir Edward Grey had no option but to act. The company directors, including some highly influential city names, were obliged to organize a commission to investigate their affairs. The Foreign Office was also determined to send a representative: Casement was the obvious choice. His knowledge of the rubber industry and his experience investigating atrocities was unrivalled, and Grey realized that his integrity would confer extraordinary authority to the investigation. After a few brief meetings at the FO, on 23 July 1910 Casement departed with the Commission on board the HMS *Edinburgh Castle*.

Sailing via the island of Madeira, the group did not arrive in Iquitos until the last day of August, after six weeks of strenuous travelling. The only casualty was the head of the company's commission, Colonel R H Bertie, who was forced to turn back because of acute dysentery. Casement also wrote privately of his concerns for a chronic eye infection, which grew progressively worse as the investigation continued.

The voyage out allowed him both time and space to assess the other commissioners. He had greatest confidence in Louis Barnes, an expert in tropical agriculture who had farmed for several years in Mozambique. The botanist, Walter Fox, had expert knowledge on the planting of rubber and was connected with the Royal Botanic Gardens at Kew. Seymour Bell was interested in aspects of 'commercial development' and how the company methods might be improved. The last and youngest member of the party, Henry Gielgud, had visited the Amazon a year earlier to check the company's books and had reported back to London favourably.

On arrival, the group made themselves known to the relevant authorities. Their presence, however, came under immediate suspicion and their movements were closely monitored by representatives of the company. Casement stayed with the British Consul while the company provided a house for the other commissioners.

The investigation began immediately. Casement met with the Prefect of Iquitos, who assured him that the stories in *Truth* were all fables. However, while discussions at an official level denied any malpractice, informal conversations revealed a very different situation. The former French Consul said that cruelty was prevalent and had been going on for years. Casement's brief specified that he was to investigate 'British colonial subjects'. He interviewed a few Afro-Caribbean overseers (mainly from Barbados and Jamaica) and employed one of them, Frederick Bishop, to serve as his guide and messenger. His efforts to find a well-known interpreter of the Indian dialects failed. On the evening of 7 September, Casement held a private dinner party for representatives of the company and the commissioners as a public relations exercise. A few days later he wrote to Tyrrell at the FO: *We are all of us acting with great caution, and secrecy even (as if we were the criminals) for it is clear the rascals are very suspicious – especially of me.*[55]

On 13 September, the eve of setting out for the Putumayo, he wrote to the FO, informing them of his concerns for his own personal safety and that of his papers: *I am keeping a diary, and part of the statement of Bishop is really a leaf of my diary – the last part. It is only sent you in case I might get lost or disappear or something up there, or die of fever, and my papers might be overhauled long before they reached Iquitos.*[56]

On 14 September, Casement and the commissioners set out from Iquitos on board the company's river launch, the *Liberal*. Nine days later, they reached the company's headquarters at La Chorrera where the real work of Casement's investigation began. He met with the company's main representative in the region and showed him various letters of permission authorizing the investigation.

Over the following ten weeks, Casement travelled extensively throughout the Putumayo region, visiting rubber stations and gathering both written and photographic evidence of the atrocities. He was to some extent hampered by his brief since he could interview only British colonial subjects. Thus, the bulk of his information was gathered from the Barbadian overseers. Their stories were gruesome and often unspeakable, describing acts that Casement admitted were even more horrific than those he had uncovered in the Congo. He recorded the details of his investigation in a journal, describing the interviews with the Barbadians and the stories of their experiences and the system of horror imposed by the chiefs of section. The investigation was often compromised by the difficulties he encountered with the other

Casement used photographic evidence in drawing attention to his investigations

commissioners, in particular Gielgud who he felt was unable to see beyond the surface of the Company's activities and lacked the intelligence to comprehend the true circumstances of the imposed regime. In his journal, he wrote dismissively: *Of course there are lots of people in this world who will defend anything that exists, merely because it exists, and they are so mentally constructed that they cannot imagine another state of things.*[57]

To his dismay, he found the most amenable of the murdering chiefs of section, who became a useful source of knowledge, had an Irish name: Andrés O'Donnell. As his investigation progressed, he began to piece together the commercial system that was leading to the outrage.

Casement discovered that the tribes had been deliberately turned against each other by the encouragement of internecine rivalries and the employment of young armed *muchachos de confianza* (confidence boys) abducted from one tribal demesne and forced to police another, with no attention to the principles of law, justice or decency. The chiefs of section were also paid a salary dependent on the amount of rubber collected, a system which led to desperate physical abuses such as flogging, confinement in stocks, and sexual atrocities. He also began to understand the economic history of the region: how the global demand for rubber had forced marauding parties of what he termed *vegetable filibusters*[58] to seek new supplies of latex-bearing trees in the most inaccessible upper reaches of the rainforest. These were regions where the tribes had been forced to retreat over centuries of gradual incursion by successive waves of exploration and conquest. Within a few decades of the earliest European and American contact, these largely peaceful communities, which possessed shamanic medicinal knowledge as complex as anywhere on earth, had been exterminated.

The most disturbing discoveries were made at the furthest rubber station of Matanzas (Slaughterhouse) presided over by the Bolivian taskmaster, Armando Normand. For several years, Normand had organized slave hunts into the Colombian territories north of the river Caquetá and driven them to their deaths at the end of a Winchester rifle. As he left Matanzas by foot to return to La Chorrera, satisfied that he had more than enough evidence to condemn the company, Casement caught up with a party of Indians transporting rubber on their backs through the forest and spent a night in their company attending to their wounds and recording their stories.

Before he left La Chorrera, Casement conducted an exhaustive analysis of the company account books and ledgers, and found longstanding evidence of fiddling, barefaced exploitation of the Barbadian overseers, deliberate inflation and bad debts. Wherever he turned he saw corruption and he sought assurances from Juan Tizon that reforms would be implemented immediately.

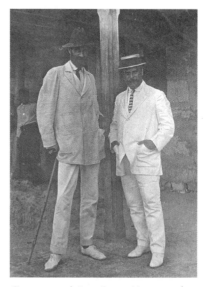

Casement with Juan Tizon, Manager of the Peruvian Amazon Company, at La Chorrera in 1910

But another dilemma was now emerging. What should he do about the Barbadians who had supplied him with the testimonies exposing the horror? He realized that if their statements were used to expose the brutal methods of the company, the company would pursue a policy of revenge and, thus, their lives would be at risk. So, he decided to offer alternative employment in Brazil to any Barbadian who wished to leave the area. At the same time, the fate of the Indians posed a different problem and one that Casement realized was insurmountable in the short term. What was required was a change of understanding in Britain towards the Amazon Indians. The British public had no idea who these people were or how they were suffering. Thus, to draw attention to their plight Casement decided to take two Indian boys with him, one a young married man, the other a 12-year-old.

On 16 November, after nearly two months investigating the Company's activities, Casement left the Putumayo with 18 Barbadians, four Indian wives, the two Indian boys and several stray dogs. At the Brazilian border, he arranged for the Barbadians to be taken to Manaus, to find the British Consul there, and to then be provided with new employment on the Madeira-Mamoré railway. Meanwhile, he continued to Iquitos to face the Peruvian authorities. There, he was met by a new type of opposition: a general indifference to what he had found, although it was agreed that a further investigation should be dispatched under the direction of the central government in Lima.

After collecting further intelligence from European businessmen engaged in the rubber business, Casement began the voyage back to London. His journal ended on 6 December as he steamed downstream, and his papers now included a large dossier of evidence along with his depositions from the Barbadians.

As his views of 'civilization' had been profoundly altered by his experiences investigating atrocities in the Congo, a similar transition emerged from what he had witnessed in the Putumayo. On his journey home, he contextualized the outrages committed against the Indians as part of a long tradition of crime meted out by successive waves of conquerors. Greed connected the activities of early Spanish and Portuguese *conquistadors* to Julio Arana and his gang; a modern prototype protected and encouraged by British investment.

THE PUTUMAYO BLUE BOOK
Casement left the two Indian boys in Barbados in the care of a Jesuit priest, intending to bring them to London once they had

some preparation for European life. He then continued back to Europe, spending a few days with Herbert Ward and other friends in Paris before reaching London. In his initial meetings with the FO, he was encouraged to write official reports and he worked intensively to deliver two separate reports on 31 January and 17 March 1911 respectively.[59] Through careful examination of the evidence, he constructed a case that became a powerful diplomatic tool in bringing pressure to bear on the Peruvian government as well as persuading the US State Department to support the Indians.

In April, with his Putumayo reports finished, Casement attended to the organization of the Morel Testimonial with the co-operation of Alice Stopford Green and Arthur Conan Doyle – an effort to give E D Morel some financial security so that he could extend his work for the Congo Reform Association to other areas of the world where slavery prevailed. A luncheon given at the end of the month to mark the occasion was a gathering of some of the most radical voices involved in the discussion of African and international affairs. Although Casement attended the lunch reluctantly, many of the guests there knew that both his financial and intellectual participation had played a vital role in the Congo reform campaign.

That summer, as part of George V's coronation honours, Casement was rewarded for his humanitarian work with a knighthood. Although this

While accepting honours publicly, Casement was not so respectful in his private correspondence

empowered him greatly, he accepted it uneasily, realizing that in the eyes of the ordinary Irishman it would be a further proof of his imperial commitment.

The summer of 1911 was politically explosive. On the domestic front, syndicalist action in Liverpool and other imperial commercial centres combined with the growing militancy of the suffragettes to generate heated exchanges in the press and parliament. More disturbing was the international situation, which brought the world to the brink of war with the Agadir crisis.

For much of this time, Casement was busy trying to rescue the Peruvian Amazon Company from financial ruin. If the company filed for bankruptcy, it would leave the Indians more vulnerable than ever. He attended a series of board meetings and at one came face to face with Arana. However, his efforts were rendered worthless when cables reached the FO at the end of July that the official Peruvian Commission of Inquiry, led by the journalist and lawyer, Dr Rómulo Paredes, had returned from the Putumayo brandishing even more disturbing evidence gathered largely from Indian witnesses. Over 200 arrest warrants had been issued against former employees of the company. Peruvian justice was endeavouring to take control of the situation.

With the backing of Grey and the Foreign Office, Casement decided to make another journey to the Peruvian Amazon. In the middle of August, he left Southampton with the two Indian boys on a return journey that for many reasons was more perilous than the first. This time he was a marked man as the contents of his reports had by now percolated up the river and his enemies were prepared for his arrival. At Barbados, he met up with an American doctor, Herbert Spencer Dickey, an old South American hand who had worked for the Peruvian Amazon Company. He became a useful source of information for Casement and the two men travelled together as far as Iquitos.

Beyond his brief to oversee the process of justice in Iquitos, a number of different agendas underpinned Casement's return journey. Due to rapidly changing economic conditions the Amazon that he re-entered in the autumn of 1911 was very different to the one he had left nine months earlier. A cholera epidemic was sweeping upriver, and the region's extractive rubber industry was about to turn from boom to bust under pressure from the plantations in British and Dutch colonies in South-East Asia.

After an arduous journey, when Casement reached Iquitos the repercussions of the crash in rubber prices were clearly visible – in local elections Arana was overthrown but no competent opposition was able to take his place. Casement prepared the way for the new British Consul and Franciscan mission. But his efforts to arrest some of the main perpetrators of atrocities came to nothing and in December, with accusations rife in Iquitos that Casement was an 'English spy', he began the difficult voyage back to Europe.

In Pará, however, his plans changed and he decided to visit Washington to discuss matters with the British Ambassador, James Bryce, an old colleague from his African days. Through Bryce, Casement managed to get a brief audience with President William Taft, and this forced the question of the Putumayo firmly on to the US agenda. Casement argued that the Peruvian government was insincere in its declared intention to bring the Arana gang to justice and the State Department listened sympathetically to his case.

After his arrival in England, Casement drafted another report for the FO recommending a series of measures to protect the Amazon Indians. He then concentrated on establishing the Putumayo Mission Fund to raise money to build a Franciscan mission in the region, believing that their presence was the only way to bring about any real protection for the indigenous population. In May 1912, he went on a brief motoring holiday to Germany with Richard Morten and visited a number of cities and villages in Belgium, France and Germany that he would next visit under very different circumstances after the outbreak of war in 1914.

In July, his reports along with the statements of the Barbadians and some of the diplomatic exchanges between the FO and Washington were published as a Blue Book: *Correspondence Respecting the Treatment of British Colonial Subjects and Native Indians Employed in the Collection of Rubber in the Putumayo District*. Around the world there was an outcry from newspaper editors, political commentators and intellectuals. Henry Nevinson wrote a piece for *The Nation* on 20 July under the heading 'The Heart of Darkness': 'We bear in mind only too clearly the misery of the Congo under Leopold's regime; we know well the atrocious system of slavery still prevailing in Portuguese Angola, and, till within the last year or two, supplying the labour for the cacao plantations of San Thomé; and we have only rather less distinct knowledge of the abominations of Mexico's Yucatan and the Valle Nacional. But in the cool atmosphere of an official document, issued with the authority of a responsible Foreign Office, we have never read anything to compare for horror with Sir Roger Casement's detailed and substantiated account of rubber-collecting by agents of a British Company under the Rule of the Peruvian Government.' [60]

Casement was universally lauded across the world as the conscience of Empire and even inspired a sermon in Westminster Abbey by Canon Hensley Henson. On 17 July 1912, he wrote that he was *bombarded with people trying to interview me*.[61] The report was dealt with in many directions. A Papal Encyclical was issued by the Vatican and published in *The Times* on 9 August asking for more humane treatment of Indian populations throughout South America. Discussion on the Putumayo echoed between pulpit and public house in England and beyond. The FO was criticized for delaying the publication. Arana's response brought a barrage of unconvincing counter-accusations and he accused

Casement with school children on Tory Island in 1912. His work amongst the Irish speaking communities of western Ireland included support for language schools and the Connemara Relief Fund

Hardenburg and Casement of manufacturing evidence and waging a deliberate campaign of calumny.

To escape the spotlight, Casement left England on 1 August and sought refuge at Ulster College in Donegal and amongst the Irish-speakers of Tory Island. He spent several weeks communicating from the isolated wilds of Ulster, maintaining the pressure on several fronts. Finally, the Foreign Office decided on two lines of action. They sent a joint consular expedition back into the Putumayo to report on implementation of reform and a joint decision was taken by Prime Minister Asquith and the Attorney-General, Sir Rufus Isaacs, to appoint a Select Committee of Inquiry to determine the level of responsibility of the company directors. Charles Roberts MP was selected as chairman of the Committee and the directors of the company were controversially represented by Raymond Asquith, son of the prime minister and a leading legal luminary. All significant officials and witnesses involved in or connected with the Putumayo affair were interrogated. During 36 sittings between the autumn of 1912 and the spring of 1913, 27 witnesses were cross-examined, including

Casement, Hardenburg and Arana. Over the next six months Casement supplied a steady stream of letters to Roberts, handing over the great body of evidence collected during his investigation and forcing it on to the official record.

On the last day of 1912, nearly crippled by arthritis, Casement left England in search of some sun and a quiet place to recover and write. He took a boat to the Canary Islands, and at the end of January sent his Putumayo journal to Charles Roberts for use as evidence in the Inquiry. He then took a ship south, along the coast of West Africa to Cape Town, boarded a train to Durban, and then turned inland to visit his brother Tom in the Drakensberg mountains of the Orange Free State. For a few brief days he relaxed in the calm of Africa's interior, making an excursion on horseback to visit ancient burial caves and passing his afternoons gardening.

With his spirits revived, in early May he returned to England with his mind already made up to leave the Foreign Office. Within days he had involved himself in a new humanitarian campaign, this time to bring relief to the neglected and forlorn Irish-speaking communities of south-west Connemara. On 11 June, after a brief visit to the region, he returned to Dublin to his rooms in Lower Baggot Street and read the news of the publication of the report by the Parliamentary Select Committee Inquiry. His Putumayo investigation had been wholly vindicated and the board of directors was found guilty of negligence. Over the next year, an amendment was made to the slavery laws making it a crime for a British company to plead ignorance in defence of the acts of its agents – making slave-owning an offence for a British subject anywhere in the world.

That same day, Casement wrote two letters to E D Morel delivering his verdict on the ten years of work carried out by the Congo Reform Association – the most popular, if radical and controversial humanitarian initiative of the early 20th century: *So the*

CRA is to say its last word in public and to lay down its arms! — but not as I think until it has won a great fight . . . Just ten years ago I was on my way up the Congo in the small mission steamer I had chartered to begin an investigation that it has taken you and those who have so bravely helped you, ten years of most strenuous effort to bring to this good end.[62]

Casement's two decades of service in the Foreign Office should be considered on a number of levels. On the surface, it led to decorations, a knighthood and long eulogies in the press. Yet beneath this, other

E D Morel, pacifist and Labour member, in 1924

agendas were at play. Through his investigations, Casement had left on the official record evidence exposing the shortcomings and brutalities of imperial and colonial systems. He was a unique witness to defining moments in the histories of both Africa and the Amazon. Together, his investigations can be considered as the final chapter in the long history of the 19th-century anti-slavery movement.

When he formally resigned from the Foreign Office on 1 August 1913, all the work that had been so publicly honoured was about to come to an end. Three years later, Casement would be dangling from a rope as the most reviled man in the Empire. It was a turnabout that only Casement himself might have prophesied as he watched the political situation in Ireland descend into a vortex of division and hatred, while the secret diplomatic dealings of the previous decade propelled the British Empire towards world war.

Irish Volunteers

Between 1910 and 1913, political positions in Ireland changed dramatically during a period of constitutional crisis. The two general elections held in 1910 returned hung Parliaments, with Unionists and Liberals winning 272 seats each and the balance of power resting with 82 Irish Nationalist MPs and 42 Labour MPs. Asquith's majority now depended on Irish support. A third Home Rule Bill was introduced with none of the idealistic vision that had inspired Gladstone back in 1886. However, the Parliament Act of 1911 meant that the ability of the House of Lords to veto any bill could now be sidelined and the Unionist ranks began to close in on the situation.

In November 1910 an armaments fund was opened and Sir Edward Carson emerged as the new leader of Unionism, prepared to fight his cause with violence to a bitter end. Gathering other influential voices to his side, including the founder of the Belfast Stock Exchange, James Craig, Carson began to rally the Protestant community of Ulster towards armed opposition, declaring Home Rule 'the most nefarious conspiracy that has ever been hatched against a free people'.[63] On 9 April 1912, a vast demonstration was held in the Balmoral district of Belfast attended by the new leader of the Conservative opposition in the

Sir Edward Carson (1854–1935) was a Crown prosecutor and went on to become a Unionist MP for Trinity College Dublin. In 1910, he became leader of the Irish Unionist Parliamentary Party and proposed the idea of insurrection to combat Home Rule. Eventually, he would also take responsibility for the Ulster Volunteers. However, Carson considered the partition of Ireland as the failure of his unionist project, because it betrayed the southern province from where he sprang.

House of Lords, Andrew Bonar Law. Two days later, Asquith introduced the Home Rule Bill. On 28 September 1912, the Solemn League and Covenant was signed in Belfast Town Hall and on New Year's Day 1913, Carson moved an amendment to the Home Rule Bill for the exclusion of the nine counties of Ulster. As secret negotiations saw the Home Rule position split, the Orange Lodges started to organize a Volunteer Force and Unionist militiamen began drilling their recruits: the division of Ireland became a political reality.

The Liberal government was not helped by the fact that their moral authority was suffering from a series of public scandals, in particular the Marconi affair, involving accusations of insider dealing against both the Attorney-General, Rufus Isaacs, and the Postmaster-General, Herbert Samuel. Even more problematic to Asquith was the now militant agitation of the suffragettes. Newspapers fed off daily stories of demonstrations, hunger strikes and attempted martyrdoms. At the same time, a revolutionary discourse was entering mainstream political discussion from several directions. Syndicalist action increased the voice of the working class. Cries of 'war' on a range of issues were shouted not just from pulpits and in parliament, but proclaimed from street corners and whispered in back alleyways, too. The most classic history of the period, George Dangerfield's *The Strange Death of Liberal England*,

In the summer of 1912, the Marconi affair rocked the Liberal Party with accusations of insider dealing by government ministers. It arose from the decision to establish a chain of wireless stations throughout the empire. The Postmaster-General, Herbert Samuel, formed the Imperial Wireless Company and opened up negotiations with the Marconi Company's managing director, Godrey Isaacs. When Marconi shares soared from £2 to £9, a whispering campaign led to a court case involving many of the legal names who would resurface at Casement's trial, including Rufus Isaacs and F E Smith. The eventual outcome of the trial was a whitewash.

commented that in 1910 'fires long smouldering in the English spirit suddenly flared up, so that by the end of 1913 Liberal England was reduced to ashes.'[64]

In Ireland, the rising political tempo was evident from the tone of the 'seditious' press. At the start of 1909, the amalgamation of two underground newspapers edited by W P Ryan and Bulmer Hobson to form *The Irish Nation and the Peasant* revealed an intellectual effort to pull together the different revolutionary strands. Although the paper was only published between 1909 and 1910, it sought deliberately to develop a new vision for an independent Irish society built on equal status for men and women and greater social justice, while nurturing pride in the Irish language. Furthermore, it was not shy of attacking the established Catholic hierarchy, which it saw as a hindrance to change and spiritual progress. Significantly, other voices of imperial dissent were also allowed to participate in this underground forum. The cause of independence was linked to struggles in both Egypt and India as anti-Imperial rhetoric began to resonate transcontinentally.

During this period, Casement's political philosophy, powerfully influenced by his experiences in Africa and South America, evolved radically. Although much of his journalism is masked by pseudonyms, some contributions that can be identified positively clearly indicate his deliberate identification of the Irish struggle with emerging movements in India, Mexico, Egypt and elsewhere. On 8 April 1911, he wrote to E D Morel from Liverpool: *These slave pits of the Earth – Congo, French Congo, Mexico, Peru, possibly Korea and Formosa under the Japanese, Angola, with São Thomé, under the Portuguese, these damnable sites of the slaver must be assailed . . . Tackling Leopold in Africa has set in motion a big movement – it must be a movement of human liberation all the world over. You must not limit your vision to the African. You concentrate on him because that's your special task for which you are fitted more than any other man – but you must remember that the cause of human freedom is as wide as the world – that if the slaver wins in Mexico or Peru, he stands, too, to win everywhere.*[65]

In his private and official correspondences on Africa, Latin America and Ireland, Casement was beginning to discreetly coordinate the intellectual struggle for social justice into a global context. At the core of his thinking was the vision of a united, neutral and peaceful Ireland, allied to the philosophy espoused by the United Irishmen. His nationalism clearly derived from his reading of Irish history and identification with ideas of social justice rooted in the Young Ireland movement and the Gaelic League. His position on international humanity derived from his investigation of the systems of Empire and the failure of the 'civilizing' project in Africa and South America. He also began to write about Empire and to define different types of imperial systems, specifically distinguishing between the British and German examples.

From 1911, Casement authored a coherent corpus of political essays articulating his views. A united Ireland, he argued, would not simply be better for Ireland but it would be equally beneficial for England and enable the Empire to reinvent itself as a commonwealth of nations. Such a reconfiguration would also benefit the power structures of Europe. Above all it would encourage a utopian discourse of peace, reconciliation and understanding rather than a dialogue of hatred, sectarianism and war. He fearlessly attacked the institutions that blocked such an approach and was particularly critical of the press, of secret international diplomacy and the betrayal of the ideals of Gladstonian liberalism.[66]

In Ireland, Casement's status was clearly understood. In the summer of 1913, when Michael J Ryan invited him to address a group of academics in Dublin he commented: 'Your worldwide reputation in the cause of liberty and freedom for all peoples stands as high if not higher in Dublin than in any other part of the British Empire.'[67] Such views ran against the tide of mainstream discussion. It was perhaps a hopeless fight for, as war approached, it brought Casement increasingly into opposition with an Empire bent on violent engagement.

From the summer of 1913, he began to openly and deliberately propel Ireland towards a position of independence and neutrality. He began by espousing his views on social justice by involving himself in the Connemara relief campaign. In May, *The Irish Independent* had published shocking pictures and stories about an outbreak of typhus which was discussed at some length in the House of Commons. Casement used the newspaper campaign for his own agenda: to define his social policies; to expose a historical lineage of misgovernment in the west of Ireland; and to promote his belief in the need for real administrative change. He referred to an *Irish Putumayo*,[68] connecting social injustices in Ireland to his South American experiences.

On 11 October, *The Nation* published a long letter from Casement pleading for unity among the people of Ireland. He argued that Ulster was the *most typically Irish province of Ireland*[69] and ancestral ties to Scotland made it no less Irish, while Ulster Protestants had a leading role to play in the affairs of an independent state. On 24 October, he entered the political arena along with Alice Stopford Green, Jack White and Reverend J B Armour at a large rally of Protestant Home Rulers held in Ballymoney to protest against the 'lawless policy of Carsonism'. Once again, he preached the politics of peace and began: *I would seek only to point a way, not to conflict and further embitterment of feeling, but to peace with honour – peace for Ireland as a whole and honour for Ulster as the first province of Ireland.* Next, he stated that his main purpose was to find within Ireland *unity of mind, singleness of purpose, and a common goodwill among all our people.* Violence was the worst option: *Civil war and sedition, bloodshed among Irishmen, are hateful to contemplate, and they settle nothing – the settlement will still have to be found.*[70]

The Times dismissed the meeting and its speakers as 'romantic nationalists', commenting that the 'dissident Protestants' represent 'the last few survivors of the Ulster Liberals of the old type'.[71] The comments enraged Casement and his reply was published in the paper's editorial page on 31 October. He argued that as someone born in Dublin and raised in Ulster, he was more representative of that province than any of the leaders behind Carsonism. He went on to deliberately combine his stance as a 'nationalist' with his work as a 'humanitarian', stating: *Whatever of good I have been the means of doing in other countries was due, in the first place, to the guiding light I carried from my own country, Ireland, and to the very intimate knowledge I possessed not only of her present day conditions, but of the historic causes that had led up to them.*[72]

On 1 November, Casement's article 'Ulster and Ireland' appeared in the *Fortnightly Review*. His attitude towards *the belligerent creed* of Protestantism was now more openly defiant. He analysed the deliberate efforts to undermine Protestant and Catholic unity with a politics designed to *make disunion perpetual* and lambasted *politics* for degenerating to a point where *sectarian hatred had taken the place of national feeling.*[73]

Casement's call for peace and understanding was little more than a *cri de coeur* engulfed by the rising tempo of the war drums beating from the Carsonist camp. If Home Rule could not be defended with common sense then it would have to be defended by force, and it was in this moment that the Irish Volunteers (*Oglaigh na-hÉireann*) were reborn. On 20 November 1913, *The Daily Chronicle* published a front-page story about the formation of the Irish Volunteers. For the first time, it spoke openly of the organization of a 'citizen force' and it identified the two leaders of the movement as 'Ulster Protestants': Sir Roger Casement and Captain James White. The article discussed how there were 'thousands of men in all parts of Ireland' ready to enrol.

The inside pages carried an interview with Casement, examining his motives for bringing the Irish Volunteers into being. When asked what prospects he had for settlement, Casement answered that the problem was the *irreconcilable mind . . . I am convinced that Catholic Ireland would shrink at no sacrifice short of the principle of self-government in order to secure the goodwill and co-operation of Irish Protestants as a whole. The present attitude of the Ulster Orangemen towards Home Rule is very much that of the Belfast man who once visited the Dublin Zoo. He saw lions, tigers, elephants, a camel and various other beasts that he was acquainted with by hearsay, and whose existence he accepted as a fact; suddenly he was confronted with a llama that spat at him, but he had never seen or heard of a llama, so after looking at it he turned away with contempt remarking, 'There's no such a beast.' That is the attitude towards Home Rule adopted by the Orangemen – 'there's no such beast.'*[74]

SECOND THOUGHTS.

Mr. John Redmond. "FULL SHTEAM AHEAD! (*Aside*) I WONDHER WILL I LAVE THIS CONTRAIRY LITTLE DIVIL LOOSE, THE WAY HE'D COME BACK BY HIMSELF AFTHERWARDS?"

From 1912 the partition of Ireland became a political reality

Five days later, on the evening of 25 November, the Irish Volunteers were founded at the Rotunda in Dublin. An hour before the meeting began, the capacity of the room had already been filled and overflow meetings were quickly arranged. Although Casement had deliberately chosen not to be present that night, his importance to the movement is indicated by a letter written by the leader of the movement, Eoin MacNeill, the scholar-revolutionary, on returning from the meeting. Having outlined the enormity of the task ahead, MacNeill ended his letter: 'In the constructive work we need the help of men like you who can stand out detached and see the whole case, and I hope we shall have your help now.'[75]

A few days later and back in Ireland, Casement helped draft the manifesto of the Volunteers: *The object proposed for the Irish Volunteers is to secure and maintain the rights and liberties common to all the people of Ireland. Their duties will be defensive and protective, and they will not contemplate either aggression or domination. Their ranks are open to all able-bodied Irishmen without distinction of creed, politics or social grade. Means will be found whereby Irishmen unable to serve as ordinary volunteers will be enabled to aid the Volunteer forces in various capacities. There will also be work for women to do, and there are signs that the women of Ireland, true to their record, are especially enthusiastic for the success of the Irish Volunteers.*[76]

In the following months, Casement was central to the raising, organizing and drilling of the Irish Volunteer units and regiments. The speed at which it happened reverberated immediately to Whitehall. Ireland was now quickly slipping towards civil war – it was too late even for a miracle.

Casement now devoted all of his energies to the effort and operated on two distinct fronts. First, he took the platform at a series of meetings as recruiter-in-chief, giving military advice where it was needed and searching for ways to encourage leadership and the training of men. Second, he helped to instigate a new

Patrick Pearse cooperated closely with Casement as both an Irish educator and rebel

The Ulster Volunteer Force was the paramilitary wing of the Ulster Unionists and founded at the start of 1913. It was led by British army officers and quickly enrolled about 90,000 recruits. At the outbreak of war, many were recruited into the 36th (Ulster) Division, which sustained severe casualties on the opening day of the Somme Offensive (1 July 1916). The UVF was revived in 1920 and again in 1966, mainly from amongst militant loyalists in the Shankhill Road district of Belfast.

propaganda offensive through his support of revolutionary newspapers and his deliberate invocation of revolutionary conspiracies.

On 10 December, the recruitment campaign kicked off in Galway with MacNeill, Casement and Pearse on the stage, flanked by academics from the university and two priests. Both MacNeill and Casement stressed their Ulster backgrounds before Casement attacked the deliberate threats uttered by the leaders of the Ulster Volunteers, citing F E Smith's taunt that 'the Nationalists would neither fight for Home Rule nor pay for it.'[77] He then explained that the founding of the Ulster Volunteers had set an example which the nationalists of Ireland might now follow in defence of their cause. If the language of anarchy had been adopted by Carson for his cause then by rights it could be adopted by others.

On 13 December, MacNeill and Casement headed for Cork and two days later held a large meeting in the City Hall. Once again, their approach was to display revolutionary solidarity for Carson in an attempt to bridge the emerging division within Ireland. When MacNeill asked for three cheers for Carson, some elements in the crowd, seated at the front of the hall, stormed the stage, there was a brief scuffle and the chairman was hit over the head with a chair, temporarily halting events.

The following day MacNeill left. Casement stayed on to gather support for his efforts to get a German steamship company, the Hamburg-Amerika line, to pass through Queenstown (Cobh). The decision by Cunard to by-pass Queenstown meant that no trans-atlantic steamers now halted in Ireland. Casement's hope was to reopen a line to the US with German co-operation. Again he opened up a long campaign in the letters columns of both *The Irish Times* and *The Irish Independent* in an effort to draw attention to what he considered to be a deliberate economic policy to disadvantage Ireland. He used the issue as a way of drawing attention to a tradition of such practices, and made reference to the famine, concluding that true independence must include economic independence. Only when Irish trade was integrated into Europe and the US would Irish sovereignty become a practical reality.

Casement spent late December at Bigger's house in Belfast with other Belfast-based nationalists. A small pageant was arranged for New Year's Eve. Young recruits in the Belfast Fianna were dressed in kilts and the uniform of the Volunteers of 1782: equipped with pikes and rifles, they made a quick march down the Antrim Road to the sound of 'A Nation Once

Johann Heinrich von Bernstorff, German Minister in the US who cooperated with Casement in his plans for Irish independence.

Again' played on the bagpipes. Early in 1914, he dispatched Hobson to the US with a memorandum outlining the position of Irish-German relations in the event of war, which Devoy passed on to the German Minister, Count von Bernstorff. By opening up lines of communication with Germany, Casement hoped to force the question of Irish independence on to the international agenda.

In early January 1914, he began conspiratorial activities by purchasing papers exposing corrupt governance in Ireland. The information had been leaked by William Henry Joyce, who had worked for the Balfour administration as a secret agent in Ireland before passing incriminating evidence to Casement, Green and MacNeill – for a price. In a letter of 30 January, Casement wrote to Green: *It is a statement that, if published, would do more to wreck the Anglo-Saxon alliance than anything I have seen – if properly edited and written up. The evidence is there, the corruption is there, the shamelessness is there, the debauchery of the 'public service' by the higher servants of the State is there; all for political ends against Ireland.*[78]

At the end of January, he visited Limerick with Patrick Pearse and led a recruitment rally at the Atheneum. He began his speech by citing the struggle of the Boers against the British Empire as an example which the Irish Volunteers should emulate, and went on to describe the need for Irishmen to bear arms to defend their property and freedom.

Beyond the noise generated by his speech-making, Casement's name was given increasing space in print. *The Irish Review* serialized the first of three articles written under the title 'From "Coffin Ship" to "Atlantic Greyhound"' allowing Casement to vent his economic views on Ireland's relationship to the Empire. He invoked the evidence of history to expose the tradition of political and administrative mismanagement. His analysis concentrated on the economic exploitation derived from decades of emigration to the US as well as recruitment into the navy and the undisclosed strategies of transatlantic shipping. He attacked a recent visit by Winston Churchill, in September 1913, whose speech to the local politicians of Cork complimented Ireland for its strategic importance and as a potential recruiting ground for sailors rather than its Irish attributes.

On 7 February, the first edition of the openly insurrectionary publication, *The Irish Volunteer* hit the streets with a lead article by Casement entitled 'From Clontarf to Berlin'. His objective was to re-define Irish manhood in preparation for war. A series of his articles were also published in *Irish Freedom*, under a variety of pseudonyms including 'The Poor Old Woman', 'Shan Van Vocht' and the familiar 'X' – one of his favourites.

In March, Casement visited Dungannon with Erskine Childers to watch Carson deliver an openly defiant attack on Home Rule. At a rally in Kilkenny not long afterwards, Casement's rhetoric turned openly to war and revolution in response to Carson's irreconcilable position and the deepening international crisis. *If the men of Ulster had a right to volunteer against Home Rule, the majority of the people of Ireland had still a greater reason to volunteer to defend it*, he raged. Volunteering had been *made lawful by the acts of their enemies*[79] and every act of aggression by the UVF brought a retaliatory response from the Irish Volunteers.

On 17 March, Casement led 1,000 Volunteers through the streets of central Limerick, as part of the St Patrick's Day parade. After assembling at the Milk Market, near Arthur's Quay, the men marched to Raheen where they were inspected. Casement was impressed by both their discipline and morale. That evening, after attending an Irish mass at St Michael's Church, he made a further inspection of the Fianna and told stories about his life in Africa, deliberately weaving his colonial experiences into the rhetoric of revolution.[80]

The political crisis had reached another flashpoint with the Curragh 'mutiny'. On 20 March, 60 British army cavalry officers, led by Brigadier-General Hubert Gough, threatened to resign their commissions rather than go to Ulster to (they wrongly believed) coerce the Ulster Volunteers into accepting Home Rule. Without seeking cabinet authority, the War Office declined to accept the resignations and reassured the officers that the government had no such intentions. Both the Secretary for War and Chief of the Imperial General Staff were forced to resign. The incident showed that the army could not be depended on to stand up to threats of action by the Ulster Volunteers in the North. A few days later, on 28 March, Casement co-signed a letter with MacNeill to *The Irish Independent*. He defined the military build-up in the North and the Curragh mutiny as preparations for a *coup d'état*, and dismissed the 'Union' as nothing more than a term to describe *the military occupation of Ireland as a conquered country*. He levelled his vociferous attack at the *unanimous endorsement of the Curragh 'pronunciamento' by the leaders and spokesmen of the English governing classes*,[81] and specifically marked out Lords Roberts, Lansdowne and Wolseley. The tone of this letter sent him down a path from which there was no return.

At Tullamore on 19 April, at another volunteer rally, Casement made a distinction between the Volunteers of 1782 and the Volunteers of the day: *The Volunteer movement of 1782 came from above – it came from the aristocracy; the movement of today originated with the people and comes from the people. It is more truly national and entirely democratic.*[82]

On 24 April, over 20,000 rifles and 3 million rounds of ammunition arrived at Larne to arm the Ulster Volunteers. The Larne gun-running destroyed any lingering hopes for reconciliation. With the Ulster Volunteers armed there were few options except to arm the Irish Volunteers. As a consequence of this act, more than in the signing of the Solemn League and Covenant, the long civil war in Ireland was born.

Obviously, the speed at which the Irish Volunteer movement had grown was having political ramifications. On 7 May, Casement visited the House of Commons with Eoin MacNeill to meet with the leading constitutional nationalists John Redmond, Joseph Devlin, John Dillon and Tom Kettle. The single question under discussion was control of the Irish Volunteers. Casement commented that he had no wish to remain in charge so long as the pledges already made could be met, including the fact that they would get rifles. 'Rifles are the last thing they should have. Anything but that,' Redmond commented.[83]

John Redmond, after his meeting with Casement at Westminster on 7 May the break in the Irish Volunteers movement seemed inevitable

However, Redmond's demand to nominate as many members to the committee as were already on it was clearly intended to split the movement in a way that was unacceptable to Casement. After the meeting, Redmond and Casement stayed behind for a private discussion. Redmond made direct objections to Casement about two of the young republican leaders, Bulmer Hobson and Patrick Pearse. When they parted, Redmond, with a hint of resignation, declared: 'Well, Sir Roger, I don't mind you getting an Irish Republic if you can.'[84]

The following day, 8 May, brought a peculiar confluence of events. A meeting was arranged at the house of Alice Stopford Green in Grosvenor Road, Westminster. In its time, the meeting room had echoed with the conversation of many of the most distinguished political and literary figures of the age: Florence Nightingale, Winston Churchill, James Bryce, Lord Morley. The decision was taken by a small inner circle including Alice Stopford Green, Erskine Childers and Darrell Figgis, to run guns into Ireland. Casement would mastermind the operation and £1,500 was raised almost entirely from the purses of Green, Molly Childers and Mary Spring Rice. Casement introduced Childers and Figgis to an arms importer. Significantly, the experience he had gained during the years spent watching for the movement of arms into Africa was now being used to overthrow the very regime for which he had done this work so diligently.

That afternoon Casement wandered over to Whitehall to make an appearance before the Royal Commission on the Civil Service which was keen to cross-examine him on his consular career and to seek his advice on how the diplomatic service might be improved. He delivered his evidence with the integrity of mind and purpose which were the hallmark of his career. This conjunction of events is indicative of the tremendously dangerous game he was playing.[85]

Over the following weeks, Casement made further preparations for the arming of the Volunteers, searching for suitable officers to undertake the training. In his search, he contacted anyone sympathetic to his cause including Wilfrid Scawen Blunt, another radical devotee of anti-Imperial causes who had published an important work entitled *Land War in Ireland*. On 14 May, Blunt and Casement lunched in the presence of a great grand-daughter of Lord Edward Fitzgerald. The meeting made an impression on both men. The main topic of discussion was the impending war. Blunt suggested that what Britain might achieve through the war was not the ruin of Germany but the break-up of the British Empire. In his diary, Blunt described Casement as 'an interesting man of the same Irish type as was Michael Davitt'.[86]

Towards the end of May, Casement and White took the

Wilfrid Scawen Blunt (1840–1922) entered the diplomatic corps and was posted to Athens, Constantinople, Frankfurt, Lisbon, Madrid, Paris and Argentina. He married Anne Isabella Noel, a direct descendant of Lord Byron, and became an ardent supporter of Irish Home Rule, for which he was briefly imprisoned. Today, he is most fondly remembered for *My Diaries* (1919 and 1920) and various poems including 'The Love Sonnets of Proteus'.

recruitment campaign into Ulster, concentrating on Derry and Tyrone. For a few days, it seemed as if the message was getting across to both Catholic and Protestant communities, and for a brief moment the threat of violence made people see sense.

On 26 May, Casement reviewed 500 Volunteers with Captain White in Celtic Park in Derry. The following day he received news about the formation of a military organization among Irish communities in south London and New York. Over the following week, he made further inspections and speeches in Strabane, Greencastle, Sixmilecross, Omagh, Carrickmacross and Cushendall. In early June, he addressed crowds in Belfast and Dungannon.

Throughout, the core of his rhetoric remained the condemnation of the two-nation theory: *These men who say that the cutting up of Ireland into two parts – Protestant and Catholic – is the solution of the difficulty are no Irishmen, and so far as I know no Irishman could put that proposal forward as a solution.* The English press also came under attack for misrepresenting the Irish as *a people incapable of peaceful discussion.*[87]

As recruitment soared, the leadership came under threat from several directions. A census taken at the end of May showed the number of Volunteers to be just short of 130,000. It was inevitable that the leadership as it was would start to feel the strain. MacNeill's negotiations with Redmond had reached an impasse. It was clear to Casement that a change was required. Still recovering from a bout of influenza, on 9 June he took the train from Belfast to Dublin and drafted a resolution that delegates from the 32 counties of Ireland should be represented on the provisional committee. Although Casement's proposal was the more democratic, Redmond was not in the mood for compromise. The following day, Redmond's response appeared in the press. After dismissing the leadership of the Volunteers as unrepresentative, he stated that unless 25 of his own nominees were elected to the provisional committee he would have no alternative but to set up an independent executive – an act which would split the Volunteer movement.

In a room in Buswell's hotel, the decision was taken by Casement, MacNeill and Maurice Moore to resign rather than split the Volunteer movement. They would issue a statement that the Irish Volunteers as originally conceived had 'ceased to exist'. Only the last-minute intervention of Bulmer Hobson reversed the situation. Hobson argued that they should appear to accede to Redmond's demands but continue to maintain control through command of the finances and arms. Casement alone decided not to attend any more provisional committee meetings and sent the veteran Fenian, Tom Clarke, in his place.

Redmond's demands not only split the original leadership of the Volunteers, it also sowed the seeds of distrust. The IRB remained suspicious of the Casement-MacNeill-Hobson alliance right up until 1916. Before leaving Dublin, Casement made final arrangements with Hobson and Childers over the Howth gun-running. He then returned to the North. When news of the capitulation reached the revolutionary leadership in the US, it was seen as a humiliating defeat. Casement had little option now but to take his fight to America and explain the position in person to the IRB/Clan na Gael chiefs, John Devoy and Joseph McGarrity.

On 28 June, he marched up the hill above Cushendun escorted by a piper to deliver the last oration from the cairn surrounding the stone of the betrayed chieftain, Shane O'Neill. During the previous decade, many of the key figures engaged in the movement for cultural nationalism had spoken from that same spot, including Shane Leslie, F J Bigger, Sean Gall and Eoin MacNeill. Casement made his last public utterance in Ireland surrounded by many of those involved in the organization of the Antrim *Feis*. After fond farewells, he left by car for Belfast and from there sailed to Glasgow for further discussions before taking one more transatlantic steamer bound for Montreal on the appropriately named SS *Cassandra*.

America and Germany

It is hard to imagine Casement's state of mind as he sailed down the Clyde, through the Sound of Moyle, towards America with a vast Volunteer army in his shadow. The journal recording these months was lost on his way back across the Atlantic several months later. The diary he started in Germany in November fondly remembered his last sighting of the Donegal *Gaeltacht*, but there was no indication of the tension of the situation in which he now found himself. When at sea he saw the world differently and his political anxieties dissolved into the mighty expanse of ocean: *On Sunday morning 5 July at 7 a.m. I looked from our port and saw far South the jagged precipices and towers of Tory Island. It was perhaps 12 miles off and beyond it rose in blue lines Muckish, Errigal and the hills of my heart. I could almost see Cloghaneely and the shining strand at Magheraroarty, whence two years before – August 1912 – I had gone over to Tory with that famous party – the fiddler, the piper and the rest.*[88]

As they passed Newfoundland, great icebergs were visible from the deck and after ten days of travelling they entered the mouth of the St Lawrence river before docking at Montreal. During the picturesque train journey to New York he reflected on the native Americans, the Mohicans and the six nations who had once roamed across this hunter's paradise: *Poor Indians, you had life – your white destroyers only possess things. That is the vital distinction I take it between the 'savage' and the civilized man. The savage is – the white man has. The one lives and moves to be; the other toils and dies to have. From the purely human point of view the savage has the happier and purer life – doubtless the civilized toiler makes the greater world. It is 'civilization' versus the personal joy of life.*[89]

In New York he found himself amongst allies, but he was also conscious of being under constant surveillance by what he referred to as the *British spy bureau*.[90] A few days after arriving, he wrote to Alice Stopford Green *we are surrounded by spies*.[91] In her memoir *Life and the Dream* (1928) Mary Colum, a leading member of the Irish-American literary scene, recalled how Casement was 'spied upon by all sides wherever he went'. Even the mail had ceased to be a safe form of communication. Casement was entering the space of rumour and suspicion that surrounds any revolutionary figurehead and intensifies in the build-up to war. Initially, he found refuge in the apartment of the cosmopolitan lawyer and art collector, John Quinn, whose penthouse at 58 Central Park West, was a frequent haunt of W B Yeats, Ezra Pound and Joseph Conrad.

Born in Ohio to a father from Limerick and a mother from Cork, the lawyer John Quinn (1870–1924) amassed one of the biggest art collections in the US. During travels to Ireland, he met the Yeats family and was introduced to the circle of Douglas Hyde, Lady Gregory and George Moore. The meetings inspired a lifelong passion for an independent Ireland based on the revival of its language and economic independence. He was the main patron of Joseph Conrad and later purchased the manuscript of James Joyce's *Ulysses*. Although his friendship with Casement was unsettled by their conflicting sympathies towards England and Germany, he always remained an honest friend.

On 20 July, Casement dined with the die-hard revolutionary John Devoy – a meeting that required delicate handling. Devoy had already made clear his fury at what he considered Hobson's capitulation to Redmond. Casement placated him by letting him in on the gun-running secret and managed to convince Devoy of the sincerity of his own revolutionary intentions.

On 22 July, Casement made his first visit to Joe McGarrity, another Clan na Gael leader, in Springfield Avenue, Philadelphia. McGarrity was keen that he should begin campaigning on behalf of the Volunteers as soon as possible. So, Casement returned to New York and with the co-operation of John Quinn organized his first public address.

On 24 July, in the sweltering convention theatre at Norfolk, Virginia, Casement, Quinn and Bourke Cochran took to the stage in a packed hall of members of the Ancient Order of Hibernians. The following day, back in Philadelphia, they waited anxiously for news about whether or not 'the picnic' (the codename for the Howth gun-running) had been successful. The story gradually filtered through.

At noon on 26 July – a warm summer's day – the *Asgard*, skippered by Erskine Childers with a crew comprising his wife, Molly, a young British soldier called Shepherd, two Donegal fishermen and Mary Spring Rice, sailed into the small port at Howth. As the boat appeared, Bulmer Hobson, at the head of 1,000 Volunteers, came into view at the other end of the jetty. It took barely half an hour for the guns to be unloaded and distributed among the men before the order to march back to Dublin was given.

The synchronization was perfect. Military intervention by the authorities was hindered by the cutting of strategic telegraph links. Although there were ham-fisted efforts to disarm the men on their return to the city, the rifles quickly disappeared into the back streets to be hidden below floor boards and in the thatch. In the evening, however, a punitive incident took place at Bachelor's Walk when the King's Own Scottish Borderers opened fire on an unarmed 'mob'. Four civilians died and 38 people were wounded. As the mastermind of the operation, Casement's popularity in the US soared. His years in Africa at 'listening posts', reporting on the movement of arms into Boer republics, was all the education he needed to prepare him for this moment.

The Howth gun-running followed by the cold-blooded shooting of civilians echoed around the world. For the Volunteer movement, it was a resounding triumph and provided a tremendous psychological boost. In the US, Casement was lauded wherever he went. In a letter to Alice Stopford Green he wrote: *The Irish here would make me into a Demi God if I let them. In Phila*[delphia] *they have christened me Robert Emmet.*[92] The arming of the Volunteers took the whole discussion to a new level. With two armed and opposing factions, the spectre of civil war was inevitable unless another military option could be found.

Casement

On 28 July, the *Philadelphia Bulletin* published a long interview with Casement. It began with his message to MacNeill on hearing of the Bachelor's Walk incident: *I beg that the victims of the lawless violence of the British Government in Dublin may be buried with public honours, and that every Irish Volunteer Corps now armed, should march to the grave with the rifles these people died to safeguard.*[93]

On 2 August, there was a great demonstration of solidarity in Philadelphia. The next day, *The Gaelic American* reported: 'The celebration was preceded by one of the most extraordinary spectacles this city has ever witnessed – a triple funeral with hearses, coffins and mourners, but no corpses. More than 1,000 men, many of them in the new uniform of the Irish Volunteers, marched from Washington Square to the theatre behind these hearses, which were symbolic of the three victims of the gun-running riots in Dublin last Sunday'.[94]

The march was led by the Seventh Regiment of Irish Volunteers, which Casement had inspected a few days before.

Their route began from beside the graves of the Irish revolutionaries who had died for American Independence in 1777–8. Casement and Devoy followed the procession in an open carriage with other leaders of the movement. When Casement stood to speak, the packed hall rose to its feet to applaud. This time, his words offered no hint of compromise and taunted both Carson and the Liberal government for inciting the political situation. Once more, Casement pleaded that the cause of both Volunteer movements was fundamentally the same. He condemned sectarian animosity as the *master curse* in preventing the emergence of a peaceful Ireland, and he scorned the press for deliberately stirring up the situation. Once more, the axis of his speech was peace and reconciliation rather than war: *I look to the day – and not far distant day – when Ulster Orangemen and Munster Nationalists will run guns together for the common defense of the shores of Ireland, and when all Irishmen will march under one banner and show the world at length, that Thomas Davis's words have been fulfilled and that Orange and Green have carried the day.*[95] At the end of the meeting, the fundraising for the Volunteer movement began. Three highly influential Irish-American attorneys, William Bourke Cochran, Morgan J O'Brien and John Quinn stepped forth and presented Casement with generous donations.

But beyond Philadelphia events were charting a different course. In the House of Commons on 3 August, the Foreign Secretary Sir Edward Grey delivered his statement on Great Britain and the European powers, announcing that 'the peace of Europe cannot be preserved',[96] and outlining the diplomatic history that had brought the world to war. The assassination of Archduke Franz Ferdinand in Sarajevo at the end of June had proved the spark to mobilize the imperial powers to war. The implications proved devastating and introduced a new set of rules into power politics and questions of loyalty and allegiance.

On 4 August, Casement met with Theodore Roosevelt to

discuss the situation. Two further fundraising meetings were organized – at Baltimore on 6 August and Buffalo on 9 August, respectively – but Casement's energies were now being forced in other directions; new alliances were necessary, different initiatives demanded. He realized that much depended on the battle for hearts and minds, and with the co-operation of McGarrity he began to prepare his political essays for publication.

Since the Agadir crisis in the summer of 1911, when European diplomats stared into the abyss but managed to delay war for another three years, Casement had authored the first of a series of essays advocating an extremely different political and diplomatic solution to the one held by his Foreign Office colleagues. Much of what he said only makes sense today, after Europe has passed through so much tragic and unnecessary history. His views were unequivocal in attacking the years of secret diplomacy, the decades of betrayal of Ireland over the Home Rule question and the potentially unhealthy state of the world if the Anglo-American alliance was allowed to dominate internationally.

In the US, his pamphlets had great currency on both a political and popular level. The titles of his published essays 'Ireland, Germany and the Freedom of the Seas: A possible outcome of the War of 1914' and 'The Crime Against Europe' advocated a path to peace and a reconfiguration of power structures to preserve such a peace.

In an article published in *The Gaelic American* on 19 September, Casement claimed that even if Germany won most of the battles *she must almost inevitably lose the final campaign.*[97] With the benefit of hindsight, Casement's analysis of global affairs was, in fact, a haunting prophecy.

On 17 September, Casement wrote an impassioned letter to *The Irish Independent* arguing that this was not Ireland's war and, thus, Irishmen should not fight: *Ireland has no blood to give to any land to any cause but that of Ireland. Our duty as a Christian people is to abstain from bloodshed.*[98] The next day, Home Rule was finally placed on the statute books although it was compromised with the provision that it would not be granted until the war was over.

On 19 September, Redmond made his Woodenbridge speech committing Ireland to the Imperial war effort 'wherever the firing line extends'. Following the orders of Lord Kitchener, the 16th (Irish) Division had been founded on 11 September under the command of General Sir Lawrence Parsons. Over the next few months, thousands of Irish Volunteers would be drafted into the British army along with many of the leaders who had earlier followed Casement on to the recruiting platform, including Tom Kettle and Erskine Childers. On 21 September Casement wrote to Quinn: *I am so distressed at Redmond's treachery, and the deplorable state of things in Ireland . . . that I am raging, like a caged animal, at the impotence enforced upon me here.*[99]

Casement now concentrated on structuring new alliances on behalf of Ireland that in the long term would guarantee international diplomatic recognition for the country's independence. On board a train on 24 September, he wrote Quinn two letters: the first about how more guns could be run from the US into Ireland; the second airing the idea of sending a jointly signed letter to the German Emperor expressing sympathy for the German people. Crucially, it was with Germany that his hopes for such guarantees were concentrated.

At the end of September, Casement began talks with the German military attaché about the formation of an Irish brigade comprised of prisoners of war. In another memorandum to the German Ambassador, Count von Bernstorff, he suggested that Germany might covertly support nationalist movements in India and Egypt as a way of overthrowing the British Empire. This cross-national dimension to Casement's revolutionary masterplan, which he had been nurturing anonymously for several years, was now introduced into German diplomatic circles.

Kuno Meyer (1858–1919), scholar and poet, was born in Hamburg but devoted his life to the study of the Irish language which he believed had made a vital contribution to early European civilization. In 1903, he founded the School of Irish Learning and trained his students in the disciplines of palaeography and manuscript editing which set the standard for modern Irish scholarship.

Casement's incipient alliance with Germany became the most controversial dimension of his diplomatic engagement and would make him many more enemies than friends. His sympathy for German culture can be traced to his friendship with the German scholar of the Irish language, Kuno Meyer. Casement had fought strongly against the Germanophobic trend preached by the British media, which he condemned as another sure way of encouraging eventual conflict.

Casement's writing also reveals a preference for the German imperial model as opposed to the British one. The former, was based on administrative federalism; the latter on commercial centralization for the benefit of the few. Finally, he considered Germany the victim of secret diplomacy and the Triple Entente, and Britain's fear that its naval supremacy was threatened. Significantly, Casement's support for Germany was not shared

Casement's views on the British and German imperial systems were set down in a pamphlet *British versus German imperialism: A contrast* published anonymously in New York (1915). He argued that British imperial power descended from a *supreme and absolute* England to subject people including *Ireland, India and Scotland*. Conversely, the German empire was founded on *state self-government* and common control of foreign policy by the constituent countries.

Casement's suggestion for a *new-modeled Empire* was not so different from the process of devolution witnessed in recent years in Britain. England, he argued, should remain the *strongest single state* but that power could always be constrained by the combined influence of Ireland, Scotland, Wales and the other states *if the necessity arose.*[100]

with the same enthusiasm by other Irish leaders and his friendship with John Quinn, in particular, suffered as a result.

On 5 October, Casement's manifesto letter was published in *The Irish Independent* but its message of neutrality was not appreciated by the increasingly pro-British Irish press. An editorial expressed surprise and sorrow that he no longer cared 'what may happen to the Empire' in what was now billed as a 'struggle for justice and righteousness'.[101]

Casement was increasingly exposed and alone. Nevertheless, the leadership of Clan na Gael saw some value in sending him to Germany. That same day he met with McGarrity and Devoy at Judge Cohalan's house and was given $3,000 in gold to finance his mission. A week later, he secured a letter of introduction from Count von Bernstorff to the Imperial Chancellor, Theobald von Bethmann Hollweg. His declared brief had three objectives: to secure a diplomatic dialogue with Germany; to educate the German government and people about Ireland; and to organize Irish prisoners of war into a competent military unit to fight for the independence of Ireland.

THE VOYAGE TO GERMANY

Casement left New York on board the *Oskar II* under an assumed name, 'James Landy', and in the company of a Norwegian manservant, Adler Christensen. As a precaution, Casement shaved his beard and tried to lighten the colour of his skin by washing it in buttermilk.

It was an eventful voyage. As they left New York harbour they witnessed the sinking of the steamship *Matapan*.

Adler Christensen, Casement's Norwegian manservant became deeply involved in the conspiracy to undermine Casement

The war became a reality on Saturday 24 October when a British cruiser, *Hibernia*, fired a gun across the bows of the *Oskar II* and ordered the ship to dock at Stornaway in the Isle of Lewis on the Outer Hebrides. Casement, believing that his cover was blown, hurried down into his cabin to hide the gold and incriminating papers and, as an extra precaution, threw the journal detailing his revolutionary activities in the US overboard. His efforts to conceal himself paid off and though six Germans were taken off the boat and interned, Casement was not recognized and the ship was allowed to continue on its way. Three nights later on 28 October they docked at Christiania (Oslo), capital of Norway.

In Christiania, events took a turn that led to one of the most shameful and confusing conspiracies of the First World War – a labyrinthine plot involving Casement and the Foreign Office that would prove to be the Achilles' heel and nemesis of both. Casement's version of events was widely publicized in his anti-imperial propaganda offensive in the pages of *The Gaelic American* and *The Continental Times* and was eventually published in diary form as *Sir Roger Casement's Diaries: His Mission to Germany and the Findlay Affair* (1922). Casement categorically accused the War Office of dirty tricks. However, his version is contradicted by documents released years later by the British security services. Although the outlines of both versions are similar, many details are in direct conflict. None the less, until the moment of his execution, Casement would recount the Findlay affair time and time again in an effort to cast the British authorities in a bad light.

It was at this point that the maze of conspiracies and counter-conspiracies that Casement had himself encouraged as far back as 1904 took another turn. Whichever version is believed, the basic plot was the same: the British Minister in Norway, Mansfeldt de Findlay, negotiated with Christensen to either capture or assassinate Casement. The war of intrigue to overthrow the renegade Irishman by any means had started in earnest. The story is further complicated by Findlay's questionable involvement in an incident in Egypt several years earlier during the Denshawi affair when his 'methods' of 'justice' had been widely denounced, most vociferously by George Bernard Shaw in his Preface to *John Bull's Other Island*.

On arriving in Christiania, Casement immediately visited the German legation to present the credentials supplied by von Bernstorff to the German Minister, von Oberndorff and then returned to the Grand Hotel. Later that afternoon, Christensen returned in an excited state and related how he had been approached in the hotel lobby by an Englishman, taken by car to the British legation and cross-examined. (The British secret service version stated that Christensen had approached the legation directly with a plan to betray Casement.) Realizing that travelling under a false passport made him vulnerable, Casement decided that the sooner they arrived in Germany the better and he made the necessary arrangements with von Oberndorff to speed up the paper work. He also decided to play the legation at its own game and enter the intrigue to protect his own position and not to raise suspicions.

The Denshawi affair did a great deal of damage to the reputation of British administration in Egypt and stirred up deep resentment amongst anti-imperialists. It began with the shooting of some sacred pigeons by four off-duty army officers in a small village in the Nile delta. It ended with a trial and the public hanging of four villagers and the flogging and imprisonment of other locals. Casement believed that the severity, authorized by Grey and Cromer, was intended to *strike terror*. Findlay, at the time attached to the British Consulate in Cairo, was closely involved in carrying out the orders, and writing up reports which were worded to cover up the incident.

The next day, Christensen was again accosted and taken this time to meet the British Minister, Mansfeldt de Findlay. In a private meeting, the Minister suggested that if Casement were 'knocked on the head',[102] Christensen would be well rewarded.

When Christensen reported back, Casement decided that they must leave that night – but not before Christensen had made one more visit to convince Findlay of his complicity. That night the two men left by train and the following day travelled through Malmö and Traelleborg to Sassnitz, where they were met by Richard Meyer, the brother of Kuno Meyer, and from there continued to Berlin.

Arthur Zimmermann

On the evening of 31 October, Casement reached the German capital. He was immediately given a new identity as an American called 'Mr Hammond' and checked into a hotel. In the following days, Casement was introduced to two high-placed officials at the German Foreign Office, the German under-secretary of state, Arthur Zimmermann, and the chief of the English Department, Count George von Wedel. He made a favourable impression on both men and became particularly close to von Wedel, who remained his staunchest ally to the end.

Casement's arrival in Germany was nothing short of a personal declaration of war and the English newspapers carried largely invented stories of his intentions and whereabouts. The journal he started on 7 November, briefly recounting some of the more significant events and dates of his life since he had left Glasgow at the start of July, was frank about both his situation and his intentions to *{p}ut on record facts connected with my journey and its objects that may be of use hereafter. For it is not every day that even an Irishman commits High Treason – especially one who has been in the* *service of the sovereign he discards and not without honour and some fame in that service.* He kept reminding himself that it was for Ireland's sake that it was done – *a free Ireland, a world nation after centuries of slavery* – and his realization that it would mean that *{t}he 'Irish Question' will have been lifted from the mire and mud and petty, false strife of British domestic politics and into an international atmosphere.*[103] In those first days he drafted a *Declaration of German Intentions towards Ireland* which became the document defining diplomatic relations between Germany and an independent Ireland.

On 17 November, it was decided that Casement should visit the Western Front to speak directly with the German Chancellor, von Bethmann Hollweg and the Secretary of State, Ivon Jugow. That evening he left Berlin with Baron von Berckheim, Richard Meyer and a Prussian escort, Count Graf von Lutterich of the Volunteer Automobile Corps. Friedrich Street station was crowded with the walking wounded and stretchers loaded with bandaged bodies returning from the Front.

Early the following morning they reached Cologne. After a brief visit to the cathedral, they climbed into the car and began the bitterly cold journey. From the Eiffel region they climbed the bleak snow-capped ridges into northern Luxembourg and southern Belgium, and from there to Charleville-Mézières via Bastogne, Neufchâteau and Sédan – a distance of 270 kilometres completed in six hours. Casement had visited much of this area in May 1912 with Richard Morten and could make interesting comparisons of how it was then to how it was now: at Sédan, the bridge over the Meuse had been blown up and in Duchery *there was scarecely a house uninjured. The whole town lay there, roofless, empty and a mass of ruins.*[104]

On arriving at the former prefecture, now the headquarters of the German General Staff, the party met with General Kurt von Lersner, whom Casement had last seen in September at the Ritz-Carlton Hotel on Madison Avenue in New York. The conversation concentrated on the question of Irish prisoners of war. Von Lersner said that efforts were underway to separate the Irish from the English although it was often difficult to tell the 'Englanders' apart.

The following day Casement had an audience with Baron von Stumm and, after exchanging mutually hostile comments about both Grey and Findlay, they talked of Ireland. Casement spoke of his dream that an independent Ireland would emerge after the war, which would be of interest not just to Germany but to Europe as a whole. After an hour of discussion about future treaty settlements, the meeting ended with Casement noticeably invigorated by the exchange.

At about noon, Casement and his escort drove out of Charleville on the road to Rocroi. Almost all of the vehicles they encountered were military or Red Cross wagons. Skirting Rocroi they entered the hill country of the Ardennes. Despite the mist and wintry gloom, the scenery was spectacular. But when they rejoined the Meuse the natural beauty was replaced by the fresh scars of battle – burned houses, ruined bridges and vagrancy. After Givet, their vehicle crossed the frontier into Belgium and Casement was impressed by the efforts to rebuild damaged property despite the proximity to the border.

After lunch at Namur, they continued to Ardenne, the scene in late August of the largest battle in the invasion of Belgium. There, Casement was told how the Germans had shot 350 men because of an ambush of a German escort by Belgian *francs-tireurs*. He was taken to the wall against which the men had been shot and was moved almost to tears by the *pitiable evidences of a sorrow . . . Sometimes, I must confess, when the present 'agony of Belgium' confronts me – and it cannot well be minimized it is in truth a national agony – I feel that there may be in this awful lesson to the Belgian people a repayment. All that they now suffer and far more, they or their king, his government and his officers wreaked on the well-nigh defenceless people of the Congo basin.*[105]

The mass grave at Ardenne triggered an anger inside Casement that was released on the page as he described the return to Cologne. He reflected on the years of diplomatic duplicity that had brought Europe to this point. If his journey to the Congo might be considered the flashpoint which turned him vehemently against Empire, then at the grave at Ardenne he was turned with equal venom against *the vast conspiracy of murder that was war*.[106] If, as Carl von Clausewitz had argued, war was no longer an affair of princes and professional armies but an affair of the people, then Casement's sympathies lay with the people; victims, as he saw it, of incompetent leadership, corrupt government and secret diplomacy.

Moreover, at Ardenne, Casement's false position became all too clear. As a man interested in ideas of freedom, peace and justice, he now found himself trapped inside a space of hatred and death. Although he had only been in Germany for a few weeks, his doubts and concerns about his situation can be traced to this inspection of a mass grave. Over the next 18 months, he would go through the motions with the German government but in truth he was a broken man – as war condemns all those who seek peace, so Casement's efforts to offer a passive solution to Ireland were starting to flounder.

Back in Berlin, on 20 November, the German press announced the arrival of Sir Roger Casement in Germany. Beside it they gave notice of the document outlining the *Declaration of German intentions towards Ireland* and confirming the view that Germany desired only 'national prosperity and freedom' for Ireland.[107]

On 28 November, Casement wrote to Devoy that although everything was being done *to keep the truth out of Ireland*, he must see that the intentions of Germany were proclaimed *far and wide*. The real significance was that he had gained *international recognition*[108] for the cause of Irish independence.

At the same time, Casement continued to fuel the Findlay

conspiracy. To mislead the War Office and stimulate the escalating intrigue with the British secret services, he sent Christensen back to Norway *with two faked letters and some pages of my 'diary' he has 'stolen'*.[109]

In Whitehall, the question of Casement was now being treated very seriously. Both Kitchener and Churchill were kept closely informed. Cyphers were dispatched to embassies throughout Europe. The prevailing view, based partly on Casement's deliberate campaign of misinformation, was that he would either try and return to the US or make a break for Ireland.

By mid-December, the two heads of intelligence who would remain closely involved with British efforts to defeat Casement,

Captain Reginald Hall, inventive Head of Naval Intelligence, whose schemes did much for Britain's war efforts. A powerful opponent of Irish activities

the Chief of Naval Intelligence, Captain Reginald Hall, and the head of Scotland Yard's Criminal Investigation Department, Basil Thomson, began to collaborate. They chartered a yacht, the *Sayonara*, to sail up the west coast of Ireland trying to establish where Casement would land. Although their intelligence indicated that he was on the point of returning to Ireland to initiate rebellion, they had no idea where, when or how. Also, Britain decided to open up diplomatic links with the Vatican to counteract Casement's own movements in that direction and selected J D Gregory, who had collaborated closely with Casement on his Putumayo Mission Fund, as part of the diplomatic mission.

With German guarantees of Irish independence in place, Casement entered the next phase of his plan: to recruit Irish prisoners of war and train an Irish brigade. On 4 December, Casement visited the camp at Limburg and addressed a body of NCOs, all of them regular soldiers. The response was not very positive. Indeed, he recruited just two men: Sergeant MacMurrough and Corporal Timothy Quinlisk. Above all, his approach was at fault. Normal methods of recruitment to the Irish revolutionary cause demanded the selective approach of individuals but Casement decided to call the prisoners together and address them openly as one.

Two weeks later, Casement met the German Chancellor, von Bethmann Hollweg. The conversation was amicable and constructive, and it inspired Casement to compose ten articles for the founding of an Irish brigade to be armed and officered by Germany. Clause 8 however quite clearly set down the idea that the Brigade could be used *to expel the British from Egypt*, apparently contradicting Clause 2 which stated that the Brigade was to fight *solely in the cause of Ireland*.[110] Gradually, Casement's international agenda was being inscribed into the negotiations for national independence; such contradictions would later leave him highly vulnerable.

The German fleet had taken a serious blow off the Falkland Islands and the war itself had become mired in the trenches of the frontline in a strategic stalemate. Casement's concerns about German sincerity were now openly expressed in his private writings. He felt they lacked the *soul for great enterprises*,[111] a possible reference to his international aspirations. On Christmas Day 1914, he wrote to John Quinn *I am a refugee, an outcast with no place to lay my head when this present war is over. The enemy would hang me – that I know – & he dominates so much of the earth that I shall not be very safe in many parts of the world – even could I get there.*[112]

On 5 January he made another visit to the Limburg camp.

This time, the reaction was openly hostile; his hopes for an Irish brigade were failing, as his confidence in the German General Staff ebbed away. Even his dependable friends Richard Meyer and Count von Wedel were trying his patience. Hints of paranoia started to permeate his journal as his recruitment efforts floundered and his despondency with the war deepened.

Casement's conspiracy with Christensen now involved the elaborate concoction of a faked plan of invasion and forged maps of minefields intended to deliberately sabotage Britain's war effort. Findlay, however, fell for the plans without hesitation and trusted Christensen to the point of writing out a receipt offering a reward of £5,000 for Casement's capture. Casement's fury might be gauged by the letter he wrote to Sir Edward Grey on 1 February in which he set down the facts of the Findlay affair and renounced all his honours including his knighthood. Copies of the letter were circulated to a number of embassies and printed up for general distribution through the German and Irish propaganda networks. Casement made his position clear: *I served the British government faithfully as long as it was possible for me to do so, and when it became impossible for me to use the pension assigned me by law I voluntarily abandoned that income as I had previously resigned the post from which it was derived.*[113]

The battle for hearts and minds became a major point of contention in Anglo-Irish relations during World War I

It is out of this situation of war-weariness and self-confessed *high treason* that his last bout of propaganda poured, writings that revealed things about Imperial foreign policy that remained 'unspeakable' until today. Besides a desperate trail of death, the winds of war also unleashed a bitter battle of representation to justify positions and mass slaughter. Efforts to exonerate military action and demonize the enemy inspired a culture of atrocity stories central to the propaganda battle.

Casement's work in both the Congo and Putumayo had made him an authority on the use of atrocity reports for political and diplomatic ends. Shortly after the outbreak of war, the highly respected historian and former British Ambassador, James Bryce, had been selected by Prime Minister Asquith to draw up a report on German atrocities in Belgium. The publication of the Bryce report in May 1915, in the same week as the sinking of the *Lusitania*, had a tremendous impact throughout the world in suffocating any pro-German sympathy. Casement and Bryce had collaborated discreetly over atrocity questions from their earliest meeting in Africa in 1894.

Casement's response to the Bryce report was published in *The Continental Times*, an English language newspaper in Berlin. He adopted a new set of pseudonyms to conceal himself and reveal the secrets of imperial government. His main attacks were launched at the most senior officials, including Sir Edward Grey and Bryce himself. The key to decrypting the bitter depths of the propaganda engagement between Casement and Whitehall leading up to his execution can be found in these writings, in particular his essay 'The Far-Extended Baleful Power of the Lie'. Here Casement attacked Bryce as a historian, as a witness, and, most controversially, as the wielder of a *lie*.[114]

Casement's accusations were counteracted through the far greater circulation of British and American newspapers. A gradual process of demonization portrayed Casement as a 'pro-Germanist' in receipt of 'German gold' and as 'mad' or 'insane'.[115] In the public mind, the status he had earned as the defender of the dispossessed began to evaporate. His position, along with the cause of advanced nationalism, was further weakened by the closure of the 'seditious' Irish papers including *The Irish Volunteer*, *Sinn Féin* and *The Irish Worker*. Until today, most of Casement's writings from this period are still unknown and remain a missing dimension of his work.

By the late spring of 1915, a number of changes were under way among the Irish nationalist leadership. Casement's lines of communication with Devoy and McGarrity were no longer safe, hampered by unpredictable time delays – some messages never arrived at all – or intercepted by British code-breakers. In late April, Joseph Mary Plunkett arrived in Berlin as the appointed emissary of the IRB and breathed new life into efforts at Zossen to make the Irish Brigade a reality. In the Volunteer movement, Pearse and Clarke were gradually starting to suborn the leadership from the control of Casement's trusted allies, MacNeill and Hobson. In London the formation of a coalition government had brought Unionist hardliners into the cabinet, including Casement's two most vehement political enemies Sir Edward Carson and F E Smith.

Casement spent part of the summer in Munich in discussion with the American Consul-General, in a futile campaign denouncing President Woodrow Wilson's foreign policy. He escaped for a few weeks of relaxation to Amersee, with another new acquaintance, Dr Charles E Curry, renting a couple of rooms in a local inn and quietly passing his days writing and walking.

Christensen returned to Berlin in October, having safely escorted Robert Monteith from the US. Monteith, a former British soldier and well known to the authorities as a trouble-maker, had personally undertaken the training of the Limerick Volunteers in 1914 and he began drilling the men immediately. Once again, plans were discussed about sending the Brigade to fight for the liberation of Egypt, encouraged by Casement's acquaintance with some Egyptian nationalists lobbying for German support.

However, Casement's deep despondency with the world crisis

was propelling him towards a state of nervous exhaustion. On 27 December 1915, he wrote: *I wish very much that Peace would come – it is dreadful to think of all the world beginning a New Year with nothing but death – killing and murdering wholesale and destroying all that makes life happy.*[116] For a man who had worked to heal differences, to enlighten governments and to unite people behind common endeavour, the war was increasingly intolerable. His nerves shattered, in mid-January 1916, he began a month of convalescence at a sanatorium near Munich.

Robert Monteith in the uniform of the Irish Volunteers designed by Casement

By early March, it was clear that revolution in Ireland was imminent. It was now a question of negotiating some final position with the German government. On 17 March, Casement began a daily journal to record his narrative of events *in order that some day the truth may be known.*[117] Plans moved quickly but the German admiralty put up objections. It was clear though that he held out little hope and saw the venture as doomed; more worthless bloodletting which had no hope of success without the right military commitment from Germany. His own position was no better, and as a self-confessed revolutionary, he had no option but to return to meet his uncertain fate.

After initial refusals, the German admiralty finally agreed to send Casement back in a submarine. Through their negotiations with Devoy in the US, they were also prepared to send a 1,200-ton steamer, the *Aud* with 20,000 guns. Casement's request for German soldiers, especially officers, was refused and it was decided that the Irish Brigade would remain in Germany.

Casement's return to Ireland aboard a submarine (U-Boat) was highly controversial. From the outset of war, Britain had tried to have the submarine outlawed as a violation of the rules of international warfare as its own submarine technology lagged behind that of the US and Germany.

The inventor of the modern submarine, John Philip Holland (1841–1914) was an Irishman with overt Fenian sympathies. In the 1870s, Holland approached Clan na Gael leaders in America with proposals to build a submarine for use against British naval vessels: various proto-types were developed for such purposes, notably the *Fenian Ram*. By the late 1890s, he was building submarines for the US navy and, later, Japan.

Holland's hope that the submarine could be used as a deterrent to war proved unrealistic after the outbreak of hostilities in 1914 when German U-Boats started sinking British cruisers including the *Lusitania*. Raimund Weisbach, Captain of the U-19 which conveyed Casement to Ireland, had fired the torpedo which sank the passenger liner.

At the end of March, Casement wrote to Count von Wedel explaining the hopelessness of the situation in which he now found himself. He realized that the decision taken by Devoy in the US to mount a revolution in Ireland was doomed without the right military guarantees from Germany. He wrote: *I have always opposed such a course unless assured of ample external military aid – an assurance wholly impossible today . . . I do not think anyone was ever put in a more atrocious position. Whatever I do must of necessity be wrong and must hurt someone no less than be contrary either to my reason, judgment or instinct.*[118]

Before leaving Berlin, Casement made careful provisions for his papers, in particular the treaty guaranteeing Irish independence. He sent a long, encrypted letter to Dr Curry from the Hotel Saxonia on 3 April, providing blunt instructions about his papers and telling him to bury his *verses* (journals and treaty) in oiled silk and publish his narrative after the war so that people would know that his actions were based *on unselfish regard for what he thought to be the welfare of his country.*[119]

On 9 April, the *Aud* cast off from Lübeck under the command of Lieutenant Karl Spindler. After initial mechanical difficulties with the first submarine, on 15 April Casement boarded the U-19 at Heligoland accompanied by Robert Monteith. Heading across the North Sea between Norway and the Shetland Islands, the great iron hulk navigated south of the Faroe Islands, passed the Hebrides and St Kilda, before arriving in Tralee bay shortly after midnight on Good Friday, 21 April.

The Irish Brigade raised from amongst the Irish prisoners of war in Germany ultimately did not return with Casement to join in *'the Rising'*

Easter Rising

In the early morning of Good Friday 1916, Casement, Monteith and a third man called Daniel Bailey, scrambled off the U-19 into a rowing boat and bade their farewells to the German crew. After almost two hours of hard rowing through the swell and waves that at one point capsized the vessel, just before dawn, soaked and

exhausted, they washed up on the long stretch of beach at Banna Strand in County Kerry. Their planned liaison with the *Aud* and the armaments shipment had failed, and no Volunteers were there to meet them. Stopping only briefly to decide their next move, they pushed on through the fog, across the grass-

Casement's Fort where he was arrested on Good Friday 1916

covered dunes and coastal marshes of Carrahane to an ancient *rath* (ring fort) where Monteith and Bailey left Casement and set off separately in search of help.

At 1.20pm, two constables from the Royal Irish Constabulary, after a tip-off about strange men on the beach, found Casement. Asked to identify himself, he replied that he was an author called Richard Morten researching a life of the mariner-monk St Brendan. The story failed to convince the policemen, and he was duly arrested.

Casement was taken in a pony and trap to the small police station at Ardfert and, later that afternoon, to Tralee where he was held overnight. He spent much of the evening chatting to

Chief Constable Kearney, who showed him much kindness, dried his clothes and warmed him by the fire. The two men talked at length about the war, politics and Irish affairs, and Kearney guessed at the prisoner's real identity. Although Casement contemplated taking his own life, the generosity shown to him by the constable counteracted such action. He was also permitted to see a priest and through him was able to communicate a message to the Volunteer command in the hope of getting MacNeill to call 'the Rising' off.

The following morning Casement was escorted openly through the streets of Tralee to the railway station and from there via Mallow to Dublin. At Arbour Hill barracks, he was taken into custody and after some rough handling endured a brief interrogation from a man Casement later described as *dressed like a gentleman – but not one*.[120] He was strip-searched but still refused to make any statement or admit his identity until he had legal representation: by now the authorities were sure they had their man. Later that afternoon, under a heavily armed escort he was accompanied in a motor ambulance to the port at Kingstown and then by boat to Holyhead. Early on Easter Sunday, he arrived in England and took the Irish mail train as far as Willesden Junction where he was handed over to the Special Branch and taken to Scotland Yard.

Later that morning, in a nondescript room in Whitehall, Casement met the three intelligence chiefs who had been tracking him

Sir Basil Thomson (1861–1939), the other Intelligence chief devoted to the overthrow of Casement

since the end of 1914: Captain Reginald 'Blinker' Hall, Basil

Room 40 was set up on the outbreak of war in 1914 to intercept and decipher enemy wireless signals. Its code-breaking activities remained closely guarded secrets, known only to the Admiralty and the Naval and Military Commanders-in-Chief. Those who worked in it were recruited mainly from the intellectual elite, such as the Cambridge historian F E Adcock. Room 40 made a vital contribution to several British naval engagements including the battle of Jutland and it was clearly aware of plans for an Irish rebellion well in advance of the outbreak.

Thomson and Major Frank Hall. Blinker Hall was a highly capable naval officer – cunning, prankish and ruthless. His intelligence strategies, devised in Room 40, proved a winning card in Britain's war effort, and his department had successfully intercepted vital cyphers about Irish revolutionary activity in the US over the previous months. Thomson was a different style of man, possessed of that air of superiority which defined the imperial ruling class and which Casement so despised. The third man, Major Frank Hall, was a senior officer in Military Intelligence who had played a leading role in the organization of the Ulster Volunteers and the running of guns into Larne for the UVF in 1914, serving as military secretary to the Ulster Volunteers.[121] Together they were a formidable team of interrogators, each of them as devoted to maintaining the British Empire as they were opposed to those who subverted it. Clearly, to all of these men, Casement represented everything they detested most about Ireland.

As the son of an Archbishop of York, Basil Home Thomson (1861–1939) was destined for high places in the British imperial hierarchy. An official in the Colonial Office, he was chosen (aged 29) to serve as Prime Minister of Tonga.

In 1896 he entered the prison service in Liverpool and built up a new career as a prison governor until his recruitment into Scotland Yard to head up Special Branch. He was particularly severe in his treatment of suffragettes, syndicalists and Irish sympathizers.

Casement was interrogated on three separate occasions over three consecutive days. According to the official transcripts which recorded some of the exchanges, the tone was generally amicable, although Casement was clearly shocked by his ordeal: *I was dazed and absolutely incapable of thinking clearly on any subject but the one – how in the name of God, to still stop the rising without doing a mean or cowardly thing or giving any man away.*[122]

Casement's preoccupation was still to forward a message to Dublin to abort 'the Rising' but it received no sympathy. His interrogators clearly had other plans claiming that they 'knew all'[123] and that it would be preferable to let the rebellion go ahead so that the insurgents could be dealt with accordingly.[124] The conversation then ranged across issues including Casement's views on Germany, his recruitment efforts and the exact nature of a 'diary' found in his possession when he was captured. At the end of the first interview, he was informed that he was being held under the Defence of the Realm Act and was then driven over the Thames and placed in Brixton prison, where he was jailed under another name so he would not be identified and the news of his capture released to the press.

Early the following morning he returned to the room for further cross-examination. This time, the interrogation took a more formal course. He was told that Bailey had also been captured and that they knew the identity of the other man, Monteith. There was then further talk of the Irish brigade and Casement's activities in Germany.

Shortly after the end of Casement's second interrogation, the Easter Rising began in Dublin. Although MacNeill tried to cancel all mobilization

The Easter Rising wreaked havoc in central Dublin for a week in 1916

plans when news of Casement's capture and the scuppering of the *Aud* had been received, those orders had been reversed by a secret military council at a meeting at Liberty Hall.

At noon, a group of Volunteers from both the *Oglaigh na-hÉireann*, led by Commandant-General Pearse, and the Citizen Army, led by Commandant-General James Connolly, took control of the General Post Office in O'Connell Street. Two flags were raised over the building: a gold harp against a green background – the emblem of the United Irish – and the now familiar tricolour of green, white and orange. Then Pearse appeared on the steps and read the Proclamation of the Republic.

Eamon de Valera (1882–1975) was Ireland's most significant politician of the 20th century. Although born in New York, he grew up in County Limerick and under Casement's influence was active in the build-up to rebellion. He served as *Taoiseach* (prime minister) from 1937–48, 1951–4 and 1957–9, before assuming presidency of the country from 1959–73.

More strategic positions were taken by other rebel battalions, as a coordinated plan of occupation took control of the city centre. The first Battalion under Edward Daly occupied the Four Courts and surrounding streets. The second Battallion under Thomas MacDonagh, took control of the Jacob's biscuit factory and posted a contingent of the Citizen Army to St Stephen's Green, under Commandant Michael Mallin and the Countess Markiewicz, before they were forced to retreat to the College of Surgeons. Boland's flour mill and the railway from Lansdowne Road to Westland Row station was held by the professor of mathematics, Eamon de Valera.

Eamonn Ceant

Commandant Eamonn Ceant and Cathal Brugha occupied the South Dublin Union and surrounding districts. Within just a few hours, Dublin had ground to a standstill and British forces, caught unawares, gradually took up siege positions in an effort to regain control of the city. By the late afternoon, 2,500 British reinforcements had arrived from the Curragh camp.

After another night in Brixton prison, Casement returned for his last interview and was immediately informed by Basil Thomson of the news from Dublin. Once again the questions concentrated on Casement's activities in Germany, his efforts to raise support in the US, how he had heard about 'the Rising' and minor details on the shipment of arms.

With his interrogators apparently satisfied that they were in control of the situation, he was escorted to the Tower of London and placed in military custody. In the afternoon, the three days of official silence were finally broken with the issuing of a statement to the press. The following day newspapers across the world carried the story of the attempted landing of arms, the capture of Casement, the bombing of East Anglia by German Zeppelins and the rebellion in Dublin. The Chief Secretary of Ireland, Augustine Birrell declared a state of emergency throughout the country.

That afternoon the Houses of Parliament were in an excited uproar; many members were dressed in fatigues. When a newly elected MP, Noel Pemberton Billing, stood up and asked the prime minister if Roger Casement had been brought to London and if could he give 'this house and the nation an assurance that this traitor will be shot forthwith'[125], Asquith answered that it was an inappropriate question. At that point, the Houses of Parliament entered a 'secret session' for the first time during the war. The Press and Strangers galleries in both chambers were cleared, and Lords and Commoners were given strict instructions as to what they might record of the ensuing debates. (At the time of writing, the official record of this session remains secret.)

On 26 April, Lord Lansdowne gave the first official account of Casement's capture. Concerns were raised in both chambers that the 'Sinn Féin Rebellion' as it was termed, had been in the making for several years and that the government had failed to act. A few members went further and suggested that the rebellion had been deliberately allowed to take place. An operation was quickly mounted in England to interrogate anyone suspected of sympathizing with the rebels. On 27 April, Alice Stopford Green's house in Grosvenor Road was searched and she was taken in for questioning.

The authorities maintained control of the situation until 3.30pm, Saturday 29 April when Commandant-General Pearse, wearing the uniform of the Volunteers, surrendered by handing over his sword. Connolly, badly wounded in the ankle, was taken to Dublin Castle along with other captured leaders. Over the next 24 hours, all remaining pockets of resistance surrendered unconditionally. The five-day insurrection had seen some random killing by both sides and some heavy shelling of rebel strongholds by the army. Hundreds were rounded up, identified and duly taken to Kilmainham Jail to be tried before a military tribunal.

By this time, Major-General Sir John Maxwell had arrived from England as Commander-in-Chief to take control of the secret military tribunals. Birrell had little option but to resign and in his final report he wrote: 'It is not an Irish rebellion. It would be a pity if *ex post facto* it became one, and was added to the long and melancholy list of Irish rebellions.'[126]

The rising had many different components. The leaders themselves comprised a number of poets and intellectuals such as the headmaster, Patrick Pearse, the university lecturer, Thomas MacDonagh, and the poet, Joseph Mary Plunkett. There were also hard-line veteran Fenians such as Tom Clarke, as well as a significant socialist element personified by the Scottish-born

Irishman James Connolly (1868–1916). Women were represented most obviously by the figure of Constance, Countess Markiewicz. Indeed, the tactical build-up to rebellion and the proclamation itself had very deliberately included women as equal citizens in the idealized vision for a new republican society.

The tactics themselves are worthy of consideration. The signs and symbols of insurrection can be detected in the first conversations of the Gaelic League in the 1890s, in the poetry and plays of W B Yeats, and, most emphatically, in the underground press. The quest for historical symbolism might also be divined in the deliberate connection of the event with the Easter cycle of sacrifice and rebirth. Although 'the Rising' is often derided for its tactical and military incompetence, it was deliberately intended to capture the imagination of both Irish and world opinion. In this way, it often seems like a piece of 'street theatre',[127] with staged effects leading to a tragic

Patrick Pearse (1879–1916), public educator and revolutionary, has become in the popular version of modern Irish history the chosen leader of the 1916 rebellion. His cultural nationalism, embodied in his writings and poetry, extends from his work for the Gaelic League and as headmaster of St Enda's school. His public rhetoric in the months leading up to 'the Rising', most notably his oration beside the grave of O'Donovan Rossa (1831–1915), and his belief in the need for 'blood sacrifice' if Ireland was to achieve its freedom, remain the most controversial aspects of his teachings.

Poster of the 1916 leaders

finale. Nineteen-sixteen was a moment which would translate well into theatre, song and ballads as well as serving as a modern foundation for the long struggle for Irish independence.

While media coverage during 'the Rising' had been scarce, once it was all over the public fascination grew. In a press largely sympathetic to the Union and Empire, 1916 was perceived as an act of insanity and the participants widely dismissed as 'mad' and full of 'crank notions.'[128] *The Cork Examiner* branded 'the Rising' a 'communistic disturbance rather than a revolutionary movement'.[129] Above all, it was an act in defiance of an Empire that was at that very moment fighting for its own survival on the Western Front. None the less, since much of the intellectual discourse underpinning the rebellion had been expressed in the underground press, the philosophies and ideologies of the rebel leaders were obscure and misunderstood.

On 3 May, Prime Minister Asquith announced that three of the signatories of the Republican Proclamation, P H Pearse, Thomas J Clarke and Thomas MacDonagh had been tried by secret military courts-martial, found guilty and shot dead in Kilmainham Jail. The statement was followed by a question from the floor inquiring about Casement who as 'the forerunner of this movement' deserved similar treatment.[130] The government, however, remained tight-lipped on the issue of Casement's ultimate fate. Over the next nine days, another dozen rebel leaders were shot following a series of secret tribunals that ended on 12 May with the execution of the badly wounded James Connolly strapped unceremoniously to a chair.[131]

Throughout this time, Casement languished in the Tower of London in solitary confinement and unable to communicate with the outside world. He refused to eat as long as he was denied legal representation and once more made an effort to commit suicide by rubbing curare into a self-inflicted wound. Outside, there were desperate efforts to extract any information from the authorities about his condition. Alice Stopford Green tried to gain access through her connections with the Home Secretary, Herbert Samuel. Pressure was exerted from the US but the situation was hampered by a death threat sent to the British Ambassador in America, Cecil Spring-Rice (the brother of Mary Spring-Rice who ran guns into Ireland with Erskine Childers in 1914) threatening that if Casement was executed he would be assassinated. On 9 May, a young solicitor sympathetic to the Sinn Féin cause, George Gavan Duffy, finally gained access to Casement. Their meeting was brief and the conversation supervised, but Duffy was instructed to represent Casement and prepare his defence. He was clearly shocked by the state of the prisoner and later recorded:

'He was suffering from acute mental strain, as a result of the rigorous confinement in which he had been kept during the previous fortnight, the interrogations to which he had (despite his appeal for independent advice) been subjected while in great distress of mind and body and the exclusion of every relative and friend. He told me that he had been allowed no change of clothing nor underclothing, and that he had worn the same garments for about four weeks, though his relations had shortly after his arrest offered in writing to supply him with everything he might need; he appeared to me to be very ill and he looked so haggard and so worn that I had difficulty persuading myself of his identity with Sir Roger Casement whom I had known some three years before.'[132]

Duffy wasted no time. First, he wrote to the director of Public Prosecutions reporting his meeting with Casement and requesting notification as to the precise legal position. The reply was that a decision had been taken to hand Casement over to the civil authorities for trial for high treason committed with and without the realm and that arrangements were underway to have him transferred from the Tower and moved from military into civil custody.

Duffy then set about engaging a legal team capable of defending Casement and selected first of all Artemus Jones, a Welsh lawyer of some prominence. Together they visited Casement in the Tower and, for the purposes of the interview, were placed in a side room with a guard posted outside the door observing everything through a glass panel. Jones later recalled the conversation and how he was struck by Casement's open avowal that he was quite happy *to die a thousand times for the sake of Ireland*[133] and well understood that a verdict of guilty for high treason meant death. In other words, the counsel for the defence was faced by a case that made a mockery of the law: a client who openly admitted to the crime for which he was being charged and was content if not eager to suffer the ultimate penalty for his political actions.

The other legal expert prepared to take up a position on behalf of Casement was another Welshman, Professor J H Morgan (1876–1955). Through Richard Morten, he had met Casement as early as 1904 and the two had corresponded on Irish constitutional matters during the Home Rule crisis.[134] In 1914, Morgan had written to Casement congratulating him on his work for Ireland and Casement had trusted Morgan enough to share many of his views on both Irish and international affairs. Moreover, his professional qualifications could not have been more appropriate. Morgan was a Professor of Constitutional Law at the Inns of Court and for some years had been at the heart of the constitutional discussion on Ireland. In 1912 he had edited a work entitled *The New Irish Constitution* containing contributions from leading political voices. At the outbreak of war, Morgan was appointed to the Adjutant-General's staff as Home Office Representative with the British expeditionary force. He was involved in the discussion on the Defence of the Realm Act and collaborated with James Bryce on the report on German atrocities. In early 1916 he put his name to a publication entitled *German Atrocities: An Official Investigation*, a work that was reprinted several times.

On 10 May Casement's name once again echoed through the Commons when the Irish MP John Dillon asked the prime minister to explain 'why Sir Roger Casement has been brought to London, and is apparently to have a public trial before a civil tribunal, whilst comparatively obscure men whom he has been largely responsible for seducing into rebellion have been sentenced and executed in Ireland by secret military tribunal.'[135] Asquith replied that since the matter was about to go to trial he preferred not to answer. However, the atmosphere of secrecy that was now building up around Casement only served to exacerbate public curiosity.

The following day, 11 May, a heated debate took place in both chambers of parliament. Strong criticism was levelled against the government policy of secrecy surrounding the executions, which Dillon claimed was 'poisoning the mind of Ireland'.[136] Asquith's defence of General Maxwell for 'discretion, depth of mind and humanity'[137] in the discharge of his duties convinced few that the government was in control. The Irish barrister and politician, T M Healy commented that the government policy was 'insane'.[138] Clearly, he argued, the reaction of the authorities was playing directly into the hands of the rebels and their cause.

Casement's defence began with his dictation of an autobiography to establish the chronology and narrative of his life. During the following weeks, this *brief* would go through a series of updates and amendments in preparation for the trial but it survives as an extraordinary insight into how Casement understood his own political evolution from loyal Imperial servant into anti-Imperial revolutionary. Although he declared that it only touched *the fringe of things*, it is revelatory as much for what it silences as for what it says.[139]

During a half century of life, Casement had walked beside the most illustrious men and women of his age. His association with Africa during that pivotal moment of the 'civilizing project' created at the Berlin conference to the exposure of the deceit of Leopold II's colonial administration backed by the false promises of the European Empire builders, had no parallel. Casement asserted that by 1900, after 16 years in Africa, *I . . . had come to look upon myself as an African.*[140] He also admitted that in 1905, after his active association with the Gaelic League and other nationalist causes *I . . . became a Sinn Féiner in political thought.*[141] In both of these confessions and in the context of his times, he transgressed the acceptable perimeters of his colour and class. He made elliptical references to his work *in other capacities*[142] while in Africa, and though there were brief comments about his 'special mission' during the Boer War there was no mention of his years spent watching for the movement of arms into enemy territory.

Casement had perfected the art of dissimulation. While seeming to be a dutiful Imperial servant of the Crown, he had, in fact, spent years undermining the very authority which he had been empowered to maintain. In the closing comments in his *brief*, he demanded that his own writings be used as evidence to expose his *treason.*[143] In other words, it was through the public understanding of his act that he sought ultimate victory.

If the Crown read out 'The Crime Against Ireland' etc. they will certainly be able to show that the idea of German help & of Germany beating England was in my mind as long ago as 1911 – August 1911. They would make a great point of that – on the other hand, the 'crime' is so damaging an exposure of English methods in Ireland & so strong an appeal to the right and duty of fighting for freedom that I am quite content to have the 'crime' figure as the chief item against me – as in truth it is. If read in court and reported in the press it goes all over the world and it will in the end bring more converts to my cause than are dreamed of today.[144]

In the secret corridors of power, the real dimensions of

Casement's 'treason' were at last becoming clear. The Imperial authorities were faced by a man who had deliberately used his official powers for his emerging revolutionary purposes. His indelible, if subversive, achievement was to have placed on the official empirical record the very evidence that would condemn those imperial systems as exploitative and reckless. His anonymous writings, hidden in the archives of seditious publications, exposed a far more extensive revolutionary network than even his most subversive Irish friends had realized. As early as 1905, Casement had penned articles linking 'causes' as diverse as the Swadeshi movement in India with colonial resistance in South America, and the Mexican revolution to progressive ideas on socialism, feminism, spirituality and ethnicity. His plan to send the Irish brigade to fight for Egypt was based on a strategy that clearly reached beyond the borders of Egypt. There was irony too in the fact that his friend and collaborator in Congo reform, E D Morel, was now running the pacifist anti-war Union for Democratic Control in Britain, supported by some of the most radical intellectuals of the day including Bertrand Russell and Norman Angell.

Over the following months, other powerful voices would weigh in behind the campaign to save Casement from the scaffold. Added to this were questions of war-weariness, a general reaction to the ruthless execution of the leaders in Dublin and the fact that many of those in the highest positions of power had formerly been great supporters and advocates of Casement's work. In their handling of their prisoner, the authorities were faced not with a regular execution of one more Irish 'rebel' but the overthrow of a revolutionary leviathan. Casement's life and spirit threatened the very reputation of the Empire as no other figure in modern British history. It was understandable that the authorities would enlist every legal heavyweight for maximum effect.

Beneath the statement by his counsel 'He will plead not guilty' Casement wrote with some confidence: *I would prefer to plead guilty, but as I am advised that would be a most improper step under such circumstances and such a charge, I would say let the Crown prove its case.*[145]

Proclamation of the Republic

The Trial and Execution

At 7am on 15 May, police officers entered Casement's cell at the
Tower of London and informed
the prisoner that they had a
warrant for his arrest. He was
then handed over to the civil
authorities, thereby passing from
military into civil custody.

Later that morning, Casement
arrived at Bow Street Police
Magistrates Court for the magisterial inquiry presided over by
the Chief Metropolitan Police

Casement arriving at Bow Street
Magistrates Court, London
15 May 1916

Magistrate, Sir John Dickinson. The cramped courtroom was
packed with both Casement's devoted allies and his inquisitive
enemies, mingling in the same space.

To the surprise of many, the case for the Crown would be conducted by the flamboyant Attorney-General, F E Smith. Smith's

F E Smith (1872–1930) was the
legal heavyweight of his age. In
January 1906 he became a
Conservative MP and by 1910 he
had formed important political
alliances with both Winston
Churchill and Edward Carson, and
opposed the Home Rule Bill. The
following year he 'galloped for
Carson' at a review of the Ulster
Volunteers. In late 1913 and early

1914, he began to negotiate the
partition and division of Ireland
into two sectarian-based statelets.
With the outbreak of war, he
accepted the post of head of the
Press Bureau, and helped to formulate the government's propaganda strategies. Towards the end
of 1915, he succeeded Carson as
Attorney-General, and later became Lord Chancellor.

leading role alongside Edward Carson in the founding of the Ulster Volunteers made his selection, to say the least, controversial. The novelist, H G Wells considered it a 'shocking conjunction'.[146] Flanking Smith sat an impressive support counsel. On one side was Archibald Bodkin, a specialist in espionage cases. On the other was Travers Humphreys, who had first come to prominence as junior counsel in the trial of Oscar Wilde. The fashionable combination of Smith, Bodkin and Humphreys sent out a psychological message to the public as to the 'type' of criminal in the dock.

The first surprise for Casement's legal representation was that he was to be tried alongside Daniel Bailey – a move that unsettled the defence and was done in order to diminish Casement's status in the public mind. On the opening day, witnesses were called to give evidence on the circumstances of Casement's arrest. In the afternoon, Casement was escorted to Brixton prison hospital, in the diocese of Southwark. On signing himself into prison he gave his religion as Catholic and that night ate his first proper meal since arriving in London almost three weeks earlier.

Back in the dock, Casement listened to soldiers openly discuss his recruitment efforts at Limburg. They were followed by what the newspapers described as 'Kerry peasants and policemen . . . evidently filled with subdued pride at the part they were suddenly called upon to play before a world audience.'[147] Throughout, Casement sat quietly scribbling pages of notes.

The last day of the hearing ended with Lieutenant-Colonel Philip Gordon, attached to the Director of Military Intelligence at the War Office, offering his opinion on the 14 sections of maps found in the rowing boat on Banna Strand. Both prisoners were then committed for trial, with the Attorney-General stressing that this should happen at the earliest opportunity.

Casement's defence was disadvantaged on almost every level. Their most immediate problem was deciding who should defend Casement. At a meeting at Duffy's rooms in the Inns of Court a few hours after the end of the hearing, it became obvious that the various discreet approaches made to barristers sympathetic to the cause of Irish nationalism, such as T M Healy, had been blankly refused. Prominent English lawyers also declined. As the options narrowed, Duffy looked more and more towards his brother-in-law, Sergeant Alexander Sullivan, as the only viable option.

Casement's defence team, including Sergeant A M Sullivan, arriving at the Old Bailey

Sullivan was the son of A M Sullivan, one of the leading intellectuals of the Young Ireland movement and best known as proprietor of *The Nation* (1855–74) and for his work *Speeches from the Dock* (1867). This book, well known

The tradition of speeches from the dock is an important source for understanding the historical differences between England and Ireland. Although the judiciary was generally reluctant to allow convicted felons the opportunity to have their oratorical moment of glory, political trials could be staged so that prisoners remained silent until after sentence, when they were allowed a brief statement.

The first edition of *Speeches from the dock or protests of Irish patriotism* by T D, A M and D B Sullivan (1867) was a bible for Irish nationalists and was widely influential in broadening public understanding of the 'sealed volume' of Irish history. It functioned as a nationalist martyrology serving above all the cause of propaganda. Its origins lie in the speeches of the United Irish leaders of 1798: William Orr, Wolfe Tone, Thomas Russell and, famously, Robert Emmet. Casement's trial speech deliberately drew on and echoed this tradition: in several later editions of the Sullivans' work published after 1916, his speech was added to the anthology.

to Casement, was an anthology of last words by leading Irish patriots who had fallen victim to British 'law and justice' in pursuit of a united and independent Ireland.

The combination of Gavan Duffy and A M Sullivan as the chief representatives of Casement's legal team inextricably connected the defence to the historical cause of the Young Ireland movement. However, while his name and pedigree might have suited Casement's 'historic' cause, Sullivan's own sympathies ran contrary to it. He had only recently worked on the council encouraging Irishmen to join the British forces and it was inevitable that there would be tensions between the two men.

The dimension of 'history' would play a central role in the proceedings and the prosecution was aware of this fact. In his opening address at the magisterial hearing, F E Smith referred to Casement's 'considerable knowledge of history'[148] – a line he chose to suppress at the trial.

From her first meeting with Casement at Brixton prison, Alice Stopford Green began compiling a list of historical precedents to support his case. She also used her knowledge and influence in other ways. She wrote to the authorities complaining of Casement's treatment under military custody and how the refusal to grant him legal representation until a week before his trial had seriously handicapped the defence. In a letter to Prime Minister Asquith, she sought to break through the blockade of censorship that prevented any of her correspondence reaching the US, where further legal and financial support might be found. But the net was clearly starting to draw around Casement and the stonewall of officialdom remained oblivious to either complaints or demands.

On 25 May, the Grand Jury was sworn in before the Lord Chief Justice, Rufus Isaacs, at the High Court. Casement was charged with six overt acts of treason and in each case true bills were found by the jury. The trial was scheduled to open at the

Old Bailey on 26 June. Gavan Duffy then applied for counsel to be assigned to Casement in accordance with the Treason Act (1747). He asked that Sergeant A M Sullivan, King's Counsel of the Irish bar, Artemus Jones and J H Morgan be appointed as counsel and that he and the American lawyer, Michael Francis Doyle, serve as solicitors. The Lord Chief Justice appointed Sullivan and Jones to the defence, saying that Morgan could act in a special advisory capacity as *amicus curiae*.

Graphic from 20 May 1916

The press, under the tight control of the hidden powers of war propaganda, played an increasingly influential role in the battle for turning public sympathy against Casement. From the moment he entered Brixton prison and his imprisonment became public knowledge, they began to construct a narrative in line with the official versions of events. On 20 May, *The Graphic*, an illustrated weekly journal with openly anti-Casement credentials, published a double-page spread intended to condemn him in advance of the trial: it stressed his pro-German rather than his pro-Irish activities; his heroic work exposing atrocities in Africa and South America was expunged from the record; and a new vocabulary emerged to fuel the increasingly lurid coverage of the story, most obviously the word 'seduce' (with its sexual connotations) became the term to describe Casement's efforts to recruit Irish prisoners of war to fight for his brigade. Whatever their form, attacks on Casement were presented as patriotic while any effort to defend him was portrayed as potentially treacherous, or sympathetic to the enemy.

As a playwright, critic and active socialist, George Bernard Shaw (1856–1950) was one of the most influential voices of the age. He made several interventions to heighten public awareness of the distinctive nature of Casement's 'treason' and the sincerity of his diplomatic mission to Germany on behalf of Irish independence. However, Shaw's views on Casement, while often original, were uninformed about the extent of his work for the Foreign Office or his involvement with nationalist activity from as early as 1904.

Nevertheless a few highly influential intellectuals and opinion-makers ignored the version propagated by the popular press.[149] Of these, Casement's most active ally was George Bernard Shaw. Although Shaw was a critic of Sinn Féin, his sympathies were changed by the secret military tribunals and the execution of the 1916 leaders, which, he felt, played directly into the hands of the extremists. In early May he was approached by Gertrude Bannister and, trusting her sincerity, he decided to become involved.

Connections between Shaw and Casement can be traced to *John Bull's Other Island,* a work to which Casement frequently referred in his prison writings, and significant for its references in the 'Preface' to the Mansfeldt de Findlay role in the Denshawi affair. Casement had himself written a short anti-Imperial pamphlet, *John Bull's Other Empire*, claiming that all empires must eventually pay a heavy price for their greed and lust for domination.

Shaw had high hopes for Casement's defence, not least a desire to write a plan for his defence and his speech from the dock in a way that would leave little doubt of the conflict of allegiances facing the Irish as a result of the war.[150] In his astute summary of the legal options, Shaw suggested that Casement had three possible lines of defence: he could plead insanity for which medical evidence would be required; he could throw himself at the mercy of the court and plead leniency based on his prior service and reputation; or he could admit to what he had done, arguing that he acted out of duty for his country and that foreign aid and the co-operation of the German empire was vital to Irish independence. It was this line that Shaw recommended and Casement developed.

Shaw also felt that the use of historical parallels was important. Casement might reasonably compare himself to the executed Scottish patriot, William Wallace, or to Giuseppe Garibaldi, the revolutionary who had mastered the techniques of guerrilla warfare in South America before returning to Italy in 1848 to raise a volunteer army. As Giuseppe Garibaldi (1807–82) was arguably the most respected freedom fighter of the 19th century, who fought in South America for the republican cause of Rio Grande do Sul against the Brazilian emperor and then for Uruguay against Argentina. In 1848 he returned to Italy and became the great hero of the *Risorgimento* and by the power of his leadership inspired Italy to unite under Victor Emmanuel of Piedmont. His legendary bravery and love for adventure inspired 'freedom struggles' and patriotic zeal across Europe well beyond his death.

Garibaldi came to embody the spirit of Italian unification, so Casement represented a similar position for Ireland.[151]

Clearly, Casement was influenced by Shaw's intervention. He even briefly entertained the idea that the historian G M Trevelyan might be persuaded into the witness box to discuss, from the historian's perspective, British support for Garibaldi's cause. Another parallel was drawn with the Asquith government's guarantees of Czechoslovakian independence in 1915.

In Casement's reply to Shaw, he agreed with him on all matters except one: *That I should never suggest to an English court or jury that they should let me off as a prisoner of war – but tell them 'You may hang me and be damned to you.'*[152] Casement was in pursuit of the martyr's crown and his prison writings began to chart his own path towards this desired end. His very 'rebellion' and the cause of Irish freedom would, he hoped, be discussed in detail at his trial. On 2 June he drafted a document for Duffy entitled 'Line of my Defence' forthrightly setting down why he had turned to rebellion. He was unequivocal in stating what his trial meant for Ireland:

I want it to be clear, then, to my counsel that it is the Irish cause – the cause of Sinn Féin and the rebels – their integrity and independence I am defending – and it is an essential part of that defence that I shirk no responsibility either for the rebellion in Ireland or the action of the German Govt. in Germany.[153]

He also wanted it to be understood that he stood for the cause of peace: *I am, possibly, serving a great cause too – the cause of peace. For peace can only come when men begin to see more clearly that there is no absolute right or wrong in this war on either side – that these hatreds and charges of horror one against the other are base and cowardly – and that peace will begin to dawn when we begin to feel that the other side, too, has a right to defend and a cause to sustain.*[154] This position coincided with the views espoused by the Union of Democratic Control, the anti-war pacifist organization run by Casement's former colleague in the Congo Reform Association, E D Morel.

Casement's effort to link his trial to the cause of peace was a departure unlikely to engender respect from the war cabinet. However, his desire to assert control over his defence began to seriously alarm Sullivan who wrote to Duffy that he must stop Casement writing, as he was being far too revelatory.

It was in this atmosphere of an increasingly adversarial if coherent response from Casement towards his trial and prosecutors that his counsel were met with the next secret weapon from Casement's opponents. On 3 June, the journalist Mary Boyle O'Reilly of the Newspaper Enterprise Association wrote to Gavan Duffy: 'Mrs Green desires me to tell you, what I have just told her, that almost a month ago a group of important American journalists were called to Whitehall and there shown letters and a diary of Sir Roger Casement's which proved him to be a "moral offender" unworthy of public sympathy.'[155] The idea that Casement's dissimulation also included a sexual double life, was one that threw his defence completely off balance. Green immediately began trying to detect where the rumours came from and after a conversation with Sir John Simon traced them to two (unnamed) sources. Casement was defenceless against the whispering campaign and the rumours spread like wildfire from the smoking rooms of gentlemen's clubs, through press rooms into mainstream gossip. In the atmosphere of 1916, with the world's largest Empire struggling for its very existence, it was not difficult to convince either the men in power or the public that if a man was capable of pro-German sympathies and of encouraging a rebellion against the Crown, then he was capable of anything.

Although today homosexuality is a generally accepted part of western liberal democracy, this certainly was not the case in 1916 when love between men was outlawed and punishable with long prison sentences. As sexual scandal wrecked the artistic achievement of Oscar Wilde for several generations, so sexuality was a useful propaganda tool adopted by all sides including the nationalist underground press against the Dublin administration. Both Morel and Casement had used sexual imagery to illustrate the extent of horror carried out by imperial systems in Africa and the Amazon and on the outbreak of war a popular adage in Britain ran: 'A dishonouring stain is worse than death.' The use of homosexuality to demonize the enemy also helped nurture a feeling of 'moral ascendancy' within the rest of society.

Casement believed that his trial was being deliberately manipulated for propagandist ends – hardly surprising since he himself was endeavouring to use it for similar purposes. On 10 June he drafted a document questioning the very legitimacy of English law.[156] He felt the whole case now was being moved towards an impeachment of Germany.

Moreover, Casement's concerns and disillusionment with Sullivan's approach were deepening daily. On 12 June, he sent a long memo to Duffy declaring that he wished to conduct his own defence to *justify the cause of Ireland before the world* and *to leave it on record*.[157] Sullivan clearly had no such intentions. Instead, he hoped to prove that no treason had been committed within the meaning of the statute by which Casement was being prosecuted. This was the Statute of Treason of 1351 – a law originally written in Norman French – which stated: '*Si homme leve de guerre contre notre dit Seigneur le Roi en son Roialme ou soit adhérant as enemys notre Seigneur le Roi en le Roialme donant a euz eid ou confort en son Roialme ou per aillours* (If a man do levy war against our said Lord the King in his realm or be adherent to the enemies of our Lord the King in his realm giving to them aid and comfort in the realm or elsewhere)'.[158] Since Casement had committed his alleged acts of treason in Germany, Sullivan hoped to win over the jury by pleading that treason had not been committed as defined by the act. It was a defence, Casement believed, that would never win.

On 13 June Michael Francis Doyle arrived from the US aboard the SS *St Paul*. Before his departure, he had communicated with the various IRB leaders and raised a considerable amount of funding from Irish-American sympathizers. Not surprisingly, the authorities were apprehensive about Doyle's presence – there had even been a suggestion within Special Branch to have him 'befriended' during his ocean voyage.[159] All of his interviews with Casement were conducted in the presence of the prison governor, while Casement's request for him to be allowed to go to Germany to gather important witnesses, material evidence and papers was peremptorily refused.[160]

The issue of collecting Casement's papers became increasingly important. He had left a vast amount of his papers scattered with various friends and allies in many different countries. Casement drafted a long memo to Gavan Duffy supplying details of his records and giving clear instructions how they should be gathered and safely placed in an Irish institution after the war. He also expressed a wish that his political and philosophical writings would be collected, edited and published to *illustrate my conception of Irish national effort.*[161] He made further reference to the trunks that he had left in Farringdon Road, containing most of his belongings and hoped that they would eventually be recovered:

These have been seized by Scotland Yard and burgled – I use the word advisedly – anything taken by Scotland Yard I presume can be legally recovered. They have no right to retain any papers or documents of mine – diaries, books or anything not used at the trial against me. I presume so. I do not see by what right or law they can retain my private writings or property of that kind, save for the 'purpose of justice' and as these are satisfied, anything of mine not so used in their hands should be recovered from them.[162]

As the trial approached, Casement began to wonder if the authorities would dare hang him for fear of possible repercussions in America and neutral European countries. It was not difficult to envisage that a process of very careful negotiation would be required, especially given the effort to highlight his pro-German sympathies rather than his dedication to Ireland:

By pretended appeal to an ancient statute they can have a first class 'drama' enacted, far more realistic than any performance of the play with all sorts of 'amazing' evidence for the press gallery and the gutter public – 'sensational' developments – 'collapse of the prisoner' – a world picture in fact to go over the whole world to exemplify the might and majesty of Britain, the 'perfidy' of her German foe and the weakness and inferiority of the Irish rebels against this British Providence.[163]

It is hard to describe the feelings and attitudes stirred by Casement's treason at almost every level of British and Irish society, ranging on one side from the deep contempt of most newspapers and the forces for war to the other, and largely unexpressed view of admiration, that Casement once more was prepared to take an independent position and suffer the consequences. During his life, Casement's work in Africa and South America had been profoundly admired by his peers, bishops and politicians of all persuasions, and his skill as an activist was to unite people behind a common cause. For some, however, he had become a hate figure. The barrister, Raymond Asquith, wrote privately: 'I am delighted that they have caught that swollen-headed, maggot-ridden idealist Casement and heartily hope they will hang him. We owe it not only to ourselves but to Belgium for the fuss he made about the Congo.'[164]

Within the corridors of the Foreign Office, the affair was an embarrassment. The Foreign Secretary, Sir Edward Grey, still believed that Casement should be portrayed as 'mad' and hoped that he could be committed to a 'lunatic asylum'.[165] During the magisterial hearing in May, he had circulated a worried memorandum to the cabinet about the bitter consequences in the US if Casement was executed, arguing that he would be proclaimed as the 'new Robert Emmet'.[166]

The impact in the US was not made any easier by Doyle's presence in London. He had already sent back reports to the American press about Casement's inhumane treatment in prison. Within the cabinet, however, a hard-core Unionist lobby bayed for Casement's blood irrespective of the consequences. Undisclosed tensions were building up on all sides, even between Morgan and Doyle in Casement's own defence team. The night before the trial opened, Casement wrote to Duffy: *I have again a fearful headache & rheumatism too – but I'll pull through please God – with the help of all who are praying for me.*[167]

THE TRIAL

Predicting the propaganda engagement, on the eve of the trial F E Smith cabled his opening address to the American press. Structural alterations had been made to the court and a new dock erected to ensure that Casement was in full view of the jury. The public demand for tickets was overwhelming – even Gavan Duffy had problems finding places for his list of Casement admirers.

The day was sunny and while the women looked cool in their summer gowns, the barristers were hot and flustered beneath their wigs and robes. Casement's faithful female cohort were out in force: Alice Stopford Green, Gertrude Bannister, Ada McNeill, Eva Gore-Booth (sister of the Countess Markiewicz who was still in prison), Alice Milligan and Sylvia Lynd. The journalist and male suffra-

Rufus Isaacs, Lord Chief Justice of England, later Viceroy of India

gette H W Nevinson sat near the front among the press gallery of special correspondents, and there were a number of churchmen present as well as the Irish Attorney-General, Sir James O'Connor.

It was to be a trial 'at bar' and held before three King's Bench judges, a legal procedure adopted in criminal cases where there was a likelihood of difficulties over specific points of law. Presiding over this impressive legal triumvirate was the Lord Chief Justice of England, Rufus Isaacs, Viscount Reading alongside the celebrated criminal judges Mr Justice Avory and Mr Justice Horridge. In advance of the trial, potentially sensitive matters had been suppressed and a prohibition placed on any mention of them during the legal proceedings. Most controversially, there was to be no reference to the running of arms into Ulster, a situation which many believed removed the last vestiges of fairness from the occasion. For it had been the running of arms into Larne and the Curragh mutiny that forced those who defended Home Rule to militarize in response to anti-Home Rule aggression. There were other obvious omissions, including details of Casement's role in the initial recruitment rallies for the Volunteers, the Findlay affair and any mention of the conspiratorial engagement in Germany or the 'seditious' propaganda writings.

Once the jury had been chosen, F E Smith took to the floor and after constructing an image of Casement informed by his sterling consular career, his loyal imperialism and his knighthood, he set about demolishing and humiliating him for his German brigade exploits, his landing and capture. The word 'seduce' rang through the court to describe Casement's efforts to recruit Irish soldiers. Much was made of the failure of those efforts before the naming of the witnesses 'to these acts of high treason and treachery'. Smith described Casement's landing in Kerry, lamenting 'that unhappy country which has been the victim in its history of so many cruel and cynical conspiracies, but surely never of a conspiracy more cruel and more cynical than this'. The ordinary folk of Kerry – men, women and children – were then applauded for displaying their loyalty to the Empire by helping to turn Casement over to the authorities. He ended with a damning statement: 'The prisoner, blinded by hatred to this country, as malignant in quality as it was sudden in origin, has played a desperate hazard. He has played it and he has lost it. To-day the forfeit is claimed.'[168]

Smith's prosecution turned ordinary Irish people – rank and file Irishmen in Germany and the rural folk of Kerry – into the main witnesses against the very man who believed he had their interests most at heart. It was an example of the inversion of positions, a tool that would become standard in the fight for the 'truth' about Casement.

Over the next two days, Irish witnesses trooped through the witness box to relate their experiences of Casement as the failed, humiliated recruiter in German prisoner of war camps or as the bedraggled and incompetent 'gun-runner' and forlorn rebel appearing on the beachfront of Kerry. Throughout, Casement watched calmly and listened intently.

The third day opened with Morgan's legal exchange with Avory and Horridge about the meaning of the treason law and his efforts to offer a motion to quash the indictment. After detailed scrutiny of the law, including long interventions from the Attorney-General and reference to a genealogy of treason trials down the ages, the Lord Chief Justice eventually intervened and ended the discourse stating that 'the point fails and that the motion to quash the indictment must be refused'.[169] As Casement had predicted, Sullivan's approach had fallen at the first hurdle.

No witnesses stepped forward to speak on Casement's behalf. Instead, he was allowed to make a statement in an effort to clear up *abominable falsehoods* and some *malicious inventions*[170] which had been made by the prosecution. First, he declared that he had never advised, as had been suggested, for Irishmen to fight alongside the Turks, nor for the brigade to fight with the Germans on the Western Front. He objected to the insinuation that he had cut the rations of those who had refused to join the brigade or that he had sent some to punishment camps. He also rejected the rumour, spread initially in the American press, that he had accepted *German Gold* and stated categorically that he had *never asked nor accepted a single penny of foreign money neither for myself, nor for any Irish cause.*[171] Finally, Casement refuted Smith's claim that Germany had financed and organized the rebellion. The Easter Rising was an all-Irish affair: *I have touched on these personal matters alone because intended as they were to reflect on my honour, they were calculated to tarnish the cause I hold dear.*[172]

Then, Sullivan began his long and circuitous address to the jury arguing that Casement's actions had to be understood within the context of his 'Irishness'; his work for the Empire was not in the service of England but for Ireland as part of that Empire. His summation then turned to the view that what had occurred in Ulster as a result of the Home Rule crisis was acutely relevant to Casement's defence. The inference was clear: Casement's prosecutor, F E Smith, and Sir Edward Carson had initiated ideas of treason and the grammar of anarchy on the founding of the Ulster Volunteers. Before 'dredging up the embarrassing past', Reading interceded and told Sullivan he had gone far enough.

Shortly after this exchange Sullivan dramatically collapsed mid-sentence ending his summary with the lines: 'My Lords, I regret to say that I have completely broken down.'[173] The court was adjourned until the following day. Some years later Sullivan described the moment: 'Half-an-hour before the crash came, I believed that I was dying. Then it appeared to me that I commenced to rave. I implored my junior to ask for an adjournment – by some strange nervous affection I resented asking myself – I was assured that I was in perfect trim and was urged to go on – again and again. I looked for the clock – it had disappeared – the jury faded away and still I raved on – the Lord Chief Justice commenced to recede down an infinite vista, until he was a pin point – then darkness fell and I crashed.'[174]

The fourth and last day of the trial began with an apology from Jones: Sullivan could not attend on doctor's orders and instead he would be completing the summation. Jones openly admitted that Casement had founded the Irish Volunteers as a consequence of the political situation that emerged in Ireland in 1911. He argued that Casement had behaved with some sense of honour in his use of the Irish brigade and asked the jury to make their decision on questions of history and humanity: 'The history of Ireland contains many melancholy and sad chapters, and not the least sad is the chapter which tells and speaks so eloquently of so many mistaken sons of that unfortunate country who have gone to the scaffold, as they think, for the sake of their native land'.[175]

Smith spoke next and after briefly paraphrasing the defence case, he appealed to the jury's imperial duty not to shirk from their responsibilities in reaching their verdict. In response to the line taken by Sullivan and Jones, he argued that the declaration of war in 1914 had changed the political situation in Ireland: 'With the outbreak of this war, with the danger to the Empire which the outbreak of this war involved, there was an arrangement and a convention between the leaders of these factions which would enable Irish soldiers to do what Irish soldiers have done in every great war in which this country has been engaged – write their names with their swords on the battlefields of Europe.'[176]

The precise nature of this 'convention' was unclear; regardless, Casement was certainly not party to it. Smith's description of loyalty as belonging exclusively to the Empire was a pointed rebuttal of Casement's anti-recruitment work rooted in his belief that Irishmen had no place fighting Britain's imperial wars.

After a brief and ambiguous exchange between the Lord Chief Justice and the Attorney-General about the nature of a 'diary found',[177] the summing up by Reading was followed by the withdrawal of the jury for 53 minutes. On their return, amid dead silence, the word 'guilty' echoed through the court. Having been sentenced to death, Casement rose to deliver his speech from the dock.

A number of drafts of rewritten passages from the speech have survived in the recent release of Casement's prison papers. They clearly indicate that he spent a good deal of time rewriting and rehearsing his speech in advance of the moment.[178] For a short time, Casement was granted permission to lay bare his soul although his body had already been claimed by the state. His words, addressed to *the people of Ireland*, demanded allegiance to God based on love rather to a monarch based on law: *The Government of Ireland by England rests on restraint and not on law: and since it demands no love, it can evoke no loyalty.*[179] He condemned his representation by the prosecution as an *evil example*: *To Englishmen I set no evil example, for I made no appeal to them. I asked no Englishman to help me. I asked Irishmen to fight for their rights. The 'evil example' was only to other Irishmen who might come after me, and in 'like case' seek to do as I did. How then, since neither my example nor my appeal was addressed to Englishmen, can I be rightfully tried by them?*[180]

With each twist of his argument, Casement attacked the legitimacy of the case against him, challenging the antiquated nature of the law and the oppressive history of English authority in Ireland. He differentiated between two types of treason: one based on a *ruthless sincerity*, the other derivative of *verbal incitements*.[181] He believed that the loyalty espoused by Carson and Smith had been achieved through verbal incitements while the cause of cultural nationalism had developed through a ruthless sincerity for independence.

Finally, Casement delivered an unrepentant and incorrigible glorification of rebellion in pursuit of a united Ireland:

If we are to be indicted as criminals – to be shot as murderers, to be imprisoned as convicts, because our offence is that we love Ireland more than we value our lives, then I know not what virtue resides in any offer of self-government held out to brave men on such terms. Self-government is our right, a thing born in us at birth; a thing no more to be doled out to us or withheld from us by another people, than the right to life itself – than the right to feel the sun or smell the flowers – or to love our kind. It is only from the convict these things are withheld for crime committed and proven – and Ireland that has wronged no man, that has injured no land, that has sought no dominion over others – Ireland is treated today among the nations of the world as if she was a convicted criminal. If it be treason to fight against such an unnatural fate as this, then I am proud to be a rebel – and shall cling to my rebellion with the last drop of my blood. If there be no right of rebellion against a state of things that no savage tribe would endure without resistance, then I am sure that it is better for men to fight and die without right than to live in such a state of right as this.[182]

During the course of the address, F E Smith ostentatiously slouched out of the courtroom, hands in pockets. None the less, the speech had a profound impact that would resonate for many years. From Bengal to Accra, nationalist leaders across the Empire would be inspired by these words. Wilfrid Blunt considered it 'the finest document in patriotic history, finer than anything in Plutarch or elsewhere in Pagan literature'.[183] And Casement's most able defendant, Artemus Jones, would later write: 'The great speech of Sir Roger Casement before [*sic*] sentence remains in the records of the law. It will be read by his fellow Irishmen generations after his judges, his prosecutors, his lawyers and his calumniators have been long forgotten.'[184]

The press was largely subdued in their reports of the speech. If Casement's message had been enshrined in law for future generations of Irish rebels, such orations were not to be encouraged. It was his immediate conviction and demonization that was most necessary for the purposes of war and Imperial patriotism: within 48 hours of the conclusion of Casement's trial, the Somme offensive began. It proved to be the most destructive battle in modern British military history and over the weeks would claim the lives of tens of thousands of men, many of them Irishmen, drafted into the 36th (Ulster) Division and 16th (Irish) Division. The Somme symbolized a commitment to victory and it 'necessitated the mobilisation of morale and the combating of war-weariness and pacifism'.[185] Casement's trial clearly served such agendas. His treason was used to help 'Ireland' redefine its 'Britishness' and to project a clearer understanding of questions of loyalty, patriotism and manhood.

However, the continued demonization of Casement was demanded not merely to demonstrate the power of the Imperial state over the individual but, more importantly, to undermine any lingering support for him as an intellectual and voice of the oppressed. As Alfred Noyes would later write, after the trial there emerged a 'cunning and elaborate misuse of associated ideas'.[186] Not only did the authorities want Casement dead, they also needed to control his historical legacy and reputation.

Immediately after sentencing, Casement's defence counsel issued a notice of appeal based on three points. First, that the offence of high treason committed outside of the realm is not an offence within the statute of Edward III. Second, that the Lord Chief Justice was wrong in law and misdirected the jury when defining 'aid and comfort'. Third, that the Lord Chief Justice misdirected the jury by not adequately putting the case for the defence to the jury.[187] In fact, Morgan felt that Sullivan had mishandled affairs badly. He later commented: 'The fact of the matter is that our main point was never put to the court but we cannot say that! One can't repudiate one's own leader.'[188]

Casement was now moved to Pentonville prison. The following day he was unceremoniously stripped of all decorations, including his knighthood. His privileges were seriously restricted. Only Catholic priests could attend him in private. Peacefully resigned to his fate, he began to prepare for physical death.

The fate of Casement split society on every level. In the cabinet, Grey and Lansdowne were opposed to his execution, while F E Smith threatened to resign his cabinet position if he was not hanged. Smith had the advantage of his legal authority as Attorney-General, a crucial factor in the eventual outcome. At the same time, in Ireland, England and around the world, countless petitions demanding his reprieve were set in motion by a variety of groups. Arthur Conan Doyle organized the most prestigious petition including names such as Arnold Bennett, G K Chesterton, Sir Francis Darwin, Sir J G Frazer, John Galsworthy, G P Gooch, C P Scott and Beatrice and Sydney Webb. Gertrude Bannister sent an appeal containing names of leading luminaries in the Bloomsbury set: Dora Carrington, Duncan Grant, Leonard Woolf and Lytton Strachey. Other important figures connected to African affairs such as Arnold Rowntree also added their support. The poet Alice Milligan submitted a petition from 'Ulster Liberals' and other local government groups sent endless petitions to try to persuade the government towards leniency. From the US, John Quinn organized a petition with a strong lobby of politicians and newspapermen while significant petitions were sent in by both the Ancient Order of Hibernians and the Negro Fellowship League.[189]

The next twist in the tale was the allegation that Casement had, in fact, come to stop 'the Rising', a position encouraged through the Vatican. The idea played neatly into the pacifist lobby and those weary with war. It also cast aspersions on the role of the security services. How much had they known in advance and why was there no effort to prevent 'the Rising' from happening?

As sympathy for Casement and arguments in his favour began to circulate, so the rumours and allegations about his sexuality and 'moral authority' were released to counteract them. Casement's most trusted political and religious allies were now made privy to the secret documents, and extracts from the 'diary' were sent to the US. Newspaper editors, churchmen, even the king were discreetly shown material that assassinated Casement's character amongst almost all of his supporters. Many of them made public announcements of their shock and disgust.

Beneath the salacious scandal-mongering, there was some good analytical reporting and opinion-making. A small biographical pamphlet, written by an academic at Trinity College and the nephew and biographer of John Redmond, L G Redmond Howard, wrote intelligently of Casement as a 'philosopher of history' and a 'prophet'. Howard argued that 'it was the indiscriminate volunteering in which Irishmen of all parties had been allowed to indulge that produced "Casement", rather than Casement who produced the chaos which was inevitably bound to occur.'[190] On 4 July, publication of the Royal Commission investigation into the Easter Rising criticized the government for failing to act earlier in preventing the lurch towards rebellion.[191]

On 10 July, Casement wrote *Some of my Objections to the Lord Chief Justice of England's Charge to the Jury – 29 June 1916* which has survived in manuscript form. In it, he strongly criticized the manner in which the press had influenced the proceedings: *I was being tried not on the evidence at all – but on the knowledge derived elsewhere than in the court.*[192]

On 17 and 18 July, Casement's appeal was heard. This time, he sat alone in the dock before the judges of the Court of Criminal Appeal – another impressive and distinguished team of legal experts. Sullivan revisited many of the same arguments he had used in the original trial and the same verdict was delivered. While the appeal again endorsed his guilt in the public imagination with a further barrage of treason-talk, other matters were under discussion at cabinet level. Memoranda were passed before the war ministers by the legal advisor to the Home Office, Sir Ernley Blackwell, setting out more reasons why Casement should be executed:

'It is difficult to imagine a worse case of high treason than Casement's. It is aggravated rather than mitigated by his previous career in the public service . . . Casement's diary and his ledger entries, covering many pages of closely typed matter, show that he has for years been addicted to the grossest sodomitical practices. Of late years he seems to have completed the full cycle of sexual degeneracy and from a pervert has become an invert – a woman or pathic who derives his satisfaction from attracting men and inducing them to use him.'[193]

Confusing 'sexual degeneracy' with references to womanhood, victimization, insanity and treason, these statements are revealing not merely of attitudes towards masculinity during the First

World War, but equally of the depth of hatred felt in some circles of government for Casement and what he represented. Through these memoranda, Blackwell inscribed into official British history a series of documents that implied that Casement was being hanged as much for his alleged sexuality as for an incitement to revolution.

Given their convenient appearance at such a vital moment, it is no wonder that those who had known Casement most closely questioned the authenticity of these documents. Casement's 'moral authority' exposing atrocities in Africa and South America had been based on his integrity as a voice for the dispossessed. He had used that authority to link his experiences of colonial outrage to Ireland's position as a conquered nation. Inevitably, suspicions of 'dirty tricks' developed in conjunction with the sexual discussion. The position of 'forgery theorists' was strengthened over the following decades by the refusal of the authorities to admit to the 'existence or non-existence' of the diaries.[194]

Over the years, the sexual dimension of the Casement case played directly into a wider sexual phobia informed by the dominant Conservative and Catholic opinion in Ireland. The discreet circulation of sexual innuendo allowed for Casement's 'martyrdom' to be undermined, and his name was rendered unspeakable on account of an activity that remained illegal in Ireland until the 1993 Criminal Law (Sexual Offences) Act.

In the US, the diaries were used to confuse and undermine all popular and political support. They destroyed Casement's respectability as well as the movement and ideals for which he had fought. In the long run, they even defined the most difficult matter of all: 'the verdict of history'. Casement was gradually expunged from the official narrative of Africa, the Amazon and Ireland.

Whether the diaries are forged or 'authentic', they successfully scuppered Casement's reputation and enabled the authorities to appropriate control of the moral high ground. More importantly, the controversy continues to obfuscate Casement's lasting significance.

EXECUTION

With the appeal refused and the cabinet confounded, Casement was fast-tracked towards the scaffold. Gavan Duffy hoped for a final plea to the House of Lords but the decision rested with the Attorney-General, F E Smith, and obviously was refused. The stream of petitions addressed to Prime Minister Asquith and the Home Secretary, Herbert Samuel, during late July failed to have an impact. Well-intentioned speeches in the US senate, comparing Casement to George Washington, brought no response from President Woodrow Wilson, who was unsympathetic to the Irish cause. W B Yeats predicted that Casement's execution would have an 'evil effect' in Ireland and America.[195] All support on behalf of Casement was answered by silence – the cold and haunting power of official silence.

W B Yeats fought for Casement's reprieve in 1916 and his 1937 poem 'The Ghost of Roger Casement-is beating on the door' became a rallying cry for those who fought for Casement's reputation

Incredibly, Casement's letters written during those last days and passed by the censor describe a man at peace with himself, confident of his fate and the fate of the cause for which he was about to die. On several occasions, he referred to his papers which would absolve him when Ireland took its place among the nations of the earth. He wrote to Richard Morten:

Don't worry what anyone says about me, Dick – it is easy to pelt the man who can't reply or who is gone – but remember no story is told till we've heard all of it – and no one knows anything about mine – including those who think they know all! But I know most – and I know the reasons for everything in my own action and many of the reasons for much in the action of my friends. I have not attempted to tell my side – there is no use to begin with in trying to do what I have not liberty to do – so I must let it be, and bear the fate that came . . . The truth is man & nations and kings and kinglets fight always, for one thing only: self interest . . . that can be done without lying and falsehood and wrecking your opponents char-acter – and without giving way to intolerable hatred.[196]

In his last letter to his sister Agnes he wrote:

I know what history will say – at least in Ireland – for I have left a very clear record behind to be made public after the war – in the hands of a good executor who will see you and other friends when peace comes and place many documents in your hands crossing the 't's' and dotting the 'i's' of many things dark to you now perhaps.[197]

Beyond his execution Casement remains the most problematic rebel in modern Irish history

In his last hours, he transcended bitterness, forgave his ene-mies and his captors and in the gesture of the martyr commented that *all are my brethren now.*[198] His words of reconciliation and peace contrast starkly with the apocalyptic discourses of war and hate that raged about him. The Catholic hierarchy, and especially Cardinal Bourne, had little sympathy for Casement and demanded a signed confession before granting his confirmation into Rome. Although the prisoner's sympathies had for many years been tilted towards mystical dimensions of Christianity, and in particular the early church fathers, he had sporadically expressed concerns for aspects of the Catholic church hierarchy. A similar dilemma was faced by Anglican and Church of Ireland bishops.

On the eve of Casement's execution, Randall Davidson, the Archbishop of Canterbury, met with the Lord Chancellor, and said that while a 'reprieve would be wiser than an execution' the 'well being and safety of the Empire' was at stake. He felt the sound argument was as follows: 'Here is a rebel who has done things worthy of death. But his case is peculiar. For many years, beyond all possibility of doubt, he battled nobly on behalf of the oppressed native folk. He had infinite difficulties to contend with, but at the cost of his health he fought on. He succeeded, and his name will always, and rightly, be held in honour for what he then did, whatever may have happened afterwards. All sorts of complications as to the rebel's real life came subsequently to light. Investigation showed perplexing contradictions in his behaviour, and though not technically (according to the experts) a man out of his mind, he is shown to have been mentally and morally unhinged.'[199]

An ordinary parish priest, uncomplicated by the interaction of politics and faith, heard Casement's last confession, gave him his first communion and accepted his soul into the church. Father McCarroll remarked later how he marched to the scaffold 'with the dignity of a prince'.[200] Though he died a Catholic in name, Casement's spiritual dimension is more honestly embodied in that unification sought by the United Irish and the Young Irelanders: a peaceful and enlightened understanding between Catholic, Protestant and dissenter.

At 9am on 3 August 1916 the body of Roger Casement was hanged.

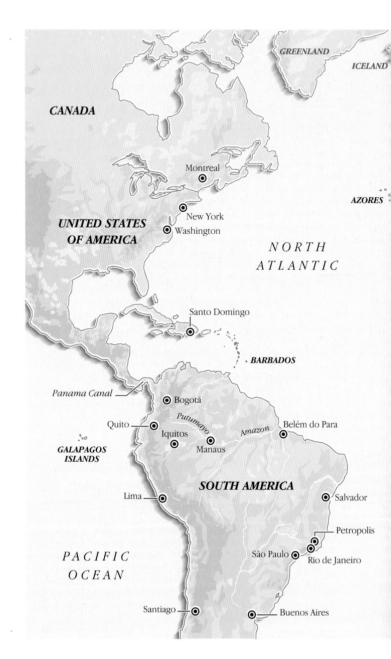

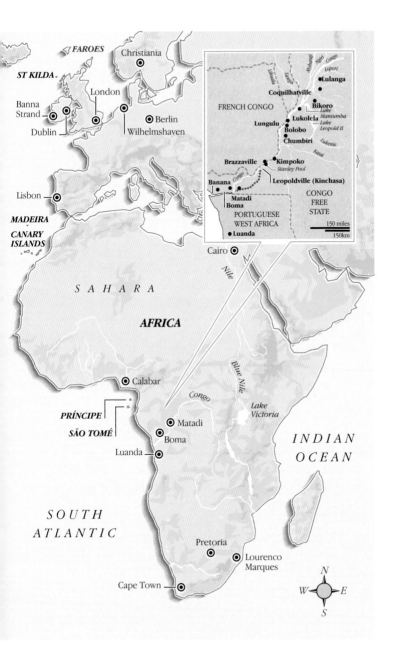

FAROES

Christiania

ST KILDA

Banna
Strand

London

Dublin

Berlin

Wilhelmshaven

Lisbon

MADEIRA

CANARY
ISLANDS

FRENCH CONGO

Lulanga

Coquilhatville

Bikoro

Lunglu

Lukolela

Bolobo

Chumbiri

Brazzaville

Kimpoko

Banana

Leopoldville (Kinchasa)

Matadi
Boma

PORTUGUESE
WEST AFRICA

Luanda

Lake
Mantumba

Lake
Leopold II

Stanley Pool

CONGO
FREE
STATE

150 miles

150km

Cairo

SAHARA

Nile

AFRICA

Calabar

Congo

Blue Nile

Lake
Victoria

INDIAN
OCEAN

PRÍNCIPE

SÃO TOMÉ

Matadi

Boma

Luanda

SOUTH

ATLANTIC

Pretoria

Lourenco
Marques

N

Cape Town

W   E

S

Notes

BL: British Library; BLPES: British Library of Political and Economic Science; CAB: Cabinet Papers; DT: Department of Taoiseach; FO: Foreign Office; HO: Home Office; NAI: National Archive of Ireland; NLI: National Library of Ireland; NYPL: New York Public Library; PRO: Public Record Office

1   NLI, MS 13,600, Casement to his sister Agnes Newman, 25 July 1916

2   L G Redmond Howard, *Sir Roger Casement* (Dublin, 1916) p.3

3   Shane Leslie, *The Irish Issue in its American Aspect* (New York, 1917) pp.106–118

4   NAI, DTS 9606A, Eamon de Valera to Julius Klein – 11 February 1934

5   *Hansard Parliamentary Debates*, 3 May 1956 Vol 552 no. 174. col. 749–760 See also HO 144/23463/311643/261 containing the various briefs prepared for the debate.

6   Maurice Moynihan (ed.), *Speeches and Statements by Eamon de Valera 1917–73* pp.603–5

7   Thomas Davis, *Literary and Historical Essays* (Dublin, 1846)

8   Dónall Ó Luanaigh 'Roger Casement, senior, and the Siege of Paris (1870) pp.33–35 – *The Irish Sword* Vol. XV no. 58 Summer 1982

9   Robert Kee, *The Green Flag* (1972) p.354

10   Roger Casement, *Some Poems of Roger Casement* (Dublin, 1918) p.xi

11   L G Redmond Howard, *Sir Roger Casement* (1916) p.54

12   NLI MS 12,114 – Manuscript Poetry Book of Roger Casement including some notes, illustrations and press cuttings

13   *Hansard – Parliamentary Debates* – 20 May 1903 Vol. CXXII Col. 1292. See also S E Crowe, *The Berlin West African Conference*

1884–85 (1942) and S J S Cookey, *Britain and the Congo Question 1885–1913* (1968)

14 J P White 'The Sanford Exploring Expedition' – *Journal of African History*, VIII, 2 (1967) pp.291–302

15 *English Historical Review* LXXVII – Jan 1962 pp.98–102

16 BLPES – Morel Papers F8/17 – 27 June 1904

17 F Puleston, *African Drums* (1930) p.40

18 Baptist Missionary Society papers – Angus Library, Regent's Park College, Oxford A/31/3 (xvi) W. Holman Bentley to Baynes – 29 November 1888

19 'Conrad's Congo Diary' in Joseph Conrad, *Heart of Darkness* (Norton Critical Edition, 1971)

20 C T Watts (ed.) *Joseph Conrad's Letters to R.B. Cunnighame Graham* (Cambridge, 1969) pp.148–52

21 F R Karl and L Davies (eds.), *The Collected Letters of Joseph Conrad* Vol. 5 (1912–16), (Cambridge, 1996) pp.595–99

22 Marcel Luwel, 'Roger Casement a Henry Morton Stanley: Un rapport sur la situacion au Congo en 1890' in *Africa-Tervuren* XIV – 1968 – 4

23 see H O Mackey, *The Forged Casement Diaries* (Dublin, 1962) pp.173–6

24 See Brian Inglis, *Roger Casement* (London, 1974) p.45

25 PRO FO 2/368 Casement to Martin Gosselin – 30.4.1900

26 Mary Kingsley quoted by Alice Stopford Green in her address on the opening of The Mary Kingsley Society of West Africa

27 NLI Acc 4902 – Casement to F H Cowper – 9 March 1901

28 NLI Acc. 4902 (6) – Casement to Francis H Cowper – June 1902

29 *Hansard Parliamentary debates* – 20 May 1903 – Vol. CXXII 1903 Col.1289–1332

30 Ibid

31 William Roger Louis, 'Roger Casement and the Congo' in *Journal of African History* vol. 1 (1964) pp.99–120. 15 September 1903 FO 10/805

32 FO 10/805

33 FO 10/805 – 5 August 1903

34 FO 10/806

35 FO 10/805–15 September 1903

36 'Manifesto of the Congo Reform Association' in Angus Mitchell (ed.) *Roger Casement in Africa* (2002)

37 Kevin Grant 'Christian Critics of Empire: Missionaries, Lantern Lectures, and the Congo Reform Campaign in Britain'. In *The Journal of Imperial and Commonwealth History*, Vol. 29 no.2 May 2001 pp.27–58

38 Wm. Roger Louis, 'The Triumph of the Congo Reform Movement, 1905–08' in *Boston University Papers on Africa* – Vol. II (Boston, 1966)

39 Kwame Nkrumah, *Challenge of the Congo* (London, 1966). NAI Department of Taoiseach 96/6/190 – S7805D

40 NLI MS 10,464 (3) – Roger Casement to Alice Stopford Green – 20 April 1907

41 Stephen Gwynn, *Experience of a Literary Man* (London, 1926) p. 260

42 R Casement 'The Prosecution of the Irish' in *Ulad* May 1905

43 Bulmer Hobson, *Ireland Yesterday and Tomorrow* (Ireland, 1968) pp.99–102

44 NLI MS 3074 (3/i) – Roger Casement to Gertrude Bannister – 31 May 1906

45 Brian Inglis, *Roger Casement* p. 149

46 Philip D Curtin, *The Atlantic Slave Trade: a Census* (1969) quotes 11,479,000. See Roland Oliver & Michael Crowder (eds.), *The Cambridge Encylopedia of Africa* (1981)

47 *Diplomatic and Consular Reports* – Brazil – Report for the year 1905–6 on the Trade of Santos no.3952

48 NLI MS 13,080 (4) – Casement to Lord Dufferin – 4 March 1908

49 *Diplomatic and Consular Reports* – Brazil – Report on the trade of the Consular District of Pará for the year 1907 and previous years – Annual Series No. 4111

50 *Freeman's Journal* – 11 December 1908

51 *Freeman's Journal* – 19 December 1908 – Mrs Green's History.

52 NLI MS 13,074 (b/i) – Roger Casement to Gertrude Bannister 31 March 1909

53 NLI MS 13,074 (b/i) – Roger Casement to Gertrude Bannister 2 July 1909

54   *Truth* – 22 September 1909

55   Angus Mitchell (ed.) *The Amazon Journal of Roger Casement* (1997) p.105

56   Ibid., p.108

57   Ibid., p.176

58   PRO FO 128/324

59   Both reports are reproduced in Angus Mitchell (ed.) *Sir Roger Casement's Heart of Darkness: The 1911 Documents* (2003)

60   *The Nation* – 20 July 1912

61   NLI MS 13,074 (7/ii) – R. Casement to G. Bannister – 17 July 1912

62   BLPES E D Morel Papers F8/25 11 June 1913

63   Robert Kee, *The Green Flag* p.467

64   George Dangerfield, *The Strange Death of Liberal England* (1970) p.14

65   Angus Mitchell (ed.) *Sir Roger Casement's Heart of Darkness: The 1911 Documents* p. 216

66   The most accessible source for these writings remains H O Mackey (ed.), *The Crime Against Europe – Writings and Poems of Roger Casement* (1958)

67   NLI MS 13,073 (14)

68   *Irish Independent* – 20 May 1913

69   *Nation* – 11 October 1913

70   A pamphlet of the speeches was produced under the title *A Protestant Protest* by A S Green. Casement's speech was reprinted in *Roger Casement in Irish and World History*, (2000)

71   *Times* – 26 October 1913

72   *Times* – 31 October 1913

73   *Fortnightly Review* DLXIII pp.799–806

74   *Daily Chronicle* – 20 November 1913

75   NLI Roger Casement Papers Acc. 4902 (23) – MacNeill to Casement – 25 November 1913.

76   Bulmer Hobson, *A Short History of the Irish Volunteers* Vol. 1 (1918) p.23

77   *Galway Express* – 13 December 1913

78   Leon Ó Broin, *The Prime Informer – A Suppressed Scandal* (London, 1971)

79 *Irish Volunteer* – 21 March 1914 Vol. 1 No. 7

80 *Limerick Leader* – 18 & 20 March 1914

81 *Irish Independent* – 28 March 1914

82 *Irish Volunteer* – 25 April 1914 Vol. 1 No. 12

83 NLI MS 10,764(i) George Gavan Duffy Papers – Notes to Counsel

84 Ibid.

85 *Report of the Royal Commission on the Civil Service* Minutes of Evidence pp.1914–16 (cd. 7749) XI

86 Wilfrid Blunt, *My Diaries – Being a Personal Narrative of Events (1888–1914)* – (London, 1919–20) p.838

87 *Tyrone Courier* – 11 June 1914

88 NLI MS 1689 – *Casement's German Journal* ff.3

89 Ibid., ff. 8–9

90 Ibid., ff. 8–9

91 NLI MS 10,464 (10) – Roger Casement to A S Green – 26 July 1914

92 Ibid. – 29 July 1914

93 *Gaelic American* – 1 August 1914

94 *Gaelic American* – 8 August 1914

95 *Gaelic American* – 8 August 1914

96 *Hansard* – 3 August 1914 Vol.LXV Col. 1809

97 *Gaelic American* – 19 September 1914

98 *Irish Independent* – 5 October 1914

99 B L Reid, *The Lives of Roger Casement* (Yale, 1976) p.206 – NYPL Quinn Collection

100 *British versus German Imperialism* was published as a pamphlet (1915) and serialized in the *Continental Times*, issues 43–45 October 9–13 1915

101 *Irish Independent* – 5 October 1914

102 Charles Curry (ed.) *Sir Roger Casement's Diaries: His Mission to Germany and the Findlay Affair* (1922) pp.41–54

103 NLI MS 1689 *Casement's German Journal* ff. 1, 7 November 1914

104 Ibid., ff. 64

105 Ibid., ff. 64

106 Ibid., 19 November 1914 ff. 58

107 Reinhard Doerries, *Prelude to the Easter Rising – Sir Roger*

Casement in Imperial Germany (London, 2000) p.56

108   Ibid., pp.66–67

109   NLI MS 1689 *Casement's German Journal* ff. 94, 17 November
        1914

110   Reinhard Doerries, Op. cit. pp.71–4

111   NYPL John Quinn Letters

112   Reinhard Doerries, Op. cit., p.75

113   The letter was published under the title: 'A black chapter of
        English perfidy – Casement's letter to Sir Edward Grey.' A
        copy is held in the National Library of Ireland pamphlet col-
        lection.

114   This essay was published in the *Continental Times* (Nov. 1915)
        and *Gaelic American* (4 December 1915) see also H O Mackey
        The Crime Against Europe (1958)

115   B L Reid, *The Lives of Roger Casement* pp.1-490

116   Franz Rothenfelder, *Casement in Deutschland* (Augsburg, 1917)

117   R McHugh, *Dublin 1916* (London, 1966) or NLI MS 5244

118   Reinhard Doerries, Op. cit., p. 200

119   Casement expressed great concern for the destiny of his papers
        and diaries before leaving Germany. A certain amount of cor-
        respondence on this matter is held in the Gavan Duffy papers.
        Relevant correspondence with Curry is held in NLI MS 17026
        and 17027.

120   NLI MS 13088 (4/iii)

121   Jeff Dudgeon, *Roger Casement: The Black Diaries with a study of
        his background, sexuality, and Irish political life* (Belfast Press,
        2002) pp.481–6

122   NLI MS 10,764 – Typed version of Notes to Counsel p.20

123   NLI MS 13,088 (4/iv) – *The Points I most wish to avoid the Crown
        making*

124   It is now generally accepted that the British Intelligence chiefs,
        aware of the Rising, wished events to take their course so that
        the Irish revolutionary leadership could be taken out. See Eunan
        O'Halpin, 'British Intelligence in Ireland (1914–21)' in
        Christopher Andrew and David Dilks (eds), *The Missing
        Dimension: Governments and Intelligence communities in the twen-
        tieth century* (1984) pp.54–77

125   *Hansard – Parliamentary Debates* – Commons – 25 April 1916 Vol LXXXI. col. 2462.

126   Leon O'Broin, *Dublin Castle and the 1916 Rising* (Dublin, 1966)

127   Declan Kiberd, *Inventing Ireland – The Literature of the Modern Nation* (Dublin, 1995) pp.191–247

128   Joe Lee, *Ireland 1912–1985* (Cambridge – 1989) pp.32–6.

129   *Sinn Féin Rebellion Handbook* (1916)

130   *Hansard Parliamentary Debates* – 3 May 1916 Vol. LXXXII Col. 31

131   Brian Barton, *From Behind a Closed Door, Secret Court Martial records of the 1916 Easter Rising* (Belfast, 2002)

132   NLI MS 13,088 (1/viia) Affidavit read by George Gavan Duffy

133   T. Artemus Jones, *Without my Wig* (Liverpool, 1944) p.163

134   Roger Sawyer, *The Flawed Hero* (1984)

135   *Hansard Parliamentary Debates* – 10 May 1916 Vol. LXXII Col. 631

136   Ibid. – 11 May 1916 Col. 945–46

137   Ibid. Col. 959

138   Ibid. Col. 960

139   Casement's brief to counsel went through a number of different versions. A manuscript version of twenty-four numbered pages, in an unidentified hand, is held in NLI MS 13,088 [1/iii] and is the original version transcribed from interviews with Casement whilst he was in the Tower of London. There are two typed versions, annotated in Casement's hand held in the George Gavan Duffy Papers NLI MS 10,764 [1]. One version (NLI MS 10,764/ii) includes an annotated and corrected version of the expanded German section which has survived in twenty-two double-sided pages of manuscript also in the Gavan Duffy Papers. This section was dated 8 June 1916.

140   Ibid.

141   Ibid.

142   Ibid.

143   Ibid.

144   Ibid.

145   Ibid.

146   H G Wells, *The Outline of History* quoted in Angus Mitchell

'Decommissioning History' – The Printer's Devil – Millenium Issue (1999)

147 *Times* – 16/17 May 1916

148 NLI MS 13,088 (i) – *Transcript of shorthand notes of opening speech by Attorney General before Sir John Dickinson* 15 May 1916

149 M L Sanders & Philip M Taylor, *British propaganda during the First World War 1914–18* (1982) pp.174–6

150 G B Shaw, *A Discarded Defence of Roger Casement* (1922)

151 G B Shaw, *The Matter with Ireland* (1962)

152 NLI MS 10,764 *Notes for Counsel* – Brixton Jail – 5 June 1916

153 NLI MS 10,764 – *Line of My Defence* – 2 June 1916

154 Ibid.

155 George Gavan Duffy Papers NLI 10,763 (6) – Mary Boyle O'Reilly of Newspaper Enterprise Association

156 NLI MS 10,764 (iii) – *Note for Counsel* 10 June 1916

157 NLI MS 10,764 (iii) – *Reason's why Sergeant Sullivan's line must fail* – 13.6.16

158 PRO – Statute of Treason 1351.

159 PRO HO/144/1636/311643/18 – Ernley Blackwell – 6 June 1916

160 NLI MS 10,764 – *What I should like Mr Doyle to do* – 5 June 1916

161 NLI MS 10,764 – *A private note for my solicitor* – 14 June 1916 Brixton Jail – ff.4

162 Ibid.,

163 Ibid.,

164 John Jolliffe (ed.) *Raymond Asquith: Life and Letters* (1980)

165 PRO CAB 37/147/33 – Confidential Cabinet memo 13 May 1916

166 Ibid.,

167 NLI MS 10,764 Letter to Gavan Duffy – Sunday 25 June 1916

168 PRO HO 144/1636/311643/33 *Rex v. Roger Casement* p.17

169 Ibid. p.158

170 Ibid. p.161

171 Ibid. p.161

172   Ibid. p.161

173   Ibid p.180

174   A M Sullivan, *Old Ireland, Reminiscences of an Irish K.C.* (London, 1927)

175   PRO HO 144/1636/311643/33 *Rex v. Roger Casement* p.190

176   Ibid. p.193

177   Ibid. pp.201–2

178   Earlier drafts of Casement's Speech from the Dock are held among his prison papers PRO HO 144/1636/311643/32A

179   PRO HO 144/1636/311643/33 *Rex v. Roger Casement* p.221

180   Ibid. p.222

181   Ibid. p.223

182   Ibid. pp.226–7

183   Brian Inglis, *Roger Casement* p.346

184   Artemus Jones, *Without my Wig* p.166

185   M Sanders and P Taylor, *British Propaganda during the First World War 1914–1918* (1982)

186   Alfred Noyes, *The Accusing Ghost or Justice for Casement* (London, 1957)

187   NLI MS 13,088 (1/xxv) – Notice of Appeal signed 29 June 1916.

188   George Gavan Duffy Papers NLI MS 10,763 (18) – Morgan to Gavan Duffy 25 July 1916

189   The main bulk of petitions are held in PRO HO 144/1636/311643/62 – 85. Another batch are held in the Asquith Papers in the Bodleian Library, Oxford.

190   L G Redmond Howard, *Sir Roger Casement* (1916) p.6

191   *The Irish Uprising 1914–21, Papers from the British Parliamentary Archive* (2000)

192   NLI MS 10,764 (i)

193   PRO HO 144/1636/311643/52 and 53

194   D Gwynn, *Traitor or Patriot, The life and death of Roger Casement* (1931) p.19 – Letter from J R Clynes to Gwynn. See also PRO HO 144/23431/331643/213

195   PRO HO 144/1636/311643/45 – Yeats to Asquith and Samuel 14 July 1916

196   NLI Acc 4902 (3) – Roger Casement to Richard Morten – 8

July 1916

197   NLI MS 13,077 (1)

198   PRO HO 144/1636/311643/32A

199   G K A. Bell, *Randall Davidson, Archbishop of Canterbury* (1935)
        Vol. II pp.786–9.

200   Herbert Mackey (ed.) *The Crime Against Europe – The Writings
        and Poetry of Roger Casement 1958*

Chronology

Year	Age	Life
1864		1 September: Birth of Roger Dave Casement in Lawson Terrace, Sandycove, Dublin the youngest of four children (Agnes, Charlie, Tom) to Roger and Anne (*née* Jephson) Casement.
1865	1	Baptism into Church of Ireland.
1868	4	Secret baptism into Roman Catholic Church in Rhyl in North Wales (Aug 5. 1868).
1873	9	Mother dies in childbirth.
1877	13	Father dies and the four children become wards in chancery to their uncle, John Casement of Magherintemple (Co Antrim).
1881	17	After finishing schooling at Church of Ireland Diocesan school in Ballymena, finds clerical work at the Elder Dempster shipping company offices in Liverpool.
1884–6	20-22	Finds temporary work in Africa in service of African International Association and as a member of the Sanford Expedition.

Year	History	Culture
1864	British, French and Dutch fleets attack Japanese in Shimonoseki Straits, Belgium. In London, Karl Marx organizes first socialist international. Henri Dunant founds Red Cross. Louis Pasteur invents pasteurization.	Anton Bruckner, *Mass No 1 in D minor*. Charles Dickens, *Our Mutual Friend*. Leo Tolstoy, *War and Peace* (until 1869). Jules Verne, *Voyage to the Centre of the Earth*.
1865	In US, Abraham Lincoln assassinated. In Belgium, Leopold I dies; Leopold II becomes king (until 1909). In South America, Paraguayan war (until 1870). End of transport of convicts to Australia.	Lewis Carroll, *Alice's Adventures in Wonderland*. Richard Wagner, *Tristan und Isolde*.
1868	In Britain, William Gladstone becomes prime minister (until 1874). In Japan, Meiji dynasty restored. In Britain, Trades' Union Congress founded.	Johannes Brahms, *A German Requiem*. Wilkie Collins, *The Moonstone*. Fyodor Dostoyevsky, *The Idiot*.
1873	In Spain, Amadeo I abdicates; republic proclaimed. In Africa, Ashanti War begins (until 1874). In Asia, Acheh War (until 1903).	Arthur Rimbaud, *A Season in Hell*. Walter Pater, *Studies in the History of the Renaissance*. Claude Monet, *Impression: soleil levant*. Tchaikovsky, *Swan Lake*.
1877	Russo-Turkish War. Britain annexes Transvaal. Japan, Satsuma Rebellion suppressed.	
1881	In Russia, Alexander II assassinated. In Japan, political parties established. Tunisia becomes French protectorate. In Algeria, revolt against the French. In Sudan, Mahdi Holy War (until 1898). In eastern Europe, Jewish pogroms.	Jacques Offenbach, *The Tales of Hoffmann*. Anatole France, *Le Crime de Sylvestre Bonnard*. Henry James, *Portrait of Lady*. Henrik Ibsen, *Ghosts*.
1884	Sino-French War (until 1885). Berlin Conference to mediate European claims in Africa (until 1885). In Mexico, Porfirio Diaz becomes president (until 1911).	Jules Massenet, *Manon*. Mark Twain, *Huckleberry Finn*. Georges Seurat, *Une Baignade, Asnières*.

Year	Age	Life
1887–9	23-25	Employed to lead survey for the Congo Railway Company. Briefly recruited by Rev William Holman Bentley to work as a lay missionary.
1890–1	26	Directed construction of the Congo Railway from Matadi to Stanley Pool.
1892	28	Enters the service of the Survey Department of the Niger Coast (Oil Rivers) Protectorate. Promoted to assistant director-general of customs at Old Calabar.
1895	31	Appointed HM Consul in the Portuguese province of Lourenço Marques, in south-west Africa.
1898	34	Appointed consul to the independent state of the Congo. First poems and short stories published in *The Outlook*.
1900	36	Returns to Lourenço Marques to report on movement of war materials and armaments into the Boer republics of Transvaal and Orange Free State. August: transferred to Kinshasa, Congo State. On return journey to Africa, stops in Belgium to meet King Leopold II.
1901	37	Consular territory is increased to include the French Congo.
1903	39	Returns to the Congo to investigate rumours of atrocities against Africans. In London, meets the crusading journalist E D Morel. Their discussions lead to the founding of the Congo Reform Association (CRA).
1904	40	February: Delivers report entitled *Correspondence and Report from His Majesty's Consul at Boma Respecting the Administration of the Independent State of the Congo*. Becomes involved in the

Year	History	Culture

1887   Victoria Golden Jubilee.   Giuseppe Verdi, *Otello*.

In Britain, Trafalgar Square riots.   Arthur Conan Doyle, *Sherlock Holmes stories*.

1890   In Germany, Otto von Bismarck dismissed.   Tchaikovsky, *The Queen of Spades*.

Paul Cézanne, *The Cardplayers*.

In Spain, universal suffrage.   Ibsen, *Hedda Gabler*.

1892   In US, Grover Cleveland wins presidential election.   Ruggiero Leoncavallo, *I Pagliacci*.

Maurice Maeterlinck, *Pelléas et Mélisande*, with Debussy's music.

In France, the Panama scandal breaks.
Rudolf Diesel patents new internal
combustion engine.

1895   In Britain, Lord Salisbury becomes prime minister.   H G Wells, *The Time Machine*.

William Butler Yeats, *Poems*.

Cuban rebellion begins.   Oscar Wilde, *The Importance of Being Earnest*.

Japan conquers Formosa (Taiwan).
Lumière brothers invent the cinematograph.
Guglielmo Marconi invents wireless
telegraphy.
Wilhelm Röntgen discovers X-rays.

1898   Spanish-American War: Spain loses Cuba, Puerto Rico and the Philippines.   James, *The Turn of the Screw*.

H G Wells, *The War of the Worlds*.

Emile Zola, *J'Accuse*.

Britian conquers Sudan.   Auguste Rodin, *The Kiss*.

1900   First Pan-African Conference.   Giacomo Puccini, *Tosca*.

In France, Dreyfus pardoned.   Joseph Conrad, *Lord Jim*.

Relief of Mafeking.   Sigmund Freud, *The Interpretation of Dreams*.

In China, Boxer Rebellion (until
1901).
First Zeppelin flight.

1901   In Britain, Queen Victoria dies; Edward VII becomes king.   August Strindberg, *The Dance of Death*.

Kipling, *Kim*.

In US, William McKinley assassinated; Theodore Roosevelt becomes president.   Anton Chekhov, *The Three Sisters*.

Pablo Picasso begins Blue Period
(until 1904).

James, *The Ambassadors*.

1903   Bolshevik-Menshevik split in
Communist Party of Russia.
In Russia, pogroms against Jews.
In Britain, suffragette movement begins.
Panama Canal Zone granted to US to
build and manage waterway.
Wright Brothers' first flight.

1904   France and Britain sign Entente Cordiale.   Puccini, *Madama Butterfly*.

G K Chesterton, *The Napoleon of Notting Hill*.

Russo-Japanese War.

Year	Age	Life
1904		Gaelic League. At end of year, temporarily resigns from the FO.
1905	41	Awarded the Companion of St Michael and St George for his humanitarian activities.
1906	42	Rejoins FO and becomes Consul for Brazilian states of São Paulo and Paraná.
1907	43	Transferred to Belém do Pará, the rubber-rich port at the mouth of the Amazon.
1908	44	Travels up the Amazon to inspect the work in progress on the Madeira-Mamoré railway line. December: Promoted Consul-General of Brazil based in Rio de Janeiro.
1910	46	July: Embarks for the Amazon with a party of commissioners representing the Peruvian Amazon Company. Spends the rest of the year travelling to and from the Putumayo, investigating allegations of atrocities.
1911	47	January: Arrives in London and starts drafting reports on Putumayo. Reports delivered to FO on 31 January and 17 March. 29 May: With Arthur Conan Doyle and Alice Stopford Greet, organizes testimonial luncheon for E D Morel. 6 July: Knighted for his human rights investigations in Africa and the Amazon. August: Embarks on a second voyage up the Amazon to oversee local elections, and to prepare the way for both the new British Consul and a Franciscan mission.
1912	48	January: In Washington, meets with US President William Taft. July: Publication of the Putumayo 'Blue Book' forces Prime Minister Asquith to open a Parliamentary Select Committee Inquiry to investigate culpability of British directors. On 13 November and 11 December respectively, cross-examined by

Year	History	Culture
1904	Photoelectric cell invented.	Jack London, *The Sea Wolf*. J M Barrie, *Peter Pan*. Chekhov, *The Cherry Orchard*.
1905	Russian revolution against monarchy fails. Bloody Sunday massacre. Korea becomes protectorate of Japan.	Richard Strauss, *Salome*. Albert Einstein, *Special Theory of Relativity*. Paul Cézanne, *Les Grandes Baigneuses*. Debussy, *La Mer*.
1906	Algeciras Conference resolves dispute between France and Germany over Morocco. Duma created in Russia. Revolution in Iran.	Henri Matisse, *Bonheur de vivre*. Maxim Gorky, *The Mother* (until 1907).
1907	Anglo-Russian Entente. Electric washing-machine invented.	Conrad, *The Secret Agent*. Rainer Maria Rilke, *Neue Gedichte*. George Bernard Shaw, *Major Barbara*.
1908	Bulgaria becomes independent. Austria-Hungary annexes Bosnia-Herzegovina.	Gustav Mahler, *Das Lied von der Erde* (until 1909). E M Forster, *A Room with a View*. Cubism begins with Picasso and Braque.
1910	George V becomes king of Britian. Union of South Africa created. Japan annexes Korea.	Constantin Brancusi, *La Muse endormie*. Igor Stravinsky, *The Firebird*. Forster, *Howards End*. Bertrand Russell, *Principia mathematica* (until 1913). Post-impressionist exhibition, London.
1911	In Britain, Parliament Act resolves constitutional crisis. In Britain, National Insurance to provide sickness benefits begins. In China, revolution against imperial dynasties. Roald Amundsen reaches South Pole. Ernest Rutherford develops the nuclear model of the atom.	Stravinsky, *Der Rosenkavalier*.
1912	Balkan Wars (until 1913). ANC formed in South Africa. *Titanic* sinks. Morocco becomes French protectorate. Dr Sun Yat-sen establishes Republic of China.	Arnold Schoenberg, *Pierrot lunaire*. Carl Jung, *The Psychology of the Unconscious*. Bertrand Russell, *The Problems of Philosophy*.

Year	Age	Life
1912		committee. 31 December: Due to poor health, leaves England to recuperate on the Canary Islands.
1913	49	Continues to South Africa to visit brother, Tom, in the Drakensberg mountains.
		11 June: After a visit to Connemara, writes to E D Morel about the end of the Congo Reform Association.
		August: Retires from the Foreign Office on a pension.
		7 October: Ceases to draw his pension. 24 October: Enters Irish politics with a speech at Ballymoney in County Antrim, before pounding of the Irish Volunteers (25 Nov 1913).
1914	50	Organizes a series of recruiting rallies for the Irish Volunteers. 24 April: Large shipment of arms successfully landed at Larne for the Ulster Volunteers.
		8 May: Meets with Erskine Childers and Darrell Figgis at the house of Alice Stopford Green in London and the decision is taken to arm the Volunteers.Extends the recruitment campaign to Ulster.
		28 June: Casement delivers the oration at the stone dedicated to Shane O'Neill at the foot of Glen Copse above Cushendun in County Antrim. Immediately afterwards, embarks for the US to continue recruitment and fundraising work.
		24 July: In Norfolk, Virginia, addresses meeting of the Ancient Order of Hibernians.
		9 August: Meets with former President Theodore Roosevelt.
		5 October: Anti-recruitment manifesto appears in the *Irish Independent*.
		15 October: Leaves the US for Norway with Adler Christensen. 31 October: Arrives in Berlin and begins negotiations with German Foreign Office over guarantees for Irish independence. 23 December: Files formal proposal of ten 'Articles' of the conditions to govern.
1916	51	21 April (Good Friday): Lands on the beach at Banna Strand. Captured and taken via Tralee and Dublin to London to be interrogated by British Intelligence chiefs. Placed under arrest in the Tower of London.
		15 May: Brought before Bow Street Magistrates Court.
		26–9 June: Tried and found guilty of treason. Sentenced to death.
		30 June: Stripped of his knighthood.
		17–18 July: Appeal opens in the Court of Criminal Appeal, at the Royal Courts of Justice.
		3 August: Executed.

Year	History	Culture
1912	Stainless steel invented.	
1913	In US, Woodrow Wilson becomes president (until 1921). In Greece, George I assassinated. In China, rebellion in Yangzi Valley. In China, Yuan Shikai elected president. Hans Geiger invents Geiger counter.	Stravinsky, *The Rite of Spring*. Guillaume Apollinaire, *Les peintres cubistes*. D H Lawrence, *Sons and Lovers*. Marcel Proust, *A la recherche du temps perdu* (until 1927).
1914	28 June: Archduke Franz Ferdinand assassinated in Sarajevo. First World War begins. Panama Canal opens. Egypt becomes British protectorate.	James Joyce, *The Dubliners*. Ezra Pound, *Des Imagistes*.
1916	Battle of the Somme. Battle of Jutland. Easter Rising in Ireland. Arabs revolt against Ottoman Turks.	Apollinaire, *Le poète assassiné*. Shaw, *Pygmalion*. Dada movement launched in Zurich with Cabaret Voltaire.

Further Reading

The Casement bibliography, which includes books, ballads, poems, films, newspaper/journal articles and thousands of 'Letters to the Editor', is vast and reflects the complexities of the man. A considerable amount of what has been published since his execution obfuscates his work and misrepresents the scale of his achievements as both humanitarian and nationalist. Over a dozen biographies have appeared, including works in Italian, Irish and German. All these works should be read sceptically with an eye to the politics underlying them.

The most readable remains Brian Inglis's *Roger Casement* (1974, 2002). The latest scholarly account is by the anthropologist, Seamas O'Siochain, *Roger Casement: from imperialist to revolutionary* (2004). Two biographies written in the 1930s: Denis Gwynn's, *Traitor or Patriot: The life and death of Roger Casement* (1931) and Gerald Parmiter's, *Roger Casement* (1936) are free of the hostility that mars Rene MacColl's *Roger Casement* (1956) and Benjamin Reid, *The Lives of Roger Casement* (1976).

Casement has been analysed intelligently by the Ulster Unionist tradition of history, most cogently by H H Montgomery Hyde in *The Trial of Roger Casement* (1960) and persuasively by Roger Sawyer in *The Flawed Hero* (1984) and *Roger Casement's Diaries* (1997). Jeffrey Dudgeon in *Roger Casement: The Black Diaries* (2002) enlivens his queer reading of his subject with his encyclopedic knowledge and experience of gay life in contemporary Belfast.

The most accessible account of Africa is by Irish historian, Thomas Pakenham, *The Scramble for Africa 1876–1912* (1991). The matter is also well treated by S J S Cookey, *Britain and the Congo*

Question 1885–1913 (1968). Morel's history of Congo reform was edited by W Roger Louis and Jean Stengers, *E. D. Morel's History of the Congo Reform Movement* (1968). Most recently, Adam Hochschild's *King Leopold's Ghost: A Story of Greed, Terror and Heroism in Colonial Africa* (1999) has provided a controversial popular overview of the extent of Leopold's crime. The most distinguished scholar of the period, however, is the former Belgian diplomat Jules Marchal, who devoted his later years to the publication of many volumes of documents from Belgium's state archive including *E. D. Morel contre Leopold II, L'Histoire du Congo 1900–10*, 2 vols (1996).

The rubber industry remains one of the great untold stories of recent history. The best general account is by Howard & Ralph Wolf, *A Story of Glory and Greed* (1936). Wade Davis in *One River: Science, Adventure and Hallucinogenics in the Amazon basin* (1997) gives a powerful account of the exploits of the Harvard botanist Richard Evans Schultes in the Amazon during the Second World War.

The controversy over the authenticity of the diaries found its most powerful voice in Dr H O Mackey, who wrote a series of books and pamphlets during the 1950s and 1960s. The most helpful is *The Truth about the Forged Diaries* (1966). A scholarly essay on the subject is by the literature specialist Roger McHugh, 'Casement: The Public Record Office manuscripts', in *Threshold*, Vol. 4, No. 1 (1960). After 1965 the forgery theory was considered 'subjected knowledge' and its exponents were driven underground, expressing their views through limited-circulation pamphlets. The relationship between truth, knowledge and power dynamics in the production of history is analysed by Michel Foucault, especially in *The History of Sexuality* (1978) and *Power/Knowledge, Selected Interviews and Other Writings 1972–77 Michel Foucault,* Colin Gordon (ed.) (1980). The history of gay and lesbian consciousness is treated in Montgomery Hyde's *The*

Other Love: An Historical and Contemporary Account of Homosexuality in Britain (1970) and Jeffrey Weeks, *Coming Out: Homosexual Politics in Britain from the Nineteenth Century to the Present* (1977).

An award-winning documentary film, *The Ghost of Roger Casement* (2002) was directed by Alan Gilsenan and financed by RTE. A reasonable dramatization of the trial was produced by Peter Wildeblood for Granada television in the *On Trial* series (1960). Brazilian film-maker, Aurelio Michilis, has made important films about the Amazon river during the rubber boom including *0 Cineasta da Selva – the film maker of the Amazon* (1997) a dramatized documentary about Julio César Arana and the success of his civilizing mission in the Putumayo. André Gide's film *Voyage au Congo*, shot during his visit in the 1920s, also has significant images of Africa's lost world.

Casement's last wish was to have a collection of his writings produced after his death: this was partially achieved by H O Mackey (ed.) *The Crime Against Europe: writings and poems of Roger Casement* (1958). Two large volumes edited by Angus Mitchell detail Casement's work in South America: *The Amazon journal of Roger Casement* (1997) and *Sir Roger Casement's Heart of Darkness: The 1911 Documents* (2003).

Acknowledgements

My thanks to Kevin Whelan and Eoin Flannery for reading through early drafts and to Barbara Schwepcke and Ravi Mattu at Haus for all their editorial work. During a decade of research on Casement and his Atlantic world I have depended on the help of countless librarians and archivists. My debt of thanks extends from the elegant little Augustinian library overlooking the Amazon in Iquitos, Peru, to the wonderfully efficient British Library inter-library lending service coordinated through the most recent library where I have found peace and refuge at Mary Immaculate College, University of Limerick. To all those libraries and library staff I salute you and say: Thank you, Gracias, Obrigado, Go raibh maith agat!

Picture Sources

The author and publishers wish to express their thanks to the following sources of illustrative material and/or permission to reproduce it. They will make proper acknowledgements in future editions in the event that any omissions have occurred.

Index

Paris Commune, 12
Parnell, Charles Stewart, 13, 38, 39, 48
Parsons, General Sir Lawrence, 95
Pearse, Patrick, 44, 80, 82, 85, 108; and Easter Rising, 116, 118, 120; biography, 119
Pedro II, Dom, 57
Penna, Affonso, 56
Pentonville prison, 1, 37, 146
Peru, 70, 75
Peruvian Amazon Company, 66
Petropolis, 57, 58; treaty (1903), 53
Philadelphia, 90–91, 92
Philadelphia Bulletin, 92
Phipps, Constantine, 35
Phoenix Park murders (1882), 16
Plunkett, Joseph Mary, 108, 118
Plunkett, Sir Horace, 42
Pound, Ezra, 90
prisoners of war, Irish, 95, 97, 102, 105, 131, 140
Public Record Office, 3, 5, 7, 36
Puleston, Fred, 21
Putumayo, 58–70, 107; Blue Book published, 68, 70; Mission Fund, 104

Quinlisk, Corporal Timothy, 105
Quinn, John, 90–91, 93, 95, 97, 105, 147; biography, 90

Rathlin island, 43
Redmond, John, 84–5, 87–8, 90, 147; Woodenbridge speech, 95
Rhyl, 11
Ribbonmen, 12
Rio de Janeiro, 56–7
Roberts, Charles, 69–70
Roberts, Lord, 26, 84
Robinson, Ronald, 18
Room 40, 114
Roosevelt, Theodore, 93
Rossa, O'Donovan, 119
Rowntree, Arnold, 146
Royal Commission on the Civil Service, 86
Royal Dublin Society, 55
Royal Irish Constabulary, 112
rubber industry: Africa, 28, 30, 31–2, 35; South America, 52, 54, 58–64
Russell, Bertrand, 125
Russell, George, 39

Russell, Thomas, 129
Ryan, Michael J, 75
Ryan, W P, 45, 74

St Brendan, 54, 55, 112
St Helena, 27
St Helier, 13
Salisbury, Lord, 34
Samuel, Herbert, 30, 73, 121, 150
Sandys, Duncan, 6
Sanford Exploring Expedition, 19–20
Santo Amaro, 50, 51
Santos, 41, 48, 49–51
São Paulo de Loanda, 24, 39
São Thomé, 68, 74
Scotland, 96
Scotland Yard, 113, 137
Scott, C P, 146
Sea of Moyle, 14
Second World War, 3
Sédan, 101
Shaw, George Bernard, 39; support for Casement, 132–3; *John Bull's Other Island*, 99, 132
Simon, Sir John, 135
Sinn Féin, 4, 13, 45, 132, 134
Sinn Féin, 107
Sixmilecross, 87
Skeffington, Hanna Sheehy, 4
slavery, 17, 31, 32, 49, 65, 68, 71; laws amended, 70
Sligo Feis, 42
Smith, F E, 2, 73, 80, 108, 150; biography, 127; prosecutes Casement, 127–8, 130, 138, 140–44; threatens to resign if Casement not hanged, 146
Smuts, Jan, 6
Solemn League and Covenant, 73, 84
Somme Offensive, 80, 145
South America, 4, 6, 7, 46, 74–5, 125; Britain's empire in, 49; Casement in, 49–64, 66–7, 131, 137, 149; Garibaldi in, 133
Spanish Civil War, 4
Spindler, Lieutenant Karl, 111
Spring-Rice, Cecil, 121
Spring-Rice, Mary, 85, 91, 121
Stanley, Henry Morton, 17, 18, 20, 23, 25
Stanley Pool, 28